Knowledge Co-Construction in Online Learning

Knowledge Co-Construction in Online Learning is a comprehensive, foundational resource that explores the study of social construction of knowledge through platforms, social dynamics, and other aspects of today's technology-enhanced education. The interactive spaces, from formal computer-supported collaborative learning settings to informal social media–integrative environments, that comprise asynchronous online learning offer a rich source of data for analyzing teaching and learning. How, then, can researchers and designers in educational technology, instructional design, the learning sciences, and beyond most effectively analyze the content and data generated by these complex co-creations of knowledge?

Grounded in sociocultural and social constructivist theories of learning and driven by the globally renowned Interaction Analysis Model, this book applies statistical and computational methods to study the group interactions and social networks that yield newly constructed knowledge during virtual learning experiences. Its unique Social Learning Analytic Methods enhance the analysis of social dynamics that support knowledge construction so often missing from mainstream learning analytics. Holistic and cyclical in its approach to online learning experiences, this essential volume written for novice and experienced researchers transcends the field's research paradigm conflicts, blends qualitative and quantitative approaches with new digital media tools, and exemplifies how research questions and designs can incorporate and automate evolving forms of inquiry.

Charlotte Nirmalani Gunawardena is Distinguished Professor Emerita of Online Education and Instructional Technology in the Organization, Information, and Learning Sciences Program at the University of New Mexico, USA.

Nick V. Flor is Associate Professor of Information Systems in the Anderson School of Management at the University of New Mexico, USA.

Damien M. Sánchez is the owner of Puerta Abierta Performance Consulting, Associate with the Return on Investment Institute, and Adjunct Faculty in the Organization, Information, and Learning Sciences Program at the University of New Mexico, USA.

Knowledge Co-Construction in Online Learning

Applying Social Learning Analytic Methods and Artificial Intelligence

Charlotte Nirmalani Gunawardena,
Nick V. Flor, and Damien M. Sánchez

Routledge
Taylor & Francis Group

NEW YORK AND LONDON

Designed cover image: Cover art by Damien M. Sánchez

First published 2025
by Routledge
605 Third Avenue, New York, NY 10158

and by Routledge
4 Park Square, Milton Park, Abingdon, Oxon, OX14 4RN

Routledge is an imprint of the Taylor & Francis Group, an informa business

ISBN: 978-1-032-34591-8 (hbk)
ISBN: 978-1-032-34919-0 (pbk)
ISBN: 978-1-003-32446-1 (ebk)

DOI: 10.4324/9781003324461

Typeset in Galliard
by Apex CoVantage, LLC

To all researchers who have analyzed with IAM and expanded our horizons, and to all who will research with IAM 2.0 in the future.

– Lani

To anyone curious about understanding how people learn and who wants to explore the realm of human-machine distributed cognitive systems, may this book serve as a stepping stone on your journey. And to my wife, Nancy, for her enduring support and motivation.

– Nick

To future generations of researchers . . . remember artificial intelligence can help us solve our most vexing problems, but it can't do the work for us.

– Damien

Contents

Figures and Tables

Figures

Tables

Authors and Guest Contributor Biographies

Authors

Charlotte Nirmalani Gunawardena is Distinguished Professor Emerita of online education and instructional technology in the Organization, Information, and Learning Sciences (OILS) program at the University of New Mexico, USA. Lani grew up in Sri Lanka and obtained her bachelor's degree in English (Honors) from the University of Kelaniya, after which she taught English as a Second Language in middle and high school and worked as a research assistant in English for Specific Purposes at the University of Colombo. She came to the United States to pursue higher studies and at the University of Kansas, Lawrence, completed her master's degree in Teaching English as a Second Language and a Ph.D. in curriculum and instruction with an emphasis in instructional technology and a minor in instructional television. After moving to the University of New Mexico as a faculty member, Lani founded and developed the graduate emphasis area in online education and taught graduate-level courses in global online learning, culture, research, and evaluation. Throughout her career, she has been passionate about researching the sociocultural context of online learning, social presence, how groups collaborate and construct knowledge online, and how to design inclusive and equitable online learning environments. In 2019, she won the First Place Book Award for her co-authored book *Culturally Inclusive Instructional Design* given by the Distance Learning Division of the Association for Educational Communications and Technology, and she received the Best Full Paper Award for her co-authored study on cross-cultural distributed co-mentoring given by the International Council of Distance Education at the World Conference in Ireland. She has directed evaluations for the United States Department of Education and the Native American Research Center for Health in Albuquerque and served on the Advisory Board for the Defense Language Institute's Foreign Language Center in Monterey, California. Lani enjoys international assignments, especially her research as a Fulbright Regional Research Scholar in Morocco and Sri Lanka, and her online program design, research, and evaluation in Brazil, Ghana, Mexico, Spain, and Turkey. She has consulted for U.S. corporations and international higher education institutions and has worked as a World Bank and Asian Development Bank consultant in Sri Lanka. She was recognized as one of the 30 worldwide women pioneers in online education in *The Encyclopedia of Female Pioneers in Online Learning*, published in 2023, and in the same year won the Carlos J. Vallejo Memorial Award for Lifetime Scholarship from the Multicultural/Multiethnic Education Special Interest Group of the American Educational Research Association.

Nick V. Flor is Associate Professor of Management Information Systems in the Anderson School of Management at the University of New Mexico, USA. Prior to UNM, he was a faculty member at Carnegie Mellon University's Graduate School of Industrial Administration. Before academia, Flor was a software engineer and project leader at Hewlett Packard in San Diego. He received his doctorate in cognitive science from the University of California, San Diego. Flor has published extensively in the areas of virtual communities and online social systems in journals such as *Communications of the ACM*, *Knowledge Based Systems*, and the *International Journal of Human-Computer Studies*. He is co-principal investigator on several grants, including from the National Science Foundation and the Defense Intelligence Agency. Flor's current research interests lie in the application of analytics, visualization, machine learning, and artificial intelligence to the study of distributed cognitive systems.

Damien M. Sánchez earned his doctorate from the Organization, Information, and Learning Sciences (OILS) program at the University of New Mexico, USA. He leverages his expertise to produce engaging learning experiences, detailed research, and thorough evaluations for his clients. As the owner of Puerta Abierta Performance Consulting, he conducts evaluations and develops online learning modules for clients like the New Mexico Department of Health. He is a Certified Return on Investment Professional and Associate with the Return on Investment (ROI) Institute where he facilitates face-to-face and online workshops on program evaluation and ROI. He teaches instructional systems design as Adjunct Professor in the Organization, Information, and Learning Sciences (OILS) Program at the University of New Mexico. Prior to completing his PhD, Damien worked as a senior instructional designer producing online and face-to-face learning solutions for the U.S. government. He also spent six months working in Sri Lanka as a content development specialist for the Asian Development Bank. Damien has published several peer-reviewed articles that investigate digital activism on Twitter. He has received awards for academic excellence, contributions to the Latino community, and citizenship.

Contributors

Monica Etsitty-Dorame is of the Diné nation originally from Fort Defiance, Arizona. She is Tábąąhá (Edge of Water) maternal clan, Tótsohnii (Big Water) paternal clan, Honágháahnii (The One Walks Around) maternal grandfather's clan and Táchii'nii (Red Running Into the Water People) paternal grandfather's clan. She is a library operations manager in government information in the College of the University Libraries and Learning Sciences at the University of New Mexico. She has 35 years of public service, instruction, and research experience with government information expertise at the UNM University Libraries. Monica is a regional representative for the New Mexico Federal Depository Library Program's regional library administered by the United States Government Publications Office. Monica received her PhD in organization, information, and learning sciences in May 2024, her master's degree in public administration, and a BA in American studies from the University of New Mexico. Monica's research interests are Indigenous and Native American culture, education, leadership, and history. Her dissertation focused on Native American women leadership in higher education utilizing a Diné informed conceptual framework examining how Native women faculty perceived leadership, their identity as leaders in higher education, their leadership in the community, and how their background and context influenced their perception of leadership.

Austin C. Megli is an alumnus of the Organization, Information, and Learning Sciences (OILS) program, where he received his doctorate degree. Austin's research delves into the realms of distance education, telework, and eLearning. His recent publications have focused on the Interaction Analysis Model (IAM) and social presence in online courses. Currently, he is a faculty member in the Business, Hospitality, and Technology (BHT) program at Central New Mexico Community College in Albuquerque, New Mexico. He also works as Principal Agreement Specialist at Sandia National Laboratories. Austin holds a Juris Doctor and is a licensed practicing attorney in New Mexico. He also holds a master's in business administration (MBA) from the University of New Mexico. Austin is a proud tribal member of the Choctaw Nation of Oklahoma. Outside his professional commitments, he continues to contribute to the academic community, encouraging the next generation of American Indian researchers.

Sharon Schaaf is Associate Professor and Clinician Educator in the College of Nursing at the University of New Mexico. She received her bachelor's degree in nursing from the University of Wyoming (1994); her master's degree as a family nurse practitioner (FNP) from the University of Texas Pan American (2002); a post master's certification in cardiology from Loyola University, Chicago (2007); a post master's certification as an adult/gerontology acute care nurse practitioner (AGACNP) from UNM (2014); her doctor of nursing practice (DNP) from Texas Woman's University (2011); and doctor of philosophy in organization, information and learning sciences at the UNM (2020). Her doctoral research focused on social network centralities, social construction of knowledge, and nurse practitioner competency. Sharon has over 25 years of experience in teaching and developing curriculum in undergraduate, graduate, and doctoral programs. She has successfully guided students through their doctoral projects. She is a Certified Healthcare Simulation Educator® and a Certified Nurse Educator®. Sharon has presented nationally and internationally on critical care, trauma, and cardiology as well as intradisciplinary nursing and digital technology.

Preface

When Terry Anderson invited me 30 years ago to conduct a professional development activity as part of a virtual pre-conference (ICDE 95 Online) to the XVI World Conference on Distance Education organized by the International Council of Distance Education (ICDE), I delightfully accepted the opportunity to try my hand at conducting a global learning experience that would provide access to topics and presenters for those unable to attend the conference in Birmingham, UK. As organizer and administrator of the pre-conference, Terry set up the technology platform, a LISTSERV, at the University of Alberta, Canada. Approximately 550 individuals subscribed to the LISTSERV.

Prior to this event, I had led GlobalEd, an inter-university collaboration where we connected graduate students in several universities in the US, Australia, and Turkey through a LISTSERV to engage in distance education research projects, and had some experience with such collaborations online. However, this invitation pushed me to a new realm to design a learning experience for practicing professionals from around the globe to explore a hotly debated topic in distance education: interaction. I was teaching a graduate-level class on distance education course design at the University of New Mexico at that time, and I invited my students to brainstorm a design that would engage participants spanning many distances. Together, we came up with the idea of a debate on "No Interaction, No Education." The challenge, however, was how to conduct a debate across international timelines. We decided to ask participants to set their clocks on their computers to Greenwich Mean Time (GMT) when they participate, posting their contributions on the day assigned for affirmative and negative arguments. The participants could post to support either the affirmative or negative, or both arguments as long as they posted on the date assigned for each argument. The participants were predominantly practicing specialists and graduate students in the field of distance education. Fifty-four participants, including the moderator, debate team leaders, and summarizers, contributed a total of 89 messages to the debate. Of the total number of contributors, 45 were from countries in which English was the predominant language, while those from Spanish-speaking countries, Brazil, Finland, Norway, Russia, Netherlands, and Germany contributed only a single message. This distribution suggested that non Native English speakers had less opportunity to participate more fully, and we noted this as an area of concern that must be addressed in future global conferences.

The tremendously positive feedback we received from participants motivated us to analyze the debate transcript. We were curious and puzzled about how people learned from each other over a period of one week. Participants discussed two types of learning at the end of the debate: first, how they learned to use computer-mediated communication to design a learning experience, especially the debate format, the technical potential and limitations, and second, what they learned from the content of messages posted, for example: "You who are participating in this conversation have made me stop and think about 'interaction.' I guess you'd call that 'learning.' Without your thoughts this would not have happened. I think this demonstrates the importance of 'interaction' to learning."

Our method of meaning-making from the debate transcript began with two questions upmost in our minds: Was knowledge constructed within the group through exchanges? Did individual participants change their understanding or create new personal constructions of knowledge as a result of interactions within the group? Initially, we employed a structured approach following a previously developed content analysis framework by France Henri. When we realized this framework did not work for our transcript, we decided to use an open-ended approach to observe how people learned from each other and constructed knowledge. The development of IAM was a messy and iterative process that took several days. Connie Lowe cut up the transcript with each post on a single piece of paper and arranged them on the floor of a vacant classroom. Then, we moved them around in different configurations and finally struck the Aha! moment when we observed a pattern of knowledge co-construction. This led to the birth of the Interaction Analysis Model, which was later referred to as the IAM by other researchers. While archaic, the process enabled us to visualize knowledge co-construction, and Connie's experience with quilting provided the metaphor for explaining the interaction we observed. As in a patchwork quilt block, the process by which the online contributions fit together is interaction, and the pattern that emerges at the end when the entire gestalt of accumulated interaction is viewed is the newly-created knowledge or meaning; thus, interaction becomes the essential process of putting together the pieces in the co-construction of knowledge.

After co-authoring a paper on the evaluation of the debate, which was presented at the VI International Conference in Distance Education at the Universidad Estatal a Distancia, in San Jose, Costa Rica, in 1995, and publishing the paper on the development of IAM in the *Journal of Educational Computing Research* in 1997, I did not follow IAM's use by other researchers, nor did I conduct research with it. It was seven to ten years later, when my doctoral students and colleagues at the Open University in Sri Lanka wanted to conduct research with the IAM, that I took another look at it. Since then, I have watched with great interest as other researchers took up the challenge of examining the social construction of knowledge (SCK) with IAM. In 2014, Margarida Lucas and António Moreira invited me to take a serious look at IAM as they had used it for their research with teachers in Portugal and noted that it was one of the most frequently used instruments to study SCK and that the extent of its use makes it one of the most coherent and empirically validated frameworks in the field. This led to a collaborative study with them to reflect on and critically examine IAM, which was published in *Computers in Human Behavior*. However, it was not until 2016, when I began a research collaboration with my current co-authors, Nick V. Flor and Damien M. Sánchez, that I commenced a concerted effort to review studies that had used the IAM and explore how the newly developed Social Learning Analytic Methods (SLAM) and artificial intelligence (AI) techniques could help us analyze SCK with IAM. Our initial publication as a team investigated how SCK in a transcript could be analyzed by employing interaction analysis, social learning analytics, and social network analysis, which was published in the *Quarterly Review of Distance Education* in 2016. This led to other publications examining how we could research SCK by integrating SLAM with qualitative analysis.

The collaboration with co-authors Nick and Damien has been one of the most fruitful and enjoyable research collaborations in my faculty career. It is a collaboration of different mindsets and expertise that developed into a culture of sharing, which encouraged feedback, peer review, and improvement. We each brought in a different set of skills, knowledge, and perspectives and co-mentored and developed each other's *zone* (as in the zone of proximal development). This collaboration met all the definitions of what a true collaboration should be, and it is what helped us to bring this book to fruition. As our collaboration grew over the years, we invited doctoral students to collaborate with us, which expanded our research through diverse perspectives and co-mentoring. Our collaborative research was published in the *American Journal of Distance Education* and in *Online Learning* in 2023. We are grateful to three of our doctoral student collaborators, Austin C. Megli, Monica Etsitty-Dorame, and Sharon Schaaf, who have contributed chapters as guest authors to this volume.

This book is the culmination of three decades of my research into the social environment of online learning, and the reconceptualized IAM 2.0 we present in Chapter 17 brings together three strands of my work related to the social environment: cultural context, social presence, and SCK. Although I was researching social presence in 1995 and 1997, at the same time when IAM was published, we did not examine social presence in the debate as the format did not generate many social messages. The research on social presence, however, has contributed to the reconceptualization of IAM 2.0, enabling us to highlight the interconnectedness and interdependence between social interaction and knowledge construction. My research on culture influenced us to assign a central role to the sociocultural context in IAM 2.0, as we emphasize the role that language and the sociocultural context play in knowledge construction. We show how the sociocultural context influences knowledge construction, especially in Phase II, cognitive dissonance. Studies conducted with IAM in China, Latin America, and Sri Lanka have pointed out that in these cultural contexts open disagreement in a public space is impolite. Therefore, participants tend to reach Phase III (negotiation of meaning and co-construction of knowledge) without passing through Phase II (cognitive dissonance). Thus, the reconceptualization of IAM integrates the three strands of my work: cultural context, social presence, and SCK, in one framework.

If you are curious about how online learners connect with each other, how they develop into a learning community, and how this connection and community support their knowledge construction in various contexts, then this book is for you. We encourage you as a researcher (perhaps as a classroom teacher, an instructional designer, or an academic in higher education) to explore analyzing knowledge construction in online transcripts using IAM 2.0 and the many SLAM and AI methods and tools we discuss in this book. The step-by-step guidance we provide on how to use these methods and tools are available in the GitHub link that accompanies this book. The SLAM and AI methods we discuss can be used to analyze transcripts with various other frameworks, not simply with IAM. We encourage you to share what you find in appropriate venues so that we can improve the methods and build a robust research community.

In conclusion, I would like to express my gratitude to my co-authors and all those who have apprenticed me to their expertise to help me develop this book and bring it to completion.

Charlotte Nirmalani Gunawardena

Part I

Theoretical Foundations

Discussion forums and interactive spaces in social media platforms and learning management systems present a rich data source for analyzing the teaching and learning process in online learning. Determining how these online discussions among groups generate knowledge has been an area of significant interest in online learning research. One framework developed to guide the analysis of interactions among online participants and the process by which they generate and construct knowledge is the Interaction Analysis Model (IAM) developed by Gunawardena, Lowe, and Anderson in 1997. In a bibliometric study examining the nature and building blocks of educational technology research spanning the time period 1966–2020, which included 30,632 articles, IAM was listed in the top 20 most-cited articles (in position #12) that shifted the paradigm of educational technology research, specifically to socially oriented theories of learning (Valtonen et al., 2022).

Part I begins with Chapter 1, which provides the theoretical foundation of IAM based on sociocultural, social constructivist, and constructivist views on learning. The IAM was developed to analyze social construction of knowledge (SCK) evident in computer transcripts when groups collaborate online. The chapter defines the interaction analysis method and elucidates the Phases of IAM, which explain the co-construction of knowledge among interacting participants. Chapter 1 concludes by providing an overview of the chapters in the book. Chapter 2 reviews the many studies that have employed the IAM for determining SCK in various contexts and concludes with a discussion of areas of improvement, specifically, the need to incorporate the context and social dynamic of online learning in any analysis of SCK. Chapter 3 explores this social dynamic, conceptualizing it as the relational nature of online social interaction, and discusses the various ways in which it is manifested online. Further, this chapter examines how social interaction is related to knowledge construction. Chapter 3 provides the path to the next section of this book, which describes the methods we can use to analyze the social environment of online learning.

References

Gunawardena, C., Lowe, C., & Anderson, T. (1997). Analysis of a global on-line debate and the development of an interaction analysis model for examining social construction of knowledge in computer conferencing. *Journal of Educational Computing Research, 17*(4), 395–429.

Valtonen, T., López-Pernas, S., Saqr, M., Vartiainen, H., Sointu, E. T., & Tedre, M. (2022). The nature and building blocks of educational technology research. *Computers in Human Behavior, 128*, 107123. https://doi.org/10.1016/j.chb.2021.107123

DOI: 10.4324/9781003324461-1

Part I

Theoretical Foundations

1 Theoretical Foundations of Social Construction of Knowledge (SCK) and the Interaction Analysis Model (IAM)

The emergence of the Internet in the early 1990s ushered in a new era for distance education. It connected people across countries and cultures with profound implications on how we think, communicate, and learn. For the first time, many-to-many communication over an extended period of time over geographical distance became possible. For distance educators, this meant the promise of assigning students group work or having them engage in collaborative learning (Dillenbourg, 1999) at a distance. The publication of Linda Harasim's seminal work on *Online Education* in 1990, focusing on the group or socially interactive nature of the online environment, set the stage for the exploration of a new form of distance education. Likewise, the field of computer-supported collaborative learning (CSCL) emerged in the 1990s to examine how groups collaborate online, share and negotiate meaning, and construct new knowledge (Koschmann, 1996). It was an exciting time when distance educators capitalized on the unique strengths of computer-mediated communication (CMC), initially using LISTSERVs and subsequently groupware to design cross-institutional, cross-country, and cross-cultural learning experiences where students were exposed to diverse perspectives and ways of learning (Collis & Heeren, 1993; Gunawardena et al., 1993; Rohfeld et al., 1991).

As they developed learning scenarios using CMC, distance educators and researchers encountered a challenge – how do you assess collaborative learning, that is, how students learn from each other, how they construct knowledge together, and how they change their perspectives through collaboration. A tremendous resource to study collaborative learning was readily available – the computer transcript. The benefit of digital technology is its ability to automatically capture communications as they are expressed, which ensures the preservation of thought processes to assist in sorting, filtering, and searching ideas. While asynchronous or time delayed text-based communication can be captured by a LISTSERV or learning management system (LMS), real-time web conferencing platforms provide a recording of the communication. Transcripts of discussion forums and social media platforms present a rich source of data for analyzing the teaching and learning process. Researching how these online discussions generate knowledge became an area of major interest, and frameworks began to emerge to help us analyze how people learn from each other online. One such framework is the Interaction Analysis Model (IAM) developed in 1997 by Charlotte Gunawardena, Constance Lowe, and Terry Anderson (hereafter referred to as IAM developers) to analyze the social construction of knowledge (SCK) online. IAM provides the foundation for this book.

This introductory chapter presents the IAM (Gunawardena et al., 1997), which has guided the predominantly qualitative analysis of discussions among online participants and the process by which they generate and construct knowledge in collaboration with each other. It was developed while analyzing the process of learning that took place in a debate

DOI: 10.4324/9781003324461-2

accessed globally via a LISTSERV. The IAM is one of the most frequently used frameworks for analyzing the process of knowledge construction as groups collaborate online (Lehtinen et al., 2023; Lucas et al., 2014). Its widespread use by researchers internationally, even as of this writing (Ho, 2024; Miyashita & Wark, 2024; Suartama & Suranata, 2024), motivated us to take a deeper look at IAM more than 25 years later. We wanted to explore its significance and determine if it can be analyzed by incorporating the newly developed Social Learning Analytic Methods (SLAM) and artificial intelligence (AI) tools and used as a framework for analyzing learning in digital spaces in a variety of contexts.

Social learning analytics is the application of statistical and computational methods to study group interactions and social networks as groups co-construct knowledge. It is different from mainstream learning analytics used by higher education to profile students and track their progress by focusing on grades, time to degree completion, etc. This led to the development of Social Learning Analytic Methods (SLAM), which we define as a collection of techniques to study group interactions on learning management systems and social networks as groups co-construct knowledge online. These techniques include frequency analysis, sentiment analysis, cluster analysis, social network analysis, and artificial intelligence (incorporating large language models, neural networks, and generative AI), which are used in a complementary fashion to analyze the social construction of knowledge. While artificial intelligence (AI) is included within the umbrella term SLAM, AI is sometimes singled out to refer to operations that only an AI architecture can perform. AI is defined as the simulation of human intelligence using computers to perform tasks that typically require human cognitive processes, like attention, memory, learning, and problem-solving. We wanted to explore how SLAM and AI can supplement and enhance qualitative analysis, which has so far been the predominant method used for the analysis of knowledge construction using IAM.

This book will show you how to research learning that happens through group interaction in both formal and informal online spaces with an understanding of your specific sociocultural context. It is written for researchers, educators, graduate students, evaluators, designers, managers, and trainers who want to explore how online participants work together and build knowledge. Researchers will benefit from the many methods and tools we discuss in this book. While we show how these methods and tools can be applied to analyzing IAM, they can also be used to analyze learning in accordance with other models and frameworks. Although technical in nature, we try to make SLAM and AI accessible to lay researchers and provide step-by-step guidance on how to use a particular software or algorithm.

We begin this first chapter by providing the theoretical foundation for IAM. We then explore interaction analysis as a method, the development of IAM, and how the five Phases of IAM can be used to analyze how people jointly construct meaning. Next, we examine how to analyze transcripts with IAM, the unit of analysis, and coding. Finally, we review the chapters in this book.

Theoretical Foundations of the Interaction Analysis Model (IAM)

As principles that describe how people learn in groups underpin the IAM framework, the next section will focus on theories and philosophies that explain how people learn from one another in diverse, networked, online environments. IAM draws from sociocultural, social constructivist, and constructivist theories about learning and other theories that explain how learning happens in computer-mediated networks, such as distributed cognition, situated learning, communities of practice, and collaborative learning.

Sociocultural Theory

The theoretical foundation of IAM rests on the pioneering work of Lev Vygotsky, the Russian psychologist and educator whose sociocultural theory holds that learning transpires in three realms: via the cultural contexts in which we live, through interactions we have with each other in our homes and communities, and within our minds (Karpov, 2014). Vygotsky (1978) observed that people make sense of the world by absorbing ideas conveyed through both direct communication and indirect cultural influences. Connections between outward social interactions and inward thought processes form the basis of learning, according to sociocultural theory. Several qualities define such learning. First, it's *distributed*. Learning can happen in many venues and time periods. Second, it's *interactive*. Learners grow by engaging with one another through reflective dialog, both one-on-one and in small and large groups. Third, it's *contextual*. The learning that happens depends on who is part of the experience, when it happens, and what transpires before and after (Gunawardena et al., 2019). From a sociocultural perspective, learning takes place within cultural contexts, through social interaction and sharing, and via language, signs, and systems. The sociocultural view of learning was supported by Greenfield and Bruner (1966) who were conducting research in the United States at that time.

Vygotsky (1978) established the dynamic interdependence of social and individual processes in learning. "Vygotsky conceptualized development as the transformation of socially shared activities into internalized processes" (John-Steiner & Mahn, 1996, p. 192). Therefore, from the sociocultural perspective on learning, the interdependence of social and individual processes in the co-construction of knowledge takes center stage. Vygotsky further extended the interdependence of social and individual processes by stating that higher mental functions are socially formed and culturally transmitted: "All the higher functions originate as actual relations between human individuals" (Vygotsky, 1978, p. 57). This clearly establishes the importance of social interaction for developing higher mental functions and for constructing knowledge.

Another very important aspect of Vygotsky's work in relation to the development of higher mental processes is his emphasis on the use of tools and signs. "Vygotsky argued that the effect of tool use upon humans is fundamental not only because it has helped them relate more effectively to their external environment but also because tool use has had important effects upon internal and functional relationships within the human brain" (John-Steiner & Souberman, 1978, p. 133). We think with, and through, artifacts; for example, the computer is an artifact that is not only capable of supporting collaborative learning but also has the potential to transform uniquely the social processes of joint problem-solving (Littleton & Hakkinen, 1999). Language is a critical tool in the mediation process. Vygotsky's emphasis on mediation by tools and signs led to the development of activity theory, which focuses on the socially distributed or collective nature of learning as well as the artifact-mediated or cultural aspects of purposeful human behavior (Engeström, 1999).

The zone of proximal development (ZPD) is another significant aspect of Vygotsky's sociocultural theory that has implications for learning. It can be defined as:

> *the distance between the actual developmental level as determined by independent problem solving and the level of potential development as determined through problem solving under adult guidance or in collaboration with more capable peers.*
>
> (Vygotsky, 1978, p. 86, emphasis in original)

In the ZPD, instructors and peers play a critical role in guiding the learning process of the individual and helping the individual bridge the gap between the knowledge he or she currently has and what he or she can attain under adult and peer guidance. This paves the way for collaborative learning.

In summary, sociocultural theory lays the foundation for the primacy of the cultural and historical context, social interaction, peer collaboration, and knowledge construction under the guidance of knowledgeable adults and peers. Guiding and mentoring become an important part of the learning process. Collaborative learning and a learning community thus play an important role in sociocultural approaches to learning and teaching.

Constructivist and Social Constructivist Theories of Learning

The two terms, sociocultural and social constructivist, are often used interchangeably. We now consider the similarities and differences between the two. Constructivism arose out of Piaget's (1964) and his collaborators' research on cognitive development. Within this group of researchers, there was a growing interest in the social nature of learning and the social context within which learning happens, which led to the emphasis on peer interaction in cognitive development. This propelled the development of social constructivist views on learning. Social constructivists subscribed to the constructivist's views of knowledge as constructed but, unlike other hard-core Piagetian constructivists, considered construction of knowledge to be a social process. Social constructivists also focus on the collaborative nature of learning (Koschmann, 1996). Therefore, compared to constructivist perspectives based on Piaget's theory of cognitive development, which emphasizes the individual's mental processes in the construction of knowledge (the active character of the learner, interacting with the environment either alone or with others, and constructing knowledge), social constructivists emphasize the social context in which the individual is acting and in which knowledge is constructed when focusing on individual mental processes in the construction of knowledge (Kumpulainen & Wray, 2002).

Perspectives on learning from constructivist, social constructivist, and sociocultural lenses are interrelated. Constructivism highlights how learners build their own meanings and knowledge frameworks. Social constructivists posit that the construction of knowledge takes place in a social context, such as in collaborative activities. The sociocultural perspective regards the individual as being part of that social and cultural environment. The learning theory foundation of IAM rests on sociocultural, social constructivist, and constructivist perspectives. These perspectives have implications for designing and assessing learning as they focus on culture; the value of real-world contexts; how to share and learn from multiple perspectives; and how tools, signs, and artifacts can aid learning when we learn together online.

We now move on to examine how theorists have expanded sociocultural perspectives on learning and the concept of the ZPD.

Distributed Cognition

Hutchins (1990), while reflecting on how ships are navigated, observed that the outcomes that mattered to the ship were not determined by the cognitive properties of any single navigator but, instead, were the product of the interactions between several navigators and a complex set of tools. He shows that the use of these tools supports "a distribution of knowledge among the members of the navigation team that makes the system very robust in the face of individual component failures" (p. 193). As a theory, distributed cognition is specifically focused on understanding interactions among people, technologies, and media in general. Hollan et al. (2000) note that distributed cognition highlights three fundamental questions about social interactions: (1) how are the cognitive processes we normally associate with an individual mind implemented in a group of individuals, (2) how do the cognitive properties of groups differ from the cognitive properties of the people who act in those groups, and (3) how are the cognitive properties of individual minds affected by participation in group activities? Another important facet of distributed cognition is that the study of cognition is not separable from an understanding of culture because agents live in complex cultural environments.

Salomon (1993) emphasizes that distribution means sharing – sharing authority, language, experiences, tasks, and cultural heritage. Unlike the positivists' view of cognition as firmly located inside the individual, Cole and Engeström (1993) argue that both cognition and culture are distributed and that cognition manifests itself as distributed activity. They show affinity between Vygotsky's sociocultural theory and the notion of distributed cognition. Distributed cognition draws attention to studying people in action and how cognition is distributed in the activities in which people interact with each other; in particular contexts and environments, and with tools, artifacts, and symbolic representations.

Situated Learning and Communities of Practice (CoP)

The sociocultural perspective on learning emphasizes the situatedness of social interaction and learning (Wertsch, 1991). Lave (1991) extends these views further by stating that we need to rethink the notion of learning, treating it as an emerging property of whole persons' legitimate peripheral participation in a community of practice (CoP). According to this view,

> Learning is a process that takes place in a participation framework, not in an individual mind. This means that it is mediated by the differences of perspectives among the coparticipants. It is the community, or at least those participating in the learning context, who "learn" under this definition.
>
> (Hanks, 1991, p. 15)

Therefore, learning is seen as situated social practice associated with the type of participation in a CoP described as legitimate peripheral participation. Legitimate peripheral participation concerns the process by which newcomers become part of a CoP. Thus, CoP became a central idea in situated approaches to learning (Lave & Wenger, 1991).

Initially, when people join a community, they learn at the periphery, and the things they are involved in and the tasks they perform may be less central to the community's activities than other participants. However, as they become more involved in the main processes of the community, they move from legitimate peripheral participation into full participation. Therefore, learning happens in the process of social participation, which is impacted by the sociocultural context. This view of learning draws from Vygotsky's ZPD (1978) discussed earlier and shows the importance of supporting newcomers who may not have the necessary skills to fully engage in the community's activities to become full, active participants in the community.

Situated learning provides the theoretical basis for organizing learning environments around ill-structured real-world problems so that learners can be engaged in the same activities they will be asked to perform in eventual practice. Both the emphasis placed by sociocultural theory on problem-solving in collaboration with others and situated cognition's emphasis on authentic, complex, ill-structured problems of practice that are encountered in the real world have led to the emergence of inquiry-based learning methods, such as problem-based learning, case-based learning, and problem-solving, as core to the design of collaborative learning environments. Ill-structured problems and inquiry-based learning support knowledge construction (Gunawardena, 2004).

Collaborative Learning

The sociocultural perspective's emphasis on the collaborative and transformative way in which knowledge is co-constructed and its view of learning as "distributed, interactive, contextual, and the result of the learners' participation in a community of practice" (John-Steiner & Mahn, 1996, p. 204) provide the theoretical foundation for collaborative learning. Vygotsky stressed that it is in collaboration with adults or more knowledgeable peers that an individual can participate in performance at a higher level of complexity than he or she can do alone. Guidance from others helps to bridge the ZPD. Vygotsky's work provided the basis for understanding how peer collaboration can facilitate learning and problem-solving through the joint construction of solutions to problems (Rogoff, 1994).

In attempting to define collaborative learning, Dillenbourg (1999) points out features that define the space of collaborative learning: "a *situation* in which *two* or *more* people *learn* or attempt to learn something *together*" (Dillenbourg, 1999, p. 2, emphasis in original), and explores this space along three dimensions: the scale of the collaborative situation (group size and time span), what is referred to as "learning," and what is referred to as "collaboration." He observes that a feature of collaborative interactions is that they are negotiable. One partner will not impose his view on the sole basis of his authority but will, to some extent, argue for his point of view, justify, negotiate, and attempt to convince. Therefore, the structure of collaborative dialogue is more complex than that of tutoring dialogue. Harasim (2017) observes that collaboration "emphasizes the key role played by discourse in knowledge creation, sharing, dissemination, application, and critique" (p. 118). Further, Harasim illustrates three processes of collaborative learning: idea generating, idea organizing, and intellectual convergence. The third phase, intellectual convergence, is reflected in shared understanding, or a mutual contribution to and construction of knowledge product or solution.

Summary of Theoretical Foundations of IAM

To summarize, IAM's foundation rests on sociocultural theory, which focuses on the social, situational, cultural, and distributed nature of learning but also accommodates social constructivist perspectives on the role of social context in individual cognition and constructivist views on how individuals construct their own meanings and knowledge frameworks. These perspectives emphasize that social interaction is part of the context and play a key role in the learning process. Knowledge is constructed within a sociocultural context. Therefore, learning designs should encourage participants to construct knowledge through interaction with one another. The ZPD emphasizes the need for scaffolding, guiding, facilitating, and mentoring to move participants to higher levels of knowledge construction. IAM subscribes to the view of distributed cognition that learning is distributed. Cognition and knowledge are distributed not only in the minds of individuals who interact but also in the tools and artifacts they use in a specific sociocultural context. As in situated learning and CoPs, the IAM acknowledges that learning happens in the process of social participation in a CoP, with newcomers gradually becoming part of the community. Learning environments should engage participants in inquiry about real-world, authentic contexts. Peer collaboration can facilitate problem-solving through the joint construction of solutions. Therefore, if learning designs focus on inquiry, it would be possible to observe higher levels of knowledge construction.

IAM recognizes (1) the influences of culture and context on learning; (2) the interdependence of the social and individual processes of learning; (3) the significant role of social interaction and collaboration in the learning process; (4) the social nature of knowledge co-construction; (5) the critical role of mentoring, scaffolding, guidance, and support to achieve the ZPD; and (6) the mediation of language, artifacts, and technology tools in the learning process.

Interaction Analysis as a Research Method

The IAM was developed while studying interactions between people and, therefore, understanding how to study these interactions will help to apply IAM in various contexts. In this section, we reflect on interaction analysis as a research method, as the IAM was developed using this method. Jordan and Henderson (1995) describe interaction analysis as an interdisciplinary method of investigating the interaction of human beings with each other and with objects in their environment. Interaction analysis holds an "explicit commitment to the existence and central importance of human social interaction, studying how individuals and communities adopt and adapt social, cultural, and historical practices" (Brown et al., 2016, p. 23). Studies that use interaction analysis see learning as a distributed, ongoing social process, in which evidence that learning is occurring or has occurred must be found in understanding the ways in which people learn collaboratively and recognize learning as having occurred. This means that we need to examine patterns of interaction and collaboration to determine interdependence in the co-construction of knowledge and how social relationships and cultural values play a role in this co-construction. Fortunately, a computer transcript provides the kind of data needed for interaction analysis.

As a research method, interaction analysis is an approach to the analysis of knowledge in use, in action, or in practice (Hall & Stevens, 2016). The characters of knowing and learning are observable in interactions shaped by what people find relevant in the activity. Hall and Stevens (2016) note that those engaging in interaction analysis rely on captured data, such as a computer transcript or video recording, which allows for close and repeated analysis. In interaction analysis, "data is analyzed *sequentially*, unfolding in time as *interaction*: as interaction among people and interaction between people and cultural artifacts (e.g., computers, cars, cookware)" (Hall & Stevens, 2016, pp. 77–78, emphasis in original). Transcripts of human interaction are generally organized into speaking turns, and the analyst moves through the transcript turn by turn, examining how one turn is related to the previous and the following turn. Interaction analysis is one means of assessing the process of perspective sharing and negotiation when people engage in knowledge construction. Stahl (2006) observes that unlike individual cognition (hidden in private mental processes) group cognition is easier to study as it is publicly visible; group interaction must be displayed for members to participate in the collaborative process. Computer transcripts of group discourse, therefore, are ideal means of studying group cognition.

The terms *interaction analysis* and *content analysis* are often used interchangeably. While both are qualitative methods, their purposes differ. Content analysis is primarily concerned with "what" is communicated. Content analysis focuses on the specific content or the meaning of the content of an individual's message (Guba & Lincoln, 1981; Merriam, 1998). On the other hand, interaction analysis is concerned with "how" communication unfolds in social settings in social interaction between people (Jordan & Henderson, 1995). It examines the dynamics of interaction between participants, focusing on their behavior, gestures, and the flow of conversation. The interaction can take place in real-time (synchronous) or delayed time (asynchronous). Content analysis and interaction analysis are similar in that both are methods for analyzing the meaning of messages. IAM's analysis procedures use both interaction analysis ("how") and content analysis ("what") of communication online.

Development of the Interaction Analysis Model (IAM)

The motivation to explore how learning occurred among a group of participants engaged in an online debate conducted as a professional development activity prior to the World Conference on Distance Education in Birmingham, UK, in 1995 provided the impetus to engage in the development of IAM. This motivation was partly fueled by the positive feedback received from participants in the debate, especially one participant's observation: "My thanks and compliments to all. For its conciseness, sophistication and clarity, this debate outshines anything I have lately experienced in any conference for which I paid good money, traveled long distances and endured fancy hotels" (Gunawardena et al., 1995, p. 202).

Preliminary Analysis

The methodology adopted to gain insight into the learning process that transpired in the debate by analyzing its transcript included several stages (Gunawardena et al., 1997). The first stage was to critically review available content analysis and interaction analysis models and select an appropriate model to analyze the debate. The IAM developers selected Henri's (1992) model, a prominent and well-recognized framework at the time, and started coding the transcript. They decided to use only three aspects of Henri's model that were applicable to the debate transcript: the interactive, cognitive, and metacognitive dimensions. They left out the other two categories of Henri's model: the participative dimension, which they felt needed to be studied separately, and the social dimension. The IAM developers, while acknowledging that the social dimension is important to study in online group learning as it can shed light on social presence, building rapport, and promoting the growth of the community, decided not to study it because "the structured debate format did not lend itself to social interaction and kept the participants task-oriented for a period of one week" (Gunawardena et al., 1997, p. 404). Soon after they began the analysis with Henri's model, they realized it was not applicable to analyzing the debate for several noted reasons and, predominantly, because "it gives us no impression of the social co-construction of knowledge by the group of individuals as a group, in a discussion or a seminar" (Lally & DeLaat, 2002, p. 161). They returned to the transcript with an open mind to observe how participants interacted and constructed knowledge. They put each post on a slip of paper and arranged them on the floor to observe the relationships. The knowledge construction process revealed itself in a pattern, and this led to the development of IAM.

Research Questions

The developers of IAM (Gunawardena et al., 1997) began with two questions:

1 Was knowledge constructed within the group by a process of social negotiation?
2 Did individual participants change their understanding or create new personal constructions of knowledge as a result of interactions within the group?

Definition of Interaction

The first step they took was to develop a new definition of interaction for the computer-mediated communication context. They used the metaphor of a patchwork quilt to describe the process of interaction in online contexts:

> The process by which the contributions are fitted together is interaction, broadly understood, and the pattern which emerges at the end, when the entire gestalt of accumulated interaction is viewed, is the newly-created knowledge or meaning. Interaction is the essential process of putting together the pieces in the co-creation of knowledge.
>
> (Gunawardena et al., 1997, pp. 411–412)

This view of interaction aligns with how communication happens online, described as transactive communication by McAteer et al. (2002). In transactive communication, participants respond to and build on each other's contributions, developing toward a mutual outcome. Transactive communication differs from the more didactic, tutor-controlled dialogue that takes place in traditional learning environments. Thus, employing the definition of interaction as the essential process of putting together the pieces of the quilt (the contributions of participants) in the co-creation of knowledge, the IAM developers proceeded to analyze the entire debate transcript to examine patterns, themes, and phases related to the SCK.

Unit of Analysis

A unit of analysis is the text block or language segment we select for analyzing the content of interactions evident in a computer transcript of an online discussion. The unit of analysis impacts how we code text. Gunawardena et al. (1997) noted the difficulty they had in determining a unit of analysis for the debate transcript. They initially used "Units of Meaning," which could signal a theme or idea, as proposed by Henri (1992). However, in their analysis of the debate transcript, they found that messages exhibited many arguments to support or refute the debate proposition, and if a message was broken down into units of meaning and each unit analyzed separately, it would be difficult to describe the process by which arguments were advanced building upon each other to support or refute propositions and negotiate meaning. They, therefore, decided to use one single message or one post as the unit of analysis, which, taken as a whole, would embody a participant's perspective and contribution toward the construction of knowledge. The fact that most studies opt for complete messages as the unit of analysis is explained by Rourke et al.'s (2001) argument that a message is the most objective identification of a unit of analysis as it is defined by the author of the message. The message embodies a participant's cognitive activity and contribution to the construction of knowledge.

Analysis of the Learning Process

As they analyzed the debate transcript, Gunawardena et al. (1997) focused on the: (1) type of cognitive activity performed by participants (questioning, clarifying, negotiating, synthesizing, etc.); (2) types of arguments advanced throughout the debate; (3) resources brought in by participants for use in exploring their differences and negotiating new meanings, such as reports of personal experience, literature citations, and data collected; and (4) evidence of changes in understanding or the creation of new personal constructs of knowledge as a result of interactions within the group.

Gunawardena et al. (1997) observed the development of the collaborative learning process in the debate transcript, which showed the interdependence of individual and social knowledge construction. They cite the work of Smith (1994) on group-mediated cognition to discuss this interdependence. According to Smith, if we take, for example, the context of a group meeting, the situation itself exerts a strong mediating effect on individual cognitive and conceptual processes. The thinking of each individual is inevitably influenced by the thinking of the other members participating in the discussion. Smith referred to this situated form of thinking as group-mediated cognition and stated that the merger of intellectual and social processes is one of the two fundamental properties of group-mediated cognition. A second fundamental property is the tension between the individual and the group – that is, the tension between the conceptual structure that is held in common and shared by the group and the slightly different versions of that structure that exist in individual working memories of the participants. Smith notes that this tension provides the energy for collective processing. When an individual voices his or her opinion on how that common or core structure is linked to additional concepts, other members can apply this new information to structures in their respective memories and perhaps change those structures. In this way, knowledge is extended. If the individual member's idea is accepted by the group, it will become part of the core conceptual structure that is shared by the group. Therefore, knowledge is created at the social level – or the level of the group, and the individual also creates his or her own understanding by interacting with the group's shared construction. Stahl (2006) argues that "in small-group collaboration, *meaning is created across the utterances of different people*. That is, the meaning that is created is not a cognitive property of individual minds but a characteristic of the group dialogue" (pp. 6–7, emphasis in original). Stahl calls "this result of collaborative knowledge building *group cognition*" (p. 7, emphasis in original).

The Interaction Analysis Model (IAM)

The analysis of the themes, patterns, and phases observed in the debate led to the development of the IAM, (Gunawardena et al., 1997). Figure 1.1 illustrates the five Phases of knowledge co-construction the IAM developers observed during the debate and which they believe characterize the negotiation of meaning when participants are engaged in the SCK. As outlined in Figure 1.1, the five Phases are (I) sharing and comparing, (II) dissonance, (III) negotiation and co-construction, (IV) testing tentative constructions, and (V) statements of agreement and application of newly constructed knowledge. Figure 1.1 identifies specific operations which may occur at each Phase of the process. The co-constructed knowledge becomes the pattern that can be viewed by looking at the interaction. "At the end, each participant is likely to take away his or her own construction, the pattern of which reflects in greater or lesser detail the pattern established in the whole" (Gunawardena et al., 1997, p. 416). The IAM developers point out that one could reasonably divide SCK into fewer or more Phases, and all these Phases may not always occur.

After the IAM was developed, Gunawardena et al. (1997) applied it to the analysis of the debate itself. The purpose was to study the process by which the new pattern of knowledge is arrived at. The questions they considered were: Did the debate as a whole move through the Phases described in Figure 1.1? Can we say that SCK occurred? They make the following observations about the knowledge construction process:

- The Phases of learning outlined in IAM occur at both the individual and social levels. Knowledge is created at the social – the level of the group – and the individual also creates

PHASE I: SHARING/COMPARING OF INFORMATION. Stage one operations include:

A. A statement of observation or opinion [PhI/A]
B. A statement of agreement from one or more other participants [PhI/B]
C. Corroborating examples provided by one or more participants [PhI/C]
D. Asking and answering questions to clarify details of statements [PhI/D]
E. Definition, description, or identification of a problem [PhI/E]

PHASE II: THE DISCOVERY AND EXPLORATION OF DISSONANCE OR INCONSISTENCY AMONG IDEAS, CONCEPTS OR STATEMENTS. (This is the operation at the group level of what Festinger [20] calls cognitive dissonance, defined as an inconsistency between a new observation and the learner's existing framework of knowledge and thinking skills.) Operations which occur at this stage include:

A. Identifying and stating areas of disagreement [PhII/A]
B. Asking and answering questions to clarify the source and extent of [PhII/B]
   disagreement [PhII/C]
C. Restating the participant's position, and possibly advancing arguments
   or considerations in its support by references to the participant's
   experience, literature, formal data collected, or proposal of relevant
   metaphor or analogy to illustrate point of view

PHASE III: NEGOTIATION OF MEANING/CO-CONSTRUCTION OF KNOWLEDGE

A. Negotiation or clarification of the meaning of terms [PhIII/A]
B. Negotiation of the relative weight to be assigned to types of argument [PhIII/B]
   C. Identification of areas of agreement or overlap among conflicting [PhIII/C]
   concepts [PhIII/D]
D. Proposal and negotiation of new statements embodying compromise,
   co-construction [PhIII/E]
E. Proposal of integrating or accommodating metaphors or analogies

PHASE IV: TESTING AND MODIFICATION OF PROPOSED SYNTHESIS OR CO-CONSTRUCTION

A. Testing the proposed synthesis against "received fact" as shared by the [PhIV/A]
   participants and/or their culture
B. Testing against existing cognitive schema [PhIV/B]
C. Testing against personal experience [PhIV/C]
D. Testing against formal data collected [PhIV/D]
E. Testing against contradictory testimony in the literature [PhIV/E]

PHASE V: AGREEMENT STATEMENT(S)/APPLICATIONS OF NEWLY-CONSTRUCTED MEANING

A. Summarization of agreement(s) [PhV/A]
B. Applications of new knowledge [PhV/B]
C. Metacognitive statements by the participants illustrating their [PhV/C]
   understanding that their knowledge or ways of thinking (cognitive
   schema) have changed as a result of the conference interaction

Figure 1.1 The Interaction Analysis Model for examining SCK in computer conferencing, developed by Gunawardena, C. N., Lowe, C. A. and Anderson, T. (1997), published in the *Journal of Educational Computing Research* (1997), 17 (4), pp. 397–431

his or her own understanding by interacting with the group's shared construction. It is important to recognize the interdependence of the individual and social processes in knowledge construction.

- Two major themes were observed when the message or post was used as a unit of analysis. One was the progression of certain strands of argument among the group from Phase I to Phase V, which could be described as the co-construction of knowledge among participants. The other was the evidence of more than one and sometimes three Phases within a single message posted by one participant, which usually progressed in sequence through the IAM Phases, providing evidence of how individuals contributed toward the co-construction.

- As the group interacted together more effectively and learned from each other, the successive stages they went through could be considered forms of higher mental functions as described by Vygotsky (1978). The movement from lower to higher mental functions could also be observed in the arguments an individual contributor presented in a single message. The IAM, therefore, begins with what could be described as lower mental functions, the sharing and comparing of information (Phase I), and moves through cognitive dissonance (Phase II) to higher mental functions described in Phase III, Negotiation of meaning and co-construction of knowledge, and Phases IV and V.

- Two types of learning were occurring. One type was where participants only provided additional examples of ideas that were already understood, learning by accretion or learning by pooling knowledge (considered lower level), as opposed to the process of negotiation, which must occur when substantial areas of inconsistency or disagreement must be resolved (considered higher level).

- The answer to the question, "Can one see evidence that the discussion proceeded through at least the first three stages?" may provide a preliminary judgment of the quality of the conference. Generally, the "more phases the conference illustrates, the more participants who are active at each phase, and the greater the variety of resources the participants call upon in the process of negotiation of meaning or construction of knowledge, the higher the quality of the conference" (Gunawardena et al., 1997, p. 417).

- Metacognitive statements by participants illustrating their ways of thinking have changed because of group interaction appeared throughout the debate but were included as a Phase V operation. These statements were closely related to cognitive activity and, in many instances, were difficult to distinguish as cognitive or metacognitive. Therefore, they were described as strategies in the co-creation of knowledge and negotiation of meaning and were included in Phase V.

- The predominant number of postings in the debate occurred in Phases II and III, which indicated high quality as several participants were involved in the exploration of dissonance or inconsistency and the negotiation of meaning and co-construction of knowledge. A few strands of argument moved the discussion from Phase III to Phases IV and V, despite the debate leaders' efforts to keep the participants from reaching a synthesis. The debate format influenced the process of co-construction by sometimes supporting and sometimes hindering the efforts made by participants to reach a synthesis (Phase III). The debate format supported Phase I by soliciting agreement on propositions, and Phase II by introducing inconsistencies between statements and moved the arguments to Phase III. What the debate format hindered was the desire of participants to reach a compromise or a synthesis on the propositions at Phase III and above. Yet, despite the format of the debate, participants negotiated and constructed new meanings and moved on to test the newly constructed knowledge (Phase IV) and determine ways to apply it and make it relevant to the real-world context (Phase V). This pattern was evident in the context of the debate as a professional development activity with experienced professionals and graduate students and may differ in discussions in varied other contexts.

While reviewing IAM as a framework for content analysis of transcripts, Lally (2001) observes:

> the analytical model of Gunawardena and her colleagues contains several important features in terms of understanding teaching and learning in networked collaborative learning environments: (a) it focuses on interaction as the vehicle for the co-construction of knowledge, (b) it focuses on the overall pattern of knowledge construction emerging from a conference, (c) it is most appropriate in social constructivist and collaborative (student-centered) learning contexts, (d) it is a relatively straightforward schema, and (e) it is adaptable to a range of teaching and learning contexts.
>
> (p. 402) (Cited in De Wever et al., 2006)

Most researchers who have used the IAM in their studies have found that a majority of discussions could be coded only at Phase I, a few at Phase II and III. Many of these discussions hardly moved beyond Phase III (De Wever et al., 2006; Sun et al., 2021). The proportion of higher-level, complex thinking is scant, with most discussions at the lowest level of sharing information (Lucas et al., 2014). This is most probably due to the way the discussions were designed. If the prompts for a discussion do not ask participants to build on each other's knowledge to arrive at a given goal, discussions may not go beyond Phase III. Therefore, the interpretation of the results of discussions needs to consider many factors, which we discuss in Chapters 17 and 18.

Coding the Transcript

When coding a transcript according to IAM (Figure 1.1), the researcher codes occurrences of the Phases and their operations (for example, Phase II Exploration of dissonance and Phase II/A Identifying and stating areas of disagreement) for every post. We have used a Microsoft Excel coding sheet for this purpose, assigning each post (the unit of analysis) to a row and the IAM code for the specific post in the column assigned to that Phase and operation. The Excel sheet we use for coding is in the GitHub repository for this chapter, https://github.com/knowledge-construction/slam-ai.

Examples of IAM Phases and operations from the coding of the debate transcript in Gunawardena et al. (1997) are summarized in a table in the GitHub repository for this chapter. After the coding was completed, the developers of IAM determined the frequencies and explained the gestalt of the overall pattern of knowledge construction observed. The purpose of the analysis was to determine the process by which the new pattern of knowledge is arrived at. We refer the reader to the original IAM publication (Gunawardena et al., 1997) for details on the coding and analysis process as we provided only a snapshot here.

Interrater Reliability and Validity

Interrater reliability when conducting qualitative interaction analysis or content analysis of transcripts is one area that has generated much debate. Interrater reliability is the measurement of the extent to which researchers assign the same code to the same sequence of text in the transcript. The question debated is whether one should use interrater reliability in qualitative coding as it is a very positivistic or quantitative way of thinking about qualitative analysis. Quantification of qualitative coding using interrater reliability statistics is not the right way to understand the data or analysis process (McDonald et al., 2019). As researchers, we acknowledge that a qualitative researcher's biases and points of view will influence the interpretation of results. Therefore, no two qualitative researchers will come up with the same results when coding a transcript. There will be areas of disagreement that need to be discussed and resolved.

However, some researchers aim for better accuracy and consistency by having multiple researchers code the same transcript and check that they are making the same interpretations. Some would argue that this lessens the subjectivity of a single coder, producing a more valid and rigorous analysis. Qualitative researchers who feel that a statistic will give better accuracy of their coding use correlational statistics like Cohen's kappa or Krippendorff's alpha to indicate agreement between coders. However, these statistics have limitations, and their acceptability has been questioned (McHugh, 2012).

There is an advantage to using multiple coders who can check each other's work and use the differences in coding to engage in a discussion about interpreting the results. This can be considered a type of triangulation process between different researchers who code and interpret the same transcript. It is this triangulation process that was used when IAM was developed (Gunawardena et al., 1997). Two researchers coded the debate transcript and resolved any discrepancies that occurred, and a third researcher reviewed the coding. They did not report an interrater reliability coefficient.

Subsequent studies using IAM have established its validity and reliability. Hall (2014) endorses the validity of IAM through a discussion of its development, use, and interrater reliability accumulated from 40 published studies spanning 14 years. Sun et al. (2021) report the IAM "has been shown to have high validity across multiple communication tools (e.g., Lucas et al., 2014; Zhang et al., 2017)" (p. 536), and the five Phase knowledge construction model is "one of the most successful" in its "adoption by a wide array of scholars" (p. 535). Schellens and Valcke (2005) reported that when three independent researchers coded IAM, the percent agreement when coding the 1428 messages was 0.69. Marra et al. (2004) employed the IAM and noted that raters reached agreement on 44 of the 47 (or 94%) of coded postings. Further, they report a Krippendorff's alpha of 0.59 for the initial IAM codes, and 0.93 during post interrater reliability discussions on coding with IAM. Lehtinen et al. (2023) stated that the IAM has been theoretically and empirically validated in asynchronous online discussions and within instructional sciences (De Wever et al., 2006, 2010; Lucas et al., 2014) and implemented in student-centered collaborative environments (Buraphadeja & Dawson, 2008).

Given the ability of a trained AI assistant to code the IAM Phases automatically, we can utilize the results from AI coding to determine interrater reliability. As each AI assistant relies on the databases it has access to, three different AI assistants based on different training datasets will have slightly different results. The same AI, however, will produce the same results with the same data for different researchers.

How IAM Compares With Other Frameworks

This section explores how IAM compares with other content analysis and interaction analysis frameworks. One such framework is Mercer's (1995) characterization of three types of classroom talk: disputational, cumulative, and exploratory talk. Disputation talk is characterized by disagreement and individualized decision-making, somewhat similar to IAM's Phase II (cognitive dissonance). Cumulative talk is when speakers build positively but uncritically on what others have said, similar to IAM's Phase I (sharing and comparing). Exploratory talk is when partners engage critically but constructively with each other's ideas and where statements and suggestions are offered for joint consideration. This is similar to IAM's Phase III (negotiation and co-construction). Mercer (1995) considers these three analytical categories representative of distinct modes of social thinking.

Lehtinen et al. (2023) note that the IAM Phases have similarities with other conceptualizations of higher-level thinking, such as *critical thinking* (Newman et al., 1995), *cognitive presence* (Garrison et al., 1999), and the concepts of *cumulative* and *exploratory talk* defined by Mercer (1995). Floren et al. (2021), in their search for a model that is not overly complex and is practical to apply to analyze synchronous discussions in an interprofessional clinical setting, compared three promising knowledge construction frameworks, the Interactive, Constructive, Active, and Passive (ICAP) Model developed by Chi and Wylie (2014), the Practical Inquiry Model developed by Garrison et al. (2001), and the IAM (Gunawardena et al., 1997). They selected the IAM given the positive associations between knowledge construction and learning quality and also because the five Phases of knowledge construction can all be observed in social interactions in a transcript. They noted that in the Practical Inquiry Model, two of the Phases (exploration and integration) are located in what the authors call a "private world" of reflection and are not easily observable. Only the triggering event and the final resolution Phase happen in a "shared world" of discourse (Floren et al., 2021).

Comparing IAM to the critical thinking model developed by Newman et al. (1995), Marra et al. (2004) observe that although the IAM focuses on knowledge creation and the Newman et al. model on critical thinking, both are concerned with qualitatively describing meaningful interactions that promote in-depth learning in online discussions. Further, they point out that IAM provides "a more holistic view of discussion flow and knowledge construction," whereas the Newman model provides "focused and segmented coding on certain potential indicators of critical thinking" (Marra et al., 2004, p. 39).

Chapter 2 continues this discussion by reviewing studies that used IAM and analyzing researcher interpretations. The following section provides an overview of the chapters in this book.

Overview of Chapters

This book is about researching learning that happens through group interaction and collaboration in both formal and informal online spaces. It is written for those who want to research how online participants work together and construct knowledge. We begin with learning theories that explain the social construction of knowledge (SCK), which forms the foundation for the Interaction Analysis Model (IAM), a framework that was developed to qualitatively analyze SCK. We take a theoretically grounded framework like IAM and show researchers how to use the more quantitative Social Learning Analytic Methods (SLAM) and artificial intelligence (AI) tools to obtain a holistic picture of knowledge construction.

The book is organized into five parts that address the theoretical foundations of the IAM, methods for researching the social environment online, procedures for analyzing the social environment, applications of IAM to data analysis, and the reconceptualized IAM 2.0 and future directions. Since we address a wide variety of topics in the chapters: theory, research, methods, software, and algorithms, the reader will encounter a variety of writing styles. For example, while the foundational chapters will focus on theory and literature, providing citations and references, the methods chapters will be more practical, explaining the methods and procedures step by step, and giving hands-on instructions on how to carry out a procedure. The analysis tools and resources for each chapter are placed in a GitHub repository. The repository can be accessed at https://github.com/knowledge-construction/slam-ai.

Theoretical Foundations and IAM

Part I addresses the theoretical foundation of SCK, the learning theory that is the basis of IAM. Chapter 1 explores SCK, defines the method of interaction analysis, and presents the five Phases and operations of the IAM, which explain the co-construction of knowledge among interacting participants. In Chapter 2, guest authors Austin C. Megli and Monica Etsitty-Dorame review the many studies that have employed the IAM for researching SCK in collaborating groups and conclude with recommendations for improving the IAM, specifically, the need to incorporate the social context and social interaction. Chapter 3 follows by exploring social interaction and how it is defined and its relationship to knowledge construction. Chapter 3 leads the way for the next section of this book, which describes the methods we can use to analyze social interaction and the social environment of online learning.

Methods for Researching the Social Environment

Part II explores methods for researching the social environment online, a landscape that is sometimes challenging for researchers to navigate. Chapter 4 discusses the SLAM for analyzing the online social environment, which, when combined with IAM, offers multiple perspectives for understanding knowledge construction, particularly in the higher IAM Phases. Methods covered include social network analysis (SNA), cluster analysis, and decision trees, which complement rather than replace qualitative analysis by explaining how the social environment influences knowledge construction. Chapter 5 explores SCK in both formal learning management systems (LMS) (like Blackboard, Moodle, and Canvas), and informal social media (like X, Reddit, and Facebook) emphasizing text-based discussions. It outlines criteria for selecting the appropriate social learning space for research, considering relevance, target audience, and access to data, and provides a detailed method for scraping and analyzing online discussions, using a case study on Reddit to illustrate the process. Chapter 6 guides researchers on using various free and open-source tools for social learning analytics, focusing on programming languages (R and Python), and integrated analysis platforms (Anaconda, RStudio). The chapter also addresses setting up programming environments, installing R and Python, package management, and choosing suitable development environments for specific research needs.

Analysis of the Social Environment and Procedures

Part III explores how to analyze the social environment by using a wide range of SLAM that can decrease the manual effort needed to work with big data. The process generally starts with establishing suitable parameters for automated inquiry which is described in Chapter 7. This chapter outlines how to build lexica using dictionary, manual, and grounded approaches, demonstrating the process with the social presence lexica we developed and emphasizing the adaptability of these methods to anchor analytics in theory. In Chapter 8, completed lexica are used to perform analytics, beginning with basic descriptive statistics. This chapter will explain sentiment analysis and demonstrate how traditional categories can be adapted to represent various research constructs, using our experience with a social presence lexicon as an example. Chapter 9 delves into clustering techniques for analyzing large datasets to determine SCK. The chapter provides a practical guide to applying K-means and hierarchical clustering, including loading libraries, data cleaning, creating a document-term matrix, performing clustering, and visualizing results. Readers will understand how to use clustering to identify discussion topics and participant roles in SCK research. Chapter 10 will discuss how social network analysis (SNA) can be applied to analyze the social environment of online learning. Using SNA with IAM Phases creates a powerful approach that adds critical relational context to online interactions. While other SLAM methods answer the "what" question of knowledge construction, SNA answers the "how" with detailed sociograms. We will examine tools like NodeXL and R, comparing their analysis procedures and evaluating their strengths and weaknesses.

Chapter 11 moves on to exploring various natural language processing (NLP) techniques to analyze and understand the SCK in online discussions. We discuss how to identify discussion topics and communication structures. We demonstrate tokenization and word frequency analysis, parts-of-speech tagging, dependency parsing and graphs, named entity recognition, topic modeling, and topic modeling with Latent Dirichlet Allocation. The chapter provides practical examples and discusses the benefits and drawbacks of each method while outlining an integrated NLP pipeline for analyzing large datasets, emphasizing the importance of preprocessing, feature extraction, semantic analysis, and visualization. Chapter 12 focuses on building predictive models to validate theories about the online social environment, for example, the potential virality of a tweet. The chapter covers various methods for creating and testing models, with a focus on linear and multiple regressions. Chapter 13 concludes Part III by exploring AI, particularly large language models, for studying SCK on social media platforms. The chapter discusses practical applications of AI in SCK research, including summarization, translation, named entity recognition, and question-answering, using Python code examples to illustrate these techniques.

Applications

Part IV provides a range of practical applications of SLAM described in the previous chapters to analyze SCK with IAM. The studies included in this section address formal learning environments (such as in the discipline of nursing) and informal learning communities in social media such as Twitter (now known as X). Each of these studies applies SLAM in a novel way to assess the social dynamic that supports knowledge construction as mapped by the IAM. Chapter 14 explores a network of practice on Twitter, analyzing the #BlackLivesMatter hashtag during the Freddie Gray protests in Baltimore in April 2015. The study's goals were to enumerate levels of SCK using the IAM and determine its relationship to social action. In Chapter 15, guest author Sharon Schaaf discusses a mixed methods study that investigated the relationships between SCK, social network centrality, and advanced practice nurse (APN) competency. She discusses the analysis procedures, which include content analysis of an asynchronous discussion using two methods: IAM to determine levels of SCK and the Expert model to determine the level of APN competency, and SNA to determine centrality of the participants. This section concludes with Chapter 16, which explores how to set up a large language model (LLM) on a personal computer and presents a study using the LLM to predict the phases of knowledge construction according to the IAM codebook. The study compared the AI's phase predictions to human coding and found that the AI could predict the phases with moderate accuracy, even achieving 100% recall for Phase II. The study suggests numerous opportunities for refinement and enhancement to achieve more reliable and accurate coding. This can be accomplished by refining the current AI model or modifying the IAM codebook to better differentiate between the various phases and operations.

Reconceptualized IAM 2.0 With SLAM and AI

Part V, the concluding section of the book, draws from the analysis and discussions in previous chapters and looks ahead to a newly reconceptualized IAM and corresponding SLAM and AI to study SCK in online learning environments. The reconceptualized IAM 2.0, discussed in Chapter 17, addresses the shortcomings of the original IAM developed by Gunawardena et al. (1997). IAM 2.0 represents a revised framework for assessing SCK in the digital age. IAM 2.0 is grounded on principles of sociocultural learning theory and assigns a central role to the sociocultural context highlighting the influence of social interaction and its three dimensions of social presence, social connectedness, and community on knowledge construction. The chapter concludes with a discussion of IAM 2.0 transcript analysis techniques and research questions for exploring the relationship between social interaction and knowledge construction using SLAM and AI. Looking to the future of learning, Chapter 18 shows how IAM 2.0, used alongside SLAM and AI, enables research into how groups and teams interact and learn across diverse contexts – formal, informal, experiential – and on various platforms, from LMS asynchronous discussions to videoconferences and social media conversations. This chapter offers advice to researchers on analyzing group knowledge construction using IAM 2.0 and SLAM and AI, providing examples of research questions, designs, and methods and suggesting ways to elevate participants to higher levels of knowledge construction in online discussions. It ends with a discussion of ethical considerations in the use of SLAM and AI.

We provide all chapter tools and resources to aid in data analysis in a repository in GitHub at https://github.com/knowledge-construction/slam-ai.

Conclusion

This chapter introduced the book and provided the theoretical foundation for the Interaction Analysis Model (IAM), the book's focus. IAM was developed to research learning that happens through group interaction and collaboration on technology platforms that can be analyzed using a transcript of the learning process. We were motivated to explore its significance 25 years later to determine if it can be used as a framework for analyzing the relational aspect of learning in digital spaces in a variety of contexts by incorporating the newly developed Social Learning Analytic Methods (SLAM) and artificial intelligence (AI) tools. After presenting IAM, we discussed its unit of analysis, coding, and issues related to interrater reliability. We also explored how IAM compares with other similar frameworks and concluded with an overview of the book and how the chapters relate to each other.

Notes

This chapter draws from the following two previously published works in the list of references: Gunawardena et al. (1997), and Chapter 2 of Gunawardena et al. (2019).

Tools and resources to aid in data preparation and analysis are in a GitHub repository at https://github.com/knowledge-construction/slam-ai.

References

Brown, N. J. S., Danish, J., Levin, M., & DiSessa, A. A. (2016). Competence reconceived: The shared enterprise of knowledge analysis and interaction analysis. In A. A. DiSessa, M. Levin, & N. J. S. Brown (Eds.), *Knowledge and interaction: A synthetic agenda for the learning sciences* (pp. 11–29). New York: Routledge.

Buraphadeja, V., & Dawson, K. (2008). Content analysis in computer-mediated communication: Analyzing models for assessing critical thinking through the lens of social constructivism. *American Journal of Distance Education, 22*(3), 130–145.

Chi, M. T., & Wylie, R. (2014). The ICAP framework: Linking cognitive engagement to active learning outcomes. *Educational Psychologist, 49*(4), 219–243. https://doi.org/10.1080/00461520.2014.965823

Cole, M., & Engeström, Y. (1993). A cultural-historical approach to distributed cognition. In G. Salomon (Ed.), *Distributed cognitions* (pp. 1–46). New York, NY: Cambridge University Press.

Collis, B., & Heeren, E. (1993). Tele-collaboration and groupware. *Computing Teacher, 21*(1), 36–38.

De Wever, B., Schellens, T., Valcke, M., & Van Keer, H. (2006). Content analysis schemes to analyze transcripts of online asynchronous discussion groups: A review. *Computers & Education, 46*(1), 6–28.

De Wever, B., Van Keer, H., Schellens, T., & Valcke, M. (2010). Roles as a structuring tool in online discussion groups: The differential impact of different roles on social knowledge construction. *Computers in Human Behavior, 26*(4), 516–523.

Dillenbourg, P. (1999). Introduction: What do you mean by "collaborative learning"? In P. Dillenbourg (Ed.), *Collaborative learning: Cognitive and computational approaches* (pp. 1–19). Oxford, UK: Elsevier Science.

Engeström, Y. (1999). Activity theory and individual and social transformation. In Y. Engeström, R. Miettinen, & R. Punamäki (Eds.), *Perspectives on activity theory*. Cambridge, UK: Cambridge University Press.

Floren, L. C., Ten Cate, O., Irby, D. M., & O'Brien, B. C. (2021). An interaction analysis model to study knowledge construction in interprofessional education: Proof of concept. *Journal of Interprofessional Care, 35*(5), 736–743. https://doi.org/10.1080/13561820.2020.1797653

Garrison, D. R., Anderson, T., & Archer, W. (1999). Critical inquiry in a text-based environment: Computer conferencing in higher education. *The Internet and Higher Education, 2*(2–3), 87–105. https://doi.org/10.1016/S1096-7516(00)00016-6

Garrison, D. R., Anderson, T., & Archer, W. (2001). Critical thinking, cognitive presence, and computer conferencing in distance education. *The American Journal of Distance Education, 15*(1), 7–23. https://doi.org/10.1080/08923640109527071

Greenfield, P. M., & Bruner, J. S. (1966). Culture and cognitive growth. *International Journal of Psychology, 1*(2), 89–107.

Guba, E., & Lincoln, Y. (1981). *Effective evaluation*. San Francisco, CA: Jossey-Bass.

Gunawardena, C. N. (2004). The challenge of designing inquiry-based online learning environments: Theory into practice. In T. Duffy & J. Kirkley (Eds.), *Learner centered theory and practice in distance education: Cases from higher education* (pp. 143–158). Mahwah, NJ: Lawrence Erlbaum.

Gunawardena, C. N., Frechette, C., & Layne, L. (2019). *Culturally inclusive instructional design: A framework and guide for building online wisdom communities*. New York: Routledge.

Gunawardena, C. N., Lowe, C., & Anderson, T. (1995). The design, implementation, and evaluation of a worldwide on-line debate. In *Proceedings of the VI Congreso Internacional: Tecnologia y Educacion a Distancia* (pp. 195–206). San Jose, Costa Rica: Editorial Universidad Estatal a Distancia.

Gunawardena, C., Lowe, C., & Anderson, T. (1997). Analysis of a global on-line debate and the development of an interaction analysis model for examining social construction of knowledge in computer conferencing. *Journal of Educational Computing Research, 17*(4), 395–429.

Gunawardena, C. N., Rezabek, L., Cochenour, J., & Dillon, C. (1993). *Inter-university collaborative learning using CMC: The globaled experience*. Proceedings of the Ninth Annual Conference on Distance Teaching and Learning (pp. 74–78), University of Wisconsin-Madison, Madison, WI.

Hall, B. M. (2014). In support of the Interaction Analysis Model (IAM) for evaluating discourse in a virtual learning community. *Education Resources Information Center (ERIC)*, ED622614. https://files.eric.ed.gov/fulltext/ED622614.pdf

Hall, R., & Stevens, R. (2016). Interaction analysis approaches to knowledge in use. In A. A. diSessa, M. Levin, & N. J. S. Brown (Eds.), *Knowledge and interaction: A synthetic agenda for the learning sciences* (pp. 72–108). New York: Routledge.

Hanks, W. F. (1991). Foreword. In J. Lave & E. Wenger (Eds.), *Situated learning: Legitimate peripheral participation*. Cambridge, UK: Cambridge University Press.

Harasim, L. M. (Ed.) (1990). *Online education: Perspectives on a new environment*. New York: Praeger.

Harasim, L. M. (2017). *Learning theory and online technologies* (2nd ed.). New York: Routledge.

Henri, F. (1992). Computer conferencing and content analysis. In A. R. Kaye (Ed.), *Collaborative learning through computer conferencing: The Najadan Papers* (pp. 117–136). London: Springer-Verlag.

Ho, Y. (2024). Enhance adult students' online knowledge construction: Exploring effective instructional designs and addressing barriers. *Journal of Computer Assisted Learning, 40*(4), 1675–1689. https://doi. org/10.1111/jcal.12983

Hollan, J., Hutchins, E., & Kirsh, D. (2000). Distributed cognition: Toward a new foundation for human – Computer interaction research. *ACM Transactions on Computer – Human Interaction, 7*(2), 174–196.

Hutchins, E. (1990). The technology of team navigation. In J. Galegher, R. E. Kraut, & C. Egido (Eds.), *Intellectual teamwork: Social and technological foundations of cooperative work*. Hillsdale: Lawrence Erlbaum.

John-Steiner, V., & Mahn, H. (1996). Sociocultural approaches to learning and development: A Vygotskian framework. *Educational Psychologist, 31*(3/4), 191–206.

John-Steiner, V., & Souberman, E. (1978). Afterword. In L. S. Vygotsky (Ed.), *Mind in society: The development of higher psychological processes* (pp. 121–133). Cambridge, MA: Harvard University Press.

Jordan, B., & Henderson, A. (1995). Interaction analysis: Foundations and practice. *Journal of the Learning Sciences, 4*(1), 39–103.

Karpov, Y. V. (2014). *Vygotsky for educators*. New York: Cambridge University Press.

Koschmann, T. (1996). Paradigm shifts and instructional technology: An introduction. In T. Koschmann (Ed.), *CSCL: Theory and practice of an emerging paradigm* (pp. 1–24). Mahwah, NJ: Lawrence Erlbaum Associates.

Kumpulainen, K., & Wray, D. (2002). *Classroom interaction and social learning: From theory to practice*. London, UK: Routledge.

Lally, V. (2001). Analysing teaching and learning interactions in a networked collaborative learning environment: Issues and work in progress. In *Euro CSCL 2001* (pp. 397–405). Maastricht McLuhan Institute.

Lally, V., & de Laat, M. (2002). Cracking the code: Learning to collaborate and collaborating to learn in a networked environment. In G. Stahl (Ed.), *Proceedings of the Computer Supported Collaborative Learning (CSCL) Conference* (pp. 160–168). Boulder, CO: International Society of the Learning Sciences (ISLS).

Lave, J. (1991). Situating learning in communities of practice. In L. B. Resnick, J. M. Levine, & S. D. Teasley (Eds.), *Perspectives on socially shared cognition* (pp. 63–82). Washington, DC: American Psychological Association.

Lave, J., & Wenger, E. (1991). *Situated learning: Legitimate peripheral participation*. Cambridge, UK: Cambridge University Press.

Lehtinen, A., Kostiainen, E., & Näykki, P. (2023, October). Co-construction of knowledge and socioemotional interaction in pre-service teachers' video-based online collaborative learning. *Teaching and Teacher Education, 133*, 104299. https://doi.org/10.1016/j.tate.2023.104299

Littleton, K., & Hakkinen, P. (1999). Learning together: Understanding the processes of computer-based collaborative learning. In P. Dillenbourg (Ed.), *Collaborative learning: Cognitive and computational approaches* (pp. 20–30). Oxford, UK: Elsevier Science.

Lucas, M., Gunawardena, C., & Moreira, A. (2014). Assessing social construction of knowledge online: A critique of the interaction analysis model. *Computers in Human Behavior, 30*, 574–582.

Marra, R., Moore, J. L., & Klimczak, A. K. (2004). Content analysis of online discussion forums: A comparative analysis of protocols. *Educational Technology Research & Development, 52*(2), 23–40. https://link.springer.com/content/pdf/10.1007/BF02504837.pdf

Mercer, N. (1995). *The guided construction of knowledge: Talk amongst teachers and learners*. Clevedon: Multilingual Matters.

McAteer, E., Tolmie, A., Harris, R. A., Chappel, H., Marsden, S., & Lally, V. (2002). Characterising on-line learning environments. *Proceedings of Networked Learning 2002*. Sheffield, UK: University of Sheffield.

McDonald, N., Schoenebeck, S., & Forte. A. (2019, November). Reliability and inter-rater reliability in qualitative research: Norms and guidelines for CSCW and HCI practice. In *Proceedings of the ACM on Human-Computer Interaction*, 3, Article 72 (pp. 1–23). https://doi.org/10.1145/3359174

McHugh, M. L. (2012, October). Interrater reliability: The kappa statistic, *Biochem Med (Biochemia Medica) (Zagreb)*, 22(3), 276–282. PMCID: PMC3900052, PMID: 23092060.

Merriam, S. B. (1998). *Qualitative research and case study applications in education* (Revised & expanded edition). San Francisco: Jossey-Bass.

Miyashita, H., & Wark, N. (2024, April). Multiple content analysis models for analyzing higher order thinking development in online forums. *International Women Online Journal of Distance Education*, 13(1), 19–40. www.wojde.org multiple content analysis

Newman, D. R., Webb, B., & Cochrane, C. (1995). A content analysis method to measure critical thinking in face-to-face and computer supported group learning. *Interpersonal Computing and Technology*, 3, 56–77.

Piaget, J. (1964). Cognitive development in children: Piaget development and learning. *Journal of Research in Science Teaching*, 2(3), 176–186.

Rogoff, B. (1994). Developing understanding of the idea of communities of learners. *Mind, Culture and Activity*, 1(4), 209–229.

Rohfeld, R., Gunawardena, C. N., Eastmond, D. V., & Davidson, W. (1991, August). *Facilitating effective computer discussion for collaborative learning at a distance*. Paper presented at the Seventh Annual Conference on Distance Teaching and Learning, Madison, Wisconsin.

Rourke, L., Anderson, T., Garrison, D. R., & Archer, W. (2001). Methodological issues in the content analysis of computer conference transcripts. *International Journal of Artificial Intelligence in Education*, 12(1), 8–22.

Salomon, G. (1993). No distribution without individuals' cognition: A dynamic interactional view. In G. Salomon (Ed.), *Distributed cognitions: Psychological and educational considerations* (pp. 111–138). Cambridge, UK: Cambridge University Press.

Schellens, T., & Valcke, M. (2005). Collaborative learning in asynchronous discussion groups: What about the impact on cognitive processing? *Computers in Human Behavior*, 21, 957–975.

Smith, J. B. (1994). *Collective intelligence in computer-based collaboration*. Lawrence Erlbaum Associates, Hillsdale, NJ: Lawrence Erlbaum Associates.

Stahl, G. (2006). *Group cognition: Computer support for building collaborative knowledge*. Cambridge, MA: MIT Press.

Suartama, I. K., & Suranata, K. S. (2024). Mastering knowledge construction skills through a context-aware ubiquitous learning model based on the case method and team-based projects. *International Journal of Education and Practice*, 12(3), 1094–1112. https://doi.org/10.18488/61.v12i3.3842

Sun, Z., Lin, C-H., Lv, K., & Song, J. (2021). Knowledge-construction behaviors in a mobile learning environment: A lag-sequential analysis of group differences. *Education Tech Research Dev*, 69, 533–551. https://doi.org.libproxy.unm.edu/10.1007/s11423-021-09938-x

Vygotsky, L. S. (1978). *Mind in society: The development of higher psychological processes*. Cambridge, MA: Harvard University Press.

Wertsch, J. (1991). *Voices of the mind: A sociocultural approach to mediated action*. Cambridge, MA: Harvard University Press.

Zhang, S., Liu, Q., Chen, W., Wang, Q., & Huang, Z. (2017). Interactive networks and social knowledge construction behavioral patterns in primary school teachers' online collaborative learning activities. *Computers & Education*, 104, 1–17. https://doi.org/10.1016/j.compe du.2016.10.011

2 A Review of the Interaction Analysis Model (IAM) Research Applications

Austin C. Megli and Monica Etsitty-Dorame

The Interaction Analysis Model (Gunawardena et al., 1997) has been widely used nationally and internationally, with over 2,700 citations as of 2024, for analyzing social construction of knowledge (SCK) online. This chapter investigates the range of research that has used the Interaction Analysis Model (IAM) as a methodology for studying the social construction of knowledge (SCK). A systematic literature review was conducted to identify, evaluate, and synthesize research studies related to the IAM's use as a method for understanding collaborative learning and SCK in the higher education context. By the beginning of 2024, the method has been used in over 113 research works by researchers across the globe in K–12, undergraduate, graduate, massive open online courses (MOOC), and professional courses. Findings suggest that IAM is robust in analyzing SCK across a variety of disciplines (Commander et al., 2016; Lucas & Moreira, 2015; Megli, 2022). This review will focus on the contexts in which IAM has been used as a method and explore its advantages and limitations for analyzing SCK.

Asynchronous discussions are extensively used in online courses. The interaction opportunity enabled by asynchronous discussions is a significant component of the educational process because it is the primary means of interaction and negotiation of meaning among a group of participants (Howell et al., 2014). Online discussion forums have offered a new medium for collaborative work, study, and community (Kanuka & Anderson, 1998). The flexible structure of online discussions also supports the notion that the growth of online education has created new opportunities and challenges (Akarasriworn & Ku, 2013; Luebeck & Bice, 2005). In many higher education online courses, students are expected to share experiences, negotiate meaning, and construct knowledge within online discussion forums (Moore & Marra, 2005). Therefore, it is important to understand which aspects of online discussions encourage learning and increase knowledge construction (Howell et al., 2014). The IAM is a flexible method that can measure both synchronous and asynchronous interactions so long as there is a transcript of that interaction (Mutiaraningrum & Nugroho, 2020; Pillutla et al., 2020).

Gunawardena et al.'s (1997) article describing the development of the IAM has been cited over 2,700 times on Google Scholar and has been the foundational method for studying SCK in numerous studies, as the IAM provides an avenue for studying the process of acquiring that knowledge – the means by which new knowledge is constructed (Luebeck & Bice, 2005). The IAM has been identified as a reliable method (Marra et al., 2004) and one of the most regularly used tools for studying knowledge construction (Beaudrie, 2000: Schellens & Valcke, 2006). In Huntley's (2008) study, which assessed how time can impact discussions that take place in a virtual forum, the IAM was preferred over Newman et al.'s (1995) Critical Thinking model because the IAM provided fewer codes (Phases I through V), easier coding

DOI: 10.4324/9781003324461-3

applications and interpretation of data, and a better view of discussion flow and knowledge construction. It is the basis for several research studies for exploring variables that may influence higher level knowledge construction in online discussion forums (De Wever et al., 2010; Guo et al., 2022; Hew & Cheung, 2011).

Gunawardena et al. (1997) developed the IAM while studying the written transcript of an online text-based debate, which was the original context for the IAM. This debate was created as a professional development experience which happened before the World Conference on Distance Learning in 1995, and the participants were primarily professionals and researchers in the field of distance learning.

The literature review explored the contexts in which the IAM was used and its strengths and weaknesses, and based on the findings, it provides recommendations for revision of the model to assess SCK.

Method

A comprehensive literature review was conducted to assess the extent and thoroughness of studies employing the IAM in the investigation of SCK. The goal was to obtain an exhaustive review of research that is relevant to the IAM. In following a social science systematic literature review, this study established, evaluated, and synthesized relevant research studies to answer this study's research interest (Petticrew & Roberts, 2006, p. 9). A Carnegie Classified Research 1 (R1) southwestern university's library databases (Academic Search Complete, Education Research Complete, ERIC, Psych INFO, Proquest Dissertation and Thesis) and the interlibrary loan service were the primary search engines for the literature review. The keywords searched include, "Interaction Analysis Model," "Social Construction of Knowledge," "Interaction," and "Interaction Analysis." The only criterion for the search was to retain works that discussed or utilized the IAM in the study. There were no limitations set on the type of works used, so data includes academic journals, books, dissertations, and conference proceedings. The literature review covered research published during the period of 1997 through 2024.

IAM Research Contexts

The IAM as a method has been used in numerous versatile research contexts across the globe in K–12, undergraduate, graduate, massive open online courses (MOOC), and professional courses in disciplines ranging from nursing, chemistry, instructional design, faculty development, leadership, religious studies, engineering, law, mathematics, educational technology, veterinary studies, learning sciences, management, psychology, gaming, history, philosophy, literature, music, computer science, physics, business administration, and communications. The IAM has been used primarily to analyze online text-based transcripts, but it has also been used to analyze video-based interactions and voice-based interactions (Kokic & Rukavina, 2017). Also, the IAM has been used to examine how knowledge co-construction can advance during post-video discourse in YouTube videos (Dubovi & Tabak, 2020). Further, the IAM has been used in the analysis of face-to-face interactions and in-person clinical learning settings in the health professions (Bao et al., 2016; Cheng et al., 2019; Socratous & Ioannou, 2018; Zhou & Yang, 2017; Floren et al., 2021). Other contexts in which the IAM has been employed to analyze interactions are virtual worlds such as Second Life (Hardesty, 2023) and informal Twitter (X) communities (Sánchez, 2018).

Studies that employ the IAM typically leverage deidentified text-data from online courses and discussions, which have been completed. Because of this, most studies do not delve into the demographics of participants in the discussion forums. Furthermore, studies employing the IAM are typically focused on the group's SCK rather than analyzing individual contributors. For example, in Yasuda's (2021) study of over 4,000 interactions over 16 weeks, there were only 4 student participants who were identified as "1 male and 3 females aged 19 to 20" which offers some information on demographics, but it can be challenging to situate these student demographics within the larger context of research studies that have employed the IAM. Similarly, Tawfik et al. (2021) described the demographics of their student participants as 121 students enrolled in an online undergraduate business course at an American Midwestern university. With the lack of demographic information and consistent ambiguity on how the contexts may be related to one another, it can be challenging to make overall observations about the type of participants who engaged and benefitted from the online experiences in the research studies. This drawback prevents researchers from identifying whether there are specific student types, such as adult learners or traditional students, who may feel most comfortable with socially constructing knowledge in a specific context via specific kinds of prompts. Researchers have also identified that student groups with specific cultural backgrounds, such as students from Latin American or Asia, may not feel comfortable with specific discussion formats such as a debate in a discussion forum (Gunawardena et al., 2018, p. 121). In analyzing discussions in the Mexican context, Lopez-Islas (2001) found that students built knowledge without going through dissonance (Phase II of IAM). Moving through the levels of SCK may not be linear in all discussions. Further, some participants may not be comfortable with all Phases of SCK in discussions, such as Phase II, which is focused on the discovery and exploration of dissonance or the inconsistency among ideas, concepts, or statements (Megli, 2022). It would be valuable for future researchers to further analyze and situate the context of their studies in relation to past research, along with analyzing the demographics of individual contributors so there would be more opportunities for researchers to contribute to the conversation around how culture, context, and demographics of participants may play a role in the SCK of a group.

Advantages of the IAM for Assessing Social Construction of Knowledge

Research studies that have utilized the IAM as their methodology have discussed and identified specific advantages of the model for analyzing SCK. A commonly identified advantage is that the IAM is a frequently used method for analyzing knowledge construction (Commander et al., 2016) and is considered to be a reliable and user-friendly model (Chai & Tan, 2009). Previous studies as well as the breadth of use by researchers support the proposition that the IAM is the most useful tool in analyzing online collaborative discussions. (Commander et al., 2016). Further, the IAM "offers a holistic view of discussion flow and knowledge construction" (Davis & Marone, 2016, p. 3), and "presents clear and validated stages for the construction of knowledge" (Lucas & Moreira, 2015, p. 1501). Hall (2014) indicated that the validity of the IAM has been established, developed, and used in over 40 different published studies nearly a decade ago. At the time of writing this chapter, over 75 research works have used the IAM as a methodology in their studies. The IAM has also had "a higher-level inter-rater reliability calculation" (Huntley & Thatcher, 2008, p. 13), which ensures a more reliable and unbiased study with resulting data that is easier to interpret (Lim & Hall, 2015). Also, Cragg et al.'s (2008) study found that the "use of a framework like social constructivism allows the distance educator to assess the efficacy of online discourse . . . and enhance the understanding of the participants" (p. 119).

When analyzing data using the IAM, the strength of the method includes "the efficacy of the model for identifying overall patterns of knowledge construction, a 'straightforward schema' for analysis" (Davis & Marone, 2016, p. 3) and makes the qualitative coding process a tool new researchers can learn and implement. In addition, the model was "found useful as a preliminary means to analyze and understand the kinds of communicative strategies taking place within a community of learners" when analyzing computer-mediated communications of working professionals in the education realm who were discussing technology implementation in the classroom (Hendriks & Maor, 2004, p. 10). Researchers have shown that the IAM can be used in combination with other analytic methods to contribute to a larger conversation around how knowledge is constructed and with learning analytics (LA), social network analysis (SNA), and other analytic methods (Gunawardena et al., 2016, 2023; Kaliisa et al., 2022; Megli, 2022; Megli et al., 2023; Ouyang et al., 2023; Saint et al., 2020).

Advantages regarding the specific Phases of the IAM include the model's ability to "explicitly conceptualize the sequential relationship between different knowledge construction Phases providing testable hypotheses of predicted knowledge construction patterns," which allows the individual Phases to be explicitly evaluated and analyzed (Wise & Chiu, 2011, p. 446). In addition, Osman and Herring (2007) determined in their study of cross-cultural learners "that differences in the frequency of each phase manifested by students in comparison to facilitators showed a trend over time toward mutual accommodation, and thus provided partial support for the negotiative spirit of the model" (p. 135). Consequently, "the strategy of counting participant contributions in general and those at each phase of construction allowed comparison of qualitative and quantitative differences in discussions occurring in these delivery methods," with those delivery methods being in-person courses and online courses (Cragg et al., 2008). In Cragg et al.'s (2008) study of master's-level nursing students discussing advanced nursing theory in an online versus face-to-face format, the researchers were able to utilize counts of specific contributions in relation to the IAM Phases in order to develop a quantitative analysis with the tool. They were one of the first researchers to show that the IAM could be used in combination with other analyses and tools. In turn, this showed that the IAM could also be used as a method in combination with other techniques for both quantitative and qualitative analysis.

Further, "the use of this [IAM] framework is intended to facilitate the comparison of findings with previous studies that consider knowledge construction in formal academic settings" (Davis & Marone, 2016, p. 3). Davis and Marone (2016) proposed that the IAM is an appropriate tool for assessing SCK in formal academic settings outside of solely the professional development environment. The IAM has been consistently used quite similarly across formal academic settings so the outcomes from those studies can be compared to one another to further the field's understanding of how students in formal academic settings socially co-construct knowledge. Essentially, the IAM is "both theoretically and empirically grounded and attempts to capture 'the complete process of negotiation' involved in knowledge construction" (Wise & Chiu, 2011, p. 446). The IAM as a methodology measures the process of SCK in online courses.

While several studies have shown the advantages of using the IAM to assess SCK, some studies have also noted the limitations of the IAM which are discussed next.

Limitations of the IAM for Assessing Social Construction of Knowledge

Despite the IAM being identified as a prominent framework to conceptualize learner-to-learner interactions, previous studies have identified common themes of limitations of the model. One of these themes is that online discussions rarely reach all five Phases as described by the IAM.

In Chai and Tan's (2009) study, which focused on studying the professional development of P–12 teachers in Singapore, they mentioned that the IAM Phases in other studies show results that learners rarely "achieve higher Phases of co-construction of knowledge" (p. 1313). This study shares the commonality with other studies that identify that most discussions operate in the lower Phases of co-construction of knowledge, specifically in IAM Phase I, II, and III. In one of the first studies that employed the IAM as a methodology when analyzing interactions in a project management course, McLoughlin and Luca (1999) identified that nearly 66%, or two-thirds, of the interactions were Phase I interactions. A few years later De Laat (2002) identified that nearly 72% of the discussion posts in their study of online interactions in a policy organization course were Phase I posts with none of the posts reaching either Phase IV or Phase V. Similarly, Jamaludin and Lang (2006) utilized the IAM in their study of K–12 students in Singapore and noted that about 65% of the posts were in Phase I with there being no Phase V posts. Lucas et al. (2014) also acknowledged that complex thinking is rarely achieved by participants and emphasized that "space for developing arguments or negotiating them becomes limited," especially "when participants only have to agree or disagree with a given statement" (p. 576). While this limitation seems to be repeated frequently in the literature, it is unclear whether it is truly a limitation of the model itself or a limitation that arises given the participants, discussion prompts, and context of the studies. Lucas et al. (2014) make the important observation that the type of discussion prompt or instructions for the assignment may limit the discussion to only the first Phase of IAM. The IAM was not created to be used with either poorly constructed discussion prompts or students who may be new to creating knowledge regarding a new topic, as it was originally developed to measure SCK of professionals in a field who voluntarily participated in a professional development debate, and therefore, it may not be a suitable tool for assessing discussions with novice participants that do not move beyond Phase I of IAM that focuses on sharing and comparing of information. There is likely a different caliber of participants when the discussion is amongst professionals working in a field with a topic they are familiar with and when the participants are K–12 students who are working around a new, unfamiliar topic.

Another limitation the researchers found when utilizing the IAM is that the IAM does not account for time constraints or intervals between interactions set by instructors or facilitators in discussions forums of working groups (Akarasriworn & Ku, 2013). In academic settings, instructors often specify the time limits for participation in a discussion. These time limits may negatively impact the time needed for a discussion to move toward knowledge construction. The IAM is unable to assess the influence of the time constraints on knowledge construction. Further, the IAM does not account for interactions happening outside of the transcripted interaction, which is a clear limitation when interaction outside the transcripted environment exists in many discussion contexts. In this regard, Ke et al. (2011) indicated that the student's knowledge is not always identifiable within a discussion post unless there is an ability to assess interactions outside formal learning environments. This can exclude outside interactions in massive open online courses (MOOCs), a recently popularized means of informal online learning, which, by their very "open" nature are inclusive of a wider array of learners (Stich & Reeves, 2017; Tawfik et al., 2017).

Interactions outside of the formal learning environment are left out of the IAM analysis, as the analysis solely focuses on text-based interactions. This inability to assess "unspoken" interactions is considered a limitation by some researchers. Another limitation identified by researchers is the IAM's inability to assess the chronological and systemic evolution of such interactions and create an accurate picture of the discussion flow or the progress and development of students' knowledge (Lucas & Moreira, 2015). Sometimes online discussion forums do not flow steadily, one after another, or they are set up through differing threads. When there is a transcript available, it is possible to analyze interactions external to the discussion such as an external WhatsApp discussion between a group of participants. Recently, Yasuda (2021) was able to analyze 4,685 mobile instant messages regarding an economics course project over 16 weeks, which were external interactions to the discussion forum environment, through utilizing the IAM in order to provide an understanding of what is happening outside of the external discussion environment. This leaves out the reality that sometimes instructors may purposefully set up rules within the learning management system that students may not view any of the discussion posts before making their own initial post. The assumption that a student has read what was posted and that the students are building off of what prior students have posted may not always, or frequently, be the case. The findings from previous studies confirm some contextual limitations of the tool developed to assess knowledge construction, which often depends on other variables. This limitation should be considered when using IAM. Wise and Chiu (2011) identified that the IAM "does not differentiate quality: a creative detailed proposed task solution may contribute more to a discussion than a simple opinion, but both are coded as knowledge construction Phase 1" (p. 467). This is a limitation of the method, as neither the quality of a post nor the roles of the variety of participants are accounted for when utilizing the IAM.

Since the development of the IAM in 1997, the five Phases have not undergone any changes. Researchers who have used IAM in their own research have not asked for the elimination of any of the five Phases, which have been considered reliable and valid in explaining the process of knowledge construction among a group (Hall, 2014). Most have pointed out that online discussions rarely reach Phases IV and V. In Osman and Herring's (2007) study of deep learning in cross-cultural contexts, students did not reach Phases IV and V as was predicted, essentially "reflect[ing] negatively on the usefulness of the Gunawardena et al. (1997) model" (p. 135). The fact that participants do not reach higher levels of knowledge construction in some discussions is not identified as a limitation of the tool itself but as an issue with the way discussion prompts are written for the participants. Therefore, it might be useful to review the IAM considering the findings of research and reconceptualize it in relation to the various contexts in which it is used.

Lastly, a major limitation of the IAM is the historical lack of analysis of the social dynamics of online interactions. Gunawardena et al. (1997) in their development of IAM, purposefully left out the analysis of social dynamics. For example, Lucas and Moreira (2010), in their study focusing on online asynchronous discussions in a first year master's degree course in multimedia in education, noticed that despite focusing on interaction as the vehicle of knowledge construction, the IAM does not have the capability of demonstrating the social dynamics that go beyond the differing categories proposed for the specific Phases for IAM. Although this limitation has been historically accounted for, recent studies have shown how social dynamics can be accounted for in future studies utilizing the IAM. For example, Megli (2022) showed that social presence lexicon analysis, developed by Gunawardena et al. (2016), can be used in combination with the IAM. Megli's (2022) study determined that an increase in social presence is significantly positively related to higher levels of SCK in online higher education courses.

Evaluation the IAM in Varied Contexts

It is important to note that the IAM framework was developed to examine the evidence of collective knowledge development in a debate forum even though it has been leveraged to analyze interactions in different contexts (Ke et al., 2011). The IAM has been used for analyzing group discussions and coding mostly open-ended and argument-natured comments, focused on collective development and meaningful thinking rather than individual cognition and content acquisition (Gee & Green, 1998; Ke et al., 2011; Marra et al., 2004).

Ke et al. (2011) proposed that more research is needed to identify variables that cannot be measured with the IAM, such as interactions outside of the online discussion forum. This endeavor implies the need to identify variables outside the discussion context that could potentially limit the analysis conducted with the tool. For example, the minimum participation requirements imposed by instructors affects how often students must participate to meet the learning objectives (Moore & Marra, 2005); therefore, their discussions may not reach the highest level of knowledge construction correlating with testing and modification of the proposed synthesis or co-construction as stipulated in the IAM (Kokic & Rukavina, 2017). Some studies had numerous participants, such as Tawfik et al.'s (2021) study which included 121 participants with 1,877 unique interactions, while Yasuda's (2021) study of over 4,000 interactions only consisted of 4 participants. There has yet to be an agreed upon way to determine whether the number of participants or interactions is appropriate for IAM analysis. This in itself limits the IAM's ability to assess all types of SCK, and particular attention should be paid toward whether the number of participants and interactions are appropriate for IAM analysis, as a minimum threshold has not been identified for the method.

Regardless of the rigor of the coding schema, the coding process is a subjective process with many nuances. Howell et al. (2014) mentioned that the IAM tool does not give individual scores that are distinguished among subcategories. Conflicts can arise when a message has evidence of multiple Phases and operations, but staying true to the IAM coding gives deference to the highest Phase identified in a message; such an approach still leaves room for nuanced subjective interpretation (Cragg et al., 2008). In turn, moving toward a more objective process with less variability may be beneficial, such as developing a lexicon to assist future researchers with the coding of the IAM Phases.

Gunawardena et al. (2016) and Megli (2022) showed the advantage of using many methods to analyze online discussions. Using multiple methods can provide insight into the social dynamics that accompany the SCK process. Other researchers (e.g., Aviv et al., 2003; Kumar & Buraphadeja, 2010; Roseli & Umar, 2015) have also used a mixed-method approach in examining the relationship between knowledge construction and other variables using multiple methods. In turn, they have gained insight into social dynamics of asynchronous online discussion forums. Further research into social dynamics in relation to knowledge construction is vital for a better understanding of SCK in online environments. Social dynamics are not often focused on in studies that have employed IAM. While Gunawardena et al. (1997) did not address the social dynamic in their development of the IAM, they have since realized its role in the knowledge construction process and, in a 2016 study, examined the social dynamic utilizing social learning analytics and social network analysis. They asserted that "social network diagrams make the social dynamics of online learning tangible which extends the IAM analysis beyond its typical capacity of focusing on cognitive processes" (Gunawardena et al., 2016, p. 42). In turn, the developers of IAM and other researchers have found that LA and SNA augment IAM by expanding understanding of the socioemotional dynamic that goes along with the SCK process. Lehtinen et al. (2023), in their study of how pre-service secondary education teachers co-construct knowledge and express socioemotional interaction in online breakout rooms during collaborative tasks, showed that other aspects of synchronous communications, such as humor and active listening, can increase the co-construction of knowledge in learning settings.

Evolution of the IAM Phases

A common consensus derived from previous studies is that the IAM provides sufficient explanatory power to accurately assess interactions among online learners when conducting content analysis on discussion posts to analyze the construction of knowledge in an online environment. To this end, it is important to explore how the IAM can be improved for analysis of SCK. Very early on, studies identified new patterns that emerged with the IAM qualitative transcript analysis, but they have not significantly changed the original model, such as the pattern that emerged in this study was one of a cognitive process involving social interchange and limited amounts of social discord (Kanuka & Anderson, 1998). In some cases, new codes were created, such as subcodes 1a or 2b, to fit the study (Chai & Tan, 2009), or a new category was developed such as Phase 0, to account for conceptual background content (Osman & Herring, 2007). The need for new categories has been proposed and recognized by researchers, as "refining the operationalization of the categories, particularly for Phase I, sharing and comparing information, and Phase III, negotiation of meaning/co-construction of knowledge, due to the difficulty in differentiating" between the Phases (Osman & Herring, 2007, p. 130). Additionally, others have found difficulties in differentiating between the lower Phases, specifically Phase II and Phase III, in some non-debate format discussions "because indicators for those Phases imply the existence of disagreement and a need to resolve a conflict" (Luebeck & Bice, 2005, p. 36). In turn, researchers should determine whether IAM Phases should be reconceptualized in some way to account for the findings from the past 25 years of research studies.

The IAM may need to be adapted depending on the culture of the participants in the online discussion forum. There seems to be a "scarcity of research reports [in conjunction with SCK and IAM] . . . from a different sociocultural context" (Gómez Jaimes & Hernández Castañeda, 2018, p. 299). For example, Chen and Starosta's (2000) study showed that leveraging the debate format created issues for some participants in specific cultures, as this context is a product of low-context culture that requires a specific expression of one's argument by using logical reasoning. Students from Asia or Latin America have found the argumentative format of a debate context to be unsettling in a formal academic context (Gunawardena et al., 2018, p. 121). Redefining the dissonance/disagreements Phase of IAM (Phase II) in accounting for cultural attributes where "cultures might not welcome dissonances/disagreements as much as stating agreements" should be a future consideration (Çardak, 2020, p. 82; Lucas et al., 2014). "Cross-cultural studies might help refine the model according to specific a culture, if distinct differences are observed between various cultures" (Çardak, 2020, p. 82). This uncomfortable feeling can further affect the students and the group of participants because the asynchronous debate is happening in a medium that does not allow for nonverbal interaction to be easily portrayed. The original development of the IAM utilized a formal debate that took place in English. Therefore, IAM did not account for other languages and their unique linguistic formats in its analysis. In turn, further adaptations of the IAM may need to be created to make for a better way to analyze SCK in cultural environments that do not comfortably lend themselves to the progression of the IAM Phases, such as developing a version of the IAM that is more appropriate to unique cultural contexts where students may regularly use languages other than English.

Findings from previous studies have consistently indicated significantly higher coding volume in Phase I, sharing and comparing information, than in any other category. This is a common finding when utilizing the IAM as Phase I is the stage when discussions begin and participants get to know each other. Regarding Phase II, researchers have observed that the "development of the IAM assumed – in fact contrived – a contentious context with the goal of resolving opposing viewpoints" (Luebeck & Bice, 2005, p. 36). Low scores in higher Phase levels could be a result of the hesitancy to assign higher values to messages due to the "lack of [IAM] indicators referring to dissonance, disagreement, and the need to negotiate opposing views" (Luebeck & Bice, 2005, p. 36). A new version of the IAM may move away from the idea that rational argument is necessary for knowledge construction, for example, "I will convince you" to leverage a more fluid process of learning through interaction "Let's pursue this together," which would be more suitable for diverse students (Luebeck & Bice, 2005, p. 36).

One early recommendation to improve the IAM was to include a more detailed and explicit boundary between the unique Phases since few discussion forums reach higher Phases of SCK (Kanuka & Anderson, 1998, p. 72). It may prove "beneficial to identify the paths of discussions that progress to the higher Phases of knowledge co-construction (e.g., the co-construction of meaning, the testing of new knowledge, and summaries and applications of new knowledge)" (Davis & Marone, 2016, p. 32) and provide indicators that would assist coding for these two Phases.

Unique Conditions Supporting the Social Construction of Knowledge

Implications for designing online discussions that reach higher levels of SCK could be better off by utilizing a few conditions which have been identified in IAM research for increasing SCK. Researchers from previous studies have regularly identified external conditions that encourage higher level discussions that enhance the learning experience in online environments (Hew & Cheung, 2011; Tawfik et al., 2021; Megli, 2022). Howell et al. (2014) point out that it is important to consider understanding which external conditions would create the most successful online discussion.

The first condition to consider is the type of online environment that will put participants at ease to contribute. Researchers have recommended utilizing an open discussion environment to prevent participants from being perceived as confrontational, which could lead to feeling afraid or hesitant to question or challenge other's ideas (Hew & Cheung, 2011). Open environments protect personal self-image from comments or opinions which could end further contributions (Hew & Cheung, 2011).

The second condition to consider is the type of discussion prompt used, or task design, to potentially promote higher levels of SCK (Howell et al., 2014; Tawfik et al., 2021). The facilitator's decision regarding the type of prompt used has also been shown to increase intersubjectivity, the experience for negotiating meaning until new knowledge is achieved, in discussion forums (Lim et al., 2017). Facilitators and developers of discussion spaces must try to ensure that participation protocols align with the specific task and intended objectives of the discussion forum prompt, which may contribute to more meaningful discussion and may assist participants in reaching higher levels of SCK (Moore & Marra, 2005). Online environments rely on online discussion forum participation as the primary form of interaction, so it is recommended to utilize the appropriate levels of expected interaction among students and instructors to produce high levels of critical thinking (Belcher et al., 2015). "A certain amount of online interaction is a necessary factor [for consideration,] but the quality of online interaction is critical for successful outcomes" (Jakubec & Campbell, 2003, p. 1391). With this consideration, attention to the number of participants, the time available for participation, and the quality of contributions from participants can help move the group to higher levels of SCK.

The third external condition to consider is understanding the social context of online discussions. An analysis of this condition was purposefully left out in the original IAM, but researchers have been able to utilize creative ways to include additional analysis to better understand the social context that happens inside and outside of the online discussion forum environment (Megli, 2022; Yasuda, 2021). The quality of online interactions can be improved by leveraging social presence techniques. The objective of creating "social presence" among participants is to reduce the feeling of isolation to increase quality participation (Moore & Marra, 2005; Gunawardena et al., 2018). In fact, it is well established that various instructor implemented techniques can increase social presence in the social environment of online learning such as using facilitator and participant introductions, cyber cafes, communities, desktop or mobile conferencing, and netiquette guidelines (Gunawardena et al., 2018). Yang et al. (2018) observed groups with higher levels of engagement were more likely to exhibit negotiation and knowledge co-construction in comparison to groups with lower levels of engagement. One recommendation by researchers is to assign participant roles, such as participant or moderator, in asynchronous group discussions and this should be introduced at the start of the discussions so that the SCK processes can be enhanced (Çardak, 2020; De Wever et al., 2010). Assigning roles to participants may help the group to reach higher levels of SCK since higher levels are so rare in discussions. Participants may also leverage social activities during knowledge construction with group members because they may lead to higher achievements (Jakubec & Campbell, 2003). Previous studies have proposed that the structure of the online discussion forums alone is not enough to influence higher levels of thinking (Luebeck & Bice, 2005) so developing social presence can be done by encouraging participants to give comments or opinions, show appreciation, contribute, and summarize more frequently, which may promote higher levels of knowledge construction in online discussions (Hew & Cheung, 2011). "Designers should create prompts that naturally encourage participants to collaborate in creating solutions and ideas or require them to choose an argument and defend their opinion" (Howell et al., 2014, p. 15). More research is needed to "investigate the association between social presence and the higher levels of knowledge construction according to the Interaction Analysis Model" (Gómez Jaimes & Hernández Castañeda, 2018, p. 300). In a recent study, Hardesty (2023) determined the relationship between social presence and knowledge construction in the Second Life virtual world and found that the more engaged the participants were in the joint activity with each other in text and in the presence of others in the same virtual space, the higher the levels of social presence and knowledge construction. Therefore, collaborative activities may lead to higher levels of knowledge construction.

This chapter recommends that future research should make a point to address social dynamics to help broaden the insights available regarding the knowledge construction process. Analyzing the social dynamics and social environment of online learning through the lens of the IAM can add a more complete understanding of how students construct knowledge in online learning environments. Social dynamics are infrequently addressed in the studies that have used IAM. Future research should explore social dynamics utilizing interdisciplinary methods such as social learning analytics (SLA) and social network analysis (SNA). In fact, Gunawardena et al. (2016) found that SLA and SNA enrich IAM by expanding understanding of the socioemotional dynamic that accompanies the knowledge construction process (Sánchez, 2018). In addition, the development of a SCK lexicon can be used as the foundation for future studies that will use the IAM and social learning analytics (Sánchez, 2018). Leveraging a social presence lexicon with the SCK lexicon in combination could increase the speed at which the analysis of the IAM and social environment could take place (Megli, 2022). SLA, SNA, and the IAM can be used in conjunction to assess multiple variables in relation to how social dynamics are associated with SCK to better account for the understanding of knowledge construction. Utilizing SLA and SNA may offer new insights, expand future research opportunities, and offer a deeper understanding of the variables that can affect the SCK. As we look ahead, our challenge as researchers is to further analyze how SCK is co-constructed in more specific education contexts and work environments so we can promote higher levels of SCK across all online learning platforms.

Conclusion

This chapter identified the various research studies in which the IAM has been used as the primary research methodology. The IAM is clearly a favorable methodology amongst researchers who conducted studies analyzing collaborative online discussion forums and SCK. The consensus amongst researchers is that the IAM is a user-friendly, reliable, and theoretically grounded model. The IAM provides sufficient explanatory power to accurately assess the knowledge construction process among online learners when researchers stay true to the IAM coding.

The limitations of the IAM are apparent and accounted for in numerous studies. A frequent limitation identified amongst researchers is that participants rarely reach higher IAM Phases (Phases IV and V) of SCK. Arguably, this is not a fault of the IAM but is likely a product of the type of discussions that took place and the knowledge level of the specific participants in the forum, as many are novice students engaging about a topic for the first time. The IAM was originally developed while analyzing a discussion forum consisting of professionals and graduate students who were familiar with the topic. Therefore, there is an unrealistic expectation for students to obtain the same higher levels of knowledge construction as experienced professionals in a field. Another limitation pointed out in studies is the inability of IAM to assess "unspoken interactions amongst the participants and their environment [which in turn] does not provide an accurate picture of the discussion flow nor the progress and development of students' knowledge" (Lucas & Moreira, 2015, p. 1501). While not a limitation of the model itself, the IAM can only be used in contexts where there is a transcript of the written or spoken discussion. Previous studies also identified the difficulty of coding messages which signal several IAM Phases. Another limitation which impacts coding with IAM is the participation level in a discussion forum. There needs to be sufficient data and communication, such as more than a couple posts, in order to effectively study a group's progression through the levels of SCK. A better understanding of external variables and conditions that impact online discussions is required to further investigate the advantages and limitations of the studies that have employed the IAM to analyze collaborative online discussions for SCK.

Ten Recommendations for Future Research

1. Integrate an understanding of the social environment in which social construction of knowledge takes place.
2. Utilize many methods in combination with IAM such as SLA, SNA, and social presence lexicon analysis to analyze online discussions, which will further inform research studies that assess SCK.
3. Compare the IAM analysis with other models that guide assessment of SCK to determine how these models converge and differ in relation to their results.
4. Identify whether the online discussion forum's design considerations, such as required posting order, threaded or unthreaded discussion forums, and ability to view other postings, affect the IAM analysis.
5. Analyze how, and which types, of discussion prompts affect whether the group will progress to higher levels of SCK.

6. Create a lexicon or dictionary classifiers and concrete examples of each Phase of IAM to increase interrater reliability when coding.
7. Determine further parsing out the Phases of the IAM by either creating new Phases or altering current Phases, such as combining Phases IV and V at the higher levels of knowledge construction.
8. Account for the cultural context of participants when analyzing SCK with IAM.
9. Determine tools that can be used to analyze the environment outside of the formal learning context that the IAM does not analyze.
10. Rethink the role of context in an IAM analysis to clearly differentiate between the contexts in which the IAM is being used, such as formal academic settings, informal academic settings, virtual work settings, mobile instant messaging, and text-based, video-based, and voice-based interactions.

References

Akarasriworn, C., & Ku, H. Y. (2013). Graduate students' knowledge construction and attitudes toward online synchronous video conferencing collaborative learning environments. *The Quarterly Review of Distance Education, 14*(1), 35–48. https://eric.ed.gov/?id=EJ1144788

Aviv, R., Erlich, Z., Ravid, G., & Geva, A. (2003). Network analysis of knowledge construction in asynchronous learning networks. *Journal of Asynchronous Learning Networks, 7*(3), 1–23. https://doi.org/10.2307/2786027

Bao, W., Blanchfield, P., & Hopkins, G. (2016). The effectiveness of face-to-face discussion in Chinese primary schools. In *EDULEARN16 Proceedings* (pp. 3863–3872). https://doi.org/10.21125/edulearn.2016.1925

Beaudrie, B. P. (2000). *Analysis of group problem-solving tasks in a geometry course for teachers using computer-mediated conferencing* [Doctoral thesis, Montana State University]. ScholarWorks. https://scholarworks.montana.edu/xmlui/handle/1/7991

Belcher, A. R., Hall, B. M., Kelley, K., & Pressey, K. L. (2015). An analysis of faculty promotion of critical thinking and peer interaction within threaded discussions. *Online Learning, 19*(4). http://doi.org/10.24059/olj.v19i4.544

Çardak, Ç. S. (2020). Revisiting social construction of knowledge in asynchronous computer mediated communications (CMC): What to change. *Anadolu University Journal of Education Faculty (AUJEF), 4*(1), 67–87.

Chai, C. S., & Tan, S. C. (2009). Professional development of teachers for computer-supported collaborative learning: A knowledge-building approach. *Teachers College Record, 111*(5), 1296–1327. www.learntechlib.org/p/106062/

Chen, G. M., & Starosta, W. J. (2000). *Communication and global society* (pp. 143–157). New York: Peter Lang.

Cheng, Y. W., Wang, Y., Cheng, I. L., & Chen, N. S. (2019). An in-depth analysis of the interaction transitions in a collaborative augmented reality-based mathematic game. *Interactive Learning Environments, 27*(5–6), 782–796. https://doi.org/10.1080/10494820.2019.1610448

Commander, N., Zhao, Y., Gallagher, P., & You, Y. (2016). Cross-national online discussions: International learning experiences with American and Chinese students in higher education. *Innovations in Education & Teaching International, 53*(4), 365–374. https://doi.org/10.1080/14703297.2015.1006524

Cragg, C. E., Dunning, J., & Ellis, J. (2008). Teacher and student behaviors in face-to-face and on-line courses: Dealing with complex concepts. *Journal of Distance Education, 22*(3), 115–128. www.ijede.ca/index.php/jde/article/view/45/773

Davis, D., & Marone, V. (2016). Learning in discussion forums: An analysis of knowledge construction in a gaming affinity space. *International Journal of Game-Based Learning, 6*(3), 1–17. https://doi.org/10.4018/IJGBL.2016070101

De Laat, M. (2002). Network and content analysis in an online community discourse. In G. Stahl (Ed.), *Computer support for collaborative learning: Foundations for a CSCL community* (pp. 625–626). Hillsdale, NJ: Erlbaum. https://doi.org/10.3115/1658616.1658755

De Wever, B., Keer, H. V., Schellens, T., & Valcke, M. (2010). Roles as a structuring tool in online discussion groups: The differential impact of different roles on social knowledge construction. *Computers in Human Behavior, 26*(4), 516–523. https://doi.org/10.1016/j.chb.2009.08.008

Dubovi, I., & Tabak, I. (2020). An empirical analysis of knowledge co-construction in YouTube comments. *Computers & Education, 156,* Article 103939. https://doi.org/10.1016/j.compedu.2020.103939

Floren, L., Cate, O., Irby, D., & O'Brien, B. (2021). An interaction analysis model to study knowledge construction in interprofessional education: Proof of concept. *Journal of Interprofessional Care, 35*(5), 736–743. https://doi.org/10.1080/13561820.2020.1797653

Gee, J., & Green, J. (1998). Discourse analysis, learning, and social practice: A methodological study. *Review of Research in Education, 23,* 119–169. https://doi.org/10.2307/1167289

Gómez Jaimes, D. R., & Hernández Castañeda, M. del R. (2018). *Paths toward social construction of knowledge: Examining social networks in online discussion forums* (Vol. 10913). Springer International Publishing. https://doi.org/10.1007/978-3-319-91521-0_21

Gunawardena, C. N., Chen, Y., Flor, N., & Sánchez, D. (2023). Deep learning models for analyzing social construction of knowledge online. *Online Learning, 27*(4), 69–92. https://doi.org/10.24059/olj.v27i4.4055

Gunawardena, C. N., Frechette, C., & Layne, L. (2018). *Culturally inclusive instructional design: A framework and guide to building online wisdom communities.* Routledge. https://doi.org/10.4324/9781315439204

Gunawardena, C. N., Flor, N. V., Gomez, D., & Sánchez, D. (2016). Analyzing social construction of knowledge online by employing interaction analysis, learning analytics, and social network analysis. *The Quarterly Review of Distance Education, 17*(3), 35–60. https://digitalrepository.unm.edu/ulls_fsp/172/

Gunawardena, C. N., Lowe, C., & Anderson, T. (1997). Analysis of a global online debate and the development of an interaction analysis model for examining social construction of knowledge in computer conferencing. *Journal of Educational Computing Research, 17*(4), 397–431. https://doi.org/10.2190/7MQV-X9UJ-C7Q3-NRAG

Guo, C., Shea, P., & Chen, X. (2022). Investigation on graduate students' social presence and social knowledge construction in two online discussion settings. *Education and Information Technologies, 27,* 2751–2769. https://doi.org/10.1007/s10639-021-10716-8

Hall, B. (2014). *In support of the interaction analysis model for evaluating discourse in a virtual learning community* [Manuscript submitted for publication, Ashford University]. www.researchgate.net/profile/Barbara-Hall-8/publication/261161448_In_support_of_the_Interaction_Analysis_Model_for_evaluating_discourse_in_a_virtual_learning_community/links/02e7e53359f2ce8234000000/In-support-of-the-Interaction-Analysis-Model-for-evaluating-discourse-in-a-virtual-learning-community.pdf

Hardesty, L. (2023). *Reconnaissance: Relationship Between Social Presence and Knowledge Construction in Second Life* (Order No. 30318606). Available from Dissertations & Theses @ University of New Mexico; ProQuest Dissertations & Theses Global. (2881083043). https://libproxy.unm.edu/login?url=www.proquest.com/dissertations-theses/reconnaissance-relationship-between-social/docview/2881083043/se-2

Hendriks, V., & Maor, D. (2004). Quality of students' communicative strategies delivered through computer-mediated communication. *Journal of Interactive Learning Research, 15,* 5–32. www.researchgate.net/publication/259080370_Quality_of_Students'_Communicative_Strategies_Delivered_Through_Computer-Mediated_Communication

Hew, K., & Cheung, W. (2011). Student facilitators' habits of mind and their influences on higher-level social construction of knowledge occurrences in online discussions: A case study. *Innovations in Education and Teaching International, 48*(3), 275–285. https://doi.org/10.1080/14703297.2011.593704

Howell, G. S., Akapnudo, U., Chen, M., Sutherlin, A. L., & James, L. E. (2014). The effect of structured divergent prompts on knowledge construction. *Journal of Asynchronous Learning Networks, 18,* 49–65. https://doi.org/10.24059/olj.v18i2.410

Huntley, B. C., & Thatcher, A. (2008). The impact of time delay on the content of discussions at a computer-mediated ergonomics conference. *The Ergonomics Open Journal, 1,* 1019.

Jakubec, S., & Campbell, M. (2003). Mental health research and cultural dominance: The social construction of knowledge for international development. *The Canadian Journal of Nursing Research, 35,* 74–88. https://pubmed.ncbi.nlm.nih.gov/12908198/

Jamaludin, A., & Lang, Q. C. (2006). Using asynchronous online discussions in primary school project work. *Australasian Journal of Educational Technology, 22*(1), 64–87. www.ascilite.org.au/ajet/ajet.html

Kaliisa, R., Rienties, B., Morch, A. I., & Kluge, A. (2022). Social learning analytics in computer supported collaborative learning environments: A systematic review of empirical studies. *Computers and Education Open*, 3, 100073. https://doi.org/10.1016/j.caeo.2022.100073

Kanuka, H., & Anderson, T. (1998). Online social interchange, discord, and knowledge construction. *Journal of Distance Education*, 13(1), 57–74. www.ijede.ca/index.php/jde/article/download/137/412?inline=1

Ke, F., Chávez, A., Causarano, P., & Causarano, A. (2011). Identity presence and knowledge building: Joint emergence in online learning environments? *International Journal of Computer-Supported Collaborative Learning*, 6, 349–370. https://doi.org/10.1007/s11412-011-9114-z

Kokic, I. B., & Rukavina, S. (2017). Learning from digital video cases: How future teachers perceive the use of open source tools and open educational resources. *Knowledge Cultures*, 5, 115–130. https://doi.org/10.22381/KC5520177

Kumar, S., & Buraphadeja, V. (2010). *Student knowledge construction in educational wikis: Challenges for interaction analysis [Conference session]*. AERA 2010 Symposium, Denver, Colorado, United States. http://plaza.ufl.edu/swapnak/AERAKumar10.pdf

Lehtinen, A., Kostiainen, E., & Näykki, P. (2023). Co-construction of knowledge and socioemotional interaction in pre-service teachers' video-based online collaborative learning. *Teaching and Teacher Education*, 133, Article 104299. https://doi.org/10.1016/j.tate.2023.104299

Lim, J., & Hall, B. M. (2015). Intersubjectivity in theoretical and practical online courses. *The Quarterly Review of Distance Education*, 16(4), 45–60. https://books.google.com/books?hl=en&lr=&id=kgcoDwAAQBAJ&oi=fnd&pg=PA45&ots=DHti4QAgBP&sig=UWph4Rs6cvvQvxVdSAY3qsmXQo4#v=onepage&q&f=false

Lim, J., Jeong, A. C., Hall, B. M., & Freed, S. (2017). Intersubjectivity and discussion characteristics in online courses. *Quarterly Review of Distance Education*, 18(1), 29–44.

Lopez-Islas, J. R. (2001, December). *Collaborative learning at Monterrey Tech-Virtual University*. Paper presented at the Symposium on Web-based Learning Environments to Support Learning at a Distance: Design and Evaluation, Asilomar, Pacific Grove, California.

Lucas, M., Gunawardena, C. N., & Moreira, A. N. (2014). Assessing social construction of knowledge online: A critique of the Interaction Analysis Model. *Computers in Human Behavior*, 30, 574–582. https://doi.org/10.1016/j.chb.2013.07.050

Lucas, M., & Moreira, A. (2010). Knowledge construction with social web tools. In M. D. Lytras et al. (Eds.), *1st International Conference on Reforming Education and Quality of Teaching*, CCIS 73 (pp. 278–284). Springer Verlag. https://doi.org/10.1007/978-3-642-13166-0_40

Lucas, M., & Moreira, A. (2015). A visual representation of online interaction patterns. *Journal of Universal Computer Science*, 21(11), 1496–1507. https://doi.org/10.3217/jucs-021-11-1496

Luebeck, J. L., & Bice, L. R. (2005). Online discussion as a mechanism of conceptual change among mathematics and science teachers. *The Journal of Distance Education/Revue de l'Éducation à Distance*, 20(2), 21–39. https://files.eric.ed.gov/fulltext/EJ807830.pdf

Marra, R., Moore, J. L., & Klimczak, A. K. (2004). Content analysis of online discussion forums: A comparative analysis of protocols. *Educational Technology Research & Development*, 52(2), 23–40. https://link.springer.com/content/pdf/10.1007/BF02504837.pdf

McLoughlin, C., & Luca, J. (1999). Lonely outpourings or reasoned dialogue? An analysis of textbased conferencing as a tool to support learning. *Proceedings of the 16th Annual Conference of the Australasian Society for Computers in Learning in Tertiary Education*, Brisbane, Australia.

Megli, A. C. (2022). *Social Presence as a Predictor of Social Construction of Knowledge in Discussion Forums in Asynchronous Online Higher Education Courses* (Order No. 29993846). Available from Dissertations & Theses @ University of New Mexico; ProQuest Dissertations & Theses Global. (2821581074). https://libproxy.unm.edu/login?url=www.proquest.com/dissertations-theses/social-presence-as-predictor-construction/docview/2821581074/se-2

Megli, A. C., Fallad-Mendoza, D., Etsitty-Dorame, M., Desiderio, J., Chen, Y., Sánchez, D., Flor, N., & Gunawardena, C. N. (2023). Using social learning analytic methods to examine social construction of knowledge in online discussions. *American Journal of Distance Education*, 38(1), 65–80. https://doi.org/10.1080/08923647.2023.2192597

Moore, J., & Marra, R. (2005). A comparative analysis of online discussion participation protocols. *Journal of Research on Technology in Education*, 38(2), 191–212. https://files.eric.ed.gov/fulltext/EJ728901.pdf

Mutiaraningrum, I., & Nugroho, A. (2020). Social construction of knowledge in synchronous text-based discussion during English language learning. *Journal on English as a Foreign Language*, 10(2), 315–336. https://doi.org.libproxy.unm.edu/10.23971/jefl.v10i2.1934

Newman, D., Webb, B., & Cochrane, C. (1995). A content analysis method to measure critical thinking in face-to-face and computer support group learning. *Interpersonal Computing and Technology, 3*(2), 56–77. www.learntechlib.org/p/80700/

Osman, G., & Herring, S. C. (2007). Interaction, facilitation, and deep learning in cross-cultural chat: A case study. *Internet and Higher Education, 10*(2), 125–141. https://doi.org/10.1016/j.iheduc.2007.03.004

Ouyang, F., Xu, W., & Cukurova, M. (2023). An artificial intelligence-driven learning analytics method to examine the collaborative problem-solving process from the complex adaptive systems perspective. *International Journal of Computer-Supported Collaborative Learning.* https://doi.org/10.1007/s11412-023-09391-3

Petticrew, M., & Roberts, H. (2006). *Systematic reviews in the social sciences: A practical guide.* Blackwell Publishing. https://fcsalud.ua.es/en/portal-de-investigacion/documentos/tools-for-the-bibliographic-research/guide-of-systematic-reviews-in-social-sciences.pdf

Pillutla, V., Tawfik, A., & Giabbanelli, P. (2020). Detecting the depth and progression of learning in massive open online courses by mining discussion data. *Technology, Knowledge and Learning: Learning Mathematics, Science and the Arts in the Context of Digital Technologies, 25*(4), 881–898. https://doi.org.libproxy.unm.edu/10.1007/s10758-020-09434-w

Roseli, M., & Umar, I. (2015). Students' levels of knowledge construction and cognitive skills in an online forum learning environment. *Procedia – Social and Behavioral Sciences, 197*, 1983–1989. https://doi.org/10.1016/j.sbspro.2015.07.574

Saint, J., Gasevic, D., Matcha, W., Nora'Ayu, U., & Pardo, A. (2020). Combining analytic methods to unlock sequential and temporal patterns of self-regulated learning. In *LAK '20: Proceedings of the Tenth International Conference on Learning Analytics & Knowledge* (pp. 402–411). https://doi.org/10.1145/3375462.3375487

Sánchez, D. M. (2018). *Building a Call to Action: Social Action in Networks of Practice* (Order No. 10841947). Available from Dissertations & Theses @ University of New Mexico; ProQuest Dissertations & Theses Global. (2133019710). https://libproxy.unm.edu/login?url=www.proquest.com/dissertations-theses/building-call-action-social-networks-practice/docview/2133019710/se-2

Schellens, T., & Valcke, M. (2006). Fostering knowledge construction in university students through asynchronous discussion groups. *Computers & Education, 46*(4), 349–370. https://doi.org/10.1016/j.compedu.2004.07.010

Socratous, C., & Ioannou, A. (2018). A study of collaborative knowledge construction in STEM via educational robotics. In J. Kay & R. Luckin (Eds.), *Rethinking learning in the digital age: Making the learning sciences count, 13th International Conference of the Learning Sciences (ICLS) 2018* (Vol. 1). London, UK: International Society of the Learning Sciences.

Stich, A. E., & Reeves, T. D. (2017). Massive open online courses and underserved students in the United States. *The Internet and Higher Education, 32*, 58–71. https://doi.org/10.1016/j.iheduc.2016.09.001

Tawfik, A. A., Koehler, A., Gish-Lieberman, J., & Gatewood, J. (2021). Investigating the depth of problem-solving prompts in collaborative argumentation. *Innovations in Education and Teaching International, 58*(5), 533–544. https://doi.org/10.1080/14703297.2021.1966821

Tawfik, A. A., Reeves, T. D., Stich, A. E., Gill, A., Hong, C., McDade, J., Pillutla, V. S., Zhou, X., & Giabbanelli, P. J. (2017). The nature and level of learner – Learner interaction in a chemistry Massive Open Online Course (MOOC). *Journal of Computing in Higher Education, 29*(3), 411–431. https://doi.org/10.1007/s12528-017-9135-3

Wise, A. F., & Chiu, M. M. (2011). Analyzing temporal patterns of knowledge construction in a role-based online discussion. *International Journal of Computer-Supported Collaborative Learning, 6*(3), 445–470. https://doi.org/10.1007/s11412-011-9120-1

Yang, X., Li, J., & Xing, B. (2018). Behavioral patterns of knowledge construction in online cooperative translation activities. *Internet and Higher Education, 36*, 13–21. https://doi.org/10.1016/j.iheduc.2017.08.003

Yasuda, R. (2021). Online knowledge construction mediated by mobile instant messaging. *Knowledge Management & E-Learning: An International Journal.* https://doi.org/10.34105/j.kmel.2021.13.002

Zhou, P., & Yang, Q. (2017). Fostering elementary students' collaborative knowledge building in smart classroom with formative evaluation. In *2017 International Conference of Educational Innovation Through Technology (EITT)* (pp. 116–117). IEEE. https://doi.org/10.1109/EITT.2017.35

3 Social Interaction and Knowledge Construction in Online Environments

Chapter 1 discussed the Interaction Analysis Model (IAM) developed by Gunawardena et al. (1997) to analyze the process of social construction of knowledge (SCK) that takes place through social interaction when groups collaborate online. Chapter 2 reviewed the studies that have employed the IAM to analyze how groups interact and construct knowledge and identified the need to address the relational and socioemotional nature of social interaction that supports group reasoning in any model that describes SCK. The chapter recommended that the IAM could be improved by paying attention to the social and relational nature of social interaction that supports knowledge construction. In Chapter 1, we pointed out that the IAM developers left out the analysis of the "social content" described by Henri (1992) as statements not related to the formal content of the subject matter, such as self-introductions or mutual encouragement that supports knowledge construction because they felt that the debate format did not support social connections between participants (Gunawardena et al., 1997). However, given the recommendation to address the relational nature of social interaction to improve the IAM, we take a fresh look at the concept of social interaction and its relationship to knowledge construction.

Chapter 3 examines social interaction from a relational and socioemotional perspective. Hod and Katz (2020) define socioemotional skills to include navigating relationships successfully, problem-solving collaboratively, and developing self-regulation and concern for others. This definition shows that the social, relational, and emotional are intertwined. Therefore, in this chapter, we selected the term *relational*, the ability to relate to each other, to refer to all three elements, social, relational, and emotional aspects of social interaction. This term also emphasizes the relational nature of social interaction in supporting SCK in technology-mediated learning environments. Chapter 3 explores why we need to study the relational nature of social interaction in online learning environments; what constitutes social interaction, such as social presence and community; how social interaction supports knowledge construction; and how the relational nature of social interaction has been studied by analyzing computer transcripts. The questions that we kept in mind as we wrote this chapter were: Why study social interaction? What is social interaction? What are the social and emotional aspects of group interaction? How do learners connect with each other in an online environment? Do these connections create community among learners? In what ways do these connections support the construction of knowledge? How have researchers analyzed transcripts to study social interaction?

DOI: 10.4324/9781003324461-4

Why Study Social Interaction?

The "embrace of sociocultural theory led to one of the most important recent theoretical shifts in education research: the proposition that all learning is a social process shaped by and infused with a system of cultural meaning" (National Academies of Sciences, Engineering, and Medicine, 2018, p. 27). Sociocultural theory emphasizes social interaction, and social interaction plays a significant role in how a group of learners will work together to construct knowledge. Therefore, studying social interaction from the perspective of its contribution to knowledge construction and from the perspective of its contribution to the relational nature of group process, keeping members connected over time, is critical if we are to develop a holistic view of SCK.

Resnick (1991) argued that the social context in which cognitive activity takes place is an integral part of that activity, not just the surrounding context for it. Much of human cognition is so varied and so sensitive to cultural context that we must also seek mechanisms by which people actively shape each other's knowledge and reasoning processes. Resnick pointed out that people build their knowledge structures on the basis of what they are told by others, orally, in writing, in pictures, and in gestures. Our daily lives are filled with instances in which we influence each other's constructive processes by providing information, pointing things out to one another, asking questions, and arguing with and elaborating on each other's ideas. Therefore, it is critical that we study social interaction not only as a vehicle that leads to the social construction of knowledge (SCK) but also as a vehicle that enables people to connect with each other, communicate, and, over time, become a community.

Theories of learning have begun to blend the social and the cognitive in explaining how learning occurs (Hod & Katz, 2020; Lehtinen et al., 2023). These are exemplified in discussions on the relationship of affect and cognition from a neurobiological perspective in which emotion is seen as an integral attribute of cognition (Adolphs & Damasio, 2001; Davidson, 2002) and in cognitive sociology (Zerubavel, 1999), which reminds us that we think both as individuals and as human beings and that what goes on inside our head is also affected by the particular "thought communities" to which we belong (Resnick et al., 1991). By stressing the interdependence of social and individual processes in the co-construction of knowledge, sociocultural approaches view semiotic tools or cultural amplifiers as personal and social resources, hence, mediating the link between the social and the individual construction of meaning (Vygotsky, 1978).

"The learning sciences of today recognize the tri-dimensional nature of learning as involving cognitive, social, and emotional phenomena" (Polo et al., 2016, p. 123). Lehtinen et al. (2023) observe that traditionally, researchers who study learning have been biased toward the cognitive at the expense of the affective but have begun to pay more attention to the socioemotional dimensions of learning. They define socioemotional interaction as that which takes place through verbal and nonverbal communication, building a cohesive and mutually respectful social and emotional atmosphere, for example, through expressions of support and active listening. Further, they note that socioemotional interaction affects participants' perceptions about social cohesion and psychological safety and is vital in supporting participants' well-being, intrinsic motivation, and creativity. Lehtinen et al. (2023) studied the co-construction of knowledge and socioemotional interaction in pre-service teachers' video-based online collaborative learning using the Interaction Analysis Model (IAM) (Gunawardena et al., 1997) and shed light on how knowledge co-construction and socioemotional activities are intertwined and how we can support the collaborative learning activities of future teachers.

We were motivated to study social interaction because it plays a key role in the process of knowledge construction both from a cognitive and relational perspective. Understanding the role of social interaction will also enable us to undertake a more comprehensive analysis of SCK using the IAM. Next, we examine what constitutes social interaction.

What Constitutes Social Interaction?

Social interaction is defined as the "ability to engage with others as persons and specifically to be equipped to engage in mutual influence over others as a fundamental capacity" (van der Aalsvoort & Harinck, 2000, p. 5). The importance of considering the interdependency between social interaction and context has been pointed out by researchers working within the sociocultural and social constructivist perspectives on learning, and according to these views, "the nature of the individual's activity and cognitive performance cannot be isolated from its social and cultural contexts" (Kumpulainen & Mutanen, 2000, p. 147).

Although the relational nature of social interaction is associated with many concepts, such as emotion, social space, social affinity, sense of community, group climate, mutual trust, social identity, etc., we selected a few concepts that we feel are the most relevant for understanding social interaction within the social context of online learning that can be analyzed in a computer or video transcript of a discussion: social presence, identity, social connectedness, and community. Everett Rogers, the pioneer of the "diffusion of innovations" theory (1962), observed that social presence is the one defining characteristic of distance education (E.M. Rogers, personal communication, 2002). Social presence is a distinguishing characteristic of distance education and an important concept that supports the social environment of online learning which we discuss next.

Social Presence

A social factor particularly significant to online education and networked learning is that of "social presence," the degree to which a person is perceived as a "real person" in mediated communication (Gunawardena & Zittle, 1997). Short et al. (1976) developed the construct of social presence and defined it as the "degree of salience of the other person in the interaction and the consequent salience of the interpersonal relationships" (p. 65). They described it as a construct that comprises a number of dimensions relating to the degree of interpersonal contact, specifically two concepts: "intimacy," and "immediacy." Intimacy is a factor of the medium used for communication, and immediacy is the psychological distance between communicators. Since its early definition, many researchers have attempted to define social presence by incorporating other constructs related to social presence. Swan (2017) notes these multiple definitions of social presence and explores how the concept has evolved through the years since the time Short, Williams, and Christie first defined it in 1976, both as a factor of the medium "intimacy" and a factor of the psychological distance of the communicators "immediacy," and observes that it is a key component of the frequently employed Community of Inquiry Framework (COI) developed by Garrison et al. (2000). Dikkers et al. (2017) discuss the Social Presence Model and its five key elements: affective association, community cohesion, instructor involvement, interaction intensity, and knowledge and experience, which build awareness of the importance of creating critical connections and cultivating relationships in learning communities. Lowenthal and Snelson (2017) investigated how researchers define social presence and summarized multiple definitions: "being there," "being real," "projecting socially and affectively," "connecting," and "belonging." They note that about 20% of the time, researchers define social presence as something more than simply being perceived as a real person, suggesting ideas of connection, belonging, and community, which can confuse what social presence is and how it is operationalized in research. They advise that it is "important not to confuse social presence with collaboration or community. Social presence, collaboration, and community are three important, yet different, constructs in the online learning literature" (Lowenthal & Snelson, 2017, p. 153).

We see social presence as grounded in its original conception by Short et al. (1976), emphasizing the "realness" of the other in the interaction. "Realness" is similar to "immediacy," a sense of the psychological closeness or distance between communicators (Wiener & Mehrabian, 1968), which Short et al. (1976) included in their definition of social presence. Immediacy is conveyed nonverbally (for example, by using emoticons, or icons that express emotion) or parenthetical metalinguistic cues (such as hmmm or yuk or lol) and verbally through the manner of expression (for example, complimenting, praising, encouraging feedback, personalizing examples, humor). Immediacy is a relationship-based construct (Bartlett Ellis et al., 2016). "Immediacy enhances social presence" (Gunawardena & Zittle, 1997, p. 9). Gunawardena and Zittle (1997) showed that participants who felt a higher sense of social presence within the computer conference they studied enhanced their socioemotional experience by using emoticons to express missing nonverbal cues in written form. From a longitudinal exploration of the effect of online students' peer interactions using social network analysis, Castellanos-Reyes et al. (2024) confirmed that social presence is a perception rather than an ability.

Online, we not only communicate with humans but also with digital assistants and other technology tools. The degree to which non-human actors generate a sense of "realness" will influence our communication with them. In some cases, realness might be desired, and, in others, it may be irrelevant. For example, when the ChatGPT chatbot by OpenAI asks, "How can I help you today?," the words create a sense of "realness" and caring by communicating someone is there to assist you.

Gunawardena and Zittle (1997) researched social presence in an inter-university computer conference and found it to be a strong predictor of learner satisfaction. Subsequent studies examining the degree of social presence desired by diverse participants found that it is key to building online relationships (Gunawardena et al., 2006; Gunawardena, 2017). Several studies have shown how social presence impacts the larger social context of an online environment, including motivation to participate, interaction, group cohesion, trust, verbal and nonverbal communication, and social equality (Kreijns et al., 2011; Richardson & Swan, 2003; Tu, 2001; Whiteside & Garrett Dikkers, 2012). Castellanos-Reyes et al. (2024) observe that social presence positively influences online students' motivation, satisfaction, retention, and learning outcomes and is crucial for successful online learning experiences. Lowenthal and Snelson (2017) caution us to consider whether social presence is essential for a meaningful educational experience and point out, "as useful as social presence might be for collaborative online learning experiences, it is not necessarily required or essential for students to learn online" (p. 153).

The degree of social presence that individuals desire may depend on individual preference or the influence of the sociocultural context. In a study of online group process and group development in Mexico and the United States, Gunawardena et al. (2001) found that U.S. participants felt that social presence was important for the smooth functioning of the group to provide a sense that the members of the group are real people. Social presence can build trust and lead to self-disclosure, and building relationships certainly enhances civility online. The Mexican focus group participants, on the other hand, felt that having personal information about the participants was not important. For these participants, how others contributed to the discussion was far more important than knowing personal information about them. This could be attributed to a cultural difference given the power distance that exists in Mexican society (Hofstede, 1980). It is possible that Mexican participants looked to the online medium as an equalizing medium that equalized status differences present in society and, therefore, did not want their peers to interject social context cues that would take away the equalizing power of the online environment. From a cultural lens, the degree of social presence desired may differ across cultures (Gunawardena, 2017). As the degree of social presence desired can be influenced by the sociocultural context, we need to broaden our understanding of this concept as online learning expands globally to ask questions such as: How does the sociocultural context influence the perception of online social presence? And what degree of social presence is necessary for interaction, learning, and or satisfaction? The answers would depend on our understanding of the sociocultural context in which learning experiences are conducted. From a cultural lens, the degree of social presence desired may differ across cultures (Gunawardena, 2017).

Online interactions are mediated through the affordances (Gibson, 1979) of a specific communication medium. Technology affordances can be described as "properties of technologies that are compatible with and pertinent to people's interactions and communications. Affordances offered by tools and technologies allow users to take some kind of action" (Rha, 2014, pp. 46–47). Lombard and Ditton (1997) pointed out that highly interactive virtual environments could evoke a greater sense of social presence. Therefore, designing system interactivity into an online system based on simulation or artificial intelligence principles, where the learner interacts with interactive pedagogical agents who communicate with students to promote meaningful learning, will be one way to enhance social presence within the online learning system when human interaction is not possible. Children's attachment to and relationship with characters or avatars in computer games may indicate that the system design itself is capable of generating social presence. Exploring the Second Life virtual world, Hardesty (2023) researched which type of social presence generated (low, medium, high) according to the Interactional Process Model of Social Presence developed by Schultze and Brooks (2019) is associated with Phases of knowledge construction as specified by the IAM (Gunawardena et al., 1997). Her findings revealed evidence of all three levels of social presence, and, further, social presence established a sense of mutual monitoring of participants that increased their sense of presence, making their virtual interactions more real. Exploring these and other similar studies will help us to establish the relationship between social presence and knowledge construction.

In summary, even though multiple definitions and constructs exist to explain social presence, we define social presence as the "realness" of the other in mediated communication. Social presence is an important relational construct that contributes to social interaction. Researchers have established that social presence can enhance learner satisfaction, learning, and the relational nature of the online environment. However, the degree of social presence desired may depend on individual preference or the influence of the sociocultural context. Next, we explore a construct closely related to social presence, that of identity, real or pseudo, in virtual environments.

Identity

Identity can be defined as "the distinguishing character or personality of an individual" (Merriam-Webster Online, 2024), or "who you are" (Cambridge Dictionary, 2024). Social presence is related to identity, as identity communicates a person's social presence. In asynchronous online discussions, identity is usually expressed through self-disclosure, which we observe when participants introduce themselves online or create profiles and disclose personal information, private life, beliefs, passions, interests, and stories. Dennen (2008) notes that to develop an online identity, an individual must be an active user of an online environment. Those who create profiles and use those profiles to share words, images, and preferences (i.e., likes and favorites) are creating their online identities. Lurkers, those who do not self-disclose or participate in discussions but only read, do not build identity and may have low social presence. Although situational lurking can be appropriate in online classes, students who lack social presence are effectively absent to their classmates and have no identity (Dennen, 2008).

Graiouid (2005), conducting studies of chat forums in Morocco, observed that communication via computers mediates the construction of cybernetic identities and promotes the rehearsal of invented social and gender relations. This inventive accommodation of the Internet acts as a contradiction to dominant patriarchal and conservative power structures. In their study of communication conventions and processes employed by users of online chat forums in Morocco and Sri Lanka, Gunawardena et al. (2009a) found that identity was expressed through language reflecting gender roles, either real or imagined. Self-disclosure of personal information, private life, or ideas or perspectives helps develop trust and the trustworthiness of the other. They note that identity was closely linked to building trust, as many participants would not reveal their true identity until they could trust the other person. We see this often when individuals introduce themselves to a group of people online. If participants communicate their identities, it is easier to connect with one another. Dwivedi et al. (2024), in their study of immersive metaverse environments (virtual platforms where users and avatars can interact with computer-mediated environments and other users, as in video games), found that building a self-image and embodied presence (how people are portrayed in a virtual world giving them a feeling of presence and identity) and co-presence is crucial to developing positive continuation intentions in the metaverse.

As we consider the expression of identity online, we need to be mindful of how the sociocultural context will influence that communication (Gunawardena et al., 2009a). Sadiqi (2003) notes that whereas the Western concept of "self" is based on the individual, the Moroccan concept of self is based on the Islamic notion of "community or group" and is, therefore, inherently plural. "One aspect of the collective self is the difficulty that Moroccans have in talking about themselves in public because it is generally considered in Moroccan society as 'lack of modesty'" (Sadiqi, 2003, p. 67). Further, Sadiqi notes that the language of introductions reveals many aspects of a Moroccan's self. Introductions involve the interplay of cultural, social, situational, and identity variables, which range from sex, local geographical origin, class, setting, participants' age, and self-interest (Gunawardena et al., 2009a).

Social presence, the realness of the other, and expressions of identity help to develop social connections and can be the foundation for group cohesion. The realness of the other is built through understanding identity and through skills – what they say in the discussion. Once the realness is established, and there is a feeling of co-presence, the relationship begins through affinity with shared characteristics or the desire to get to know someone who has unique, intriguing characteristics. Social presence and identity, although different constructs, are closely related. Together, they lead to social connectedness, which we will discuss next.

Social Connectedness

Tu and McIsaac's (2002) study found that "social presence is necessary to enhance and foster online social interaction" (p. 146). Social presence is also a foundational facet of social connectedness. Social connectedness happens through interaction. Social connectedness is an individual's belief that a relationship exists between that individual and others. Social connectedness ensues when interacting participants relate to each other through mediated communication in an online social network. Riedl et al. (2013) investigated the interplay between three fundamental constructs of social interactions conceptualized as social presence, social awareness, and social connectedness. We perceive social awareness as a reflection of social presence and conceptualize social connectedness as taking place through interaction.

Discussing the theoretical foundations for social connectedness in online environments, Slagter van Tryon and Bishop (2009) note that the underlying process involved in the development of social connectedness is social cognition, which is defined as how people make sense of the online environment. "It is social cognition that provides context and shapes behavior for all participants in an interaction through the expectations that each has of the other's intentions and predicted *next move* during an encounter" (Slagter van Tryon & Bishop, 2009, p. 293, emphasis in original). "Learners' feelings of social connectedness may be a key factor in predicting online course success" (Slagter van Tryon & Bishop, 2012, p. 347). From their research into e-mmediacy, which they associate with social connectedness, Slagter van Tryon and Bishop (2012) identified three broad categories of expert-recommended strategies for overcoming social connectedness problems in the online learning environment: increased interactions, comprehensive technical support, and persistent follow-up.

Social connectedness can be described as the feeling of belonging to a social group and implies the creation of bonding relationships. Communication is often seen as a means of feeling connected and being in touch. Communication can be classified as connectedness-oriented communication, where the focus is mainly on maintaining and enhancing social relationships, and content-oriented communication, where the goal is an exchange of information. Connectedness-oriented communication allows people to be aware of each other and contribute to maintaining social relationships (Riedl et al., 2013). Connected-oriented communication, across time, will also lead to the development of the community.

Whiteside et al. (2017) provide practical guidance for designers and instructors on how to enhance connectedness in online and blended learning environments to overcome isolation. Some of the strategies involve cultivating connections to build community and connecting content to applied and authentic learning experiences. Other strategies involve integrating social activities to establish connections and relationships before academic work and creating social areas in online spaces to encourage community-building. They see connecting as "social negotiating" and encourage creating a nurturing and safe environment online where social negotiation can take place.

Community

Social presence, identity, social connectedness, and community are related but different constructs that describe social interaction. If social connectedness continues over a period of time within large or smaller sub-groups, it signals the formation of an online community. We define a community as a network of stable connections over time within a group. Jones (2002) points out that the length of residence in a community is directly correlated to the strength of attachment to it. Communities support the social dimension of online learning and engage in the negotiation of culture, norms, and values among community participants.

McMillan and Chavis (1986) observed that online learning communities evolve from simple cohorts when learners elevate their engagement with one another to an emotional sense of community – when there is "a feeling that members have of belonging, a feeling that members matter to one another and to the group, and a shared faith that members' needs will be met through their commitment to be together" (p. 9). When group members begin to use "we" in a communication sequence, it communicates immediacy and community instead of "you" and "I," which maintains separation between the communicators, which is less immediate or communicates non-immediacy (Wiener & Mehrabian, 1968). Community interaction can be understood at two levels: active participation and engagement in a task and good sociability, where participants interact not only academically on a task but also socially.

Wenger et al. (2002) defined communities of practice (CoPs) as "groups of people who share a concern, a set of problems, or a passion about a topic, and who deepen their knowledge and expertise in this area by interacting on an ongoing basis" (p. 4). According to Wenger (1998), a CoP defines itself along three dimensions: what it is about – its joint enterprise as understood and continually renegotiated by its members; how it functions – mutual engagement that binds members together into a social entity; and what capability it has produced – the shared repertoire of communal resources that members have developed over time (see also Wenger, 1998, pp. 73–84). The three structural elements of CoPs described by Wenger et al. (2002) – domain, community, and practice – apply to social networking environments as well as to face-to-face CoPs. They note that when these three elements function well together, they make a CoP an ideal "knowledge structure – a social structure that can assume responsibility for developing and sharing knowledge" (p. 29).

Based on their experience collaborating on writing a journal article about social networking using several social networking tools, Gunawardena et al. (2009b) proposed that in addition to an individual zone of proximal development (ZPD) (Vygotsky, 1978) scaffolded by technological tools, social networking sites create a collaborative ZPD among participants or a Group ZPD. Goos et al. (2002) distinguish between the traditional expert–novice interaction and the interaction between individuals of equal status. They define this peer collaboration as "mutuality," an interactive process encompassing varied reasoning and viewpoints that builds a shared understanding of the learning goal. As viewpoints are challenged within the group, individuals may clarify their reasoning, comparing their own ideas with others. Peer feedback and peer mentoring enhance this learning process. Smith (1994) uses the term group-mediated cognition (GMC) to describe the form of situated thinking whereby the thinking of each individual is inevitably influenced by the thinking of the other members taking part in the activity, even if it is only to disagree. He notes that GMC takes place within basic cycles of interaction between the individual and the group. While some GMC processes are intellectual, others are social, but many include both intellectual and social dimensions. Mason and Rennie (2008) point out that what is different about collaborative technologies is that interaction, peer commentary, and collaborative research actually happen in a distributed global environment. "Knowledge is created, shared, remixed, repurposed, and passed along" (p. 10).

Dialogue, discourse, and language play a critical role when individuals learn with each other in an online CoP. When studying a community, we need to pay attention to its discourse and language. Each CoP has its own discourse, which can affect how a person negotiates meaning. Discourse is often synonymous with language. It is in examining discourse that we can see "how a community is shaped by language use and how language use shapes a community" (Creese, 2003, p. 55). Each discourse is shaped or, in Wenger's terminology, "negotiated" (Wenger, 1998, p. 52) to help shape meaning, and it is in analyzing these discourses that one can see how identity and power intertwine to negotiate meaning. A CoP has its own way of using language to determine meaning. The nuances of a language can confuse an issue or situation. Therefore, engaging in definitions, explaining acronyms, providing context for messages, and focusing on clarity in writing will enable learners to participate more fully in a learning community or CoP. Barton and Tusting (2005) argued that we must incorporate models of language in use – language as part of social practice, power, and hierarchy, in the negotiation of meaning, and resolution of conflict, as they are often overlooked areas in CoPs. They advise us to pay attention to issues of power and conflict within communities, including risk, stigma, and equity, that would impact learning. They recommend incorporating the broader social context in learning design.

To summarize, this section discussed the relational aspect of social interaction and emphasized the need to study it and the social context within which cognitive activity takes place. Although the relational nature of social interaction is associated with many concepts, we selected a few constructs for exploration which we felt were the most relevant for understanding social interaction and which can be observed in the transcript of a computer or video discussion. The selected constructs were social presence, identity, social connectedness, and community. While these constructs are related to each other, they are separate constructs, and we discussed them in terms of their contribution to social interaction in the online social environment.

How Does Social Interaction Influence Knowledge Construction?

The interdependence between social and individual processes in the construction of knowledge is a founding principle of sociocultural and social constructivist approaches to learning that emphasize the social and contextual nature of learning. This means that learning involves both individual and social processes, a point of view that requires "the study of social interaction as a means and as a contributor to learning outcomes" (van der Aalsvoort & Harinck, 2000, p. 5). Sociocultural perspectives, which see learning from a cultural point of view, emphasize the role of social interaction in the movement from interpersonal to intrapersonal functioning (Vygotsky, 1978; John-Steiner & Mahn, 1996). This means that social interaction plays a critical role in individual learning and knowledge construction. Interactions occur both at the level of the individual and the group. Individual members influence themselves, other group members, and the group as a whole.

"Sociocultural theory is used by many authors to explain how the negotiation of meaning leads on to the joint construction of knowledge. Collaborative problem solving is often used as a source of data for studying this phenomenon" (van der Aalsvoort & Harinck, 2000, p. 216). Collaboration means that participants are engaged in a coordinated effort to solve a problem together; it involves the construction of a solution that otherwise could not be produced alone. There must be reciprocal understanding between collaborators, which involves individuals establishing mutually shared or common knowledge through negotiation of meaning (Littleton & Hakkinen, 1999). Lally and DeLaat (2002) observe that in collaborative learning settings, students can criticize their own and other students' contributions, ask for explanations, give counterarguments, stimulate themselves and other students, and motivate and help each other to finish the task. During collaboration, learners can become teachers, and teachers can become learners with their roles interacting and changing over time. The teacher becomes a facilitator and a guide by the side, moving away from the role of the sage on the stage.

Leseman et al. (2000) observe that the concept of "co-construction," which unites the converging (neo) Piagetian and (neo) Vygotskian lines of thinking, explains the process of knowledge construction. They note that co-construction processes in social interaction involve three basic notions: (1) knowledge acquisition and development involve active construction processes; (2) the construction processes of an individual are coherently linked with the construction processes of others; and (3) there is reciprocity between the participants. Construction means that new knowledge is acquired on the basis of old knowledge structures, where available knowledge (e.g., categories, schemata, strategies) provides the basis to understand new information and to integrate it into the existing knowledge structures. "Coherent links of individual construction processes with other minds is a necessary assumption to understand social-cultural influences on learning and development" (Leseman et al., 2000, p. 106). Smith (1994) used the term *collective intelligence* to describe "how groups of individuals can occasionally and under particular circumstances meld their thinking into a coherent whole" (p. 1).

Cole (1991) believes that the "two analytic categories we label *individual* and *social* are constituted in a unique medium – human culture" (p. 411, emphasis in original). For Cole, culture is the meeting point of the individual and the social. He argues that we need to develop studies "that treat neither the group nor the individual as the primary unit, but rather examine the ways in which cognitive and social activity unfold in a culturally mediated setting" (Resnick, 1991, p. 18). When we research SCK with IAM, we must keep in mind that the sociocultural context will influence social interaction and the way in which knowledge is constructed. Participants bring with them their own cultural ways of constructing knowledge, some avoiding dissonance, others engaging in it as shown in studies that used the IAM for analysis in international contexts with international participants (Lopez-Islas, 2004; Öztok, 2016). There are multiple approaches to constructing knowledge; therefore, the role of the sociocultural context is key to understanding how knowledge is constructed through social interaction in a specific environment. Öztok's (2016) investigation into the cultural ways of constructing knowledge utilizing the IAM showed that the four individuals' "unique identity trajectories determine the nature of the discourse, and shape the process of knowledge construction" (p. 181). The study also showed that individuals do not experience online learning through just one identification category but use multiple identities to collaborate and learn.

Focusing on the role of dialogue, Scardamalia and Bereiter (1994) discuss three characteristics of knowledge-building discourse. First, the focus is on problems rather than on categories of knowledge or on topics. Second, inquiry is driven by questions and desire for understanding, and negotiating ideas is marked by purposeful and constructive engagement with each other. More knowledgeable others do not stand outside the learning process (as teachers often do) but rather participate actively. Less knowledgeable participants in the discourse play an important role pointing out what is difficult to understand and, in turn, inadequacies in explanations. To the extent novices can push the discourse toward definition and clarification, their role is as important as more knowledgeable peers. Emphasis should be on the creation of a climate and desire to advance understanding rather than to display individual brilliance. Third, it is important to work with ideas in contexts broader than one's immediate working community such as engaging in peer review for scientific publication. Working within the broader knowledge-building community enables participants to view ideas from multiple perspectives. Therefore, implications for the design of learning environments that fosters knowledge construction include: (1) designing learning centered on problems rather than topics, (2) creating an environment where students with diverse expertise and knowledge can work together, (3) engaging the teacher in the learning process, and (4) engaging the learning community in examining ideas in broader contexts to enable understanding from multiple perspectives and expertise.

Goos et al. (2002) reconceptualized metacognition as a social collaborative process. In their three-year study of patterns of student– student social interaction that mediated metacognitive activity in mathematics classes, they attempted to capture the interactive nature of the groups' metacognitive monitoring and regulation, highlighting the reciprocal character of collaborative interactions, where mutuality was expressed through a balance of utterances labeled as self-disclosure, feedback request, and other monitoring. Goos et al. (2002) noted that "collaborative metacognitive activity proceeds through offering one's thoughts to others for inspection and acting as a critic of one's partner's thinking" (p. 207). This illustrates the critical role that social interaction plays in SCK.

Researching Social Interaction

As complex social relationships and different cultural values shape the intellectual interdependence in the co-construction of knowledge, as explained in sociocultural theory, John-Steiner and Mahn (1996) emphasize the need to examine patterns of interaction and collaboration that occur in collaborative learning environments to understand how learning takes place. Hence, discourse analysis, content analysis, conversation analysis, and interaction analysis became popular methods for researching social interaction and collaborative group process and development. In this section, we briefly reflect on transcript analysis methods used by researchers to explore social interaction in collaborative learning, as analyzing readily available transcripts is the focus of this book.

Bales (2001), in one of the early attempts to measure social interaction, emphasized that individuals' mental processes and social interactions take place in systematic contexts that can be measured. He was a pioneer in the development of methods for observing and measuring the interaction processes of groups. Since then, many coding schemes have been developed to analyze the social and relational processes and document change and transformation within the collaborative process in computer or video transcripts of discussions. Most of these methods focused on researching social presence, groups, and community.

Rourke et al. (1999) viewed social presence as one of the three "presences" that support learning in online environments and developed one of the earliest coding schemes in the field to assess social presence. They defined social presence as "the ability of learners to project themselves socially and affectively into a *community of inquiry*" (p. 50, emphasis in original). The other two presences defined were cognitive presence and teaching presence. They identified three indicators of social presence: affective responses, cohesive responses, and interactive responses, and analyzed them in online discussions. Affective responses included personal expressions of emotion, feelings, beliefs, and values. Cohesive responses were communication behaviors that build and sustain a sense of group commitment, such as greetings and salutations and group or personal reference. Interactive responses provided evidence that others were attending, such as agreement/disagreement, approval, and the referencing of previous messages. Rourke et al. (1999) developed protocols for coding online discussion transcripts based on these indicators. They noted their reliability in the pilot content analysis of two online class discussions. Based on their work, Swan (2002) and Swan and Shih (2005) developed an extensive coding schema to identify fifteen immediacy indicators that represent social presence, five each for affective, cohesive, and interactive responses in the discussion.

Their affective indicators, which reflected personal expressions of emotion, feelings, beliefs, and values, included the use of paralanguage, expressions of emotion, statements of values, humor, and self-disclosure. The cohesive indicators that support the development of community include greetings and salutations, the use of vocatives, group reference, social sharing, and course reflection. Their interactive indicators, which provide evidence that the other is attending and supporting interactions among communicators, included acknowledgment, agreement/disagreement, approval, invitation, and personal advice. Their coding of transcripts of computer discussions based on this scheme led them to the conclusion that students participating in online discussions strove to create a community of learning by employing text-based verbal immediacy behaviors to reduce the psychological distance among themselves. The coding schemes developed by Rourke et al. (1999) and Swan (2002) and Swan and Shih (2005), and later modified by them, were used by other researchers to analyze the relational social environment of online learning employing content analysis of transcripts.

Lowenthal and Dunlap (2020) used these coding schemes to analyze social presence in online discussions and observed that studying social presence is complex, as situation variables such as group size, instructional task, and previous relationships influence how social presence is established and maintained. Further, Lowenthal and Snelson (2017) pointed out the problems related to defining social presence and their impact on the development of research constructs. Kreijns et al. (2022) agreed that the conceptualization of social presence is problematic and identified two other constructs closely related to social presence: sociability (as a medium attribute) and social space (as a group attribute). They note that careful definition of research constructs will enable a more accurate understanding of interpersonal communication and group dynamics online.

Transcript analysis coding schemes were developed by other researchers to analyze social cues and social interaction. Lehtinen et al. (2023) combined content analysis of co-construction of knowledge and socioemotional interaction in online breakout rooms when studying pre-service secondary teachers during a collaborative task. They used the IAM to analyze SCK and developed categories of socioemotional interaction in their content analysis coding scheme, which included active listening, laughter/humor, life outside, encouraging participation, and expressing feelings. In order to understand social presence in situated interaction and how it is accomplished in virtual environments, Schultze and Brooks (2019) developed the Interactional Process Model of Social Presence to code transcripts of virtual interaction. This model included three constructs that could be used to code transcripts. They are copresence, where participants see each other and are aware of another's presence in a shared space; focused interaction through joint engrossment in a cooperative endeavor; and interlocking involvement obligation, highlighting the extent of interdependency between the focal actor and the other in focused interaction, which signals a high degree of social presence by supporting the other's involvement and validating the existence of the other's social self. Many of these content analysis schemes provide important insights into how computer or video transcripts can be analyzed to determine social interaction.

A predominant number of studies that have analyzed the social environment of online learning have conducted quantitative analysis using surveys of students or qualitative content analysis using interviews. For example, Gunawardena and Zittle (1997) developed a social presence scale and, using survey data and regression analysis, demonstrated that social presence is a strong predictor of learner satisfaction. Kreijns et al. (2020) aimed at a unidimensional social presence measure, but the Rasch test for multidimensionality revealed two dimensions for social presence, namely, "awareness of others" and "proximity with others"; the former dimension indicating low perceptions and the latter higher perceptions of social presence. Rovai (2002) developed a Classroom Community Scale, which generates an overall classroom community score as well as two subscales: connectedness and learning and showed that "sense of community and perceived cognitive learning are related" (p. 329).

Researchers have begun to use automated Social Learning Analytic Methods (SLAM) such as social network analysis (SNA) and lexica analysis to research the social environment of online learning (Gunawardena et al., 2016; Castellanos-Reyes et al., 2024). The following two sections of this book focus on researching social interaction with SLAM and are devoted to examining how to research the social environment of online learning that supports knowledge construction.

Conclusion

This chapter examined the concept of social interaction in online environments from a relational and socioemotional perspective. It explored why we need to study the social aspect of interaction in online learning environments, what constitutes social interaction, and how the relational nature of social interaction supports knowledge construction. The chapter showed that social presence, identity, social connectedness, and community are important dimensions of social interaction and need to be studied further while also examining their relationship to SCK. The chapter concluded with a discussion of transcript analysis methods using qualitative content analysis to examine social presence, connectedness, and community and looked forward to the next chapters addressing how social interaction can be researched employing SLAM.

References

Adolphs, R., & Damasio, A. R. (2001). The interaction of affect and cognition: A neurobiological perspective. In J. P. Forgas (Ed.), *Handbook of affect and social cognition* (pp. 27–49). NJ: Lawrence Erlbaum Associates.

Bales, R. (2001). *Social interaction systems: Theory and measurement.* New York: Routledge.

Bartlett Ellis, R. J., Carmon, A. F., & Pike, C. (2016). A review of immediacy and implications for provider-patient relationships to support medication management. *Patient Prefer Adherence*, 7(10), 9–18. https://doi.org/10.2147/PPA.S95163. PMID: 26792985; PMCID: PMC4710167.

Barton, D., & Tusting, K. (2005). *Beyond communities of practice: Language, power, and social context.* New York, NY: Cambridge University Press.

Cambridge Dictionary. (2024). Identity. In *Cambridge dictionary online.* https://dictionary.cambridge.org/us/dictionary/english/identity

Castellanos-Reyes, D., Richardson, J. C., & Maeda, Y. (2024). The evolution of social presence: A longitudinal exploration of the effect of online students' peer-interactions using social network analysis. *The Internet and Higher Education*, 61, 100939. https://doi.org/10.1016/j.iheduc.2024.100939

Cole, M. (1991). Conclusion. In L. B. Resnick, J. M. Levine, & S. D. Teasley (Eds.), *Perspectives on socially shared cognition* (pp. 398–417). Washington, DC: American Psychological Association.

Creese, A. (2003). Language, ethnicity and the mediation of allegations of racism: Negotiating diversity and sameness in multilingual school discourses. *International Journal of Bilingual Education and Bilingualism*, 6(3–4), 221–236.

Davidson, R. (2002, April). *Emotion, plasticity and the human brain: An overview of modern brain research and its implications for education.* The Decade of Behavior Distinguished Lecture Presented at the American Educational Research Association Annual Conference, New Orleans, LA.

Dennen, V. P. (2008). Pedagogical lurking: Student engagement in non-posting discussion behavior. *Computers in Human Behavior*, 24, 1624–1633. https://doi.org/10.1016/j.chb.2007.06.003

Dwivedi, Y. K., Balakrishnan, J., Mishra, A., De Bock, K. W., Adil, S, & Al-Busaidi, A. S. (2024). The role of embodiment, experience, and self-image expression in creating continuance intention in the metaverse. *Technological Forecasting & Social Change*, 203. https://doi.org/10.1016/j.techfore.2024.123402

Garrett Dikkers, A., Whiteside, A. L., & Tap, B. (2017). Social presence: Understanding connections among definitions, theory, measurements, and practice. In A. L. Whiteside, A. Garrett Dikkers, &

K. Swan (Eds.), *Social presence in online learning: Multiple perspectives on practice and research* (pp. 11–25). Sterling: VA: Stylus.

Garrison, D. R., Anderson, T., & Archer, W. (2000). Critical inquiry in a text-based environment: Computer conferencing in higher education. *The Internet and Higher Education, 2,* 87–105. http://dx.doi.org/10.1016/S1096-7516(00)00016-6

Gibson, J. (1979). *The ecological approach to visual perception.* Boston, MA: Houghton Mifflin.

Goos, M., Galbraith, P., & Renshaw, P. (2002). Socially mediated metacognition: Creating collaborative zones of proximal development in small group problem solving. *Educational Studies in Mathematics, 49*(2), 193–223.

Graiouid, S. (2005). Social exile and virtual *H'rig*: Computer-mediated interaction and cybercafé culture in Morocco. In M. Wiberg (Ed.), *The interaction society: Practice, theories, and supportive technologies* (pp. 57–92). Hershey, PA: Idea Group.

Gunawardena, C. N. (2017). Cultural perspectives on social presence: Research and practical guidelines for online design. In A. L. Whiteside, A. Garrett Dikkers, & K. Swan (Eds.), *Social presence in online learning: Multiple perspectives on practice and research* (pp. 113–129). Sterling: VA: Stylus.

Gunawardena, C. N., Bouachrine, F., Idrissi Alami, A., & Jayatilleke, G. (2006, April). *Cultural perspectives on social presence: A study of online chatting in Morocco and Sri Lanka.* Paper presented at the Annual Meeting of the American Educational Research Association, San Francisco, CA.

Gunawardena, C. N., Flor, N. V., Gomez, D., & Sánchez, D. (2016). Analyzing social construction of knowledge online by employing interaction analysis, learning analytics, and social network analysis. *The Quarterly Review of Distance Education, 17*(3), 35–60.

Gunawardena, C. N., Hermans, M., Sánchez, D., Richmond, C., Bohley, M., & Tuttle, R. (2009b). A theoretical framework for building online communities of practice with social networking tools. *Educational Media International, 46*(1), 3–16. http://dx.doi.org/10.1080/09523980802588626

Gunawardena, C. N., Idrissi Alami, A., Jayatilleke, G., & Bouacharine, F. (2009a). Identity, gender, and language in synchronous cybercultures: A cross-cultural study. In R. Goodfellow & M. N. Lamy (Eds.), *Learning cultures in online education* (pp. 30–51). London, UK: Continuum.

Gunawardena, C. N., Lowe, C., & Anderson, T. (1997). Analysis of a global on-line debate and the development of an interaction analysis model for examining social construction of knowledge in computer conferencing. *Journal of Educational Computing Research, 17*(4), 395–429.

Gunawardena, C. N., Nolla, A. C., Wilson, P. L., López-Islas, J. R., Ramírez-Angel, N., & Megchun-Alpízar, R. M. (2001). A cross-cultural study of group process and development in online conferences. *Distance Education, 22*(1), 85–121.

Gunawardena, C. N., & Zittle, F. (1997). Social presence as a predictor of satisfaction within a computer mediated conferencing environment. *The American Journal of Distance Education, 11*(3), 8–25.

Hardesty, L. A. (2023). *Reconnaissance: Relationship between social presence and knowledge construction in second life* [Ph.D. Dissertation, University of New Mexico]. https://digitalrepository.unm.edu/oils_etds/66

Henri, F. (1992). Computer conferencing and content analysis. In A. R. Kaye (Ed.), *Collaborative learning through computer conferencing: The Najadan Papers* (pp. 117–136). London: Springer-Verlag.

Hod, Y., & Katz, S. (2020). Fostering highly engaged knowledge building communities in socioemotional and sociocognitive hybrid learning spaces. *British Journal of Educational Technology, 51*(4), 1117–1135. https://doi:10.1111/bjet.12910

Hofstede, G. (1980). *Culture's consequences: International differences in work-related values.* Beverly Hills, CA: Sage.

John-Steiner, V., & Mahn, H. (1996). Sociocultural approaches to learning and development: A Vygotskian framework. *Educational Psychologist, 31*(3/4), 191–206.

Jones, S. G. (2002). Afterword: Building, buying, or being there: Imagining online community. In K. A. Renninger & W. Shumar (Eds.), *Building virtual communities: Learning and change in cyberspace* (pp. 368–376). Cambridge, UK: Cambridge University Press.

Kreijns, K., Bijker, M., & Weidlich, J. (2020). A Rasch analysis approach to the development and validation of a social presence measure. In M. Khine (Ed.), *Rasch measurement.* Singapore: Springer. https://doi.org/10.1007/978-981-15-1800-3_11

Kreijns, K., Kirschner, P. A., Jochems, W., & Buuren, H. (2011). Measuring perceived social presence in distributed learning groups. *Education and Information Technologies, 16*(4), 365–381.

Kreijns, K., Xu, K., & Weidlich, J. (2022). Social presence: Conceptualization and measurement. *Educational Psychology Review, 34*(1), 139–170. https://doi.org/10.1007/s10648-021-09623-8

Kumpulainen, K., & Mutanen, M. (2000). Mapping the dynamics of peer group interaction: A method of analysis of socially shared learning processes. In H. Cowie & G. van der Aalsvoort (Eds.), *Social interaction in learning and instruction: The meaning of discourse for the construction of knowledge* (pp. 144–160). Oxford, UK: Elsevier Science.

Lally, V., & de Laat, M. (2002). Cracking the code: Learning to collaborate and collaborating to learn in a networked environment. In G. Stahl (Ed.), *Proceedings of the Computer Supported Collaborative Learning (CSCL) Conference* (pp. 160–168). Boulder, CO: International Society of the Learning Sciences (ISLS).

Lehtinen, A., Kostiainen, E., & Näykki, P. (2023, October). Co-construction of knowledge and socioemotional interaction in pre-service teachers' video-based online collaborative learning. *Teaching and Teacher Education*, 133, 104299. https://doi.org/10.1016/j.tate.2023.104299

Leseman, P. P. M., Rollenberg, L., & Gebhardt, E. (2000). Co-construction in kindergartners' free play: Effects of social, individual and didactic factors. In H. Cowie & G. Van der Aalsvoort (Eds.), *Social interaction in learning and instruction: The meaning of discourse for the construction of knowledge*. Amsterdam, Netherlands: Pergamon/Elsevier Science Inc.

Littleton, K., & Hakkinen, P. (1999). Learning together: Understanding the processes of computer-based collaborative learning. In P. Dillenbourg (Ed.), *Collaborative learning: Cognitive and computational approaches* (pp. 20–30). Oxford, UK: Elsevier Science.

Lombard, M., & Ditton, T. (1997). At the heart of it all: The concept of presence. *Journal of Computer-Mediated Communication*, 3(2). https://doi.org/10.1111/j.1083-6101.1997.tb00072.x

Lopez-Islas, J. R. (2004). Collaborative learning at Monterrey Tech-Virtual University. In T. Duffy & J. Kirkley (Eds.), *Learner-centered theory and practice in distance education: Cases from higher education* (pp. 297–319). Mahwah, NJ: Lawrence Erlbaum.

Lowenthal, P. R., & Dunlap, J. C. (2020). Social presence and online discussions: A mixed method investigation. *Distance Education*, 41(4), 490–514. https://doi.org/10.1080/01587919.2020.1821603

Lowenthal, P. R., & Snelson, C. (2017). In search of a better understanding of social presence: An investigation into how researchers define social presence. *Distance Education*, 38(2), 141–159. https://doi.org/10.1080/01587919.2017.1324727

Mason, R., & Rennie, F. (2008). *E-learning and social networking handbook*. New York: Routledge.

McMillan, D. W., & Chavis, D. M. (1986). Sense of community: A definition and theory. *Journal of Community Psychology*, 14(1), 6–23.

Merriam-Webster. (2024). Identity definition & meaning. In *Merriam-Webster dictionary online*. www.merriam-webster.com/dictionary/identity

National Academies of Sciences, Engineering, and Medicine. (2018). *How people learn II: Learners, contexts, and cultures*. Washington, DC: The National Academies Press. https://doi.org/10.17226/24783

Öztok, M. (2016). Cultural ways of constructing knowledge: The role of identities in online group discussions. *International Journal of Computer-Supported Collaborative Learning*, 11, 157–186. https://doi.org/10.1007/s11412-016-9233-7

Polo, C., Lund, K., & Plantin, C. (2016). Group emotions: The social and cognitive functions of emotions in argumentation. *International Journal of Computer-Supported Collaborative Learning*, 11, 123–156. https://doi.org/10.1007/s11412-016-9232-8

Resnick, L. B., Levine, J. M., & Teasley, S. D. (1991). *Perspectives on socially shared cognition*. Washington, DC: American Psychological Association.

Rha, I. (2014). Emerging visual culture in online learning environments. In I. Jung & C. N. Gunawardena (Eds.) *Culture and online learning: Global perspectives and research*. Stylus.

Richardson, J. C., & Swan, K. (2003). Examining social presence in online courses in relation to students' perceived learning and satisfaction. *Journal of Asynchronous Learning Networks*, 7(1), 68–88.

Riedl, C., Köbler, F., Goswami, S., & Krcmar, H. (2013). Tweeting to feel connected: A model for social connectedness in online social networks. *International Journal of Human-Computer Interaction*, 29(10), 670–687. https://doi.org/10.1080/10447318.2013.768137

Rogers, E. M. (1962). *Diffusion of innovations*. New York: The Free Press.

Rourke, L., Anderson, T., Garrison, D. R., & Archer, W. (1999). Assessing social presence in asynchronous text-based computer conferencing. *The Journal of Distance Education/Revue de l'ducation Distance*, 14(2), 50–71.

Rourke, L., Anderson, T., Garrison, D. R., & Archer, W. (2001). Methodological issues in the content analysis of computer conference transcripts. *International Journal of Artificial Intelligence in Education, 12*(1), 8–22.

Rovai, A. P. (2002). Development of an instrument to measure classroom community. *The Internet and Higher Education, 5*(3), 197–211. https://doi.org/10.1016/S1096-7516(02)00102-1

Sadiqi, F. (2003). *Women, gender, and language in Morocco.* Leiden and Boston: Brill Academic Publishers.

Scardamalia, M., & Bereiter, C. (1994). Computer support for knowledge-building communities. *The Journal of the Learning Sciences, 3*(3), 265–283.

Schultze, U., & Brooks, J. A. M. (2019). An interactional view of social presence: Making the virtual other "real". *Information Systems Journal, 29*(3), 707–737. https://doi.org/10.1111/isj.12230

Short, J., Williams, E., & Christie, B. (1976). *The social psychology of telecommunications.* London, UK: John Wiley.

Slagter van Tryon, P. J., & Bishop, M. J. (2009). Theoretical foundations for enhancing social connectedness in online learning environments. *Distance Education, 30*(3), 291–315.

Slagter van Tryon, P. J., & Bishop, M. J. (2012). Evaluating social connectedness online: The design and development of the social perceptions in learning context instrument. *Distance Education, 33*(3), 347–364.

Smith, J. B. (1994). *Collective intelligence in computer-based collaboration.* Hillsdale, NJ: Lawrence Erlbaum.

Swan, K. (2002). Immediacy, social presence, and asynchronous discussion. In J. Bourne & J. C. Moore (Eds.), *Elements of quality online education* (pp. 157–172). Volume 3 in the Sloan-C Series. Boston, MA: The Sloan Consortium.

Swan, K. (2017). Multiple perspectives on social presence in online learning: An introduction to this volume. In A. L. Whiteside, A. Garrett Dikkers, & K. Swan (Eds.), *Social presence in online learning: Multiple perspectives on practice and research* (pp. 3–10). Sterling: VA: Stylus.

Swan, K., & Shih, L. F. (2005). On the nature and development of social presence in online course discussions. *Journal of Asynchronous Learning Networks, 9*(3), 115–136. https://doi.org/10.24059/olj.v9i3.1788

Tu, C. H. (2001). How Chinese perceive social presence: An examination of interaction in online learning environment. *Education Media International, 38*(1), 45–60.

Tu, C. H., & McIsaac, M. (2002). The relationship of social presence and interaction in online classes. *American Journal of Distance Education, 16*(3), 131–150. https://doi.org/10.1207/S15389286AJDE1603_2

van der Aalsvoort, G., & Harinck, F. J. H. (2000). Studying social interaction in instruction and learning: Methodological approaches and problems. In H. Cowie & G. van der Aalsvoort (Eds.), *Social interaction in learning and instruction: The meaning of discourse for the construction of knowledge* (pp. 5–20). Oxford, UK: Elsevier Science.

Vygotsky, L. S. (1978). *Mind in society: The development of higher psychological processes.* Cambridge, MA: Harvard University Press.

Wenger, E. (1998). *Communities of practice: Learning, meaning, and identity.* Cambridge, UK: Cambridge University Press.

Wenger, E., McDermott, R., & Snyder, W. M. (2002). *Cultivating communities of practice: A guide to managing knowledge.* Cambridge, MA: Harvard Business School Press.

Whiteside, A. L., & Garrett Dikkers, A. (2012). Maximizing multicultural online learning experiences with the Social Presence Model, course examples, and specific strategies. In K. St. Amant & S. Kelsey (Eds.), *Computer-mediated communication across cultures: International interactions in online environments* (pp. 395–413). Hershey, PA: IGI Global.

Whiteside, A. L., Garrett Dikkers, A., & Lewis, S. (2017). Overcoming isolation online: Strategies to enhance social presence in practice. In A. L. Whiteside, A. Garrett Dikkers, & K. Swan (Eds.), *Social presence in online learning: Multiple perspectives on practice and research* (pp. 180–187). Sterling: VA: Stylus.

Wiener, M., & Mehrabian, A. (1968). *Language within language: Immediacy, a channel in verbal communication.* New York: Appleton-Century-Crofts, Meredith Corporation.

Zerubavel, E. (1999). *Social mindscapes: An invitation to cognitive sociology.* Cambridge, MA: Harvard University Press.

Part II

Methods for Researching the Social Environment Online

The online social environment can be a complex virtual landscape for researchers to navigate. This section is designed to help researchers not only understand it but also feel confident and capable of conducting research using a variety of methods in conjunction with the Interaction Analysis Model (IAM). Chapter 4 explores Social Learning Analytic Methods (SLAM) and discusses several key approaches to researching the social environment that will complement qualitative research. These methods, including social network analysis (SNA), cluster analysis, and decision trees, are techniques that researchers can use to understand how the social environment influences knowledge construction. Chapter 5 explores the social construction of knowledge (SCK) in both formal learning management systems (LMS) (like Blackboard, Moodle, and Canvas), and informal social media (like Twitter (now known as X), Reddit, and Facebook) emphasizing text-based discussions. It outlines criteria for selecting the appropriate social learning space for research, considering relevance, target audience, and access to data, and provides a detailed method for scraping and analyzing online discussions, using a case study on Reddit to illustrate the process. Chapter 6 guides researchers on using various free and open-source tools for social learning analytics, focusing on programming languages (R and Python), and integrated analysis platforms (Anaconda, RStudio). The chapter also addresses setting up programming environments, installing R and Python, package management, and choosing suitable development environments for specific research needs, ensuring that researchers feel capable and prepared for their research endeavors.

DOI: 10.4324/9781003324461-5

4 Social Learning Analytic Methods (SLAM) for Examining Online Social Dynamics

This chapter will describe the Social Learning Analytic Methods (SLAM) that can be used to analyze the online social environment and how these methods are different from pure learning analytics, which does not take the relational aspect of online learning into account. We define SLAM as a collection of techniques to study group interactions on learning management systems and social networks as groups co-construct knowledge online. These techniques include frequency analysis, sentiment analysis, cluster analysis, social network analysis, and artificial intelligence (incorporating large language models, neural networks, and generative AI), which are used in a complementary fashion to analyze the social construction of knowledge (SCK). Combining SLAM with the Interaction Analysis Model (IAM) developed by Gunawardena et al. (1997) provides multiple perspectives from which to understand knowledge construction especially at the higher phases of the IAM. This chapter introduces sentiment analysis, cluster analysis, decision trees, and social network analysis (SNA) that can enhance our understanding of the social environment that supports knowledge construction online. Though powerful analytic tools, SLAM is not intended to replace the qualitative analyst but, instead, provide additional tools to understand the social dynamics of knowledge construction as well as facilitate time-consuming qualitative analysis.

Learning Analytics

Learning analytics is a subset of the broader field of analytics. Therefore, it is necessary to first define *analytics* before considering *learning analytics*. Note that the term analytics is a new way to describe something many people are familiar with, data analysis. However, analytics go far beyond foundational and straightforward analysis techniques such as applying measures of central tendency (mean, mode, median) or descriptive statistics. Analytics encompass technology enabled methods that include but are not limited to social network analysis (SNA), cluster analysis, and decision trees. "Analytics marries large datasets, statistical techniques, and predictive modeling. It could be thought of as the practice of mining institutional data to produce "actionable intelligence" (Campbell et al., 2007, p. 42). An example of such actionable intelligence is Amazon's use of recommenders which work by tracking user behavior and using specific algorithms to provide content based on those choices (Konstan & Riedl, 2012). Internet users should all be familiar with recommenders that are behind online advertisements encouraging the purchase of a protective phone case after purchasing a new phone. Another key aspect of the definition of analytics is its focus on institutional data because analytics is commonly applied in educational institutions. This flows into the definition of learning analytics, which traditionally focuses on large datasets that originate from school systems of all different levels. According to the 1st

DOI: 10.4324/9781003324461-6

International Conference on Learning Analytics and Knowledge, as cited by Long and Siemens (2011), "learning analytics is the measurement, collection, analysis and reporting of data about learners and their contexts, for purposes of understanding and optimizing learning and the environments in which it occurs" (p. 34). Of course, data about learners is more available than ever with so many formal learning institutions turning to the use of learning management systems (LMS). Learning resource usage statistics, grades, and the content of discussions are all easily accessible on an LMS. The availability of these data presents a rich opportunity to apply learning analytics in order to enhance student performance. One good example of learning analytics applied to this end is found in Arnold and Pistilli (2012) where a proprietary algorithm was used to provide students a red, yellow, or green light, like a traffic stoplight, indicating their potential success in a course given the points earned in the course to date, effort, prior academic history, and demographic factors. Learning analytics focuses on analyzing institutional student data in an effort to achieve institutional goals such as enhancing overall student success.

Social Learning Analytics

Social learning analytics is "a distinctive subset of learning analytics that draws on the substantial body of work demonstrating that new skills and ideas are not solely individual achievements, but are developed, carried forward, and passed on through interaction and collaboration" (Buckingham Shum & Ferguson, 2012, p. 5). Social learning analytics do not include data that comes from institutional records of schools or universities. Datapoints like grades, time spent in a course, and meeting syllabus deadlines are left aside for a focus on datapoints like social presence, synthesis, and testing new knowledge. Social learning takes place both within traditional classrooms and in informal spaces like social media, so social learning analytics is applied to data that comes from both spaces. The focus of social learning analytics is on the process of SCK. The foundations of SCK were largely established by Vygotsky (1978) and are discussed in Chapter 1. Within SCK, we focus on the process of knowledge construction using the Interaction Analysis Model (IAM) (Gunawardena et al., 1997) and how it is supported by social interaction, specifically by the construct social presence defined by Gunawardena and Zittle (1997) as the extent to which a person perceives another as a real human. Much research has been done regarding SCK and social presence, but none has fully applied social analytics techniques as a research methodology. This book presents a novel approach to analyzing these phenomena using analytics techniques we call Social Learning Analytic Methods (SLAM).

Social Learning Analytic Methods (SLAM)

SLAM was first coined as a collection of techniques in Gunawardena et al. (2018). Prior to this publication, the analytic methods that are part of SLAM were mostly applied on their own to serve the individual needs of researchers. For example, Levin et al. (1990) used descriptive statistics from their intermessage reference analysis to build message maps which show the ebb and flow of messages over time. What we propose is a strategic approach to employ SLAM to understand the knowledge construction process and how social interaction influences knowledge construction. In so doing, we aim to realize the potential identified by Lucas et al. (2014) who wrote, "More detailed procedures will not only help researchers to compare results of different studies, but could also be used to enable automatic analysis tools" (p. 581) when envisioning how the IAM could be improved.

Perhaps one of the most important works that led to the reconceptualization of the IAM and the SLAM we present in this book is the work of Lucas and Moreira (2010), who pointed out that while the IAM was strong in its ability to identify knowledge construction, it did not account for social interaction that supports knowledge construction. Indeed, Rourke et al. (1999), conducting research on communities of inquiry, identified that cognitive presence, teaching presence, and social presence all play a key role in an educational experience. Cognitive presence is effectively the social construction of knowledge which can be assessed by the IAM. Teaching presence has to do with the design of the learning experience and facilitation techniques. Social presence is "defined as the ability of learners to project themselves socially and affectively into a community of inquiry" (Rourke et al., 1999, p. 50). The paper by Lucas et al. (2014) allowed the IAM's original author and the researchers who initially identified the gap in the IAM to acknowledge the IAM's inability to assess the social context of SCK and explore how to address this shortcoming. It was not until Gunawardena et al. (2018) that we began to develop methods to address the social context.

Each of the SLAM procedures can be used both to conduct automatic analysis and to perform a content analysis. In reconceptualizing the IAM in Chapter 17, we wanted to take advantage of the affordances of new technologies, by introducing SLAM, and also remain true to the original qualitative roots by updating our coding framework. Allowing qualitative researchers to continue using methods they are comfortable with and opening the analysis up to quantitative researchers enhances the utility of the IAM to researchers of all methodological proclivities. Figure 4.1 presents a summary of SLAM and the levels at which data should be used to understand SCK.

In order for SCK to occur, people must interact with one another. Thus, the person is the basic level of SLAM analysis. Including the human elements of the SCK process roots the analysis in context and humanizes the learning experience that is the subject of the analysis. The next level of SLAM analysis is the message, which is the product of the people who are participating in a collaboration moving toward SCK. The message is the unit of analysis for the IAM. To create knowledge, people interact with the messages created by others. These

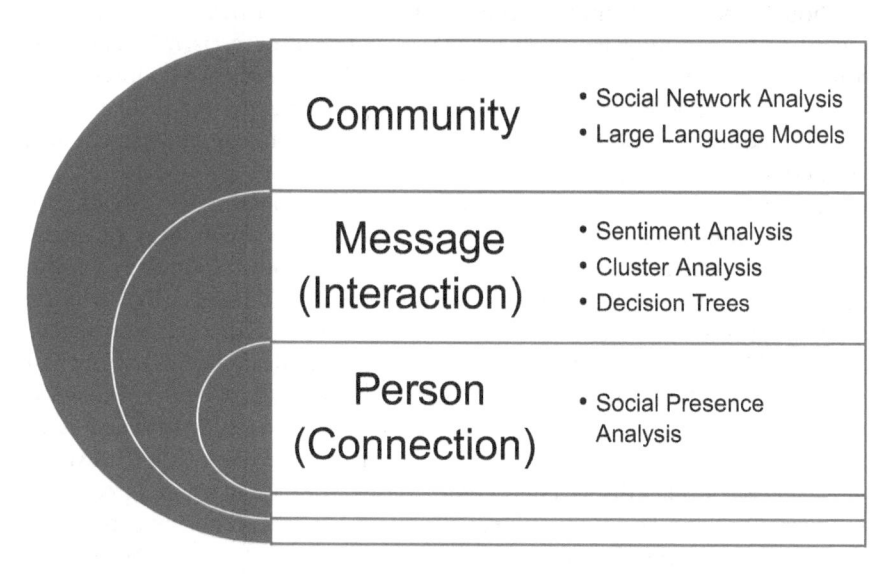

Figure 4.1 Levels of SLAM analysis and associated methods

artifacts of cognitive and social processes can be directly analyzed using the IAM. The final level of SLAM analysis is the community, which is focused on the connections people make with one another via social presence and the connections people make with the knowledge shared by those in the group. This macro level of analysis allows researchers to find patterns that are not easily identifiable when looking at the detailed content of messages. Community level analysis allows us to see interaction patterns like the comparison of how influential network participants are in relationship to one another or the points at which the SCK process reaches higher phases.

Sentiment Analysis

Sentiment analysis "is the field of study that analyzes people's opinions, sentiments, evaluations, appraisals, attitudes, and emotions toward entities such as products, services, organizations, individuals, issues, events, topics, and their attributes" (Liu, 2012, p. 1). Descriptive statistics are the foundation of sentiment analysis. Note that descriptive statistics are the most basic way we have to understand data trends. For the purpose of this book, the most important method is a word frequency count. This sounds like what it is, counting the number of similar words within a dataset. One of the early contributions to analyzing online interactions using these types of frequency counts was made by Levin et al. (1990), who proposed a multipronged model to illustrate the social environment and participation patterns in online interactions. Their study focused on the Intercultural Learning Network comprising mostly primary, secondary, and university students and instructors. One of their analytical techniques involved a qualitative content analysis that required a coder to read messages between participants to determine whether a given message referenced others. This included determining whether someone agreed with a previous statement. Assessing agreement is similar to sentiment analysis. As a foundation for other SLAMs, a word frequency analysis will tell researchers what is being discussed.

The most common method of sentiment analysis is based on word counts. Sentiment analysis differs from a word count because it focuses on specific words that indicate a given sentiment about something. Sentiment can be either positive or negative. Positive sentiment can be identified by counting words like *happy, wonderful,* or *perfect.* Negative sentiment aligns with words like *angry, terrible,* or *disgusting.* Once words are counted, they are assigned a score. Positive words get a +1 while negative words get a –1. The totals in each category are added up and the result is known as a sentiment score. Sentiment analysis can tell us how people feel about a given subject.

A sentiment analysis can become a construct analysis by changing the categories of words being counted. A construct is an abstract variable that is a central focus of research. Just about any research construct can fit the sentiment analysis model. So long as a construct can be associated with keywords that exemplify it, the construct can be analyzed automatically using the procedures we will describe in later chapters. Some examples of constructs that are relevant to the IAM are affective responses, self-disclosure, disagreement, and the list goes on. Sentiment analysis helps understand the social environment when sentiment keywords are replaced by keywords that identify social presence. For example, words like *affection, care,* and *love* are indicators of emotion. This is exactly what we have done with SLAM to conduct analysis at the person level as displayed in Figure 4.1. In the case of a social presence analysis, the keyword frequencies reveal how often and how people are establishing social presence.

The power of sentiment analysis is twofold: word counts become the foundation for other types of analytics because they are used to establish the parameters used by automated methods to classify data, and the basic methods used to conduct sentiment analysis can fit a wide variety of research constructs when traditional positive and negative words are replaced. For more information about how to customize sentiment analysis to fit other research constructs, see Chapter 7. To determine how word counts are related to one another, one must conduct a cluster analysis.

Cluster Analysis

The purpose of a cluster analysis is to classify data for which there are no clear labels or existing trends (Weiss et al., 2015). Cluster analysis is considered an unsupervised classification method because it uses the data itself as the input for the identification of labels and trends as it groups data. Specifically, the most common method of cluster analysis uses the counts of words within data to create its groupings which is how it builds upon word counts produced via sentiment analysis. The unit of analysis for clustering varies and can include entire documents, paragraphs, and even sentences. Clustering primarily considers similarity in order to group data. Similarity is determined by an examination of the contents of a document and assigning a score for a document according to the frequencies of the words in it. In the case of documents, clustering groups documents whose content is most similar. In the case of sentences, clustering will focus on the proximity of the words themselves as well as their frequencies to determine their similarity. Clustering is not guided by a specific framework or goal. Clustering takes an open-ended approach to its grouping of unstructured data.

According to Manning and Schütze (1999), clustering can be used for:

- Exploratory data analysis
- Generalization

Exploratory data analysis applies to the context of examining the social environment because it can be used as a preliminary step in understanding large datasets by creating groupings. Furthermore, clustering also gives researchers a clear illustration of how the things that are being discussed are related to one another. One way of visualizing clusters is using a dendrogram. The clusters in a dendrogram will clearly show how near or far various elements of a discussion are from one another as shown in Figure 4.2.

Dendrograms are hierarchical in nature and should be interpreted from top to bottom. Figure 4.2 includes numbers that are associated with the individual posts from the transcript of a computer discussion. So, post 92 (in the top left corner) is extremely different from the large number of posts all clustered together in the bottom center of the graphic. The bulk of the discussion involves topics that are highly related to this large central cluster. Posts from clusters that are further away from this central cluster have commonalities with the central cluster but differ enough to be separated by the clustering algorithm. Examining the contents of the posts reveals what is being discussed within a given cluster and thus can become exploratory data analysis.

The generalization application of clustering applies because clusters in dendrograms are formed based on frequencies of words. This allows researchers to use the clusters as themes in and of themselves because they were not produced using an interpretive coding process. The ability of clusters to serve as themes reveals a connection between clustering and grounded theory (Glaser & Strauss, 1967). Grounded theory is a qualitative data analysis method that asks the analyst to use only the data from a given study to guide the creation of a theory. Applying grounded theory involves a manual review and coding of the data

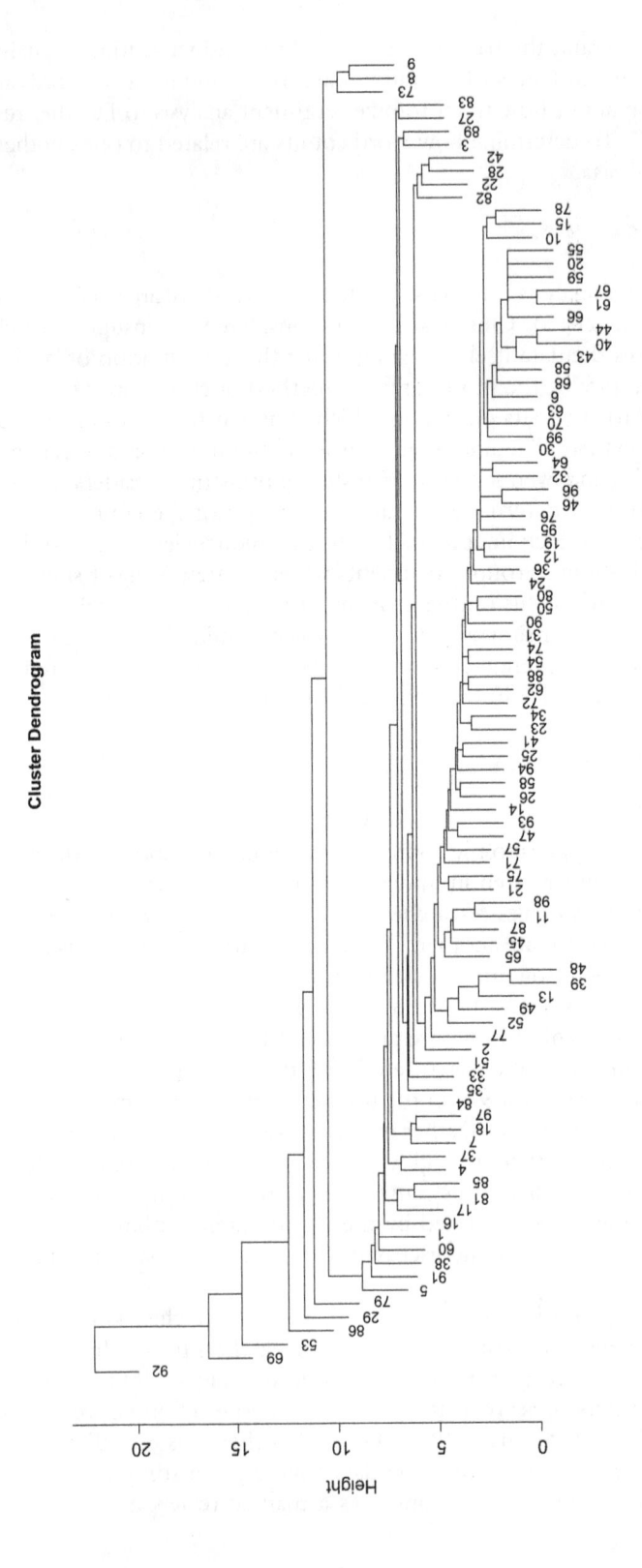

Figure 4.2 Dendrogram

based on the researcher's interpretation. As coding progresses, various themes emerge from the data, which are used as building blocks in theory building. Using grounded theory is time-consuming, and it also can be influenced by the subjectivity of the analyst. Cluster analysis can serve the purpose of the analyst who is applying grounded theory because it uses the data to create themes, and it will also save the qualitative analyst the time of developing the codes using content analysis.

The output of clustering must be reviewed by an analyst to evaluate the efficacy of this unsupervised method, but this verification is straightforward and does not take hours to complete, even for large datasets. Using clustering to conduct a type of grounded theory analysis can also potentially remove the subjectivity that hand coding the data might introduce. Using clustering to conduct an analysis similar to grounded theory might provide an objective view of the codes and categories. Two qualitative researchers who are coding the same dataset using the same grounded theory procedures will likely produce somewhat different results. However, the same two researchers who apply the same clustering technique to a dataset will produce exactly the same results. This means that using clustering methods to support a grounded theory analysis increases the replicability of the research.

Cluster analysis is useful for understanding the social environment of online learning because it clearly illustrates the relationships between ideas and subjects being discussed. Furthermore, it provides a time-saving option to traditional grounded theory research that reduces the researcher's subjectivity. The groupings of data that result from a cluster analysis can also be useful because decision trees can be grown using the rules identified by examining clusters (Witten et al., 2011).

Decision Trees

Decision trees are visual representations of classification rules determined by the researcher that are applied to data. The rules help the decision trees identify topics or themes in data. Decision trees are aptly named as they are comprised of the following elements:

- Root – initial query being considered by the decision tree like how text should be classified according to the IAM
- Node – individual grouping of data like a topic or theme
- Branch – entire arm of the decision tree that stems from the main node. Branches include other nodes, branches, and leaves
- Leaf – smallest level grouping like a subtopic or subtheme that is not split by rules

Generally, decision trees are applied to the task of text categorization. At their root, decision trees are algorithmic classifiers because they use rules to (1) define criteria that are used to split nodes into branches and (2) when to stop breaking them down. Decision trees grow just like real trees according to these criteria. Generally, nodes are split into branches when the split will result in a large amount of new branches and leaves (Weiss et al., 2015).

Like real trees, decision trees must be pruned. To prune a decision tree, leaves and branches are evaluated by the researcher. The involvement of the researcher in pruning makes it clear that decision trees are a supervised classification method. Pruning is done to make sure the tree does not use sparse data to classify new inputs and to optimize performance (Manning & Schütze, 1999). For example, if an IAM dataset had the one and only instance of the phrase "I disagree" in Phase III, subsequent data would also be classified as Phase III regardless of whether or not "I disagree" would be best suited for classification in this IAM Phase. When pruning decision trees, researchers must be careful not to remove data that is actually well represented because this will introduce inaccuracies. For example, deleting instances of the phrase "my opinion" as representations of IAM Phase I when it happens to be the most common Phase I phrase will cause the decision tree to rely on other less common phrases to classify data as Phase I.

Social Network Analysis (SNA)

SNA can be defined as a method of identifying the relationships among social entities (e.g., dyads, triads, and larger groups) and analyzing the implications of these interaction patterns (Wasserman & Faust, 1994). Visualizing interactions that buttress SCK is of interest to some scholars who use the IAM because it can provide a holistic view of discussions (Lucas et al., 2014). The key output of SNA is the sociogram which was first introduced by Moreno (1953). The intent behind the sociogram is to illustrate the relationships between people by connecting points representative of people or groups in a network. The connections themselves represent communications like texts, emails, or discussion posts that are sent between the people or groups in the network. Figure 4.3 provides an example of a sociogram that serves as a visual reference to the primary features of a sociogram which are as follows:

- Actors – individuals in a network represented as circles with names in them. Generally, actors are people but they can also be groups. When appropriate, SNA can also focus on the words within a dataset and use them as the actors in a sociogram. Actors are also known as "nodes."
- Relational tie – the connections between actors represented as lines between the circles with names on them. Connections are communications like texts, emails, or discussion posts that are sent between actors. Ties can be directional, which indicates who sent whom the communications like in Figure 4.3. Relational ties are also known as "edges."
- Centrality – nodes that are in the middle of the sociogram. Nodes that are most central have the highest number of connections going to and from them. In Figure 4.3, Alice has the highest centrality followed by Charlie. Eve has the lowest centrality.

The use of the sociogram has changed little since it was first introduced but it has become much easier to create due to advances in technology. Levin et al. (1990) conducted a foundational study to SNA with their use of "message maps" that displayed the interrelationships among messages using directional arrows. These message maps bear a strong resemblance to modern sociograms, which also use directional arrows to illustrate the relationships between groups of people. For an in-depth discussion of some technologies that are used to conduct SNA, see Chapter 10.

SNA is useful because it illustrates the interaction dynamics of a group that is building knowledge by clearly showing how participants in an activity are related to one another. SNA easily identifies contributors who are most important to the group's SCK with nodes that have many connections to them and those that also exist within the primary cluster of nodes. Sociograms also reveal contributors who play a minor role in the group's social construction of knowledge with nodes that have few connections and exist on the periphery of the visualization.

The sheer number of connections and the relative position of an individual node are useful, but greater detail is possible when focusing on the sociogram. For example, the sociogram can focus on the entire dataset to illustrate the gestalt of the group's knowledge construction process. Alternatively, sociograms can be examined according to the individual IAM Phases that are found within coded data. This approach allows researchers to isolate the contributors

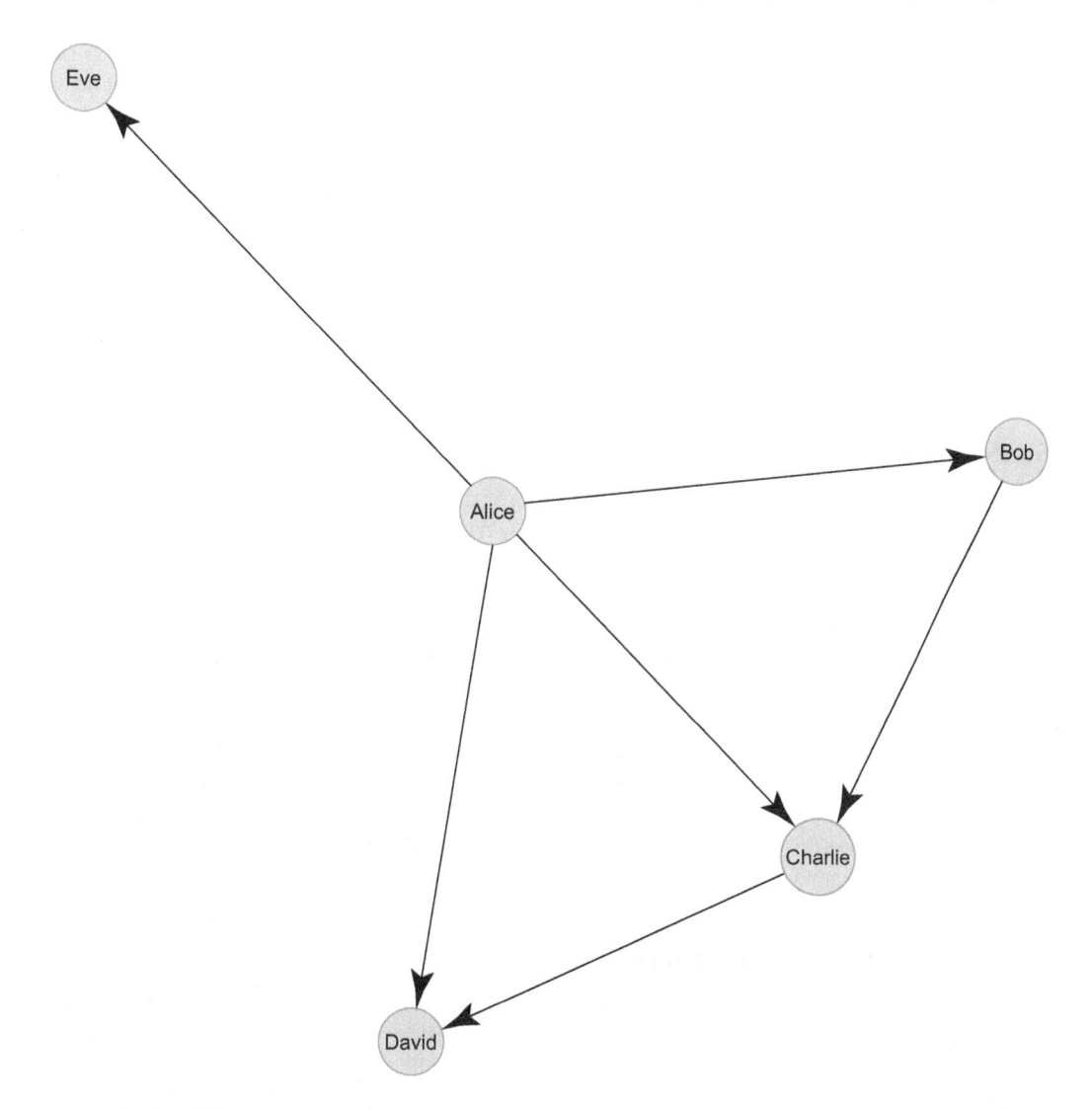

Figure 4.3 Social network analysis sociogram

and to clearly see which ones are the most important to the network's knowledge creation process as the group's process evolves.

Including social presence in the analysis accounts for yet another variable that is key to SCK. Researchers can use these visualizations to quickly determine the role social presence plays by determining how frequently people who are central to the network exemplify social presence. This is done by using word frequencies as a unit of analysis for social presence along with the IAM Phases. Note that connections between people denote some type of social presence in and of itself, but the nature of the social presence must be coded qualitatively to ensure accurate interpretation. SNA is a central method that is used to enumerate social presence by providing a way to visualize both the associations between people in the network as well as content.

Relationships certainly exist between people, but they can also exist between subjects or ideas as the knowledge construction process unfolds. SNA can also be useful in showing how knowledge is built and the specific content that is needed to construct the path to higher levels of understanding. To use a sociogram to illustrate the connections between ideas, we should use the words within the messages as the network's nodes and their coded IAM Phases. The resulting visualization will illuminate pathways that were followed during the course of social knowledge construction. Note that using SNA in this fashion does not relate to the social context of a group's knowledge construction process, but it is a novel use of the technique that is valuable in tracking how an idea evolves, gets stuck, or remains the same. Such knowledge is useful for researchers and teachers when evaluating the success of instructional interventions and considering modifications to improve outcomes.

SLAM Analysis Sequence

So far this chapter has described each SLAM in light of how they can be individually used to analyze social interaction in the process of the SCK. While the individual methods are effective in their own right, using them together allows researchers to maximize their ability to understand SCK. For example, a researcher who is using the IAM to understand SCK would first conduct a word frequency analysis and sentiment analysis to quickly determine the contents and sentiment of their data, respectively. Next, the analysis moves to an LLM and automatic classifications. Knowledge of the data's contents and sentiment will help the researcher evaluate the output. Further support is provided in the next step which is to use a cluster analysis to differentiate between noisy data. In this case, the LLM might have produced some inaccurate IAM classifications that could be visually identified using the cluster analysis dendrogram. The final step is to conduct SNA because the entirety of the analysis should be interpreted through the lens of the sociocultural context. See Chapter 18 for a full treatment of how SLAM can be used in a complimentary fashion to answer a variety of research questions.

SLAM in Practice – Analytics Supporting Not Replacing Researchers

Some of the techniques described in this chapter and elsewhere in this book might seem complex and intimidating. However, we agree with Witten et al. (2011), who wrote that when analyzing analytics "simple ideas often work very well, and we strongly recommend the adoption of a 'simplicity-first' methodology when analyzing practical datasets" (p. 86). We urge researchers to adopt this mindset as well and to make use of the code we provide in this book that can be used to employ the methods we describe in the chapters. Starting small with the SLAM that is most accessible, perhaps a word count, is a meaningful first step.

In proposing SLAM to buttress the IAM, our intent is to provide researchers of all backgrounds and skill sets with accessible tools that can be used to enhance the breadth and depth of analysis. Qualitative researchers should find that SLAM provides them with a time-saving approach to analysis that can help them complete the coding of data much more efficiently. Quantitative researchers should find SLAM a comfortable place to start understanding big data and extending existing skill sets to conduct analysis. In Gunawardena et al. (2016), we included a figure that proposed analytic tools should not replace, but rather assist, qualitative researchers. We have updated this figure in Figure 4.4 to illustrate the relationship we believe should exist between the IAM 2.0 qualitative analyst (a researcher who is using the IAM 2.0 presented in Chapter 17 to perform qualitative analysis) and SLAM tools.

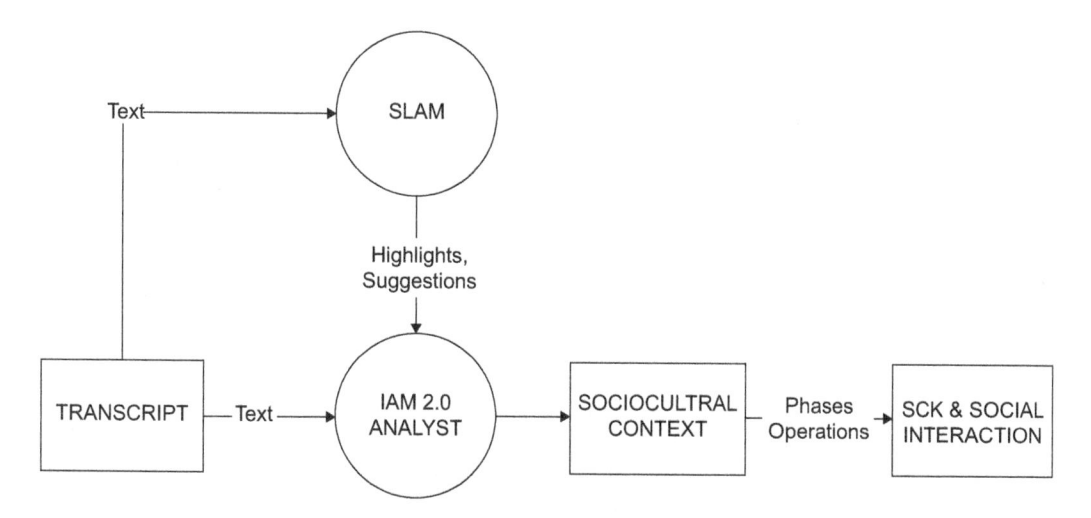

Figure 4.4 SLAM as a process that assists, not substitutes for, the analyst

The transcript is the foundation of the analysis as text is the primary input for SLAM and content analysis conducted by the IAM 2.0 analyst. SLAM provides highlights in the data and can make suggestions for the analyst to consider. The final results must pass through the IAM 2.0 analyst because they will first need to view the results provided by SLAM through the lens of the sociocultural context from which the data originates. Finally, the analyst must check the automatic classifications produced by SLAM to ascertain the levels of SCK and social interaction that were identified. Regardless of a researcher's expertise with quantitative or qualitative methods, SLAM should be used to inform and reveal trends. Findings should be verified to ascertain their veracity because even the best analytics and artificial intelligence will not be able to replace the perspective and insights provided by IAM 2.0 analysts.

We ultimately view SLAM using the lens of distributed cognition (Hutchins, 1995). The distributed aspect tells us that people mediate their cognition using external resources like tools. Indeed, it is impossible to memorize every single bit of knowledge one encounters in a lifetime. Knowing where to find the information or how to discover new answers using tools is the key. In this case, SLAM are the tools that can be used to achieve high levels of insight that are not possible without using them. The role of the researcher using analytics tools to solve problems is irreplaceable in this view of cognition because the tools themselves are not useful until someone puts them to use for a particular purpose. SLAM provides a set of tools that researchers can use together or piecemeal to answer complex questions.

One major benefit of using SLAM is that they can quickly perform tasks that were typically relegated to very time-consuming grounded theory or content analysis. In environments where formal researchers are often pressured with teaching and service duties and when educators simply want to discover new ways to improve learning experiences for their students, time is of the essence. SLAM offers a set of tools that can be used to alleviate the pressures of time and produce informative results that can be used for both the design and development of instructional interventions and to conduct cutting-edge research.

Conclusion

This chapter differentiated between learning analytics and social learning analytics. It then introduced SLAM as a novel way to analyze SCK with each technique providing unique insights. SLAM techniques including sentiment analysis, cluster analysis, decision trees, and SNA were also described. Each of these techniques is intended to assist researchers in their work with qualitative data rather than replace their role in research. In the forthcoming chapters, we further expand on the SLAM methods introduced in this chapter so researchers are able to work with them to conduct their own research.

References

Arnold, K., & Pistilli, M. (2012). *Course signals at purdue: Using learning analytics to increase student success.* International Conference on Learning Analytics and Knowledge, Vancouver, BC, Canada.

Buckingham Shum, S., & Ferguson, R. (2012). Social learning analytics. *Educational Technology & Society, 15*(3), 3–26. www.ifets.info/journals/15_3/2.pdf

Campbell, J. P., DeBlois, P. B., & Oblinger, D. G. (2007). Academic analytics: A new tool for a new era. *EDUCAUSE Review, 42*(4), 40–57. http://er.educause.edu/~/media/files/article-downloads/erm0742.pdf

Glaser, B. G., & Strauss, A. L. (1967). *The discovery of grounded theory: Strategies for qualitative research.* Aldine.

Gunawardena, C. N., Flor, N. V., Gómez, D., & Sánchez, D. (2016). Analyzing social construction of knowledge online by employing interaction analysis, learning analytics, and social network analysis. *Quarterly Review of Distance Education, 17*(3), 35–60. (e-Learners and Their Data, Part 1: Conceptual, Research, and Exploratory Perspectives).

Gunawardena, C. N., Flor, N. V., & Sánchez, D. M. (2018). *Learning analytics and social construction of knowledge online.* Distance Teaching and Learning Conference, Madison, WI.

Gunawardena, C. N., Lowe, C. A., & Anderson, T. (1997). Analysis of a global online debate and the development of an interaction analysis model for examining social construction of knowledge in computer conferencing. *Journal of Educational Computing Research, 17*(4), 397–431.

Gunawardena, C. N., & Zittle, F. J. (1997). Social presence as a predictor of satisfaction within a computer-mediated conferencing environment. *American Journal of Distance Education, 11*(3), 8–26.

Hutchins, E. (1995). *Cognition in the wild.* MIT Press.

Konstan, J. A., & Riedl, J. (2012). Deconstructing recommender systems: How Amazon and Netflix predict your preferences and prod you to purchase. *IEEE Spectrum, 49,* 55–58.

Levin, J. A., Kim, H., & Riel, M. M. (1990). Analyzing instructional interactions on electronic message networks. In L. M. Harasim (Ed.), *Online education: Perspectives on a new environment.* Praeger.

Liu, B. (2012). *Sentiment analysis and opinion mining.* Morgan & Claypool.

Long, P., & Siemens, G. (2011). Penetrating the fog: Analytics in learning and education. *EDUCAUSE Review, 46*(5), 30–41. https://net.educause.edu/ir/library/pdf/erm1151.pdf

Lucas, M., Gunawardena, C. N., & Moreira, A. (2014). Assessing social construction of knowledge online: A critique of the interaction analysis model. *Computers in Human Behavior, 30,* 574–582.

Lucas, M., & Moreira, A. (2010). *Knowledge construction with social web tools.* International Conference on Technology Enhanced Learning, Berlin Heidelberg.

Manning, C. D., & Schütze, H. (1999). *Foundations of statistical natural language processing.* MIT Press.

Moreno, J. L. (1953). *Who shall survive? Foundations of sociometry, group psychotherapy and socio-drama* (2nd ed.). Beacon House, Inc.

Rourke, L., Anderson, T., Garrison, D. R., & Archer, W. (1999). Assessing social presence in asynchronous text-based computer conferencing. *Journal of Distance Education, 14*(2), 50–71.

Vygotsky, L. S. (1978). *Mind in society: The development of higher psychological processes.* Harvard University Press. www.marxists.org/archive/vygotsky/index.htm

Wasserman, S., & Faust, K. (1994). *Social network analysis: Methods and applications.* Cambridge University Press.

Weiss, S. M., Indurkhya, N., & Zhang, T. (2015). *Fundamentals of predictive text mining* (2nd ed.). Springer.

Witten, I. H., Frank, E., & Hall, M. A. (2011). *Data mining: Practical machine learning tools and techniques* (3rd ed.). Morgan Kaufmann.

5 Social Construction of Knowledge (SCK) Platforms, Scraping, and Methods

Exploring the social construction of knowledge (SCK) online is a journey that begins with a crucial first step: gathering data pertinent to your research question. This task involves tapping into the abundant data available across various learning management systems (LMS), like Blackboard and Canvas or social media platforms like Reddit, Facebook, and X (formerly Twitter). Let us refer to any online space where SCK can take place as a "social learning space." The main challenge lies in selecting the most suitable social learning space for mining data. This selection is crucial because most social learning spaces specialize in discussing different topic areas. In this chapter, we'll equip you with the essential concepts and criteria necessary to make informed decisions about which social learning space to data mine.

In deciding on a social learning space for studying SCK, there are three main criteria:

Relevance to Your Topic. The first criterion for selecting a social media platform is its relevance to your research question or topic of interest. Not all platforms will have discussions or content related to your research question. Therefore, it's important to choose a platform where your topic is being actively discussed. For instance, if your research is about professional networking behaviors, LinkedIn might be more relevant. If your topic is related to coding or software development, platforms like GitHub or Stack Overflow would be more relevant. For research about educational practices or pedagogy, platforms like Edmodo, Google Classroom, or the subreddit r/education on Reddit could be valuable sources of data. Always consider the main purpose and user demographic of the platform when assessing its relevance to your topic.

Target Audience. The second criterion is the target audience. You need to consider whether the platform has the audience you want to study. Different platforms attract different demographics, so the platform you choose should align with the demographic you're interested in. For example, if you're studying the behavior of young adults, platforms like Instagram or TikTok, which have a younger user base, might be more suitable. On the other hand, if you're interested in professional behaviors, LinkedIn, with its professional user base, would be a better choice. For studying educational practices, platforms used by educators and students, like Edmodo or Google Classroom, would be relevant. Always consider the demographic profile of the platform's users when making your selection.

Computerized Access. The third criterion is bulk or computerized access to downloading discussions. Learning management systems like Canvas typically do not have provisions for the bulk downloading of posts and replies – you must copy and paste the data manually. Some social media platforms provide application programming interfaces, or APIs. These APIs allow you to programmatically download their data, which can be a significant advantage when dealing with large amounts of data. For instance,

DOI: 10.4324/9781003324461-7

Reddit offers extensive and free API access for downloading posts and user information. X, formerly Twitter, also provides API access, but unlike Reddit, it comes at a cost. Facebook has an API as well, but it comes with more restrictions, especially on personal data. Conversely, platforms like Instagram have more limited API access, making it more challenging to download data in bulk. It's important to note that not all platforms provide such access, and those that do may impose limitations on what you can do with their API, how much data you can download, and what costs might be involved. Given the volume of data that often needs to be downloaded for research, computerized access or some form of automated downloading is likely the most important factor to consider.

Limitations of Using Social Media Platforms for Studying Social Learning

While social media platforms provide a wealth of data for studying social learning, they also come with inherent limitations, particularly when compared to controlled experiments. In a controlled experiment, researchers have precise control over subjects, materials, and procedures, which is not the case with social media research. Here, the environment is dynamic and unpredictable, and the data is influenced by numerous external factors. Understanding these limitations is crucial for accurately interpreting research findings and effectively navigating the potential challenges that may arise during your study.

General Limitations

Lack of Control Over Audience Demographics

On social media networks, it is challenging to target specific audience demographics, which can lead to biased results. Unlike controlled experiments, where participants can be selected to match your research needs, social media platforms require you to focus on communities or spaces that are likely to attract your desired participants. For example, if your research involves studying teachers, you might gather data from a dedicated forum like the Reddit r/teachers subreddit. However, even within these spaces, the users may not represent a random or diverse sample, introducing potential bias into your findings.

Data Availability

Access to data on social media platforms is often limited. Platforms may restrict the types of data you can retrieve, such as allowing access to public posts while excluding private messages. There may also be limits on the volume of data you can download, or the speed at which you can access it. Geographic and account-based restrictions might further limit data access to certain regions or specific users. Additionally, user actions, such as post deletions, can create gaps in your dataset. If you plan to analyze discussions surrounding a particular event in time, keep in mind these data availability limitations, as they can impact the completeness and accuracy of your analysis.

Data Quality

Social media data may not always be reliable or accurate. Users can provide misleading or false information, whether intentionally or unintentionally. Some users may be role-playing, posting content based on fictional personas rather than personal experience. Others may engage in trolling, posting provocative content to elicit reactions rather than genuine responses. Furthermore, trends, bots, or spam can distort the content, making it less reflective of authentic beliefs. The absence of context or nonverbal cues in online posts can also lead to misinterpretations of intent or meaning.

Research Restrictions

Many social media platforms have specific guidelines governing the use of downloaded data. These guidelines typically require researchers to avoid publishing user-identifiable information, refrain from singling out individuals in publications, ensure that platform data is not combined with external datasets without appropriate permissions, and present data analyses in aggregate form. While these restrictions are usually outlined on the Developer Policy page – primarily for developers – they are equally applicable to researchers using the data.

Finding a Discussion Topic on Social Media

All social media platforms have some kind of search functionality, which can return both a list of discussions and a list of groups dedicated to the search topic. On Reddit, for example, suppose you searched for "using AI in education" because you're interested in researching how teachers are applying this new technology. Figure 5.1 shows the search results in the middle, and a list of groups related to the topic of AI in education on the right-side panel. At this point, you can search one of the groups, like r/Using_AI_in_Education, for a possible discussion thread, or you can browse the search results and select a discussion thread for analysis.

For the sake of instruction, let us say we want to analyze the first item in the search results, "Using AI in schools." This post has been upvoted (liked) over 7,500 times and has 313

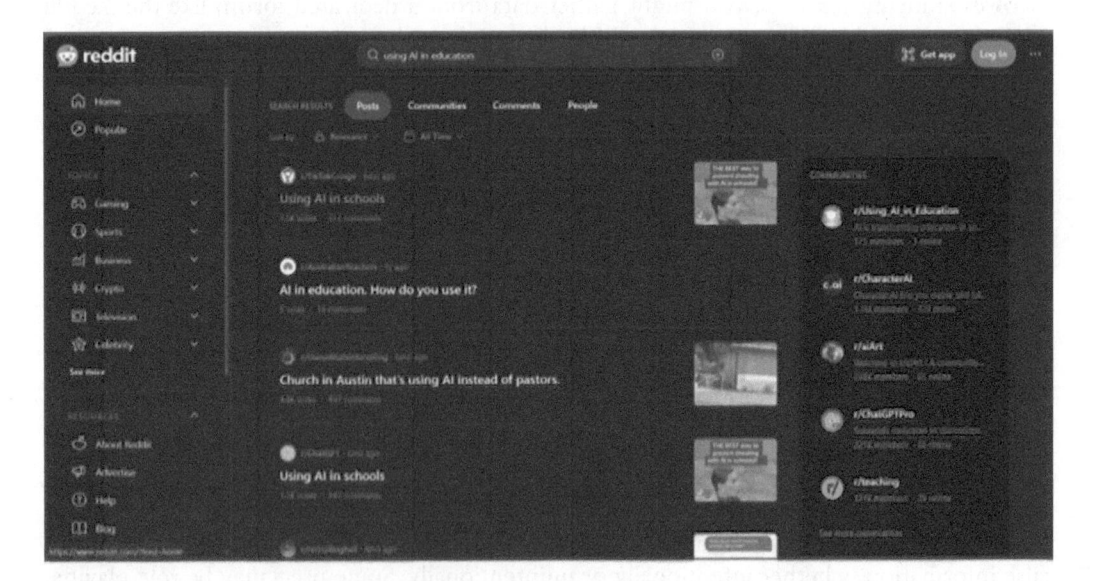

Figure 5.1 Reddit search page

comments. Downloading each post and reply manually, then reading through and analyzing the posts, would take a lot of time. Data-mining techniques, analytics, and AI can greatly assist in the downloading and analysis process.

The following section describes how to develop an app that downloads the entire discussion into a file for subsequent analysis, a process known as *scraping*. The code for the entire app is available as a notebook at:

https://github.com/knowledge-construction/slam-ai/blob/master/Chapter-5/python-reddit-discussion-scraper.ipynb

Scraping Social Media: A Case Study of Reddit

For the study of SCK, Reddit serves as an excellent platform. It hosts a multitude of groups, known as "subreddits," covering a wide array of topics, and fostering an environment where users can learn from each other. Furthermore, when it comes to scraping subreddits, Reddit provides an application programming interface (API). This API simplifies the process of automating data scraping.

In the following, we use Python and several packages to demonstrate how to develop your own custom scraper.

One-Time Setup

First, follow the steps on the Wiki to get authentication and authorization to run a scraper on Reddit. You must complete these steps first, or the subsequent code will not work. The steps are at:

https://github.com/knowledge-construction/slam-ai/wiki/Chapter-5-Reddit-Apps-One-Time-Setup

Import Packages

To scrape Python, you need the following packages:

- *os*: for reading and writing files
- *praw*: a library of functions for accessing the Reddit API
- *pandas*: for creating and manipulating data frame, which will hold the scraped data
- *dotenv*: holds the user's login information for accessing the python API programmatically
- *datetime*: utilities for manipulating data with time stamps

```
import os              # contains code for doing file operations
import praw            # main package for scraping python
import pandas as pd    # used to create data frame to hold data scraped

from   dotenv   import load_dotenv # contains code to manage connections
from   datetime import datetime    # routines for handling dates and times
```

Set Global Parameters

After importing packages, create variables that specify the URL representing the discussion thread that you want to scrape (*url_of_interest*), as well as where to store the scraped data including the folder (*folder*), and the file name (*filename*).

```
# Step 0. Set the global parameters
###################################################################
url_of_interest = "www.reddit.com/r/TikTokCringe/comments/16ir9c7/using_ai_in_schools/"

filename        = 'using-ai-in-schools.csv' # GLOBAL PARAMETER
folder          = "./" # GLOBAL PARAMETER
```

Log in to Reddit

After specifying what to scrape and where to place the data, you need your app to log into Reddit, just as you would have to log into Reddit using your username and password. For the app, its username and password are the *client_id* and *client_secret*, respectively, stored in the .env file. The variable *user_agent* describes your app to Reddit:

```
# Step 1. Login to Reddit (Authentication)
###################################################################

# load all the variables from .env file into environment variables
load_dotenv()

client_id     = os.getenv("reddit_client_id")
client_secret = os.getenv("reddit_client_secret")
user_agent    = os.getenv("reddit_user_agent")

reddit = praw.Reddit(
    client_id     = client_id,
    client_secret = client_secret,
    user_agent    = user_agent,
)
```

Scrape the Discussion

With your app logged into Reddit, it can now download the entire thread. This is accomplished by submitting the url representing your thread to Reddit to get the original post, then getting all the comments underneath the post:

```
# Step 2: Scrape the URL of interest
####################################################################

post = reddit.submission(url=url_of_interest)
post.comments.replace_more(limit=None)   # Grab original post
comments = post.comments.list()          # Grab comments
```

Store the Discussion in a Data Frame

The previous step pulled the topic post and all comments into memory. In order to save these results to a file, you need to first format the results in a data frame. This is analogous to arranging your data in a spreadsheet.

```
# Step 3: Create data frame of results
####################################################################

thread = []

# Add original post (OP) to the data frame-customize to add columns of interest
thread.append({
    'reply'     : 0,
    'id'        : post.id,
    'parent_id' : "null",
    'date'      : datetime.utcfromtimestamp(post.created_utc).strftime("%Y-%m-%d
%H:%M:%S UTC"),
    'author'    : post.author,
    'title'     : post.title,
    'score'     : post.score,
    'replies'   : len(comments),
    'text'      : post.selftext,
})

# Add all comments to the data frame
for i, comment in enumerate(comments):
    thread.append({
        'reply'     : i+1,
        'id'        : comment.id,
        'parent_id' : comment.parent_id,
        'date'      : datetime.utcfromtimestamp(comment.created_utc).strftime("%Y-
%m-%d %H:%M:%S UTC"),
        'author'    : comment.author,
        'title'     : post.title,
        'score'     : comment.score,
        'replies'   : len(comment.replies),
        'text'      : comment.body,
    })
```

Save the Data into a File

With the topic and replies stored in a data frame, the last step is to write out the data frame as a comma-separated-value (CSV) file. In a CSV file, the first row is the header, and every other row is data, with data items separated by commas.

```
# Step 4: Write out data frame
##################################################################

df        = pd.DataFrame(thread)
fullpath = f'{folder}/{filename}'
df.to_csv(fullpath, index = False)
```

Having returned a file, you can start analyzing your data using the Social Learning Analytic Methods (SLAM) techniques in this book. We will use this data as a case study for applying the SLAM and AI techniques in this book.

Assuming you have downloaded discussion data for analysis, you can start writing up the methods section of your research. It will not be complete at this point, as you need to do some computation to determine important information like how many users participated or how long the discussion lasted, to name a few, but you can get most of it written down.

Writing Up Your Methods Section

When using an online platform for your research, the traditional APA-focused approach to writing your methods section may need some adjustments. Here is a suggested structure:

- **Data.** In traditional studies, this section would be titled "Participants." However, in the context of researching SCK online, it's more appropriate to discuss the data you're analyzing. Describe the source of your data (e.g., which social media platform), the timeframe during which the data was collected, and any criteria used to select the data. For example, you might only analyze tweets containing a certain hashtag or posts made within a specific group. Any data anonymization, privacy, or ethical considerations should also be listed in this section.
- **Materials.** This section should detail the tools you used to collect your data. If you used a social media scraper, specify which one and provide information about where it can be accessed (if publicly available). If you developed your own tool, describe it and consider providing the code in an appendix or a public code repository.
- **Procedure.** Describe the steps you took to collect and analyze your data. This should include any preprocessing steps (e.g., cleaning the data, handling missing data), how you handled ethical considerations (e.g., anonymizing data), development environment, programming languages, packages or libraries used, and the specific analyses you conducted. Be as detailed as possible to allow other researchers to replicate your study.

This is only an outline of some of the items to include. Remember, the goal of the Methods section is to provide enough detail that other researchers can replicate your study. This not only helps to validate your findings but also contributes to the cumulative nature of scientific research.

Case Study: Reddit and the Topic of AI in Education

Suppose you want to study SCK, using the Interaction Analysis Model (IAM) as the theoretical framework. Further suppose you have the specific research question: How can AI be effectively used to help students learn and not merely to plagiarize?

Method

The following method was used to scrape the data used in this analysis.

Data

A post on the subreddit r/education with 70 replies and the subject: "Should education embrace AI?" There were a total of 39 unique participants, including the author.

Materials

An app was created at www.reddit.com/prefs/apps, and the credentials returned were used to populate the custom Reddit scraper (https://github.com/knowledge-construction/slam-ai/blob/master/Chapter-5/python-reddit-discussion-scraper.ipynb). The thread started on 2023-05-08 14:58:22 UTC, and the last reply scraped was 2023-09-29 19:49:11 UTC.

Conclusion

In this chapter, we explored the process of selecting an appropriate social learning platform for studying SCK. We emphasized the significance of choosing platforms based on relevance to your topic, target audience, and computerized access for efficient data collection. Social media platforms such as Reddit and Facebook, along with learning management systems, offer rich data sources but have limitations that must be navigated thoughtfully. We outlined a methodology for scraping and analyzing discussion data, using a case study on AI in education from Reddit to illustrate these concepts. The Appendix contains the code for developing an automated Reddit scraper.

To help analyze your datasets, subsequent chapters will guide you through the analysis of your data by applying SLAM and AI techniques.

6   Analytics Tools

Suppose you have a research question on the general topic of social learning, such as "How can educators effectively use AI to improve learning?" Further suppose that you have completed Chapter 5 on SCK platforms and have downloaded a dataset from social media that you believe has answers to your research question. The next step is to choose a development environment to help you do the analysis.

While there are existing statistical programs, like Statistical Analysis System (SAS) and Statistical Package for the Social Sciences (SPSS) that you could use, if you want to stay at the forefront of analytics, which often involves using a mix of constantly evolving algorithms, you should use a programming language along with its associated development environment. Your main choices for programming languages are R and Python, and there are several possible development environments.

This chapter aims to familiarize the researcher with the concepts necessary to set up a programming language and a development environment for exploring and for making predictions from large volumes of data. This is usually a one-time choice and setup that you do prior to either data collection or analysis.

Is Programming Needed?

One question we often hear is, "Can I get by without programming? I'm not very good at it." To be completely honest, the answer for researchers is generally, "No, not if you want to apply the latest analysis and visualization techniques to your data." As social learning researchers, we work with large volumes of culturally rich discussions, and the techniques for analyzing and visualizing this data are constantly evolving. Knowing how to program enables you to use these techniques as soon as they become available, rather than waiting for a company to incorporate them into an app with a user-friendly interface.

The good news is that the programming you need to know is at a level where you are primarily formatting your data and calling pre-existing functions to process or visualize it.

For example, suppose you have collected 1 million posts on a discussion, and you want to identify the 5 main topics and the 10 keywords associated with each topic. In the programming language R, using a technique known as Latent Dirichlet Allocation (LDA), the code would be:

```
# Assuming you have a data frame 'df' with a column 'text'
dtm <- DocumentTermMatrix(Corpus(VectorSource(df$text))) # Format data
lda_model <- LDA(dtm, k = 5)                              # 5 topics
terms(lda_model, 10)                                      # 10 words
                                                          # per topic
```

DOI: 10.4324/9781003324461-8

There is a similarly short snippet of code in Python to find the top 5 main topics and the 10 keywords used in discussing each topic. Both R and Python offer pre-existing functions within libraries or packages that you can use to perform the latest analyses on your data.

So, the answer to the question, "Is programming needed?" is yes. The next question is: Which programming language should you use – R or Python?

Programming Languages: R or Python?

Looking briefly at their history and design goals, R was designed by statisticians for statisticians, making it an excellent tool for statistical analysis and visualization. In contrast, Python was created as a general-purpose programming language that allows programmers to write code efficiently with using lines. A general truth in programming is that what can be accomplished in one language can usually be accomplished in another. The choice between programming languages often comes down to factors such as ease of learning, ease of implementing your designs, and the capabilities of the surrounding ecosystem of support tools and libraries. Key considerations when choosing between R and Python include:

Ease of Learning. There is no clear consensus in the research literature on whether R or Python is easier for beginners to learn, as both languages are commonly used to teach programming. If you are already familiar with a programming language like C or its variants (C#, C++, Java), you may find R's syntax quite similar. On the other hand, if you are comfortable with basic programming concepts like expressions, conditionals, loops, and functions, and prefer a concise programming language, you might find Python more appealing.

Libraries and Packages. A library or package is a collection of pre-existing code that programmers bundle for others to use, saving you the effort of writing algorithms from scratch to analyze and visualize your data. You simply call a function, much like using a macro or built-in function in Excel. R offers a comprehensive set of packages for statistical analysis and data visualization. Python has a vast ecosystem of libraries for data analysis and visualization, with additional strengths in machine learning and artificial intelligence, supported by packages like Scikit-learn, TensorFlow, and PyTorch.

Communities and Support. Both R and Python have active user communities that continuously contribute and maintain these libraries, ensuring they stay up-to-date with the latest analysis and visualization techniques. R has a particularly strong presence in academia and research, while Python's broader user base extends beyond analytics into areas like software engineering and artificial intelligence. When choosing a library or package, it is essential to consider the strength and activity of the community that supports it, as an active community often means higher-quality and more reliable code.

Data Visualization. After analyzing your data, you often visualize it. R is well-known for its packages like ggplot2, which allow you to quickly create high-quality statistical graphics. Python also offers powerful visualization libraries such as Plotly and Matplotlib, but R's ggplot2 is often considered superior for creating complex visualizations.

Performance. When analyzing large datasets, where discussions can involve thousands or even millions of postings, performance becomes a key consideration. The speed at which your data can be processed depends not only on the programming language but also on the efficiency of the libraries you use. Many R and Python packages for processing large datasets are actually written in lower-level languages like C for improved speed. Generally, Python's data analysis libraries, such as Pandas and NumPy, are known for their speed and efficiency, especially when handling large datasets. In contrast, R can be less efficient for large-scale data processing, especially using the default DataFrame object, but there are packages that significantly improve performance and are well-suited for handling big data.

Research Popularity. R is particularly popular in academia and research for data analysis and statistical work, while Python is widely used for data science, machine learning, and computational research. Both languages are strongly supported in academic circles, but the choice often depends on the specific field and type of analysis being conducted. Choose the language that best enables you to conduct your research effectively and to share your findings with colleagues and with the broader research community.

To summarize, choosing between R and Python often depends on the specific needs of your project, your familiarity with programming languages, and the type of data being analyzed. We recommend using both languages, depending on which one offers the necessary libraries or packages for your analysis. However, if your analysis involves extensive artificial intelligence processing, Python and its associated ecosystem of libraries may be the more suitable choice.

Choosing an Integrated Development Environment

Similar to writing papers in the English language using a word processor app, a development environment for a programming language is a set of tools that include an editor for writing your code, a debugger for testing your code, and tools for helping the programmers improve the code. These environments are designed to streamline the coding process, making it easier to write, test, and optimize your code. When a development environment includes an editor, debugger, and utilities for improving code, all-in-one, it is known as an *integrated development environment* (*IDE* for short). For both R and Python, there are multiple IDEs available for your use, and some IDEs work with both languages. In the following sections, we will explore two popular development environments for R and Python, respectively, and discuss how to choose the one that best fits your needs.

For R: RStudio

RStudio is widely recognized as the most popular IDE for the R programming language. It was developed specifically around R, with the goal of making analysis and visualization straightforward for researchers. The IDE provides a user-friendly interface and a collection of tools that help researchers more easily model, analyze, and visualize their data. In addition to a friendly user interface, social construction of knowledge (SCK) researchers will find these other features helpful:

Integrated Analysis and Visualization Tools. Some of the key tools RStudio offers include *code completion*, suggesting functions and their parameters, which is invaluable for analytics involving functions from various packages. It also provides *syntax highlighting* to identify typos and coding mistakes. RStudio provides extensive *debugging* capabilities, allowing you to set breakpoints on lines, which allow you to stop the code at and examine variables. For *visualizing* results, RStudio has integrated panels that hold current and previous plots. Finally, RStudio offers easy *package management* for downloading and updating packages.

Computational Notebooks. In the context of an integrated development environment, a computational notebook is a tool that allows you to combine text, code, and output, including graphs, all in a single file. It is the digital analogy of the researcher's hand-written notebook, which combined hand-drawn text, calculations, and graphs. Notebooks allow easy exploratory data analysis, as you can write code, execute it, and see the results immediately within the same document. By allowing you to intersperse text comments before and after code and results, notebooks become an important tool for learning and discovery, both for the researcher and research collaborators.

For Python: Jupyter Notebook

There are many IDEs for Python, including PyCharm, VS Code, Spyder, Atom, and IDLE, to name just a few. These IDEs generally provide similar useful features to those listed for RStudio. For SCK researchers, we recommend using Jupyter Notebook as an IDE for several reasons. First, and most importantly, Jupyter Notebook is a computational notebook which, as mentioned, allows you to combine code and code output (which includes graphs). This capability affords the writing of code and the visualization of results in small chunks, which facilitates the *testing and exploring of different research questions and hypotheses*. In addition to assisting exploratory analysis, the ability to combine code and results in a single document *facilitates reproducible research*, ensuring that others can follow and replicate your analyses. Jupyter Notebooks can be shared, *fostering collaborative research efforts*. Finally, the ability to intersperse text comments with code and output makes it easy to document your thought process, methodologies, and findings, enhancing the clarity and understandability of your research.

Cross-Language IDEs: Visual Studio Code

For SCK researchers working with both R and Python, an IDE like Visual Studio Code (VS Code) is worth considering. VS Code is a free, open-source IDE that supports a multitude of languages including R and Python. At its core it is a lightweight editor, allowing you to quickly open and edit files without consuming a lot of your computing resources. However, it is highly customizable through its free marketplace, enabling you to add capabilities for supporting multiple languages, multiple file formats, debugging, and different kinds of visualizations, among many other extensions.

Ultimately, the decision on which IDE to use should be based on your experience level with coding, the type of analyses your current and future research questions require, and any specific capabilities you need to support your workflow. In this book, we will use RStudio as the IDE for R, and Visual Studio Code as the IDE for Python. In our experience both IDEs provide an easy-to-use interface and the flexibility to expand capabilities to support answering complex research questions.

Setting Up an R IDE on Your Personal Computer

For detailed and the latest instructions on setting up R on your personal computer, visit the book Wiki at:

https://github.com/knowledge-construction/slam-ai/wiki/Chapter-6-Setting-up-R

As a last note, there are services like Google's Colaboratory (*https://research.google.com/colaboratory*) that provide a cloud-based IDE, allowing you to program in R in a web browser without installing any software. These services also provide GPUs to accelerate computationally intensive tasks. While most of these cloud-based IDEs offer basic functionality for free, they charge for tiered packages containing advanced features along with increased storage and performance.

Setting Up a Python IDE on Your Personal Computer

For detailed and the latest instructions on setting up a Python IDE on your personal computer, visit the book Wiki at:

https://github.com/knowledge-construction/slam-ai/wiki/Chapter-6-Setting-up-Python-and-Miniconda

Similar to R, there are online services that allow you to program in Python without having to install any software on your computer such as Google Colaboratory, which supports programming in both R and Python. If you do not want to install software on your personal computer, this is an option, but make sure the free tier level is sufficient for your data, analysis, and visualization needs.

Learning Resources for Programming

While it is outside of the scope of this book to teach programming, there are numerous online resources available, including tutorials and entire courses, to help you learn R and Python for data analysis.

One of the best free online resources for learning R, with an emphasis on data science, *R for Data Science* (Wickham et al., 2023; https://r4ds.hadley.nz/). This book not only teaches the R programming language but also teaches the RStudio IDE and covers a set of packages known as TidyVerse for data manipulation (data wrangling), analysis, and visualization.

Similarly there are free books for learning Python with an emphasis on data science including, *Python Data Science Handbook* (VanderPlas, 2016; https://jakevdp.github.io/PythonDataScienceHandbook/). This book also teaches Python in the context of data science, and is focused on the packages: Pandas, for data wrangling; Numpy and Scikit-Learn, for data representation and analysis; and Matplotlib for visualization. Another good book is *Python for Data Analysis* (McKinney, 2022), which uses Jupyter Notebook as an IDE and focuses on data wrangling (https://wesmckinney.com/book).

The book Wiki also provides an updated list of programming resources for both R and Python:

https://github.com/knowledge-construction/slam-ai/wiki/Chapter-6-Resources-for-Learning-to-Program-in-R-Python

Conclusion

In Chapter 6, we examined the key tools and environments necessary for conducting data analysis in social learning research. Given the constantly changing landscape of analytics, it is crucial to choose the right programming language and development environment to leverage the latest techniques. While existing statistical software like SAS and SPSS are options, this chapter emphasizes the importance of programming languages such as R and Python for their flexibility and advanced capabilities. We discussed the advantages of each language and how integrated development environments (IDEs) like RStudio for R and Jupyter Notebook for Python can enhance the coding process by offering features tailored to data analysis. The chapter provides links to the book Wiki that guides you through setting up these environments, ensuring you are equipped to handle large datasets and apply state-of-the-art methods for analysis and visualization.

References

McKinney, W. (2022). *Python for data analysis.* Sebastopol, CA: O'Reilly Media. https://wesmckinney.com/book/

VanderPlas, J. (2016). *Python data science handbook: Essential tools for working with data.* Sebastopol, CA: O'Reilly Media. https://jakevdp.github.io/PythonDataScienceHandbook/

Wickham, H., Çetinkaya-Rundel, M., & Grolemund, G. (2023). *R for data science.* Sebastopol, CA: O'Reilly Media. https://r4ds.hadley.nz/

Part III

Social Environment Analysis Procedures

There are many Social Learning Analytic Methods (SLAM) that researchers can leverage to support decision-making from big data as they analyze the social environment. This section describes how to use a wide range of SLAM. The process generally starts with establishing suitable parameters for automated inquiry, as described in Chapter 7. Specific SLAM that can decrease the manual effort to work with big data are the focus of the rest of the chapters in this section and include clustering, social network analysis, natural language processing, and other analytic methods. Chapter 7 outlines how to build lexica using dictionary, manual, and grounded approaches, demonstrating the process with the social presence lexica we developed and emphasizing the adaptability of these methods to anchor analytics in theory. In Chapter 8, completed lexica are used to perform analytics, beginning with basic descriptive statistics. This chapter will explain sentiment analysis and demonstrate how traditional categories can be adapted to represent various research constructs, using our experience with a social presence lexicon as an example. Chapter 9 delves into clustering techniques for analyzing large datasets to determine SCK. The chapter provides a practical guide to applying K-means and hierarchical clustering, including loading libraries, data cleaning, creating a document-term matrix, performing clustering, and visualizing results. Readers will understand how to use clustering to identify discussion topics and participant roles in SCK research. Chapter 10 will discuss how social network analysis (SNA) can be applied to analyze the social environment of online learning. Using SNA with IAM Phases creates a powerful approach that adds critical relational context to online interactions. While other SLAM methods answer the "what" question of knowledge construction, SNA answers the "how" with detailed sociograms. We will examine tools like NodeXL and R, comparing their analysis procedures and evaluating their strengths and weaknesses.

Chapter 11 moves on to exploring various natural language processing (NLP) techniques to analyze and understand the SCK in online discussions. We discuss how to identify discussion topics and communication structures. We demonstrate tokenization and word frequency analysis, parts-of-speech tagging, dependency parsing and graphs, named entity recognition, topic modeling, and topic modeling with Latent Dirichlet Allocation. The chapter provides practical examples and discusses the benefits and drawbacks of each method while outlining an integrated NLP pipeline for analyzing large datasets, emphasizing the importance of preprocessing, feature extraction, semantic analysis, and visualization. Chapter 12 focuses on building predictive models to validate theories about the online social environment, for example, the potential virality of a tweet. The chapter covers various methods for creating and testing models, with a focus on linear and multiple regressions. Chapter 13 concludes Part III by exploring AI, particularly large language models, for studying SCK on social media platforms. The chapter discusses practical applications of AI in SCK research, including summarization, translation, named entity recognition, and question-answering, using Python code examples to illustrate these techniques.

DOI: 10.4324/9781003324461-9

Part III

Social Environment Analysis Procedures

7 Lexical Foundations
Rooting Analysis in Theory

This chapter describes the first step in working with Social Learning Analytic Methods (SLAM). The process of building lexica following various approaches will be described. We will advocate for a mix of these approaches to create the most robust lexicon possible. Our own experience creating lexica for social presence will serve as a tangible example of how to build lexica starting with a theory of interest. The chapter will include a brief review of lexica that can also be used to examine the social environment as well as examples of research questions and designs with lexica. It will conclude with a focus on the flexibility of lexica building making it clear how to turn established theories into lexica that can be used to conduct analytics.

The foundation of SLAM is the lexicon. SLAM is defined as a collection of techniques to study group interactions on learning management systems and social networks as groups co-construct knowledge online. These techniques include frequency analysis, sentiment analysis, cluster analysis, social network analysis, and artificial intelligence, which are used in a complementary fashion to analyze the social construction of knowledge (SCK). There are various technical definitions that describe what a lexicon is but the simplest and most straightforward way to think about a lexicon is as a list of words and phrases. It's just not any list. Instead, it is a list that is focused on a particular idea, theme, or research construct. Ultimately the lexicon provides a framework that is used along with other SLAM methods to automate analysis of large bodies of text. For example, the words and phrases within the lexicon are the parameters used by sentiment analysis to search for positive, negative, or neutral sentiments. A lexicon can be focused on very simple or very complex phenomena. The key is to provide sufficient information so that SLAM methods can effectively use those parameters to parse through otherwise unwieldly datasets and make sense of them to ascertain social knowledge construction and key elements regarding the social environment and context.

Types of Lexica

Research has identified four primary types of lexica as follows:

1. Sentiment
2. Subjectivity
3. Connotation
4. Construct

Next, we will provide brief descriptions of each type of lexicon focusing mostly on sentiment and subjectivity lexica. We also provide some examples of studies dealing with these lexica

DOI: 10.4324/9781003324461-10

in the coming sections. Note that links to various lexica that have been previously used in research are available at the end of this chapter.

Sentiment

This lexicon typically contains a positive and a negative category (Pang & Lee, 2008). The positive category contains words and phrases that indicate a positive sentiment (excellent, wonderful, happy, etc.) while the negative category contains words that indicate a negative sentiment (poor, awful, sad, etc.). Each word within the positive and negative category are equally important. Sentiment lexica are the most basic type of lexicon.

In the study conducted by Pang et al. (2002), two graduate students were asked to independently come up with words that indicated positive or negative sentiment in movie reviews. These lexica were then used to count the instances of the positive and negative words they contained in movie reviews. This provided a useful baseline which they used to compare the performance of lexica that were created using automatic classifiers. The automatic classifiers were able to outperform the lexica established by the graduate students.

Subjectivity

This type of lexicon can contain a variety of different categories because it focuses on both positive and negative words and phrases as well as the degree to which the word or phrase is positive or negative. The subjectivity lexicon differs from the sentiment lexicon because it includes the degree to which words and phrases are positive or negative. The degree of positive or negative sentiment is represented with a score that is given to each word or phrase.

The study conducted by Taboada et al. (2011) describes how they created a Semantic Orientation Calculator (SO-CAL) by extracting adjectives, nouns, verbs, and adverbs from sources like Epinions and using them to calculate semantic orientation scores. Note that each part of speech was its own lexicon such that all adjectives were in one lexicon, all nouns were in another, and so on. The researchers manually assigned scores for the adjectives, nouns, verbs, and adverbs lexica between –5 for extremely negative to +5 for extremely positive. Their work also accounted for negation and intensification. Ultimately the final subjectivity lexicon was validated by human annotators and dictionaries and was found to be robust.

Connotation

Connotation lexica go beyond surface level sentiment by understanding the connotation of statements. The connotations of words and phrases is determined by exploring the overall perception of a word or phrase. Connotation lexica are inclusive of traditional sentiment lexica because connotation would carry the same polarity of the sentiment and also because of the difficulty of drawing a distinction between the connotation and sentiment.

The work of Feng et al. (2013) developed a lexicon that determines the connotation of words using graph-based algorithms that determine collocations. These graphing techniques illustrate relationships between adjectives, nouns, verbs, and adverbs that yield association scores. Their work ultimately established positive, negative, and neutral lexica.

Construct

Construct lexica can have the largest number of categories in them because they map to the elements of various research constructs. One example is the social presence lexicon that was created in Gunawardena et al. (2016). In fact, the majority of the work that the authors of this book have done falls under the category of construct lexica. This includes operationalizing the IAM using SLAM. We describe our work creating a construct lexicon later in this chapter.

Building Lexica

An in-depth treatment regarding methods that are used to build lexica can be found in Liu (2012). However, we will describe them briefly here to inform the upcoming discussion of how various lexica have been developed and used to implement SLAM in a variety of contexts. What follows are descriptions of these methods of lexica building:

- Manual
- Dictionary
- Corpus
- Combined

Manual Approach

The manual approach of creating a lexicon will be very comfortable for researchers who are familiar with qualitative research methods. The simplest, and most time-consuming of qualitative methods, is the content analysis. Performing a content analysis involves reading transcripts and reviewing documents. It is a straightforward review of source documentation paired with a classification task that allows the person reviewing the source documents to produce a summary. The manual approach to lexicon development is a content analysis. However, those who have not performed qualitative research or are not familiar with these methods can easily use a manual approach to lexicon creation. All that is required is time and an ample amount of source documentation. Developing codes for the document analysis is a necessary first step before reviewing large volumes of information. Qualitative research software such as Atlas.TI can also be of use because they provide a straightforward method for researchers to keep track of their work.

Dealing With Coding Bias

The primary benefit of using a manual approach is that researchers have a great deal of control over the parameters that are included in the lexicon. The researcher will be able to accurately classify all words and phrases according to the construct of choice. Taboada et al. (2011) asserts that the manual method of lexicon creation is superior to others. The manual approach depends on the expert opinion of the researcher to interpret the context of the words and phrases and assign them to lexica categories as appropriate. However, this is a double-edged sword because even expert opinions introduce subjectivity and thus the potential for coding bias to be built into the lexicon. Researchers performing manual lexicon creation should be wary of this reality and can easily remedy it by having other researchers cocreate the lexicon.

Researchers can also have colleagues create the lexicon using similar source documentation independently of one another and later compare the results. A final strategy to address bias that the manual approach to lexicon creation can introduce is to use clustering to develop the themes in the data as described in Chapter 4.

The other primary drawback to employing a manual approach to lexicon creation is the fact that it is quite time intensive. Researchers who wish to use a manual approach must take care to estimate the true level of effort they will have to dedicate to produce a robust lexicon.

Dictionary Approach

The dictionary approach offloads some of the time-consuming analysis required by the manual approach to lexicon creation by using dictionaries as a primary asset. When using the dictionary approach to lexicon creation, traditional dictionaries like Merriam-Webster can be useful. However, incorporating tools that are specifically oriented for the task of lexicon creation such as WordNet (Fellbaum, 1999) can be more useful. For that matter, dictionaries can also be developed using very finite sets of data. For example, this specific approach was popularized by a paper written by Hu and Liu (2004), who used it to create a sentiment lexicon based on movie reviews. At the time, there were many reviews online that were freely available for analysis. This body of information provided the foundation that the researchers used to create their lexicon.

The dictionary approach depends on the identification of seed words. Taboada et al. (2011) define seed words as "a small set of words with strong negative or positive associations, such as excellent or abysmal" (p. 271). Obviously, this definition comes from the context of a sentiment analysis. Seed words can be associated with any type of simple or complex research construct. The reason they are called seed words is because they provide the most basic state and general description of the phenomenon being investigated. Taking the example of the IAM, a seed word for the first Phase could be "definition." The phrase could be "I think." The researcher should compile a list of the seed words as a first step in applying the dictionary approach.

With a list of seed words in hand, the researcher can then consult dictionaries in order to expand their lexicon. The purpose of consulting dictionaries is to make sure the lexicon is able to cast a wide enough net to make the SLAM method applied worthwhile and assure it will yield useful findings. Using online dictionaries, such as the ones listed and at the end of this chapter, can quickly and easily yield large numbers of words and phrases to expand the lexicon. This expansion can be done in roughly half the amount of time as if the researcher was performing a manual lexicon generation.

However, Liu (2012) notes that the resulting expanded lexicon can include a number of different errors which must be manually reviewed to correct. Sánchez experienced the same results when he used a dictionary-based approach for his dissertation research. One of the main disadvantages of using a dictionary approach is that the words and phrases within the lexicon are often very domain and context specific (Liu, 2012). This is a concern when trying to use the lexicon to perform analysis outside of the domain from which it was created but can be ignored when outside applications are not needed.

Corpus-Based Approach

A corpus is a large collection of documents. The documents can be just about anything including but not limited to articles, web pages, social media posts, and entire books. A benefit of using a corpus-based approach to lexicon creation is that it pulls in very large volumes of text as unique entities that are classified based on the contents of the documents. The limitation of this approach is the corpus needs to be very large to cover all possible language combinations. However, computing power continues to grow as evidenced by ChatGPT, which used millions of documents to train it. Thus, processing the documents is not so much of a barrier as hand-picking the documents that are appropriate for a corpus-based lexicon construction. Using a corpus-based approach can also lack specificity to analyze finite data like individual posts because the lexicon will be constructed using vectors that will not necessarily match small-scale analysis. Disambiguation can also be a challenge across various sized documents because specific words within a given domain can have different meanings, which creates an ambiguity that will become a problem when trying to automatically classify new documents.

Combined Approach

Liu (2012) ultimately recommends combining the various techniques to create lexica. Assuring the final lexica are sensitive to context is job number 1 for anyone who wants to use SLAM. The best way to assure human-like classification is to create the lexica first using the manual approach because this allows researchers to create the overall framework for the lexica. During the validation of the initially created lexica, it can be useful to include multiple coders to remove subjectivity (Taboada et al., 2011). Lexica should be context-sensitive while avoiding bias. Once various coders have worked to a consensus, the result can be expanded using a dictionary approach. A corpus-based approach can also be substituted for a dictionary approach depending on the ultimate unit of analysis being considered.

Building Domain-Specific Lexica

Building a lexicon is effectively a classification task. Oftentimes, there are many different themes within a lexicon. The common example of a sentiment analysis has three different categorizations; positive, negative, and neutral (Liu, 2012). More complex phenomena are going to include many more categories. For example, the lexicon that we have developed for the IAM includes each of the five Phases of this research framework. However, it could easily include all of the operations also associated with the Phases. How our research group created the IAM lexicon will be discussed in this section as well as how we have created other lexica for different domains that span a wide range of different applications.

Social Presence

The work of creating an IAM lexicon started with social presence. Our initial aim in Gunawardena et al. (2016) was to examine the association between social presence and knowledge construction since the IAM examines SCK. Our dataset was a transcript containing 42 postings generated by 15 students who were discussing the topic of "culture" from a master's level college course focusing on eLearning. We wanted to apply SLAM to this work as a novel way to conduct the analysis. We created a social presence lexicon using two categories of words that are common in sentiment analysis: positive and negative. By leveraging existing research on social presence and conducting some class-based activities, we were able to populate the categories of our social presence lexicon.

We started our work with the five element Social Presence Model by Whiteside and Dik-kers (2012), which provides examples for the various aspects of each of the five elements. The examples helped us to identify language that would fit the elements of the model. These examples were very useful as we coded our data later on, but we got a head start on our lexicon because one of the elements of the Social Presence Model is affective association. Research identified an article (Barrington, 1963) containing a list of words that describe affective reactions. The words in this article provided us with a treasure trove of potential additions to our social presence lexicon. We worked together as a group and identified the words that were most salient to our analysis according to the Social Presence Model and added them to either the positive or negative category of our lexicon. Note that this technique is an example of a dictionary-based method to lexicon creation.

Next, we conducted an IAM analysis of the transcript by highlighting IAM operations in the transcript and noting the number of their occurrences. Having coded the transcript for SCK, our next task was to apply the Social Presence Model's coding scheme to identify words that contributed to social presence within the context of our study. Our content analysis yielded further words that we added to either the positive or negative lexicon categories. This is an example of a manual method of lexicon creation. With a completed lexicon in hand, we shared our work with a group of students who were very familiar with IAM coding and asked that they validate our work. Gunawardena facilitated this brainstorming validation session, which resulted in some minor modifications to the lexicon. The final version was used to conduct a social presence analysis (which is similar to a sentiment analysis with the exception that it uses words rooted in social presence instead of opinion) with Microsoft Excel and a custom social presence analyzer written in Visual Basic by Flor (2014). The number of matches for each of the 42 postings showed which posts had the greatest influence on social presence.

In completing this review, we recognized the potential for SLAM to enrich the traditional content analysis required to complete an IAM analysis. We proposed a process regarding how SLAM could be incorporated with IAM analysis such that the analytic methods would assist rather than substitute for the analyst. Our vision was that SLAM could provide preliminary findings and general themes prior to the analyst completing the IAM content analysis. These preliminary findings could be verified by the analyst or even used as a quick way to validate the qualitative analysis coding. We applied our proposed process and extended our use of SLAM in Gunawardena et al. (2018). We were encouraged by how easy it was to customize our work to a new theoretical construct. In this case, social presence. We also realized that SLAM had the potential to reduce time-consuming qualitative coding and saw the potential to remove this challenge by creating a lexicon for IAM because it would enable automated processing according to the framework. So, we decided to go beyond social presence and create an IAM lexicon.

IAM

The first IAM lexicon was created as part of Sánchez (2018a). This doctoral dissertation focused on how people engage in social action via conscientization (Freire, 1970) and examined how people build knowledge as they engage via the IAM in the context of an online movement. The dataset contained Twitter posts from several days surrounding the organizing and protests associated with the killing of Freddie Gray in Baltimore, MD. Note that Freddie Gray was an African American man who sustained deadly injuries to his spine while he was in police custody. The lexicon was created using a manual approach that involved reading tweets and viewing associated media, coding the tweet for the IAM, and adding words and phrases to the lexicon. This effort was applied to several days within the dataset to establish seed words that exemplified all five Phases of the IAM. Once the initial coding was completed, the lexicon was expanded using a dictionary approach with WordNet.

The study successfully identified all five Phases of the IAM, but the final lexicon was very context specific. This means that for studies outside of the realm of social action and organizing, it would have a difficult time producing comprehensive results. That being said, the IAM lexicon was the foundation for the work completed by Megli et al. (2023) in the arena of education and online discussions. The lexicon was modified first by pursuing a corpus-based approach. The research group used various library databases to search for previous studies using the IAM by searching for keywords such as "Interaction Analysis Model," "Social Construction of Knowledge" and "Interaction," and "Social Construction of Knowledge" and "Interaction Analysis." In total, 15 articles were identified to extract words and phrases from that signaled various IAM Phases. The next step was to apply a manual approach via a qualitative analysis of three study transcripts from graduate online courses for study-specific language related to the IAM. Two of the transcripts came from the learning sciences and the other came from nursing. Upon completion of the manual coding and analysis, researchers met in pairs and finally as a whole group to reach a consensus regarding how the words and phrases in their coding would be classified. The final lexicon was used to perform SLAM on the study data.

The work that has been completed to date creating, modifying, and applying the IAM lexicon illustrates how lexica can be developed for theories that have been widely applied in the domain of online learning within formal learning environments. Lexica have also been created that can analyze informal learning environments.

Social Action

Lexica can also be created for applications that are outside of the realm of education. Sánchez (2016) created a lexicon for social action based on the typology of roles identified by Penney and Dadas (2014) for how people used Twitter in relationship with an online movement. The first step in creating this lexicon was to gather social media data that was relevant to the study of the online organizing surrounding the death of Tony Robinson.[1] Once the data were gathered, words and phrases that fit the roles identified by Penney and Dadas (2014) were identified within the data gathered from Twitter. The lexicon was used to conduct a sentiment analysis, which produced frequencies with the roles that were used to run correlations. The analysis ultimately revealed that people who share information online are dissimilar from people who participate in online protests and/or face-to-face protests.

Conscientization

The study by Sánchez (2018b) of social media postings about the inauguration of the 45th President of the United States used a similar technique to develop a new type of lexicon to determine the level of conscientization (Freire, 1970) of tweets. This lexicon also included a binary variable indicating whether people supported the former president or not. This study also included a traditional sentiment analysis. Supporters of the former president were found to be highly negative in nature and levels of conscientization were found to be highly associated with being retweeted. To extend the previous work, Sánchez (2018a) used the same lexicon that was added to using the aforementioned process.

It should be clear that lexica can certainly be developed to fit a number of different academic and social phenomenon that occur in both formal and informal educational environments. They can also be created to analyze data from technical domains.

Medical Documentation

The research conducted by Lamers-Johnson et al. (2021) used a lexicon that was created to automate the analysis of medical documentation using the OILS Twitter Scraper (Flor, 2014). This research successfully modified a tool that was initially created to analyze social media data and outfit it for use in a medical setting. This lexicon was created in a partnership between Sánchez and a team of subject matter experts who supplied the correct terms that needed to be found in each of the categories of the nutrition care process (NCP). The focus of this study was on the extent to which dieticians were adhering to the NCP, and indeed, the tool provided away for medical documentation to be checked to quickly determine the match. The completed lexicon and subsequent automatic analysis were validated by a team of nutrition experts who found that the automatic analysis was acceptable for conducting audits of nutrition documentation to assess alignment with recommendations for evidence-based care.

The initial research was such a success that Lamers-Johnson et al. (2022) was conducted using a similar technique to create a new lexicon that evaluated evidence-based nutrition practice guidelines (EBNPG) for Type 1 and Type 2 diabetes. The new lexicon and analyzer, called the Diabetes ECP Analyzer, was again based on the original tool by Flor (2014). It was created via a collaboration between a team of EBNPG experts and Sánchez. The Diabetes Expected Care Plan (ECP) Analyzer ultimately contained a category for evidence, diagnosis, intervention, and monitoring and evaluation. The tool was used on a real-world dataset from 562 patients and effectively identified the extent to which nutrition practice guidelines were implemented.

Improving Performance of Lexica

A lexicon provides the foundation for various types of SLAM analyses by outlining the criteria the methods will use to analyze text so these assets do not have specific performance metrics to improve in and of themselves. However, since they contain the criteria that other SLAM depend on they have a direct influence on the performance of the other methods. If SLAM are not as accurate as desired, most of the time reworking the lexica that they are based on will remedy the issue. Researchers should ultimately apply the following methods in such a way that they will be able to balance the accuracy of their results with the amount of time that is needed to achieve the desired results. The following are recommendations for the enhancement of lexica.

Use Existing Literature

When creating a new lexicon, it is important to avoid recreating the wheel. Existing literature beckons the savvy researcher to look for trends in language that exemplify the phenomenon of interest. Coding schemes are also of great value because they provide clear categorizations and examples of the codes. Language from these examples can be pulled into the new lexicon as unigrams, bigrams, or n-grams.

Include Context-Specific Language

Performing a manual approach to lexicon creation via a brief content analysis of the study data is a good way to make sure that the new lexicon accounts for the specific subjects that are being discussed in a given context. The content analysis can include reading and coding the study data. However, researchers can also consider using SLAM to facilitate this work. This entails producing a list of the most frequent words and phrases within the study data. Order the lists from highest to lowest frequencies and focus on nouns and noun phrases. These "trends" should be topics of interest to the researcher because adding them to the lexicon will increase the accuracy of the automatic analysis. The frequency list guides the researcher to the instances of them within their full context in the study data. When considering the full context, the researcher can determine how to classify the words and phrases within the new lexicon.

Iterate

The process of building a lexicon and trying it with the SLAM of choice is a primary component of building strong automatic classification systems. Researchers should first set a bar for the accuracy of their work by looking at applicable research. If the accuracy leaves something to be desired, additional refinements should be made to the lexica to help increase the performance until it reaches the desired levels. Potential changes include but are not limited to adding or removing n-grams and clarifying n-grams to remove ambiguous terms that cause noise in the data classification. It is also useful to examine the extent to which automatic classifications match the coding of humans. In fact, the ultimate test for automatic classification is how well it mimics human coding. Developing models of this nature is the ultimate goal of automatic classification and this end goal can only be reached by iterating on the lexica and making changes until it produces satisfactory results.

Add Items to the Lexicon

Generally speaking, the accuracy of a lexicon is a function of how many items it has in it. So, if the first version of a lexicon is not classifying lots of data or is classifying data incorrectly, then it is likely time to enhance the lexicon using some combination of the lexicon-building approaches described earlier in this chapter. However, it is also true that the larger the number of n-grams within the lexicon, the greater the likelihood of the automatic classification yielding inaccurate results. Researchers need to exercise caution when working outside of the data produced after the first analysis is complete because new parameters could decrease the accuracy of the initial analysis.

In order to avoid this potential complication, use the data that is either not classified or is classified incorrectly to refine the lexicon. Liu (2012) recommends finding frequent nouns and noun phrases as one way to improve the performance of a lexicon. This can be done by using a program to produce counts of the nouns and noun phrases from the data itself. Those that are most frequent in the data that were not classified or were not classified correctly should be added to the lexicon in the appropriate categories. Using the results of the initial data classification to refine the lexicon assures that refinements will only improve upon the initial results.

Researchers should exercise caution when adding items to a lexicon because adding words and phrases that are the same or very similar in different categories will make it more difficult for the automatic classification to distinguish between the categories. This will introduce inaccuracies when using methods like custom sentiment analysis and those inaccuracies will be magnified further when working with a large language model (LLM). Note that using synonyms in different categories is not the best solution because words and phrases that mean the same thing will threaten the validity of the measurement for the given categories. If particular words and phrases that are similar must be included in more than one category, add additional words and phrases to create a meaningful differentiation between them. The additional detail will focus the automatic classification and assure a solid foundation for other SLAM.

Add Items to the Training Set

Higher level forms of SLAM like naïve Bayes, machine learning, and support vector machines depend on having a coded dataset to educate the AI regarding what to look for as it classifies inputs. The more data the AI has to work with, the better it can analyze new inputs and produce highly accurate classifications. This particular suggestion starts to get into the realm of what is covered in Chapter 11 and 12 so look there for a more detailed discussion of how training datasets are used to educate AI.

Include Detailed Examples in Sentence Form

In Megli et al. (2023), we attempted to use a LLM to classify the five Phases of the IAM. We tried two different approaches to construct our lexica to maximize the performance of our LLM:

1. General high-level descriptions of each Phase
2. Specific examples of the text that relate to how a human coder would classify the text

Some examples of what we devised in each approach are provided in Table 7.1.

Table 7.1 General and Specific Examples of IAM Phases

General Descriptions	Specific Examples
#1, "I define the concept this way. Or I believe the concept is that."	#1, "A 'Phase 1 post' example is: I believe culture is a set of rules."
#2, "I disagree with how you have defined the concept."	#2, "A 'Phase 2 post' example is: Your definition of culture doesn't make sense."
#3, "I want to modify your definition of the concept."	#3, "A 'Phase 3 post' example is: I would accept your definition of culture if you add in experience."
#4, "I want to test your definition of the concept."	#4, "A 'Phase 4 post' example is: Let's see if your definition of culture explains foreigners."
#5, "Let us now apply your definition of the concept."	#5, "A 'Phase 5 post' example is: We should apply your definition of culture to other things."

The general descriptions were based off of the classic IAM table found in Gunawardena et al. (1997). The specific examples were taken from the coded dataset we were working with. As we proceeded through various iterations, we found that we were able to improve the accuracy of our classifications by 35% when we provided the LLM with specific sentences that described each IAM Phase. This is curious because the LLM seemed to learn best when provided with these types of concrete examples.

Note that including such detailed and verbose examples is best when paired with the LLM SLAM, while using the n-gram approach is more suitable for traditional sentiment analysis. The reason that the LLM performs well using the examples is because it already has been trained on numerous examples of the terms contained in the example. It effectively has an internal dictionary for each of the terms in the example. More traditional sentiment analysis approaches do not include pre-existing dictionaries, so researchers need to establish these parameters when conducting these types of analyses.

Using a Custom Lexicon to Perform an Analysis

So far, this chapter has provided researchers with examples of how various phenomena can be made into their own lexica. Now it will provide the R code that is needed to employ the customized lexicon to analyze data.

Prior to working in R, the data will need to be formatted as a CSV file. This will allow R to read and load the file to use to conduct the analysis. Use the Save As function in a program like Microsoft Excel to format the lexicon as a CSV.

The customized lexicon will need to be built in a specific fashion to be used in the code provided in this chapter. The words and phrases to be classified need to be in the first column and it should be labeled "word" while the second column should label each word or phrase for the "category" it belongs to.

word	category
I think	Phase/IA
Opinion	Phase/IA
Define	Phase/IA

All words and phrases should be listed in this two-column format. Simply change the value of the category in the second column to indicate a change in the category for the corresponding word or phrase.

Note: If your lexicon has been previously loaded in a data frame, you can directly use it in R.

Install and Load Required Packages

To perform sentiment analysis in R using a customized lexicon, you can create your own sentiment lexicon and then use it with the *tidytext* and *dplyr* packages using the following code:

```
install.packages("tidytext")
library(tidytext)
install.packages("dplyr")
library(dplyr)
```

Load CSV Data and Group Data

The first step is to load the data into R and group it so it is ready for analysis. Note that the data in the CSV needs to have a column titled "id" that includes some kind of identifiers to work with the code provided here. If a researcher is working with data that does not have an ID, something else will need to take its place and *id* in the *group_by(id) %>%* command will have to change to match the value of the grouping variable.

```
# Stores the CSV data within R in groups according to the columns in the CSV and dis-
plays a summary of what is loaded
grouped_data <- read.csv("your_data.csv") %>%
group_by(id) %>%
mutate(line = row_number()) %>%
ungroup ()
grouped_data
```

Note: Data loaded directly into R should have at least two columns as follows to work with the code provided here:

id	text

Tokenize Text Data

Tokenization involves breaking the text into individual words or tokens. These tokens are eventually matched to the criteria provided in the lexicon that the researcher selects to analyze their data. Tokenize the data using the following code:

```
# Assuming 'grouped_data' is your text data stored in a data frame with a 'text' column.
If there is not a column named 'text', change this value to match where your data is
stored
        tokens <- grouped_data %>%
  unnest_tokens(word, text)
```

Load the Custom Lexicon

A customized lexicon formatted as a CSV can be read by R using *read.csv()*. The code needed to load the customized lexicon is as follows:

```
# Read the customized lexicon
custom_lexicon <- read.csv("custom_lexicon.csv")
```

Join Lexicon With Tokenized Data

Once the custom lexicon has been loaded in R, the parameters of the lexicon must be associated with the data that needs to be analyzed. The code to perform this step is as follows:

```
# Join the custom lexicon with the tokenized data
        phenomenon <- tokens %>%
  inner_join(custom_lexicon, by = "word", relationship = "many-to-many")
```

Conduct Analysis

The title of the second column can be whatever is desired but "category" will need to match this value in the program when running *group_by(category) %>%*, the value must match the name of a category column in the lexicon CSV file.

```
# Summarize scores
analysis_summary <- phenomenon %>%
  group_by(category) %>%
  summarize(count = n())
```

Display Sentiment Scores

In order to display the text-based results of the custom analysis, the variable that is storing the analysis must be called in R. This simply requires entering the name of the variable. In this case the code to display results is as follows:

```
analysis_summary
```

Researchers can also opt for a visual representation of the results by using the *ggplot2* package. After installing and loading the package, use the following code to display the results of the analysis:

```
# Visualize sentiment scores (optional)
install.packages("ggplot2")
library(ggplot2)
ggplot(analysis_summary, aes(x = category, y = count)) +
    geom_bar(stat = "identity", fill = "skyblue") +
    labs(title = "Custom Analysis", x = "Categories", y = "Count")
```

A Complete Program

Previous sections have described an entire program that can be used to conduct a sentiment analysis in a piecemeal fashion. In order to bring all of these concepts together, here we present a complete picture of what the entire program could look like from loading data to producing an exported file for a custom analysis.

```
# Load necessary packages
install.packages("tidytext")
library(tidytext)
install.packages("dplyr")
library(dplyr)

# Stores the CSV data within R in groups according to the columns in the CSV and
displays a summary of what is loaded
grouped_data <- read.csv("your_data.csv") %>%
group_by(id) %>%
mutate(line = row_number()) %>%
ungroup ()
grouped_data

# Assuming 'grouped_data' is your text data stored in a data frame with a 'text'
column. If there is not a column named 'text', change this value to match where your
data is stored
    tokens <- grouped_data %>%
  unnest_tokens(word, text)

# Read the customized lexicon
custom_lexicon <- read.csv("custom_lexicon.csv")

# Join the custom lexicon with the tokenized data
      phenomenon <- tokens %>%
      inner_join(custom_lexicon, by = "word", relationship =
      "many-to-many")

# Summarize scores
analysis_summary <- phenomenon %>%
  group_by(category) %>%
  summarize(count = n())

analysis_summary

# Visualize sentiment scores (optional)
install.packages("ggplot2")
library(ggplot2)
ggplot(analysis_summary, aes(x = category, y = count)) +
   geom_bar(stat = "identity", fill = "skyblue") +
   labs(title = "Custom Analysis", x = "Categories", y = "Count")
```

In this example, replace "custom_lexicon.csv" with the file path of your customized lexicon. Adjust the code according to the structure of your lexicon and the specifics of your sentiment analysis task.

Research Questions

1. How can multiple methods of building lexica be used to improve the quality of automatic classification?
2. How does the performance of a given lexicon apply to different datasets?
3. What words and phrases improve the performance of analysis conducted using a lexicon?
4. To what extent did the automatic classification based on the lexicon match the coding of a human researcher?
5. What combination of different lexica should be used to describe phenomena?

Sample Lexica Resources

It is useful to review the work of others in an effort to start building lexica that are applicable to one's own research. Here are a number of freely available lexica that have been published online. Many of them include access to the full lexica as well as sample analyzers.

- General Inquirer lexicon (Stone, 1966)

  https://inquirer.sites.fas.harvard.edu/

- Sentiment lexicon (Hu & Liu, 2004)

  www.cs.uic.edu/~liub/FBS/sentiment-analysis.html

- MPQA subjectivity lexicon (Wilson et al., 2005)

  http://mpqa.cs.pitt.edu/lexicons/subj_lexicon/

- SentiWordNet (Esuli & Sebastiani, 2006)

  https://github.com/aesuli/SentiWordNet

- Emotion lexicon (Mohammad & Turney, 2010)

  www.purl.org/net/emolex

Conclusion

This chapter described how to build a lexicon. This list of words and phrases is the first step in working with SLAM because the lexicon provides the framework that guides the specific SLAM techniques. An example of how we created a social presence lexicon was also presented. Lexica are very flexible and allow researchers to create parameters that can focus SLAM on just about any research construct.

Note

1 Tony Robinson was an unarmed 19-year-old African American teenager who was shot and killed by a police officer during a civil disturbance in 2015. News of Robinson's death spread quickly and protests demanding justice soon followed. The Twitter data used to create the lexicon came from people participating in the Tony Robinson protests.

References

Barrington, B. L. (1963). A list of words descriptive of affective reactions. *Journal of Clinical Psychology*, *19*(2), 259–262.

Esuli, A., & Sebastiani, F. (2006). *SentiWordNet: A publicly available lexical resource for opinion mining*. Paper presented at the Proceedings of the 5th International Conference on Language Resources and Evaluation, Genoa, Italy.

Fellbaum, C. (1999). *WordNet: An electronic lexical database* (2nd ed.). MIT Press. EBSCOhost. http://search.ebscohost.com/login.aspx?direct=true&scope=site&db=nlebk&db=nlabk&AN=48571

Feng, S., Kang, J. S., Kuznetsova, P., & Choi, Y. (2013). *Connotation lexicon: A dash of sentiment beneath the surface meaning*. Proceedings of the 51st Annual Meeting of the Association for Computational Linguistics (Volume 1: Long Papers), Sofia, Bulgaria.

Flor, N. V. (2014). *OILS Twitter Scraper*. Creative Commons Attribution-ShareAlike 4.0 International License.

Freire, P. (1970). *Pedagogy of the oppressed*. Continuum.

Gunawardena, C. N., Flor, N. V., Gómez, D., & Sánchez, D. (2016). Analyzing social construction of knowledge online by employing interaction analysis, learning analytics, and social network analysis. *Quarterly Review of Distance Education*, *17*(3), 35–60. (e-Learners and Their Data, Part 1: Conceptual, Research, and Exploratory Perspectives).

Gunawardena, C. N., Flor, N. V., & Sánchez, D. M. (2018). *Learning analytics and social construction of knowledge online*. Distance Teaching and Learning Conference, Madison, WI.

Gunawardena, C. N., Lowe, C. A., & Anderson, T. (1997). Analysis of a global online debate and the development of an interaction analysis model for examining social construction of knowledge in computer conferencing. *Journal of Educational Computing Research*, *17*(4), 397–431.

Hu, M., & Liu, B. (2004). *Mining and summarizing customer reviews*. Proceedings of the Tenth ACM SIGKDD International Conference on Knowledge Discovery and Data Mining (KDD '04), Seattle, WA, USA.

Lamers-Johnson, E., Kelley, K., Knippen, K., Feddersen, K., Sánchez, D. M., Parrott, J. S., Colin, C., Papoutsakis, C., & Jimenez, E. Y. (2022). A quasi-experimental study provides wvidence that registered dietitian nutritionist care is aligned with the academy of nutrition and dietetics evidence-based nutrition practice guidelines for type 1 and 2 diabetes. *Frontiers in Nutrition*, *9*(969360). https://doi.org/10.3389/fnut.2022.969360

Lamers-Johnson, E., Kelley, K., Sánchez, D. M., Knippen, K. L., Nadelson, M., Papoutsakis, C., & Jimenez, E. Y. (2021). Academy of nutrition and dietetics nutrition research network: Validation of a novel nutrition informatics tool to assess agreement between documented nutrition care and evidence-based recommendations. *Journal of the Academy of Nutrition and Dietetics*, *122*(4).

Liu, B. (2012). *Sentiment analysis and opinion mining*. Morgan & Claypool.

Megli, A., Fallad-Mendoza, D., Etsitty-Dorame, M., Desiderio, J., Chen, Y., Sánchez, D., Flor, N. V., & Gunawardena, C. N. (2023). Using social learning analytic methods to examine social construction of knowledge in online discussions. *American Journal of Distance Education*. https://doi.org/10.1080/08923647.2023.2192597

Mohammad, S., & Turney, P. (2010). Emotions evoked by common words and phrases: Using mechanical turk to create an emotion lexicon. Paper presented at the Proceedings of the NAACL HLT 2010 workshop on computational approaches to analysis and generation of emotion in text (pp. 26–34).

Pang, B., & Lee, L. (2008). *Opinion Mining and Sentiment Analysis* (Vol. 2). Now Foundations and Trends. https://doi.org/10.1561/1500000011

Pang, B., Lee, L., & Vaithyanathan, S. (2002). *Thumbs up? Sentiment classification using machine learning techniques*. Proceedings of the ACL-02 Conference on Empirical Methods in Natural Language Processing,

Penney, J., & Dadas, C. (2014). (Re)Tweeting in the service of protest: Digital composition and circulation in the occupy wall street movement. *New Media & Society*, *16*(1), 74–90.

Sánchez, D. M. (2016). Digital justice: An exploratory study of digital activism actions on Twitter. *Journal of Educational Technology Development and Exchange*, *8*(2), 1–22. http://tnet1.ioe.tsinghua.edu.cn/evaluate/DSS_DD/infoSingleArticle.do?articleId=1334431&columnId=306708

Sánchez, D. M. (2018a). *Building a call to action: Social action in networks of practice* [Doctoral Dissertation, University of New Mexico]. Albuquerque, NM.

Sánchez, D. M. (2018b). Concientization among people in support and opposition of President Trump. *Educational Technology & Society, 21*(1), 237–247.

Stone, P. J. (1966). *The General Inquirer: A computer approach to content analysis.* Cambridge, MA: MIT Press.

Taboada, M., Brooke, J., Tofiloski, M., Voll, K., & Stede, M. (2011). Lexicon-based methods for sentiment analysis. *Computational Linguistics, 37*(2), 267–307.

Whiteside, A. L., & Dikkers, A. G. (2012). Maximizing multicultural online learning experiences with the social presence model, course examples, and specific strategies. In *Computer-mediated communication across cultures: International interactions in online environments* (pp. 395–413). IGI Global.

Wilson T., Hoffmann P., Somasundaran S., Kessler J., Wiebe J., Choi Y., Cardie C., Riloff E., & Patwardhan S. (2005). *OpinionFinder: A system for subjectivity analysis.* Paper presented at the Proceedings of HLT/EMNLP 2005 Interactive Demonstrations, Vancouver, BC.

8   Sentiment Analysis

This chapter will describe sentiment analysis and its basic tenants. Next, we will illustrate how traditional positive, negative, and neutral categories within sentiment analysis can be reworked to represent any number of research constructs based on our own experience of using a social presence lexicon to analyze data. An initial and fundamental step in working with Social Learning Analytic Methods (SLAM) is using lexica to parse through data via sentiment analysis. Note SLAM is defined as a collection of techniques to study group interactions on learning management systems and social networks as groups co-construct knowledge online. These techniques include frequency analysis, sentiment analysis, cluster analysis, social network analysis, and artificial intelligence. Completed lexica are used to conduct analytics starting with basic descriptive statistics.

What Is Sentiment Analysis?

"Sentiment analysis, also called opinion mining, is the field of study that analyzes people's opinions, sentiments, evaluations, appraisals, attitudes, and emotions toward entities such as products, services, organizations, individuals, issues, events, topics, and their attributes" (Liu, 2012, p. 1). This technical definition of sentiment analysis provides a useful foundation with which one can understand this method. However, it might be overly complex and clouds the true simplicity of a sentiment analysis. Another definition of sentiment analysis is provided by Batrinca and Treleaven (2015) as "the application of natural language processing, computational linguistics and text analytics to identify and extract subjective information in source materials" (p. 90). This definition asserts the important detail of sentiment analysis being about subjective information which is in line with the previous definition's focus on opinions. An even more straightforward way to understand sentiment analysis is to review the two primary categories of analysis that are part of a sentiment analysis. They are:

1. Positive
2. Negative

Each of these categories is scored with words appearing in the data from the positive lexicon being valued a +1 and words from the negative lexicon being valued a –1 (Hu & Liu, 2004). The values are added together and the result is the sentiment score. At times, the data being scored will result in a neutral sentiment which is denoted by a score of 0. Sentiment analysis is a method that is used to determine the extent to which people feel positive, negative, or neutral about a given topic. At its core, sentiment analysis is an automated word count that uses lexica to guide what is being counted. The opinion-based aspect of sentiment analysis

DOI: 10.4324/9781003324461-11

from the first definition comes into play when this chapter turns its focus to ways in which sentiment analysis can be extended.

Relationships Between Lexica and Sentiment Analysis

Lexica are the foundation of sentiment analysis. Indeed, it is not possible to conduct a sentiment analysis without knowing what words and phrases should be counted as positive or negative. Take the following lists for example:

Positive

- Good
- Wonderful
- Excellent

Negative

- Bad
- Terrible
- Woeful

A sentiment analysis performed using these lexica will be able to identify and score instances of the three words in each list in any dataset. However, the sentiment analysis will be limited to only the six total words. In order to enhance the analysis, more words will have to be added for the positive and negative categories. The more comprehensive the words in these categories become, the more accurate the results of the sentiment analysis will be. Care must be taken to assure the correct assignment of words to the categories to avoid introducing errors into the sentiment analysis. Lexica provide the parameters for the automatic analysis performed by the sentiment analysis. Note that conducting a sentiment analysis does not usually require the creation of a customized lexicon because there are many freely available on the Internet. One example that we have used in past research can be found in Liu et al. (2005). Refer to Chapter 7 for a complete description of how to build and refine lexica.

Applications of Sentiment Analysis

Early applications of sentiment analysis used a lexical database called WordNet (Fellbaum, 1999) in concert with programed routines to summarize customer product reviews (Hu & Liu, 2004). Applications have grown exponentially over the years. Liu (2012) says sentiment analysis has a range of applications in almost every domain including "management sciences, political science, economics, and social sciences" (p. 2). Indeed, sentiment analysis is a method with great utility for almost any conceivable application so long as one goal of the inquiry is to determine the nature of peoples' opinions. Some examples cited by Pozzi et al. (2017) include how former President Obama used sentiment analysis during his 2008 campaign, how people responded to terrorism using Twitter data, and how messages about a smoking cessation drug influenced use behaviors. Liu (2012) even suggests that businesses can skip conducting surveys to do market research because they can determine public opinions using automated sentiment analysis systems that focus on data that comes from social media platforms. Sentiment analysis is a useful technique for quickly determining how people feel about a given topic. It can achieve even greater utility as its basic features can be used to conduct customized analysis as described in the next section of this chapter.

Extending Sentiment Analysis

The mechanics of sentiment analysis are universal because the word counts that are at the heart of the method can be retrofit to count words that represent just about any category imaginable. For example, if researchers are interested in knowing whether people feel positive or negative about something, they will simply create lexica that have positive and negative words and conduct a traditional sentiment analysis. When researchers want to know more about opinions, they can create lexica that represent the range of possible opinions. The lexica can even be changed to interrogate data for more specific phenomenon so long as the phenomenon can be represented using language. Some examples include verbal aggressiveness, negotiation skills, racist language, and many more. Note that while sentiment, whether people feel positive or negative about something, is subjective, research constructs like the ones just mentioned are not. Thus, sentiment analysis moves from subjective to a more objective focus as lexica are created that adhere to strong theory regarding a phenomenon of interest. Our research has focused on social presence and the social construction of knowledge. What follows are descriptions of how we have extended sentiment analysis to work in these domains.

Social Presence

Our research group's first attempt at extending sentiment analysis focused on the phenomenon of social presence in Gunawardena et al. (2016). Our work investigated social presence using data from online courses at a university. The first and most critical step was to create new lexica to fit social presence. The process we used to create the lexica is described in detail in Chapter 7.

When the lexica were completed, we next moved to operationalize them using a customized tool called the OILS Twitter Scraper (Flor, 2014). This Visual Basic tool was written for Excel to facilitate the data analysis by focusing on a program that is more comfortable to a majority of researchers because it doesn't require any coding like sentiment analyses that are conducted using R. The OILS Twitter Scraper includes a sentiment analyzer that depends on unique tabs within an Excel workbook. These tabs are used to hold the lexica such that there is a tab for positive words and negative words. In the case of social presence, we placed words and phrases that contributed to establishing social presence in the positive tab and words and phrases that detracted from social presence in the negative tab. The data was placed on a sheet of its own for analysis. After selecting all of the data, the sentiment analysis macro was executed which ultimately produced counts of all the words and phrases from the lexica which were easily summed using Excel's built-in descriptive statistic functions to determine an overall score.

We used the same version of the OILS Twitter Scraper that was customized to analyze social presence in Gunawardena et al. (2018). Words and phrases were selected from the study data transcripts to add to the existing lexicon. The lexicon was operationalized by adding the positive and negative words into sheets in the tool. Next, a routine was run on all 42 rows of study data that produced the number of words or phrases that matched the contents of the lexicon. The routine also produced a social presence score for each post in the data.

IAM and Conscientization

To complete the sentiment analysis, the lexica for the IAM and conscientization (Freire, 1970) was first developed using the methods described in Chapter 7. Note that this was the second time the conscientization lexicon was used and that the first study that developed it (Sánchez, 2018) is described later in this chapter. The lexica were implemented to conduct a customized analysis by inputting them into the OILS Twitter Scraper which entailed including the unigrams (single word) and bigrams (two words) associated with each construct into specific sheets in this Excel-based tool. These lists then had the spaces within them replaced with dashes using Find & Replace. Next the lists were added to another sheet that uses a routine to count the spaces in each bigram or n-gram (three or more words). Then a routine in the OILS Twitter Scraper was used to replace all instances of unigrams and bigrams with versions that contain dashes. Finally, another routine was used to count the instances of each unigram and bigram in the dataset. As part of the counting process, the OILS Twitter Scraper codes tweets that were not manually coded during the content analysis for IAM and conscientization.

Social Action

Sánchez (2016) adapted sentiment analysis to identify various actions associated with digital activism as identified by Penney and Dadas (2014) in the context of #BlackLivesMatter organizing for Tony Robinson. The words and phrases associated with digital activism were added to their own tabs within the OILS Twitter Scraper worksheet. Each of these elements of the lexicon were used to analyze the Twitter study data and produced counts of each category. The counts were then used to produce a correlation matrix that determined the relationships between them.

Conscientization

Sánchez (2018) was the first study to develop the conscientization lexicon and implement it. Chapter 7 describes how the lexicon was developed. The lexicon was operationalized with the OILS Twitter Scraper using methods similar to what have already been described for previous studies. Counts of words and phrases that matched the criteria in each of the four stages of conscientization were produced by the tool as it analyzed the Twitter dataset. This study also included a specific sentiment analysis question that examined how the sentiment of people who supported the 45th President of the United States compared to those who opposed him. The traditional positive and negative words and phrases were used to analyze the data to answer this question by producing a sentiment score.

Medical Documentation

To operationalize the lexicon that was developed in Lamers-Johnson et al. (2021) to analyze the Nutrition Care Process described in Chapter 7 and extend the typical sentiment analysis, it was necessary to add some functionality to the OILS Twitter Scraper. This required adding additional tabs to the OILS Twitter Scraper because it only had two built-in tabs for the positive and negative words. This also required adding additional code to the original sentiment analysis macro to accommodate the additional inputs. Once these modifications were complete, it was only a matter of including the words in their appropriate tabs as they related to the gold chain language. The new tool was called the diabetes mellitus (DM) Expected Care Plan (ECP) Analyzer. It was concluded that the DM ECP Analyzer was highly accurate (98.3%) and sensitive (99.1%). The study asserted that the DM ECP Analyzer was acceptable for conducting automated audits of nutrition documentation as they pertain to evidence-based care recommendations.

Lamers-Johnson et al. (2022) built on the work completed in the previous study to create a customized analyzer to evaluate the Evidence-Based Nutrition Practice Guidelines. There were tabs for evidence, diagnosis, intervention, monitoring and evaluation. It was used to score data from 787 medical visits that were documented according to the NCP to ECPs that were developed after first visits and diagnosis. A score of 0–4 was assigned to data based on the pattern of matching terms such that a match in one category was worth 1 point. 4 matches equaled a score of 4. Finally, a classification indicating the extent to which the ECP was implemented was assigned based on a combination of the score and the pattern of matches within the levels in the lexicon.

How to Conduct a Sentiment Analysis

Thus far, this chapter has discussed traditional sentiment analysis as well as provided examples of studies that have used its basic tenants in an expansive fashion to conduct a custom analysis. The focus of the chapter will now turn to providing readers with what they will need to conduct their own sentiment analysis. This chapter has previously stated the relationship between lexica and sentiment analysis. The majority of the work that is required to conduct a sentiment analysis occurs when creating the lexica. The sentiment analysis itself can be run rather easily using a tool like the OILS Twitter Scraper or R. Steps on using R to conduct sentiment analysis will be provided later because there are some steps that must be completed prior to working with the analysis tools to improve the quality of the findings.

Data Cleaning

The old saying "garbage in, garbage out" applies strongly to sentiment analysis. Specifically, the data that goes into the analysis needs to be of the highest quality possible in order to assure the highest quality results. General issues that impact the quality of data include but are not limited to misspellings, extra spaces, punctuation errors, inconsistencies in expressing common topics like using different formats for a date, and using words or phrases that come from foreign languages. General solutions for these issues include but are not limited to running a spell check, using Find & Replace, identifying variations in expressing common topics and standardizing them, and translating foreign words and phrases.

Additional issues arise when working with data the comes from social media because some data might contain only hashtags making a given item impossible to classify because it does not contain natural language. Filtering data so that these types of datapoints are left out of the analysis is generally a good practice. Another issue that arises when working with social media data is that of attribution. Analysis should focus on data that comes from people instead of bots that are automatically generating content and thus creating large amounts of noise in the overall dataset. Spam detection is a topic onto itself and readers are encouraged to dive deeper into this subject. The most accessible method that can be used to identify data that does not come from real people generally involves content analysis. Diving deep into the profile of a user that generated the suspicious content can provide clues regarding whether they are bots or not.

Performing basic data cleaning is important because sentiment analysis works by checking a given structure established in the lexicon that guides it on a dataset. The more varied and unstructured the data that is being analyzed, the less accurate and complete the results will be. Automatic analysis can be performed quickly but it is subject to the degree to which their parameters match the data they are being applied to. This means that in each analysis performed there will always be some data that does not get coded. The objective is to ensure as much data is pulled into the analysis as possible and that it is done accurately. This is accomplished by assuring data is of high quality before conducting the first analysis. Subsequently, researchers should analyze their results and see whether large portions of their data did not get coded by the first analysis. If the data in question needs further cleaning, it should be performed. If not, the researcher should apply content analysis and/or clustering to these non-coded data and refine the lexicon in an effort to increase the accuracy of their results.

Software Used to Conduct Sentiment Analysis

This section will illustrate how to conduct a sentiment analysis using R. We focus on R instead of on the OILS Twitter Scraper that was used to conduct many of the examples in this chapter because R is a standard and widely available tool. R is a free platform that requires a bit of computer coding savvy to use. It is a command line program which means it works by entering text-based commands. This might make it somewhat intimidating to use for some researchers so this chapter will provide the basics that anyone needs to get started. Keep in mind that researchers have the option of installing an integrated development environment like RStudio if working in the command line is not ideal. RStudio works with R and provides a more user-friendly interface that will make the capabilities of R more accessible to a wider audience. The official websites are as follows (see Chapter 6 for instructions on installing R and RStudio):

R

www.r-project.org/

RStudio

https://posit.co/downloads/

Currently, there does not appear to be a comprehensive volume on R that is dedicated to sentiment analysis. Many practitioners scour the web and kludge together various snippets of code to meet their needs. This section presents a summary of basic techniques.

How to Conduct a Sentiment Analysis Using R

The samples of code that are provided in this section are provided as templates. Researchers should feel free to copy and paste the code directly into their own versions of R. Note that code provided in this section includes notations in the code that begin with a #. These are comments that explain what the following line(s) of code will do. When a line of text begins with a #, R will skip the line and go to the next command. That means that lines of code that begin with a # can be copied without impacting how the program will function.

Sentiment analysis in R can be performed using a variety of different packages including *tidytext*, *sentimentr*, and *textblob*. This chapter will cover *sentimentr* and *tidytext*.

Sentiment Analysis Procedure for Sentimentr

The *sentimentr* package provides a straightforward method researchers can use to analyze data that is input directly into R. This package provides researchers with the ability to display and visualize the results of the analysis as well.

Install and Load Required Packages

As with all analysis done in R, the first step is to make sure that the appropriate package that is used to conduct the analysis is installed and loaded into the workspace. Use the following code to install and load the *sentimentr* package:

```
# Load necessary packages
install.packages("sentimentr")
library(sentimentr)
```

Entering Data

Next specific data to be analyzed should be entered by the researcher. Data, in the form of sentences, should be entered within quotation marks. The following is a sample of what the code should look like:

```
text_data <- c("I adore this product! It's the best ever!",
               "The service was the worst. I will never return.")
```

Conduct Sentiment Analysis and Display Sentiment Scores

After inputting data, the next step is to conduct the sentiment analysis and display the results. The first line of code in the following example runs the sentiment analysis while the second displays the results formatted by positive, negative, and neutral sentiment, as well as an overall sentiment score.

```
sentiment_scores <- sentiment_by(text_data)
print(sentiment_scores)
```

Visualize Sentiment Scores

Researchers can also opt to display the results of the sentiment analysis for easier interpretation in a scatter diagram using the following code:

```
plot(sentiment_scores$ave_sentiment)
```

Sentiment Analysis Procedure for Tidytext

The *tidytext* package allows researchers to customize the lexica they use to analyze data. The options are described later in this section. Using different lexica will yield different results and the appropriate lexicon should be selected for its match to the research questions. This package also requires researchers to load data into R rather than entering it directly into the program like with *sentimentr*. The procedure that is required to load data into R is also described in this section.

Install and Load Required Packages

First make sure to install and load the *tidytext* and *dplyr* packages using the following code:

```
# Load necessary packages
install.packages("tidytext")
library(tidytext)
install.packages("dplyr")
library(dplyr)
```

Data Entry for Sentiment Analysis

Data can be loaded into R either by using a pre-existing CSV and loading it in or by manually typing the data into R. Manual data entry is best for small scale analysis while loading a CSV lends itself best to big datasets.

Load CSV Data and Group Data

```
# Stores the CSV data within R in groups according to the columns in the CSV and displays a
summary of what is loaded
grouped_data <- read.csv("your_data.csv") %>%
group_by(id) %>%
mutate(line = row_number()) %>%
ungroup ()
grouped_data
```

Manual Data Entry

Data can be entered manually in R for small-scale analysis. Simply use the following code as a framework and add as many statements as desired within quotes and separate statements using commas.

```
grouped_data <- data.frame(
  text = c("I love this product! It's fantastic!",
          "The service was terrible. I will never come back.")
)
```

Tokenize Text Data

Tokenization involves breaking the text into individual words or tokens. These tokens are eventually matched to the criteria provided in the lexicon that the researcher selects to analyze their data. Tokenize the data using the following code:

```
# Assuming 'grouped_data' is your text data stored in a data frame with a
'text' column. If there is not a column named 'text', change this value to
match where your data is stored
tokens <- grouped_data %>%
  unnest_tokens(word, text)
```

Load Sentiment Lexicon

A sentiment lexicon contains words or phrases annotated with sentiment scores (positive or negative).

```
# Load the Bing lexicon included in tidytext
get_sentiments("bing")
```

Note: Researchers have many lexica available to apply to their sentiment analysis work with the *tidytext* package. *Bing* is included and the other packages are available for download by installing the *textdata* package. Once the package has been installed and loaded using the *install.packages* and *library* commands, simply replace *bing* with the name of the desired lexicon to download it before using it in the data analysis. For example, researchers would use the following code to load the National Research Council (NRC) lexicon:

```
get_sentiments("nrc")
```

Note that future references to *bing* in the upcoming code have to be replaced by the name of the lexicon of choice in order to function. The lexica available for use as well as descriptions of them are as follows:

1. bing: The Bing lexicon includes positive and negative sentiment words.
2. afinn: The AFINN lexicon, described in Nielsen (2011), is the name used for the Affective Norms for English Words lexicon which contains a list of English words rated for sentiment on a scale from –5 to 5.
3. nrc: The NRC Emotion lexicon associates words with eight basic emotions (anger, anticipation, disgust, fear, joy, sadness, surprise, trust) and two sentiments (positive and negative).
4. loughran: The Loughran-McDonald Financial Sentiment lexicon contains words related to financial sentiment often used in financial documents.

Join Lexicon With Tokenized Data

Once the appropriate lexicon has been loaded in R, the parameters of the lexicon must be associated with the data that needs to be analyzed. The code to perform this step is as follows:

```
# Join the sentiment lexicon with the tokenized data
sentiment <- tokens %>%
inner_join(get_sentiments("bing"), by = "word", relationship = "many-to-many")
```

Conduct Sentiment Analysis

At this point, R has already performed all of the steps needed to prepare for the analysis. All that is left is to produce sentiment scores. These lines will perform the sentiment analysis:

```
# Summarize sentiment scores
sentiment_summary <- sentiment %>%
   group_by(sentiment) %>%
   summarize(count = n())
```

Display Sentiment Scores

In order to display the text-based results of the sentiment analysis, the variable that is storing the analysis must be called in R. This simply requires entering the name of the variable. In this case the code to display results is as follows:

```
sentiment_summary
```

Researchers can also opt for a visual representation of the results by using the *ggplot2* package. After installing and loading the package, use the following code to display the results of the sentiment analysis:

```
# Plot sentiment scores
install.packages("ggplot2")
library(ggplot2)
ggplot(sentiment_summary, aes(x = sentiment, y = count)) +
   geom_bar(stat = "identity", fill = "skyblue") +
   labs(title = "Sentiment Analysis", x = "Sentiment", y = "Count")
```

A Complete Program

Previous sections have described an entire program that can be used to conduct a sentiment analysis in a piecemeal fashion. In order to bring all of these concepts together, here we present a complete picture of what the entire program could look like from loading data to producing an exported file.

```
# Load necessary packages
install.packages("tidytext")
library(tidytext)
install.packages("dplyr")
library(dplyr)

# Stores the CSV data within R in groups according to the columns in the CSV and
displays a summary of what is loaded
grouped_data <- read.csv("your_data.csv") %>%
group_by(id) %>%
mutate(line = row_number()) %>%
ungroup ()
grouped_data

# Assuming 'grouped_data' is your text data stored in a data frame with a 'text' column. If
there is not a column named 'text', change this value to match where your data is
stored
tokens <- grouped_data %>%
  unnest_tokens(word, text)

# Load the Bing lexicon included in tidytext
get_sentiments("bing")

# Join the sentiment lexicon with the tokenized data
        tokens <- grouped_data %>%
        unnest_tokens(word, text)
inner_join(get_sentiments("bing"), by = "word", relationship = "many-to-many")

# Summarize sentiment scores
sentiment_summary <- sentiment %>%
  group_by(sentiment) %>%
  summarize(count = n())

sentiment_summary
```

Research Questions

1. How does sentiment vary across different levels of SCK?
2. How does the cultural setting of an instructional activity influence the predominant emotions expressed by participants?
3. How does the sentiment influence the development of community?
4. How has the sentiment used in online discourse evolved over time?
5. How does dissonance influence the sentiment of participants in instructional activities?

Conclusion

This chapter reviewed how to conduct a sentiment analysis. Sentiment analysis is the most basic SLAM technique. It provides researchers information regarding whether the sentiment of data is positive, negative, or neutral. Numerous examples of how sentiment analysis was applied in diverse domains were provided. Sentiment analysis is also extremely flexible because the lexica that are the foundation of this technique can be modified to quantify just about any research construct.

References

Batrinca, B., & Treleaven, P. C. (2015). Social media analytics: A survey of techniques, tools and platforms. *AI & Society: Journal of Knowledge, Culture and Communication, 30*(1), 89–116. https://doi.org/10.1007/s00146-014-0549-4

Fellbaum, C. (1999). *WordNet: An electronic lexical database language, speech, and communication* (2nd ed.). Cambridge, MA: MIT Press. EBSCOhost. http://search.ebscohost.com/login.aspx?direct=true&scope=site&db=nlebk&db=nlabk&AN=48571

Flor, N. V. (2014). *OILS Twitter Scraper*. Albuquerque, NM: Creative Commons Attribution-ShareAlike 4.0 International License.

Freire, P. (1970). *Pedagogy of the oppressed*. New York, NY: Continuum.

Gunawardena, C. N., Flor, N. V., Gómez, D., & Sánchez, D. (2016). Analyzing social construction of knowledge online by employing interaction analysis, learning analytics, and social network analysis. *Quarterly Review of Distance Education, 17*(3), 35–60.

Gunawardena, C. N., Flor, N. V., & Sánchez, D. M. (2018). *Learning analytics and social construction of knowledge online*. Paper presented at the Distance Teaching and Learning Conference, Madison, WI.

Hu, M., & Liu, B. (2004). *Mining and summarizing customer reviews*. Paper presented at the Proceedings of the Tenth ACM SIGKDD International Conference on Knowledge Discovery and Data Mining (KDD '04), Seattle, WA, USA.

Lamers-Johnson, E., Kelley, K., Knippen, K. L., Feddersen, K., Sánchez, D. M., Parrott, J. S., Colin, C., Papoutsakis, C., & Jimenez, E. Y. (2022). A quasi-experimental study provides evidence that registered dietitian nutritionist care is aligned with the academy of nutrition and dietetics evidence-based nutrition practice guidelines for type 1 and 2 diabetes. *Frontiers in Nutrition, 9*(969360). https://doi.org/10.3389/fnut.2022.969360

Lamers-Johnson, E., Kelley, K., Sánchez, D. M., Knippen, K. L., Nadelson, M., Papoutsakis, C., & Jimenez, E. Y. (2021). Academy of nutrition and dietetics nutrition research network: Validation of a novel nutrition informatics tool to assess agreement between documented nutrition care and evidence-based recommendations. *Journal of the Academy of Nutrition and Dietetics 122*(4).

Liu, B. (2012). *Sentiment analysis and opinion mining*. San Rafael, CA: Morgan & Claypool.

Liu, B., Hu, M., & Cheng, J. (2005, May 10–14). *Opinion observer: Analyzing and comparing opinions on the web*. Paper presented at the Proceedings of the 14th International World Wide Web Conference (WWW-2005), Chiba, Japan.

Nielsen, F. Å. (2011). *A new ANEW: Evaluation of a word list for sentiment analysis in microblogs*. Paper presented at the ESWC2011 Workshop on "Making Sense of Microposts": Big Things Come in Small Packages, Heraklion, Crete.

Penney, J., & Dadas, C. (2014). (Re)Tweeting in the service of protest: Digital composition and circulation in the occupy wall street movement. *New Media & Society, 16*(1), 74–90.

Pozzi, F., Fersini, E., Messina, E., & Liu, B. (2017). Challenges of sentiment analysis in social networks: An overview. In F. Pozzi, E. Fersini, E. Messina, & B. Liu (Eds.), *Sentiment analysis in social networks* (pp. 1–13). Cambridge, MA: Morgan Kaufmann.

Sánchez, D. M. (2016). Digital justice: An exploratory study of digital activism actions on Twitter. *Journal of Educational Technology Development and Exchange, 8*(2), 1–22.

Sánchez, D. M. (2018). Concientization among people in support and opposition of President Trump. *Educational Technology & Society, 21*(1), 237–247.

9 Cluster Analysis

When studying the social construction of knowledge (SCK) in large datasets, which can range from hundreds to possibly millions of posts, a common question arises: What are the participants discussing? If you are unfamiliar with the dataset, your goal is to identify the overarching topics. However, if you have some context – such as the posts originating from a specific forum or all containing the same hashtag – you may be more interested in uncovering the subtopics within that dataset. To discover topics and subtopics, one could read each post individually, take notes, and then analyze the notes, but that would be prohibitively time-intensive. Fortunately, there are several automated techniques available for determining topics, subtopics, and, generally, categories of discussion, with cluster analysis being one of the most common methods.

Cluster analysis is a method that groups similar data together, and it is widely used in the learning and educational sciences (Dutt et al., 2017; Le Quy et al., 2023). For SCK researchers, where the data typically consists of text postings, cluster analysis can group texts based on several criteria, including common words, shared meanings, and sentiment, to name a few. For example, cluster analysis might group posts that frequently use words like *culture, tradition,* and *learning* together, while another cluster might form around posts that include terms such as *technology, online courses,* and *eLearning.* When grouping according to shared meanings, one cluster might consist of posts discussing how culture influences participation in online courses, while another cluster could include posts about how eLearning platforms need to be adapted to different cultural contexts.

In short, in the context of analyzing text to understand SCK, "clustering" encompasses a set of methods that group data based on specific similarity criteria. A typical clustering algorithm takes text as input, transforms it into a format conducive to the application of similarity measures, and then uses those measures to group the data. Once grouped, the data can be visualized.

Clustering Algorithms

In the context of SCK research involving discussion on learning management systems or on social media platforms, several clustering algorithms are commonly used (see also Le Quy et al., 2023). These include:

K-means Clustering. This algorithm partitions the data into k distinct, non-overlapping clusters based on their distances to the k centers. The algorithm iteratively assigns each data point to the nearest center and updates the center as the mean of the points in the cluster. K-means is a popular choice due to its simplicity and efficiency. The method is great for partitioning data into a predefined number of clusters, and it works well when the clusters are roughly spherical. However, its performance can decline with clusters of different sizes and densities.

DOI: 10.4324/9781003324461-12

Hierarchical Clustering. This algorithm builds a hierarchy of clusters by either a bottom-up approach (agglomerative) or a top-down approach (divisive). The result is a tree structure that can be cut at different levels to form different clusters. Hierarchical clustering is useful for understanding the data's structure and does not require specifying the number of clusters in advance. However, it can be computationally intensive for large datasets.

Topic Modeling (e.g., Latent Dirichlet Allocation). While not a traditional clustering algorithm, topic modeling can be used to group texts into different topics, which can be interpreted as clusters. Each document is considered a mixture of topics, and each topic is considered a mixture of words.

These algorithms can be applied to the text data from discussion boards and from social media platforms in order to identify common topics, track changes in the discussion over time, and understand the structure of the conversation.

Case Study: K-means

Step 1: Load Libraries

To begin clustering your data using the K-means algorithm in R, the first step is to load the necessary libraries that can assist with clustering. Two popular libraries for this purpose are *tm*, a text mining library, and *cluster*, a library that provides various clustering algorithms:

```
# Load required libraries. If you have not installed these libraries,
# prior to running the code you must do:
#    install.packages('tm')
#    install.packages('cluster')
#    install.packages('Rtsne')
#    install.packages('plotly')
#    install.packages('ggplot2')
library(tm)
library(cluster)
library(Rtsne)
library(plotly)
library(ggplot2)
```

Step 2: Read Dataset into Data Frame

Next, you must read the data from your discussion dataset into a data frame. Here, we use the dataset from Chapter 5, *using-ai-in-schools.csv*, and read the postings into a data frame named df:

```
df = read.csv('using-ai-in-schools.csv', encoding = 'UTF-8')
```

Step 3: Data Cleaning

Before clustering, R requires that the text of the discussion is converted into a Corpus object. A Corpus object, or simply corpus, in R is part of the *tm* package. A corpus serves as a container for managing and manipulating collections of text documents efficiently. All documents within a corpus can be processed and analyzed as one entity, allowing for efficient text analysis. Once the text data is converted into a corpus, various preprocessing tasks like removing punctuation, converting to lowercase, removing stop words, and stemming can be performed to prepare the data for analysis. After these preprocessing steps, the corpus can be converted into a document-term matrix or a term-document matrix for further analysis like clustering.

The following code demonstrates converting the discussion text into a corpus, and then preprocessing the data to make it all lowercase, remove punctuation, remove numbers, remove stop words, and strip out excess whitespace.

```
# Create a corpus from the text
corpus <- Corpus(VectorSource(df$text))
# Preprocess the text data
corpus <- tm_map(corpus, content_transformer(tolower))
corpus <- tm_map(corpus, removePunctuation)
corpus <- tm_map(corpus, removeNumbers)
corpus <- tm_map(corpus, removeWords, stopwords("english"))
corpus <- tm_map(corpus, stripWhitespace)
```

Step 4: Create a Document-Term Matrix (DTM)

Once the corpus is preprocessed, it needs to be transformed into a different structure known as a document-term matrix (DTM). In the context of R programming, a DTM is a table in which each row signifies a document (or a posting in our dataset), and each column represents a term or word from the document. The value in each cell of the matrix indicates the frequency of a term in a specific document. The DTM serves as a common input for numerous text-mining techniques, including clustering, because it provides a structured, numerical representation of the text data that can be readily processed by these algorithms. The *tm* package in R includes a function, DocumentTermMatrix(), which is used to convert a corpus object into a DTM. This transformation is a pivotal step in the text-mining process as it transposes our text data into a format suitable for analysis.

In more specific terms, text is transformed into a numerical vector in a multidimensional space, where each word constitutes a separate dimension. When employing natural language processing algorithms, this vector representation is often referred to as an "embedding," and the transformation process is known as "vectorization."

```
# Create a document-term matrix
dtm <- DocumentTermMatrix(corpus)
```

Step 5: Perform K-means Clustering

Finally, K-means clustering on the dataset using the following block of code. As this is the key code block, the detailed explanation of each line is as follows:

- k <- 3: This sets the number of clusters that the K-means algorithm will create. You can change this to any number you want.

- set.seed(123): This sets the seed for the random number generator, which is used in the K-means algorithm. Setting a seed ensures that the results are reproducible.
- clusters <- kmeans(dtm, centers = k): This line performs the K-means clustering on the dataset *dtm* with k number of clusters. The result is stored in the clusters variable.

```
# Perform K-means clustering
k <- 3 # Change this to the number of clusters you want
set.seed(123) # For reproducibility
clusters <- kmeans(dtm, centers = k)
```

Step 6: Display Cluster Assignments

The following code block allows you to view the cluster assignments for each document and extract the documents belonging to the first cluster. It prints the cluster assignments for each document, indicating which cluster they belong to.

```
# Print the cluster assignments
print(clusters$cluster)
```

The output for all 317 posts is as follows, with the post number underlined, and the cluster number for the post directly below it:

```
  1   2   3   4   5   6   7   8   9  10  11  12  13  14  15  16  17  18  19  20  21  22  23  24  25  26  27  28
  3   3   3   3   3   3   3   3   3   3   3   3   3   3   3   3   3   3   3   3   3   3   3   3   3   3   3   3

 29  30  31  32  33  34  35  36  37  38  39  40  41  42  43  44  45  46  47  48  49  50  51  52  53  54  55  56
  3   3   2   3   3   3   3   3   3   3   3   3   3   3   3   3   3   3   3   3   3   3   3   3   3   3   2   3

 57  58  59  60  61  62  63  64  65  66  67  68  69  70  71  72  73  74  75  76  77  78  79  80  81  82  83  84
  3   3   3   3   3   3   3   3   3   3   3   3   3   3   2   3   3   3   2   3   3   3   3   3   2   3   3   3

 85  86  87  88  89  90  91  92  93  94  95  96  97  98  99 100 101 102 103 104 105 106 107 108 109 110 111 112
  3   3   3   2   3   3   3   3   1   3   3   3   3   3   3   3   3   2   3   3   3   3   3   3   3   3

113 114 115 116 117 118 119 120 121 122 123 124 125 126 127 128 129 130 131 132 133 134 135 136 137 138 139 140
  3   3   1   3   3   2   3   3   2   3   3   3   3   3   3   3   3   3   3   3   3   3   3   3   3   3

141 142 143 144 145 146 147 148 149 150 151 152 153 154 155 156 157 158 159 160 161 162 163 164 165 166 167 168
  3   3   3   3   3   3   3   3   3   3   3   3   3   3   3   3   3   3   3   3   3   3   2   3   3   3

169 170 171 172 173 174 175 176 177 178 179 180 181 182 183 184 185 186 187 188 189 190 191 192 193 194 195 196
  2   3   3   3   3   3   3   2   3   3   2   3   3   3   2   3   3   3   3   3   3   3   3   3   3   3

197 198 199 200 201 202 203 204 205 206 207 208 209 210 211 212 213 214 215 216 217 218 219 220 221 222 223 224
  3   3   3   3   3   3   1   3   3   3   3   3   3   3   3   2   3   3   3   3   3   3   3   3   3   3

225 226 227 228 229 230 231 232 233 234 235 236 237 238 239 240 241 242 243 244 245 246 247 248 249 250 251 252
  3   2   3   3   3   3   3   3   3   3   3   2   3   3   3   3   3   2   3   3   3   3   3   3   3   3

253 254 255 256 257 258 259 260 261 262 263 264 265 266 267 268 269 270 271 272 273 274 275 276 277 278 279 280
  3   3   3   3   2   3   3   3   3   3   3   3   3   3   3   3   3   3   2   3   3   3   3   3   3   3

281 282 283 284 285 286 287 288 289 290 291 292 293 294 295 296 297 298 299 300 301 302 303 304 305 306 307 308
  3   3   2   3   3   3   3   3   3   3   3   3   3   2   2   3   2   3   3   3   3   3   3   3   3   3

309 310 311 312 313 314 315 316 317
  2   3   3   3   3   3   3   3   2
```

Step 7: View Posts in Cluster

Typically, you want to see the posts assigned to a cluster. The following code retrieves and prints the documents in the first cluster. This provides a way to inspect and analyze the results of the clustering analysis, allowing you to see which documents were grouped together by the clustering algorithm. Change the cluster number to see the data in other clusters.

```
# Get the indices of the documents in the first cluster
cluster1_indices <- which(clusters$cluster == 1)

# Subset the original data to get the documents in the first cluster
cluster1_documents <- df$text[cluster1_indices]

# Print the documents in the first cluster
print(cluster1_documents)
```

The output for the posts in cluster 1 is as follows:

```
[1] "ChatGPT can be a valuable tool for schools in several ways. Firstly, it can
provide personalized assistance to students, offering explanations, clarifications,
and additional practice on various subjects. This tailored support can help strug-
gling students catch up, and challenge high-achievers to excel further.\n\nMoreo-
ver, ChatGPT can assist teachers in creating and refining educational materials. It
can generate custom worksheets, essay prompts, and even suggest creative lesson
plans. This saves teachers time and allows them to focus on other critical aspects
of education.\n\nAdditionally, ChatGPT can be used for language learning and im-
provement. It can engage students in interactive language exercises, correct grammar
and vocabulary usage, and facilitate conversations in a chosen language.\n\nFur-
thermore, it can foster inclusivity by providing support to students with diverse
learning needs. For instance, it can offer alternative explanations, formats, or re-
sources for students with varying learning styles or accessibility requirements.\n\
nLastly, ChatGPT can facilitate distance learning. It can serve as a virtual tutor,
offering guidance and support to students studying remotely, ensuring they have ac-
cess to educational resources and assistance even outside of traditional classroom
settings.\n\nOverall, ChatGPT's adaptability, scalability, and personalized assis-
tance make it a valuable asset for schools, enhancing the learning experience for
both students and teachers."

[2] "This is literally the dumbest thing I have ever heard. Genuinely, this is no
way similar to a calculator. A calculator tells you what 2(5+7)/6(8-9) is with-
out having to do take the time to do it yourself with room for error, while every
kid can still take the time and break it down themselves, the calculator just
```

simplifies it with 100% accuracy. AI in this scenario will legitimately comes up with the points/arguments and articulates them for the writer, that's not similar at all. The AI equivalent of a calculator would be spell checking and grammar checking, AI to write whole essays is the equivalent of taking a picture of math problem and writing down the answer it gives you. Doesn't take a genius to see the difference in the two.\n\nThis lady is great at saying stupid shit and making it seem smart, make the kids write essays in class. Simple. Critiquing a paper does nothing, I can critique and edit literally any paper after reading it 2 times, even if it's covering a topic I know nothing about. How does this help kids in any way? The answer? It doesn't, it doesn't *at all*. I'm gonna sound like a boomer, but this a sure fire way to make kids dumb as fuck and impossible to create their own arguments, but will create a whole generation of "well akshually . . ." kids. This is beyond fucking stupid. Writing an essay is not hard at all, a 2 page essay can be done in 30-50 minutes depending in writing typing speed, and the writer will be knowledgeable about what they wrote with the ability to defend it."

[3] ">while every kid can still take the time and break it down themselves\n\nAnd can the kid not still take the time to break the essay down in this scenario?\n\n>Critiquing a paper does nothing, I can critique and edit literally any paper after reading it 2 times, even if it's covering a topic I know nothing about.\n\nThis is incredibly ignorant, trying critiquing a full PhD level thesis on astrophysics when you don't even know what Kepler's laws are, you wont get very far.\n\n>Writing an essay is not hard at all, a 2 page essay can be done in 30-50 minutes depending in writing typing speed, and the writer will be knowledgeable about what they wrote with the ability to defend it.\n\nThis is completely subjective. Personally, essays take an incredibly long time and are arduous to write, even on topics I am knowledgeable about. I can have an academic conversation easily on the matter, but essay writing really only tests your ability to convert your thoughts and ideas into succinct phrasing. I would argue the understanding of the concepts themselves are far more important than the actual essay writing. \nAdditionally, people can 100% bullshit essays. Kids do that literally all the time in school, and bullshit essays are just as easy to spot as bullshit critiques."

Step 8: Visualize Clusters

Finally, you can visualize clusters by reducing the dimensionality of the document-term matrix and representing points with different colors based on their cluster assignment. There are multiple packages for reducing dimensionality including *umap*, *pca*, and *tsne*. The following code uses *tsne*:

```
# Remove duplicate rows for tsne
duplicate_rows = duplicated(dtm)
dtm_unique = dtm[!duplicate_rows,]
clusters_unique <- clusters$cluster[!duplicate_rows]
```

```
# Perform t-SNE
tsne_model <- Rtsne(as.matrix(dtm_unique), dims = 2, perplexity=30, verbose=TRUE,
max_iter = 500)

# Create a data frame with t-SNE dimensions and cluster assignments
tsne_data <- data.frame(
  x = tsne_model$Y[, 1],
  y = tsne_model$Y[, 2],
  cluster = factor(clusters_unique),
  text = df$text[!duplicate_rows]
)

# Create a ggplot
p <- ggplot(tsne_data, aes(x = x, y = y, color = cluster, text=text)) +
geom_point() +
theme_minimal()

# Convert the ggplot object to a plotly object
plot <- ggplotly(p, tooltip = "text")

# Print the plot
plot
```

Figure 9.1 is a graphical representation of the K-means clustering analysis:

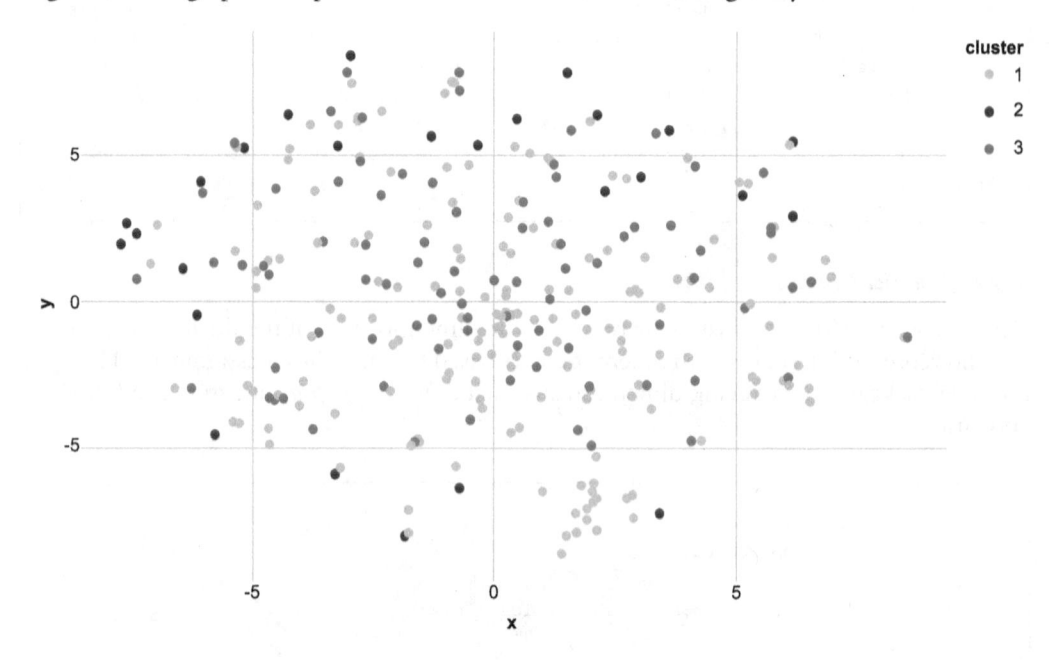

Figure 9.1 An example of a cluster diagram. Each dot represents a post and dots near each other indicate posts that are similar.

Case Study: Hierarchical Clustering

Hierarchical clustering is the other popular technique for grouping text based on similarity and for discovering possible topics of discussion in a thread.

Step 1: Load Libraries

To begin clustering your data using the hierarchical clustering algorithm in R, the first step is to load the necessary libraries that can assist with clustering. Two popular libraries for this purpose are *tm*, a text mining library, and *cluster*, a library that provides various clustering algorithms:

```
library(tm)
library(cluster)
library(Rtsne)
library(plotly)
library(ggplot2)
```

Step 2: Read in Dataset

Next, you must read the data from your discussion dataset into a data frame. Here, we use the dataset from Chapter 5, *using-ai-in-schools.csv*, and read the postings into a data frame named df:

```
df = read.csv('using-ai-in-schools.csv', encoding = 'UTF-8')
```

Step 3: Data Cleaning

Before clustering, R requires that the text of the discussion is converted into a corpus object. A corpus object, or simply corpus, in R is part of the *tm* package. A corpus serves as a container for managing and manipulating collections of text documents efficiently. All documents within a corpus can be processed and analyzed as one entity, allowing for efficient text analysis. Once the text data is converted into a corpus, various preprocessing tasks like removing punctuation, converting to lowercase, removing stop words, and stemming can be performed to prepare the data for analysis. After these preprocessing steps, the corpus can be converted into a document-term matrix or a term-document matrix for further analysis like clustering.

The following code demonstrates converting the discussion text into a corpus, and then preprocessing the data to make it all lowercase, remove punctuation, remove numbers, remove stop words, and strip out excess whitespace.

```
# Create a corpus from the text
corpus <- Corpus(VectorSource(df$text))

# Preprocess the text data
corpus <- tm_map(corpus, content_transformer(tolower))
corpus <- tm_map(corpus, removePunctuation)
corpus <- tm_map(corpus, removeNumbers)
corpus <- tm_map(corpus, removeWords, stopwords("english"))
corpus <- tm_map(corpus, stripWhitespace)
```

Step 4: Create a Document-Term Matrix (DTM)

Once the corpus is preprocessed, it needs to be transformed into a different structure known as a document-term matrix (DTM). In the context of R programming, a DTM is a table in which each row signifies a document (or a posting in our dataset), and each column represents a term or word from the document. The value in each cell of the matrix indicates the frequency of a term in a specific document. The DTM serves as a common input for numerous text-mining techniques, including clustering, because it provides a structured, numerical representation of the text data that can be readily processed by these algorithms. The *tm* package in R includes a function, DocumentTermMatrix( ), which is used to convert a corpus object into a DTM. This transformation is a pivotal step in the text-mining process as it transposes our text data into a format suitable for analysis.

In more specific terms, text is transformed into a numerical vector in a multidimensional space, where each word constitutes a separate dimension. When employing natural language processing algorithms, this vector representation is often referred to as an "embedding," and the transformation process is known as "vectorization."

```
# Create a document-term matrix
dtm <- DocumentTermMatrix(corpus)
```

Step 5: Perform Hierarchical Clustering

To perform hierarchical clustering, you first compute a distance matrix from the document-term matrix, then apply the hierarchical clustering algorithm, and finally cut the resulting dendrogram to define the desired number of clusters:

```
# Compute the distance matrix
dist_matrix <- dist(dtm)

# Perform hierarchical clustering
hc <- hclust(dist_matrix)

# Cut the dendrogram to create a specified number of clusters
k <- 3 # Change this to the number of clusters you want
clusters <- cutree(hc, k)
```

Step 6: Display Cluster Assignments

At this point, it is straightforward to display the cluster assignments simply:

```
# Print the cluster assignments
print(clusters)
```

Step 7: Display Posts Associated With a Cluster

You can display the documents associated with a specific cluster by subsetting the original data based on the cluster assignments. Here's how you can do it for the first cluster:

```
# Get the indices of the documents in the first cluster

# Subset the original data to get the documents in the first cluster
cluster1_documents <- df$text[cluster1_indices]

# Print the documents in the first cluster
print(cluster1_documents)
```

Step 8: Display Hierarchical Clusters

For a small number of posts, you can display the clusters as follows (see Figure 9.2):

```
plot(hc)
```

But for larger plots, you need to do dimensionality reduction, similar to the previous clustering example using K-means, and color the resulting 2D plot points according to the group (see Figure 9.3).

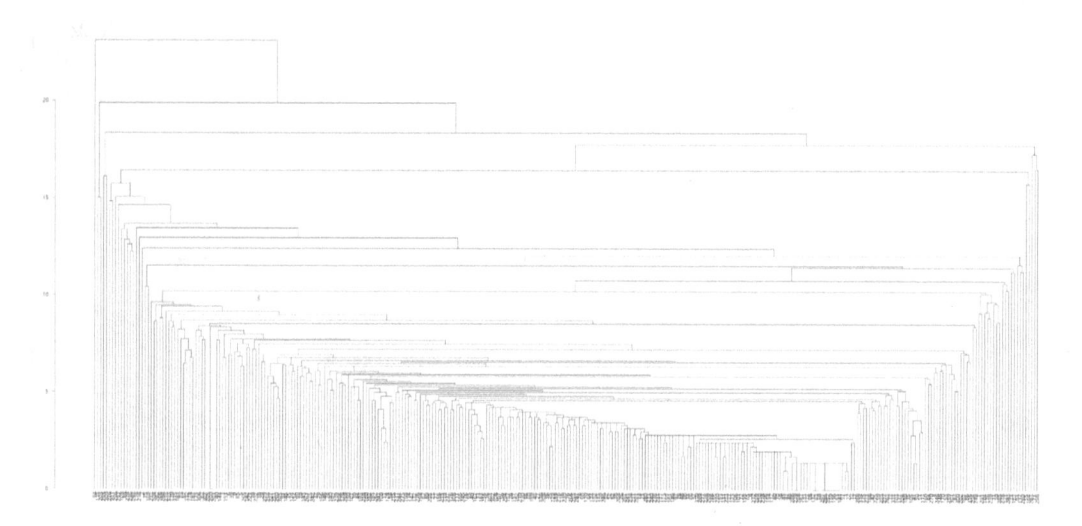

Figure 9.2 An example of a hierarchical cluster diagram, also known as a dendrogram

```r
# Remove duplicate rows for tsne
duplicate_rows = duplicated(dtm)
dtm_unique = dtm[!duplicate_rows,]
clusters_unique <- clusters[!duplicate_rows]

# Perform t-SNE
tsne_model <- Rtsne(as.matrix(dtm_unique), dims = 2, perplexity=30, verbose=TRUE,
max_iter = 500)

# Create a data frame with t-SNE dimensions and cluster assignments
tsne_data <- data.frame(
  x = tsne_model$Y[, 1],
  y = tsne_model$Y[, 2],
  cluster = factor(clusters_unique),
  text = df$text[!duplicate_rows]
)

# Create a ggplot
p <- ggplot(tsne_data, aes(x = x, y = y, color = cluster, text=text)) +
  geom_point() +
  theme_minimal()

# Convert the ggplot object to a plotly object
plot <- ggplotly(p, tooltip = "text")

# Print the plot
plot
```

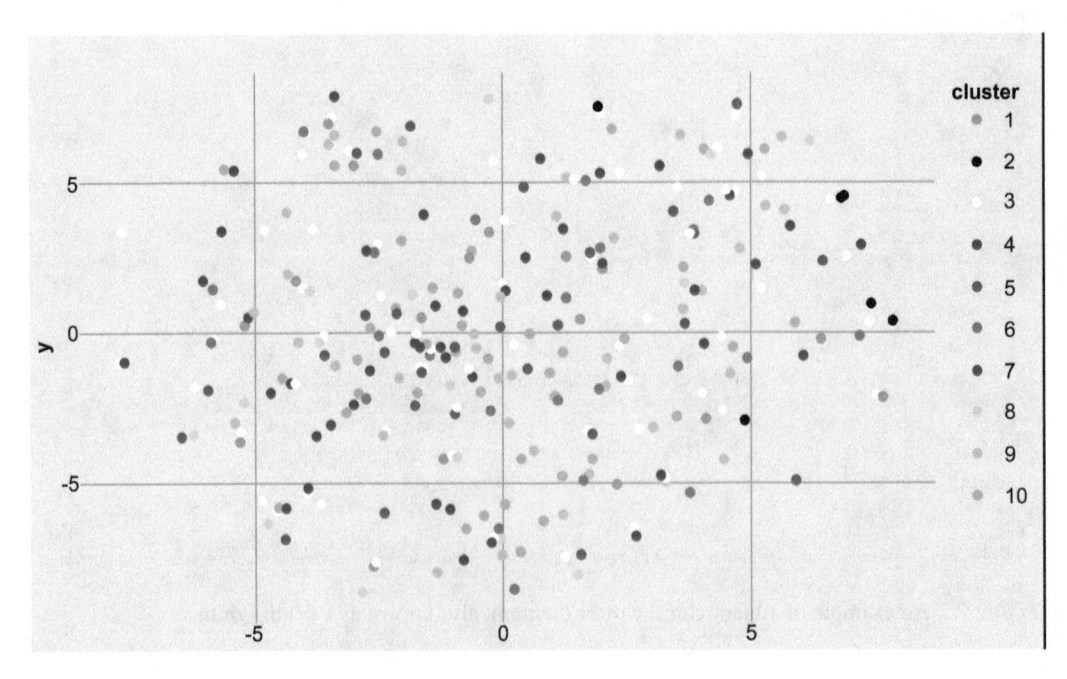

Figure 9.3 Another example of a cluster diagram. Each dot represents a post and dots near each other indicate posts that are similar.

Conclusion

In Chapter 9, we discussed the role of clustering in analyzing large datasets, particularly in the context of understanding SCK. We explored various methods for clustering posts to depict groups of similar posts, including K-means, hierarchical clustering, and dimensionality reduction. Clustering allows us to identify potential themes in our data, visually represented by posts that are close to one another, and explore relationships within the data. These groups provide insights into the topics being discussed and, when analyzed over time, reveal how these topics evolve. This chapter has provided a detailed guide on implementing clustering techniques, from preparing text data to clustering the data and visualizing the clusters.

References

Dutt, A., Ismail, M. A., & Herawan, T. (2017). A systematic review on educational data mining. *IEEE Access*, 5, 15991–16005. IEEE Access. https://doi.org/10.1109/ACCESS.2017.2654247

Le Quy, T., Friege, G., & Ntoutsi, E. (2023). A review of clustering models in educational data science toward fairness-aware learning. In A. Peña-Ayala (Ed.), *Educational data science: Essentials, approaches, and tendencies: Proactive education based on empirical big data evidence* (pp. 43–94). Springer Nature. https://doi.org/10.1007/978-981-99-0026-8_2

10 Social Network Analysis (SNA)

This chapter will describe how social network analysis (SNA) can be used to analyze the social environment of online learning. Using SNA along with the IAM Phases is a powerful technique that adds needed relational context to online interactions that take place within the social environment. Other Social Learning Analytic Methods (SLAM) answer the "what" question about knowledge construction while SNA answers the "how" question with detailed sociograms. Note that SLAM is defined as a collection of techniques to study group interactions on learning management systems and social networks as groups co-construct knowledge online. These techniques include frequency analysis, sentiment analysis, cluster analysis, SNA, and artificial intelligence. We will discuss popular tools for producing sociograms, NodeXL and R. We will differentiate between the two tools in terms of analysis procedures and also discuss the strengths and weaknesses of both tools.

What SNA Adds to SLAM

Previous chapters have described other SLAM including lexicon analysis and sentiment analysis. These methods can be used in a complimentary fashion such that the lexicon and sentiment analysis will answer the "what" question while SNA will answer the "how" question about social knowledge construction. The "what" question is concerned with the content of messages. It determines the topics being discussed. The "how" question is concerned with the ways in which people talk about various topics. Haythornthwaite (1996) sets SNA apart writing, "The focus on patterns of relationships, such as who works with whom or who exchanges information with whom, distinguishes social network analysis from other analysis techniques" (p. 324). SNA examines the social environment that supports discussions.

Evolution of SNA

The First Sociogram

The work of Moreno (1953) on sociometry represents one of the first times researchers considered methods that were specifically suited for sociological studies. "The chief methodological task of sociometry has been the revision of the experimental method so that it can be applied effectively to social phenomena" (Moreno, 1951, p. 31). Moreno developed the idea of sociometry within the broad context of psychology. Sociometry includes a method to illustrate the relationships between people. He called the graphic that was the output of this method a sociogram. Moreno's aim was to provide a method that could map social structures in the service of helping to modify them. This initial work focused on directly asking

DOI: 10.4324/9781003324461-13

members of a group about their favorable or unfavorable impressions of others in the group as well as the degree of their impressions. In other words, group members would be asked to rank others according to how favorable or unfavorable they found each person. This data would be used to construct a sociogram by representing men and women with different symbols and using different colored lines to represent the various favorable or unfavorable impressions between each group member. If the sociogram revealed various members were isolated or had many unfavorable associations, interventions could be considered to remedy the situation. Modern SNA carries this same purpose as isolated members of the network are often encouraged to engage more fully in activities. Moreno's work in this area was not widely popular and eventually further research largely came to a halt after he made the decision to give the American Sociological Society control of his journal called *Sociometry* (Nolte, 2014). Regardless, the field owes the creation of the term *sociogram* to Moreno and, although not directly related, modern SNA has many similarities to Moreno's initial ideas. The field and this chapter use the term *sociogram* to describe network graphics.

The Blueprint

The seminal text in SNA is Wasserman and Faust (1994). This comprehensive volume defines the host of statistical measures that are associated with complex SNA. It also lays the foundation for modern SNA including defining key concepts like actors, network types, centrality, directional and nondirectional relations, network density, and relational ties. The definitions for these key terms are provided here:

- Actors – "discrete individual, corporate, or collective social units. Examples of actors are people in a group, departments within a corporation, public service agencies in a city, or nation-states in the world system" (Wasserman & Faust, 1994, p. 17). In sociograms, actors are usually named shapes. These named shapes are commonly called "nodes."
- Centrality – "Centralization measures the extent to which a set of actors are organized around a central point" (Haythornthwaite, 1996, p. 333).
- Directional relationships – "the relational tie between a pair of actors has an origin and a destination; that is, the tie is directed from one actor in the pair to the other actor in a pair" (Wasserman & Faust, 1994, p. 44).
- Nondirectional relationships – ties between actors that do not have a direction such as countries that share borders (Wasserman & Faust, 1994). The countries would be related but not in a directional fashion say, for example, if John sends Sara an email.
- Network density – "The density of a network indicates the degree to which members are connected to all other members" (Haythornthwaite, 1996, p. 332).
- Relational tie – "The defining feature of a tie is that it establishes a linkage between a pair of actors" (Wasserman & Faust, 1994, p. 18). Ties are shown on sociograms as lines that connect various actors.

This book is intended to provide an introductory understanding of SNA so readers who would like to learn more are encouraged to refer to Wasserman and Faust (1994).

Initial Steps: Frequencies and Message Maps

An important step in using SNA to examine online learning was taken in Levin et al. (1990). Their work used data from an online conference much like numerous studies from that era. Their study included two methods that bear many similarities to SNA: intermessage reference analysis and message flow analysis. The intermessage reference analysis requires a researcher to code messages according to who referenced whom in a table format. This coding also captures the direction (incoming or outgoing) of the message. Descriptive data like how many messages received a given number of references and the role of the person whose messages were referenced are outcomes of this coding. Levin et al. (1990) also created an "influence" measure by adding all of the direct and indirect message references. This is similar to how modern SNA counts messages that are sent and received by a given person and scales the size of their node according to that frequency.

The final coded data is presented in a message map that shows all the members of the group and uses arrows to show the directionality of the references between the member messages. The directionality of messages is also important to modern SNA because it helps identify whether people are both contributors and consumers of information. Levin et al. (1990) note that depending on the size of the network, the final message map can be quite difficult to understand because of the web of nodes and connections that can be difficult to decipher. For this reason, they suggest focusing on specific clusters (multiple messages that reference one another) of the network to get a more detailed look at the phenomenon happening within the network. Clusters are used as guideposts to foster further inquiry into the contents of those messages. Using references as a datapoint allows the researcher to visualize how people are communicating. The benefit of seeing communication patterns is that it allows for the identification of people who are most and least central to a discussion. Answering the "what" question requires looking into the content of the messages. See our chapter on sentiment analysis for methods that should be used to analyze the content of messages.

Clusters that are identified using the intermessage reference analysis can be analyzed using the message flow analysis. This level of analysis focuses on the density of messages over time. Messages are plotted by placing the number of messages on a vertical axis and time increments like days on a horizontal axis. The resulting figure is similar to how modern SNA displays the number of messages people send within a network. The benefit of visualizing message frequency is to determine what timeframe generates more or less activity which can direct further investigation to identify important variables that influence the context of the discussion.

Of specific relevance to measuring the social construction of knowledge (SCK) is the work of Howell-Richardson and Mellar (1996), who set out to test whether course design and moderator actions influenced participant interaction. Their method included identifying messages sent in an online course that were identified using a specific computer command or specific lexical references to messages. The authors focused on the lengths of messages, how they were distributed, and the relationship between the messages. Message maps were created to show the relationship between incoming and outgoing messages. These maps contained numbers to represent participants and lines and arrows to show the connections between them similar to Figure 10.1.

Modern SNA follows this practice by mostly using people and groups as their unit of analysis and arrows of various kinds to show how they are connected. However, messages and words are sometimes used. The various units of analysis that are used in modern SNA will be discussed later in this chapter.

SNA + Mixed-Methods Approaches to Evaluate SNA

One of the first attempts that was made to evaluate SCK using social learning analytics, including SNA, was proposed by Martinez et al. (2003). Their research focused on information

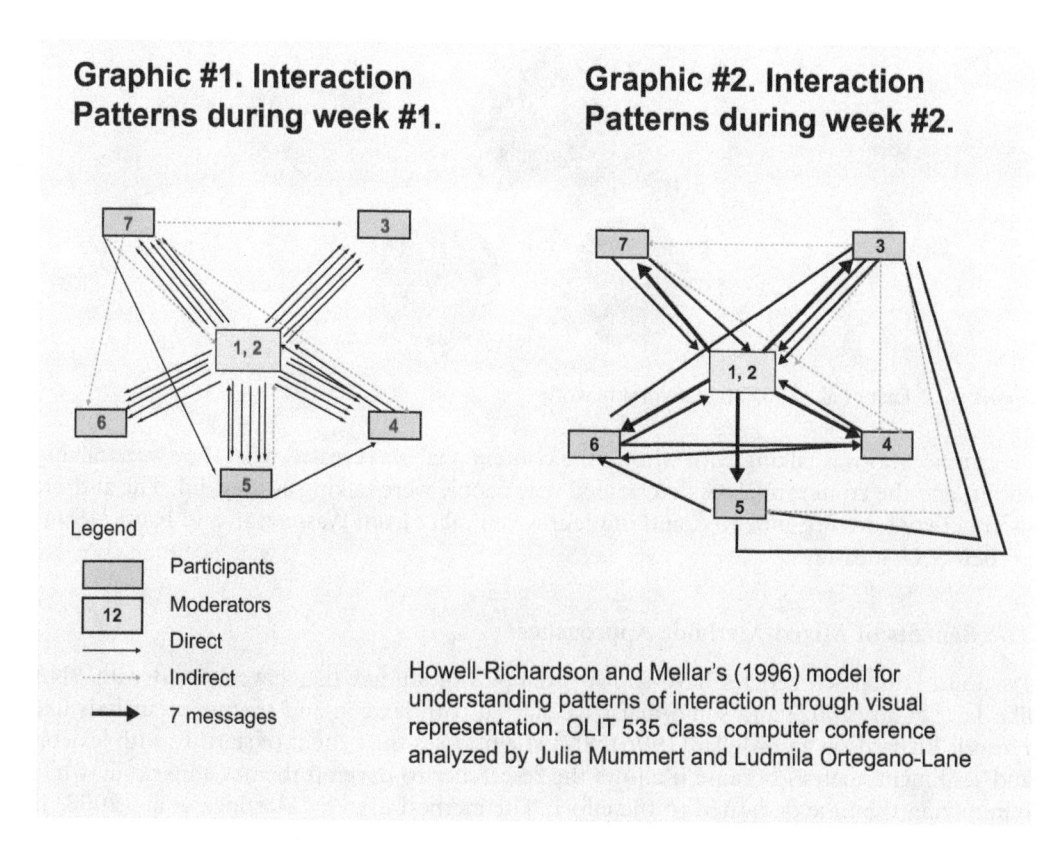

Graphic #1. Interaction Patterns during week #1.

Graphic #2. Interaction Patterns during week #2.

Legend

Participants

12 Moderators

Direct

Indirect

7 messages

Howell-Richardson and Mellar's (1996) model for understanding patterns of interaction through visual representation. OLIT 535 class computer conference analyzed by Julia Mummert and Ludmila Ortegano-Lane

Figure 10.1 OLIT 535 interaction patterns

sharing as their vehicle for social knowledge construction. This study took place on the backdrop of an online course in a Spanish telecommunications engineering school and was inspired by the principles of case study research. The method also includes automated tools and other analytic methods, which makes it similar to SLAM. This point will be expanded upon in this chapter.

SNA begins with what the authors call "sociometries," which require students to list the people who they have some kind of a relationship with. The authors proposed completing SNA several times during the course as a formative evaluation but at least at the start and end of the course. Indeed, Martinez et al. (2003) had students provide their prior relationships at the beginning of the course. Their proposed SNA also used data from course event logs to construct the final sociograms, which provides an objective data source to balance out the initial self-reported "sociometries" coming from students. Martinez et al. (2003) include network density, degree centrality, and network degree centralization from Wasserman and Faust (1994) as their SNA measures.

Another work that used SNA to investigate SCK was Laat et al. (2007), who used SNA to analyze virtual learning communities. In order to study networked learning, the authors used a multimethod research framework as shown in Figure 10.2.

Again, we have an example of authors using a variety of methods to compliment and validate findings that were produced by other methods. In this case, the SNA was used to

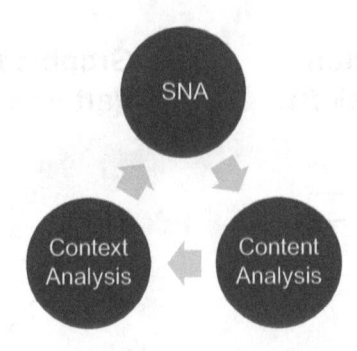

Figure 10.2 Laat et al. (2007) research framework

determine who was talking with whom, the content analysis revealed what they were talking about, and the context analysis determined why people were talking as they did. The authors used network density, indegree, and outdegree centrality from Wasserman and Faust (1994) as their SNA measures.

The Benefits of Mixed-Methods Approaches

Previously discussed articles have shown examples of studies that have started with SNA like Laat et al. (2007) and some that have started with lexicon and sentiment analysis like Howell-Richardson and Mellar (1996). SLAM embodies the benefit of starting with lexicon and sentiment analysis because it allows the researcher to develop themes empirically while minimizing the time dedicated to the effort. The method used by Martinez et al. (2003) is similar to SLAM because it first identifies a scheme of categories empirically, theoretically, or even according to evaluation objectives. However, SLAM provides a deeper level of analysis especially for researchers who do not already have a coding scheme or theoretical framework in mind.

All of the methods previously discussed (Howell-Richardson & Mellar, 1996; Laat et al., 2007; Levin et al., 1990; Martinez et al., 2003), including SLAM, employ numerous methods that complement one another and look at the SCK in different ways. For example, the approach established by Martinez et al. (2003) is meant to develop over time such that one method is meant to complement and/or refine the previous method's findings.

> The overall evaluation process evolves cyclically so that in the first phase each one of the analysis methods is performed independently, yielding partial conclusions that can be confirmed or rejected by triangulation or can produce a new cycle of the evaluation process, in order to gain insight about an emergent aspect.
>
> (Martinez et al., 2003, p. 359)

Another example is provided by Laat et al. (2007), who says their combination of SNA, content analysis, and context analysis "are used to triangulate and contextualise our findings" (p. 268). The relationship between SNA and lexica and sentiment analysis is that they look at the social environment of a discussion from different angles and provide different points of view that paint a comprehensive picture of the phenomenon being studied. Discussing studies that examine the social environment is important but more germane are studies that use the IAM.

IAM and SNA – Exploring the Social Environment of Knowledge Construction

This section focuses on a selection of studies that use the IAM to answer "what" types of questions and SNA to answer "how" types of questions. Each study looks at a slightly different phenomenon but all ultimately explore the social environment that supports their phenomenon using SNA. The first study is Heo et al. (2010), who used SNA to examine interaction patterns, which they called the macro level, and an IAM content analysis for analyzing team messages, which they called the micro level. The authors saw the IAM analysis as a way to determine the quality of online instruction. The SNA used the number of links between actors and an overall density score. They also calculated the betweenness scores for their teams. Note that betweenness is another way of saying that the authors calculated the centrality of the teams in their study. The findings used SNA to answer a "how" question as Heo et al. (2010) determined that the social environment exhibited high levels of interaction and influenced communication, mutual support, and team cohesion. They also answered a "what" question because the group with the highest level of interaction also scored the lowest on their group project. The IAM analysis provided the "what" in this case because the group in question was focusing mostly on Phase I communications.

Similar to Heo et al. (2010), Aviv et al. (2003) conducted a SNA and paired it with an IAM content analysis. Their study focused on a business ethics course at a university in the Middle East. They administered the course using a structured and unstructured approach hoping to determine how the presence or absence of structure would influence knowledge construction. Their SNA involved a cohesion analysis which identifies strong ties between various actors and membership to various small groups called cliques. They also performed a typical IAM content analysis. Aviv et al. (2003) answered a "how" question by identifying how communications in structured and non-structured environments differed from one another. Specific to the social environment, they found connections were much stronger within a structured environment and also identified how important the specific structure was to their outcomes. Their study answered a "what" question by determining the levels of knowledge construction in each study condition. Pairing these two findings together, the authors determined that structure was associated with higher Phases of knowledge construction and cohesion as opposed to non-structured environments.

Lin et al. (2016) used the IAM and SNA like other studies but also included questionnaires and focus groups as part of their research design. The authors did not use automated techniques to analyze data from their questionnaires or focus groups. This is the utility of SLAM as they could have saved themselves time during the analysis phase of the study. At any rate, the mixed-method analysis was conducted mostly to triangulate their findings. The researchers were successful in this regard. They established the "how" of their networks using SNA showing that their social environment was supported by a key actor, who was an important leader. They also found that their social environment was balanced between online and real-world activities. The authors subsequently validated the "how" using questionnaires and focus groups. Lin et al. (2016) used their methods to establish validity across the methods employed. This is also a trait of SLAM. All of the studies presented in this section focus on people and groups as their unit of analysis. Such a focus unlocks the first elements of social presence by clearly showing how a community is connecting. However, SNA can also be expanded to focus on other units of analysis and thus reveal the trust and community elements of social presence as described in the next section.

Unit of Analysis: Actors

Traditional SNA is focused on people or groups (also known as actors). These sociograms illustrate the nature of the relationships between the actors and how they are connected. Wasserman and Faust (1994) make an important point writing

> the unit of analysis in network analysis is not the individual, but an entity consisting of a collection of individuals and the linkages among them. Network methods focus on dyads (two actors and their ties), triads (three actors and their ties), or larger systems (subgroups of individuals, or entire networks).
>
> (p. 5)

From the perspective of SCK, SNA is concerned with the network and how its members communicate with one another. SNA allows researchers to form vibrant communities by illustrating where connectivity should be increased or decreased (Cross et al., 2006). This is the key benefit of conducting SNA on people and groups.

Our research team has used a method similar to Martinez et al. (2003) in sharing sociograms with classes. Our approach involves structuring the SNA around specific discussion-based activities and taking multiple SNA snapshots during a course. The first time a facilitator should conduct and share a SNA with students is at the beginning of the course. The discussion-based activity that could be the focus of the SNA could be a formal graded class activity or it could even be the introduction forum. This initial sociogram might show that the facilitator is among the most central members of the discussion with many connections to the students as efforts are made to spark interactions and knowledge-building. The sociogram should be shared with students along with the facilitator's commentary regarding how the interactions unfolded. The second SNA should come in the middle of the course and again be focused on a discussion-based activity. From the previous SNA and accompanying commentary, students will be familiar with SNA and should be intrinsically motivated to take steps to improve or maintain their position within the network. A final SNA should be conducted at the end of the course and again shared with students. The final sociogram should be shared with further commentary from the facilitator regarding the evolution of the community during the course. This final sociogram could display the students as the most central in the discussion while the facilitator is displayed on the periphery. It is ideal to have students with the highest centrality because that means that they are driving the discussion without the interjections of the facilitator.

One key variable in the evolution of community is the role played by the facilitator. Prior research like Aviv et al. (2003) has already made this point, but it is worth revisiting because we have learned the value of a facilitator that focuses on community-building in our own experiences. Oftentimes, students will not build community, or knowledge for that matter, unless they are specifically prompted to do so by the facilitator. Most often, students will simply stay within Phase I and provide their own definitions or opinions simply to meet the activity requirements of many discussion-based activities. We are proponents of specifically including a statement like "In this discussion, you are expected to build on the comments provided by your classmates" in the directions that go with discussion-based activities. Focusing on key actions like citing your peers and synthesis have also been useful in our practice. Facilitators can also structure their activities such that students will be more likely to build community and knowledge. One of our favorite strategies is to have a designated student provide an overall summary of an entire discussion when it is nearing its conclusion. Another strategy is to have students produce a mind map of the contents of a discussion-based activity. Taking actions such as these helps students become more central to any discussion and fosters both community and knowledge-building.

However, the intervention of a facilitator can confound the overall findings regarding the authenticity of the community formed during a given course. The method we propose with SLAM aims to present an objective view of community based on typical SNA metrics. In terms of social presence, SNA that focuses on people and groups reveals how people are connecting with one another. We define social presence as the extent to which someone is perceived as a real person by their peers (Gunawardena & Zittle, 1997). The more people are perceived as real people, the more connections they will make with one another. The evolution of connections within a discussion are especially clear when multiple sociograms are produced.

Researchers should also feel free to question students directly regarding their perceptions of the community and to what extent they feel the structure of activities or interaction of the facilitator influenced the overall outcomes. Taking an action such as this would balance the findings with another viewpoint that increases credibility. Researchers should not rely solely on SNA to determine the extent to which community or knowledge was built. Instead, researchers should incorporate various methods within SLAM to triangulate findings. An additional strategy that involves SLAM uses sentiment analysis along with SNA to focus on words and phrases as the actors in a network.

Unit of Analysis: Words

SNA when applied to words as the unit of analysis, instead of people or groups, helps to illustrate how concepts are related to one another. It reveals evidence of interaction in the form of trust-building and language related to community. These final two components of social presence are revealed when sentiment analysis, described in Chapter 8, first identifies the words that are related to each of these constructs. In the case of trust building, they are words such as *trust, swear, confidence, believe,* and *rely.* In the case of community, they are words like *we, us,* and *let's all.* Running a sentiment analysis that focuses on trust-building and community allows researchers to first develop the descriptive statistics associated with each category. Using SNA to illustrate the connections between and within these constructs is a matter of creating a sociogram as we will describe in this section.

Qualitative research has set some precedent in producing visuals that relate words and concepts with tools like Atlas.TI. Graphics such as Figure 10.3 are the result of the time-consuming process of conducting a content analysis, which requires reading all transcribed materials and coding them into themes. Sentiment analysis would take the place of a content analysis in the case of SLAM. Atlas.TI uses the resulting hierarchy of codes and how they overlap to produce graphics like Figure 10.3.

SNA produces something similar only without the suggested relationships between the nodes. Another key difference is that Figure 10.3 uses codes as nodes directly from the transcribed materials, whereas SNA uses the words and phrases from its automated analysis. A sample sociogram that was produced using this method is shown in Figure 10.4.

SNA applied to words and phrases can also reveal how the knowledge that a group created is related. Sociograms taken over a period of time can show how relationships evolve and also make it clear when new knowledge is developed. To illustrate this point, we should take the example of an academic course. Every course is based on a syllabus that outlines the content to be covered each week. This means that the content has a linear

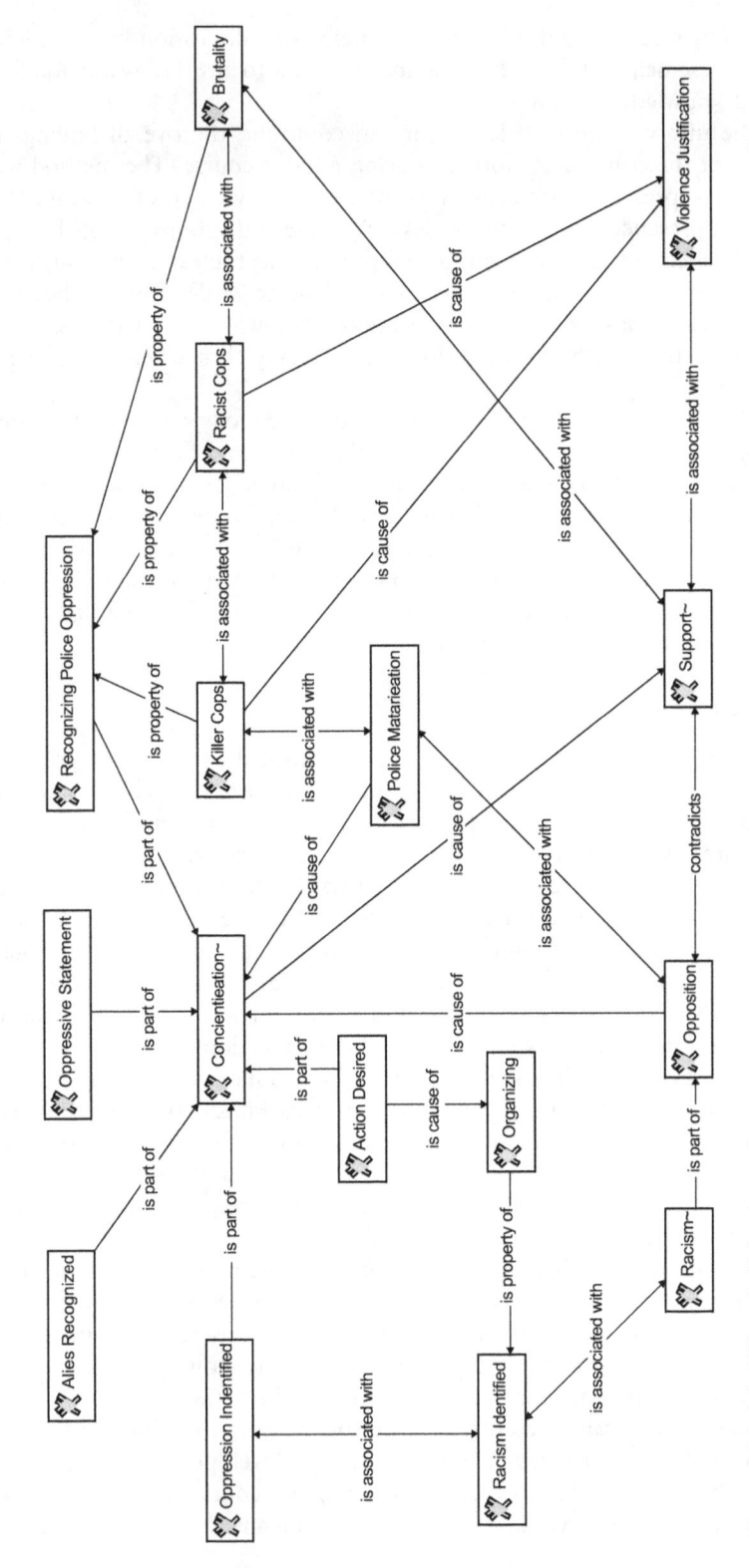

Figure 10.3 Atlas.TI code links network

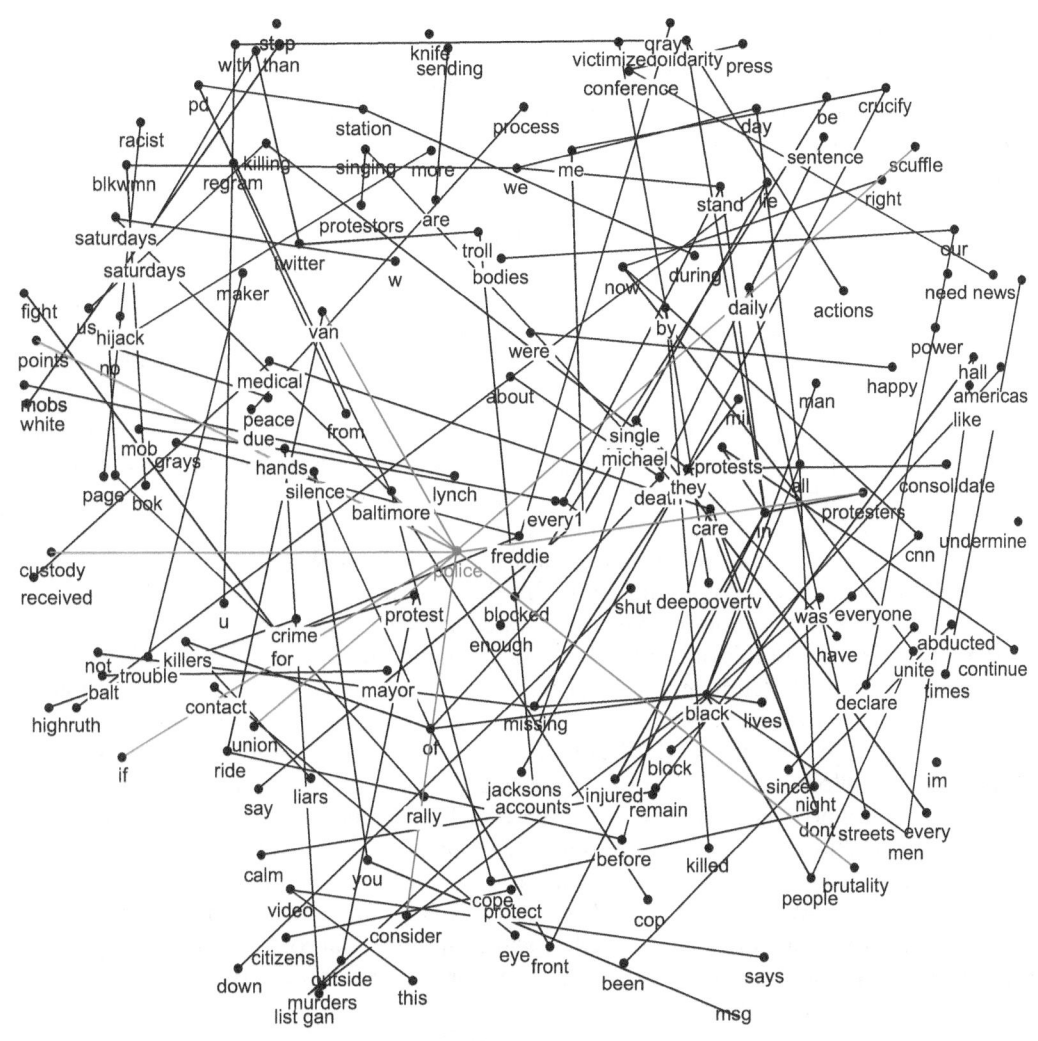

Created with NodeXL (http://nodexl.codeplex.com)

Figure 10.4 SNA focused on words

structure already imposed upon it. The course's facilitator might expect concepts that are covered in each week to be grouped together but students might make connections between the content and weave the concepts together in ways that go beyond the linear syllabus structure. This type of relationship is easily seen using SNA. New knowledge can also be clearly identified because new nodes will appear in one sociogram as compared to previous ones.

SNA that focuses on language as its unit of analysis sheds light on how trust and community are built by visualizing the connections between language that exemplifies these activities. SNA can also be used to ascertain the tangible value of community and knowledge-building. This is beyond the scope of SLAM but is worth mentioning as it represents the ultimate level of evaluation for which SNA can be applied.

Unit of Analysis: Organizations

Some readers might have heard the term *organizational network analysis* (ONA). Do not be fooled. An ONA is simply an SNA applied to a very large unit of analysis: organizations. ONA seeks to illustrate the network of connections within and sometimes between organizations:

> The organizational network is understood as a system of connections between people or organizational units (e.g., departments), created in order to exchange information, knowledge, ideas, and resources. Significant aspects of this network are internal relations, creation, flow, and use of information and knowledge.
>
> (Ujwary-Gil, 2020, p. 37)

SNA is between actors while ONA includes actors but expands the unit of analysis to include organizational entities and tangible/intangible resources. ONA has a specific outcome that is oriented toward achieving business results (Cross et al., 2010).

Attending a web conference in Winter 2024 by a multinational Fortune 500 company provides an example of how one business is using ONA to achieve business results. This company involved 13,000 employees in their ONA of an online venue that allowed their employees to post and work on projects that were created by other employees. The company made sure that participants in this online venue provided their skills and capabilities as part of their profiles which helped identify expertise. The projects posted by employees were required to have specific objectives and intended results. As employees posted projects and signed up to work on them, the company used ONA to identify people who were most central to various networks. This allowed the company to make connections between the most central individuals and people who could most use their expertise. The efforts of the company ultimately led to lots of international collaboration and helped them to create many cross-functional teams. The organization also used the ONA on an individual level by regularly providing each participating employee with a customized report of their position within the larger network. According to the company, this resulted in some employees becoming more engaged and reaching out to others more in order to become more central to the network. This increased the organization's productivity.

Results such as these are not uncommon. A study of 15 communities of practice across various industries by Cross et al. (2006) revealed that using SNA/ONA can decrease time wasted on reinventing the wheel, improve quality, and leverage distributed expertise. Unlocking the potential of SNA requires familiarity with the tools of the trade. The next section focuses on building capacity with software used to conduct SNA.

Software Used to Conduct Social Network Analysis

This section will provide step-by-step directions for researchers who would like to conduct a SNA. Steps will be provided for both NodeXL and R.

NodeXL

NodeXL is a Microsoft Excel-based tool that is maintained by the Social Media Research Foundation. NodeXL offers a free version and a paid version with advanced features. The free version is a good place to start and later determine if having the advanced features will be advantageous. The fact that NodeXL does not require knowledge of coding and the general familiarity many researchers have with Excel makes this an attractive option for beginners. For an in-depth treatment of how NodeXL can be used to conduct SNA, see Hansen et al.

(2020). This chapter will present the basics of conducting SNA with NodeXL to illuminate the social environment of knowledge construction.

R

R is a free platform that requires a bit of computer-coding savvy to use. It is a command line program which means it works by entering text-based commands. This might make it somewhat intimidating to use for some researchers, so this chapter will provide the basics that anyone needs to get started. Keep in mind that researchers have the option of installing an integrated development environment like RStudio if working in the command line is not ideal. RStudio works with R and provides a more user-friendly interface that will make the capabilities of R more accessible to a wider audience. The official websites are as follows (refer to Chapter 6 for detailed installation instructions):

R

http://www.r-project.org/

RStudio

https://posit.co/downloads/

Currently, there does not appear to be a comprehensive volume on R that is dedicated to SNA. Many practitioners scour the web and kludge together various snippets of code to meet their needs. This section presents a summary of basic techniques.

How to Conduct a Social Network Analysis Using NodeXL

Downloading and Installing NodeXL

In order to download either the free or paid versions of NodeXL, researchers must register using the following link:

www.smrfoundation.org/nodexl/installation/

This page provides a detailed set of instructions that should be followed to install the program. Note that NodeXL does not work on Mac computers.

In order to load all of NodeXL's functions, you might need to add the folder where it is located to Excel's list of trusted folders. Visit the Trust Center within Excel to do this. Alternatively save the file on your local hard drive.

When NodeXL installs, it will add a tab to Excel where researchers can work with all of the functions described in this section.

Importing Data

If researchers already have data that they would like to analyze in Excel format, it can be imported into NodeXL. If researchers do not have any existing data, skip to the next section.

1. Open the Excel file where the data is stored.
2. Open the NodeXL Excel template.
3. Click the **NodeXL Basic** tab.
4. Click **Import**. The **Import** drop-down menu will appear.

   Note: The majority of the options are only available in NodeXL Pro.

5. Choose **From Open Workbook**. The **Import from Open Workbook** dialog box appears.
6. Choose the columns from the original data file that correspond to Vertex 1 and Vertex 2 from the dropdown menus.
7. Click **Import**.

Entering Data

1. Enter names in the **Vertex 1** column.
2. Enter names in the **Vertex 2** column.

> **Note**: These names are the actors in your sociogram and names entered in the **Vertex 1** column will be connected to the names in **Vertex 2** column, row-by-row.

Displaying Sociograms

1. Click **Show Graph**. The sociogram will display in the **Document Actions** panel.

> **Note**: The **Show Graph** button turns into the **Refresh Graph** button when a sociogram has been displayed. To update the sociogram after making changes, click **Refresh Graph**. The graph will have to be displayed again after any of the changes in the following section are made.

Changing Sociogram Format

Display a Directed Network

1. Choose **Directed** from the drop-down menu to add directional arrows to the sociogram.

Modify Sociogram Layout Type

1. Choose an option from the **Layout** drop-down menu.

> **Note**: The Layout drop-down menu can also be found in the **Document Actions** panel.

Changing Sociogram Visual Properties

Researchers can customize their sociograms using the options on the **Edges** and **Vertices** tabs. The **Edges** are the connections between the actors. The **Vertices** are the actor nodes.

The **Visual Properties** columns on each tab display their own tooltips that guide users. Some of the most common are presented here.

Change Edge Color

1. Right-click a cell in the **Color** column that corresponds to an edge.
2. Click **Select Color**. The **Color** dialog box opens.
3. Choose a color.
4. Click **OK**.

> **Note**: The color of vertices can be changed in the same fashion on the **Vertices** tab.

Change Edge Size

1. Enter a number between 1 and 10 in the cells in the **Width** column.

   Note: The color of vertices can be changed in the same fashion by entering a number between 1 and 1,000 in the **Size** column on the **Vertices** tab.

Display Actor Labels

1. Click the **Vertices** tab.
2. Copy the names in column A (**Vertex**) and paste them in column H (**Label**).

Change Actor Shapes

1. Click a cell in the **Shape** column. A drop-down arrow appears.
2. Click the drop-down arrow.
3. Choose a shape from the drop-down menu.

How to Conduct a Social Network Analysis Using R

The samples of code that are provided in this section are provided as templates. Researchers should feel free to copy and paste the code directly into their own versions of R. Note that code provided in this section includes notations in the code that begin with a #. These are comments that explain what the following line(s) of code will do. When a line of text begins with a #, R will skip the line and go to the next command. That means that lines of code that begin with a # can be copied without impacting how the program will function.

Importing Data

Tip: To revise lines of code that were entered previously, use the up and down keyboard buttons. Pressing the up button will cycle up through previous lines of code and pressing down will cycle down through previous lines of code.

Researchers will either have the option to enter data manually into R or to load a CSV (comma delimited text file) with the social network relationships into R for analysis. This section describes how to load a CSV into R. Manual data entry will be covered in the next section.

To load a CSV into R, researchers must use the *read.csv* function. Here is an example of what the code should look like:

```
# Specify the file path to your CSV file
file_path <- "path/to/your/file.csv"

# Load the CSV file into a data frame
my_data <- read.csv(file_path)
```

Note: Researchers should replace "*path/to/your/file.csv*" with the actual path to the CSV file. The absolute path or a relative path will work. To make things simpler, save the CSV to the R folder on your computer so the path will not have to be very complex.

To check the working directory for R, use the following code:

```
# Get the current working directory
current_directory <- getwd()

# Print the current working directory
print(current_directory)
```

To change the working directory, use the following code with the path to the desired directory within the quotes:

```
# Set a new working directory
setwd("path/to/your/new/directory")
```

In order to check the data that was loaded, researchers should use the following commands:

```
# Display the structure of the loaded data frame
str(my_data)

# View the first few rows of the data frame
head(my_data)
```

Making sure that the data was loaded into R correctly is a best practice prior to conducting any analysis.

Creating a Sociogram Using a CSV

Once the data has been loaded, it can be prepared for display as a sociogram. The *igraph* package is the most commonly used. Load it using the following code:

```
install.packages("igraph")
library(igraph)
```

Note that R will provide a prompt for the researcher to select a Comprehensive R Archive Network from which to download the package.

Next, enter the following code to prepare the sociogram making sure to enter the name of your CSV file instead of *your_data.csv*:

```
# Load CSV data
edges <- read.csv("your_data.csv")

# Create a graph object from the edge data
graph <- graph_from_data_frame(edges, directed = FALSE)
```

Now the sociogram is ready to display. Use the following command to display it:

```
plot(graph)
```

Note that there are many customizations that can be applied to this step of the process. Changes to the look and feel of the sociogram will be covered in a later section.

Manual Social Network Data Entry

Oftentimes, it is advantageous to create social network data in a CSV format because entering lots of data into Excel is less time-consuming as compared to entering the data directly into R. Researchers who are working with smaller datasets might opt to enter their data directly into R. This section describes how to manually enter social network data in R.

First, make sure to load the *igraph* package if it is not already in the workspace by running the following code:

```
install.packages("igraph")
library(igraph)
```

The next step entails entering the social network data. Sample names have been used in this example and should be replaced with real data that follow the same punctuation format. Manual entry requires data in both the *from* and *to* lines of code which represent the source and target for the SNA. The code is as follows:

```
edges <- data.frame(
    from = c("Alice", "Bob", "Charlie", "Alice"),
    to = c("Bob", "Charlie", "David", "Eve")
)
```

The final step is to create the sociogram and display it using the following lines of code:

```
graph <- graph_from_data_frame(edges, directed = TRUE)
plot(graph)
```

Changing Sociogram Display Properties

There are many ways to change the way that sociograms look within the *igraph* package. Changes to the default display properties can add much value to a sociogram and should be guided by research questions.

Layout Options

The sociogram can be displayed using a variety of different layouts. Each of the options have their own advantages. All of the options are accessed by adding *layout* = to the *plot* property.

The Fruchterman Reingold option is the default option. It is good for simulating a physical system where nodes that are connected are closer to one another and nodes that are not connected appear farther away.

```
plot(graph, layout = layout.fruchterman.reingold)
```

The Kamada Kawai option minimizes the space on the sociogram and tends to place nodes closer together.

```
plot(graph, layout = layout.kamada.kawai)
```

The Circle option lays the nodes out in a circular orientation, which is advantageous for visualizing cyclical relationships.

```
plot(graph, layout = layout.circle)
```

The Random option places the nodes in random positions. This can be useful when trying to explore data and think creatively.

```
plot(graph, layout = layout.random)
```

The Star option will attempt to create a star out of the nodes such that the distance between them is maximized.

```
plot(graph, layout = layout.star)
```

The Grid option attempts to create a grid out of the nodes. This is suitable for exploring data and producing sociograms that are linear in orientation.

```
plot(graph, layout = layout.grid)
```

The Sugiyama option uses the properties of the sociogram (spectral embedding of the adjacency matrix) to determine the node positions.

```
plot(graph, layout = layout.sugiyama)
```

The Reingold Tilford option will arrange the nodes in a tree-like fashion. This can help to visualize hierarchical relationships.

```
plot(graph, layout = layout.reingold.tilford)
```

The Graphopt option will display the nodes while focusing on minimizing the crossings of edges.

```
plot(graph, layout = layout.graphopt)
```

Customizing Node and Edge Attributes

The simple changes to the look of sociograms can be added to *plot(graph)*, the code that displays the sociograms. Adding various properties to this code can adjust the node size, color, and shape. Researchers can also change the edge color, thickness, and arrow styles. Here is an example of the required code:

```
plot(graph,
        vertex.size = 25,
        vertex.color = "lightblue",
        vertex.shape = "square",
        edge.color = "black",
        edge.width = 3,
        edge.arrow.size = 0.5,
        main = "Sociogram Customizations")
```

Export Sociograms as Images

To export a sociogram to an image file in R, researchers must use a special combination of commands that write the sociogram to the image file. The first command opens the data frame by specifying the file type (e.g., png, pdf, jpeg) and file name. The command *dev.off* signals that the input has finished and writes the file. The following is a simple example of where these lines of code should go:

```
# Open a graphics device (e.g., PNG)
png("sociogram.png")

# Plot the sociogram
plot(graph)

# Close the graphics device
dev.off()
```

Note that the *plot(graph)* line of code can contain any number of customizations described in previous sections of this chapter. However, when these commands are used, R will not display the output. It will only write the file. Create the sociogram desired before adding the lines of code that will export it.

A Complete Program

Previous sections have described an entire program that can be used to produce a sociogram in a piecemeal fashion. In order to bring all of these concepts together, here we present a complete picture of what the entire program could look like from loading data to producing an exported file.

```
# Load necessary packages
install.packages("igraph")
library(igraph)
# Load CSV data
edges <- read.csv("your_data.csv")

# Create a graph object from the edge data
graph <- graph_from_data_frame(edges, directed = TRUE)

png("sociogram1.png")

plot(graph, layout = layout.fruchterman.reingold,
     vertex.size = 25,
     vertex.color = "lightblue",
     vertex.shape = "square",
     edge.color = "black",
     edge.width = 3,
     edge.arrow.size = 0.5,
     main = "Sociogram Customizations")

dev.off()
```

Concluding Thoughts: The Value of Learning Communities

SNA is a key method within SLAM because it is flexible enough to illustrate all three components of social presence by focusing on actors of different kinds. To some researchers, it might seem like too much work to produce multiple sociograms over the life of a given learning activity. However, the process by which knowledge is created is of immense value to academic and business concerns. The answer to "how" knowledge is being created is something that can be improved and recreated. The end result is learning communities that can bring immense value to the people within them and to the overall domains in which they exist.

Cross et al. (2006) writes about one value-driven impact of community: "Typically the real value proposition of a community lies with increasing knowledge transfer and learning across some natural fragmentation point in the networks – ties across function, physical distance, expertise, or key projects" (p. 53). People themselves can be assets to people who are having challenges because reaching out and removing the fragmentation is not as expensive as recreating the wheel. Indeed, the process behind creating cohesive learning communities is of great value.

This relates to the IAM in that the SCK can, at times, become bogged down in dissonance. When people are mired in disagreement, they will remain fragmented and caught in cycles of conflict. SLAM can measure this using a sentiment analysis and show how the disagreement is taking place using SNA. The combination of the two analyses will allow researchers to identify ways to break the impasse and help the group reach Phase III. At this point, it can be said that knowledge has been created. Ideally, groups will eventually engage in knowledge validation as well.

As groups reach these higher Phases of the IAM, they are going to produce knowledge assets that are high quality. These knowledge assets can be reused to create more knowledge and, in some instances, they can drive value creation in organizations. At the end of the day, the value proposition of tracking the evolution of the SCK is high. As people build more knowledge, they create knowledge assets that others can use to solve problems more effectively. Subsequent members of a community can enter at any time and make their own contributions to the knowledge assets, which can be tracked with the IAM. Indeed, the cycles of knowledge construction and validation can be effectively tracked with SLAM and using the SNA component of SLAM will show researchers how social presence has contributed to the final production of knowledge. The creation and maintenance of a learning community is the ultimate goal. SLAM, in concert with the IAM, provides the tools.

Research Questions

1. How does the structural composition of a social network influence the flow of information within a community?
2. What are the distinct communities or subgroups within an online social network? How do these communities evolve over time?
3. How do individuals with high centrality and influence within a social network impact decision-making processes or opinions within the community?
4. How do patterns of social interactions and network structures change over time in response to external events or interventions?
5. To what extent do individuals in a social network tend to form connections with others who share similar characteristics or opinions (homophily)?

Conclusion

This chapter described how SNA can be used to explore the social environment associated with SCK. It presented a brief history of sociograms and how other researchers have used the technique. SNA allows researchers to answer questions about "how" knowledge is being constructed. It can also be focused on words and phrases to show how knowledge develops over time. SNA is a powerful technique that can help researchers establish how the social environment influences SCK.

References

Aviv, R., Erlich, Z., Ravid, G., & Geva, A. (2003). Network analysis of knowledge construction in asynchronous learning networks. *Journal of Asynchronous Learning Networks, 7*(3), 1–23.

Cross, R. L., Laseter, T., Parker, A., & Velasquez, G. (2006). Using social network analysis to improve communities of practice. *California Management Review, 49*(1), 32–60.

Cross, R. L., Singer, J., Colella, S., Thomas, R. J., Silverstone, Y., Cokins, G., & Flemming, B. (2010). *The organizational network fieldbook: Best practices, techniques and exercises to drive organizational innovation and performance* (1st ed.). John Wiley & Sons, Incorporated.

Gunawardena, C. N., & Zittle, F. J. (1997). Social presence as a predictor of satisfaction within a computer-mediated conferencing environment. *American Journal of Distance Education, 11*(3), 8–26.

Hansen, D. L., Smith, M. A., Schneiderman, B., & Himelboim, I. (2020). *Analyzing social media networks with NodeXL: Insights from a connected world* (2nd ed.) [Book]. Morgan Kaufmann.

Haythornthwaite, C. (1996). Social network analysis: An approach and technique for the study of information exchange. *Library & Information Science Research, 18*(4), 323–342. www.sciencedirect.com/science/article/pii/S0740818896900031

Heo, H., Lim, K. Y., & Kim, Y. (2010). Exploratory study on the patterns of online interaction and knowledge co-construction in project-based learning. *Computers & Education, 55*(3), 1383–1392.

Howell-Richardson, C., & Mellar, H. (1996). A methodology for the analysis of patterns of participation within computer mediated communication courses. *Instructional Science, 24*(1), 47–69. www.jstor.org.libproxy.unm.edu/stable/23371467

Laat, M., Lally, V., Lipponen, L., & Simons, R.-J. (2007). Online teaching in networked learning communities: A multi-method approach to studying the role of the teacher. *Instructional Science, 35*(3), 257–286. http://download.springer.com/static/pdf/719/art%253A10.100 7%252Fs11251-006-9007-0.pdf?auth66=1422390996_b71318d7ecb58861006b8a3d82e2b97c&ext=.pdf

Levin, J. A., Kim, H., & Riel, M. M. (1990). Analyzing instructional interactions on electronic message networks. In L. M. Harasim (Ed.), *Online education: Perspectives on a new environment*. Praeger.

Lin, X., Hu, X., Hu, Q., & Liu, Z. (2016). A social network analysis of teaching and research collaboration in a teachers' virtual learning community. *British Journal of Educational Technology, 47*(2), 302–319.

Martinez, A., Dimitriadis, Y., Rubia, B., Gomez, E., & de la Fuente, P. (2003). Combining qualitative evaluation and social network analysis for the study of classroom social interactions. *Computers & Education, 41*(4).

Moreno, J. L. (1951). *Sociometry, experimental method and the science of society*. Beacon House.

Moreno, J. L. (1953). *Who shall survive? Foundations of sociometry, group psychotherapy and socio-drama* (2nd ed.). Beacon House, Inc.

Nolte, J. (2014). *The philosophy, theory and methods of J. L. Moreno: The man who tried to become God*. Taylor & Francis Group. http://ebookcentral.proquest.com/lib/unm/detail.action?docID=1707400

Ujwary-Gil, A. (2020). *Organizational network analysis: Auditing intangible resources*. Routledge.

Wasserman, S., & Faust, K. (1994). *Social network analysis: Methods and applications*. Cambridge University Press.

11 Natural Language Processing

Natural language processing (NLP) is a multidisciplinary subfield of computer science and computational linguistics that bridges the gap between human language and machine understanding and is a growing research area in the educational and learning sciences (Shaik et al., 2022; Wu et al., 2024). It encompasses a range of techniques designed to allow computers to interpret, generate, and process human (natural) language in a meaningful way. This involves tasks such as understanding the semantic and syntactic aspects of text, extracting relevant information, analyzing sentiment and thematic trends, and even generating text that mimics human communication. NLP leverages machine learning, linguistics, and artificial intelligence to tackle these complex challenges, enabling more intuitive and effective interactions between humans and machines.

In the context of social media platforms, where textual data is abundant and the social construction of knowledge (SCK) is a dynamic process, NLP proves to be an invaluable tool for researchers. It offers the capability to analyze vast datasets at scale, identifying patterns, trends, and the evolution of discussions over time. By employing techniques like sentiment analysis, topic modeling, and entity recognition, NLP helps in understanding the emotional tone, underlying themes, and key actors within online communities. This analysis provides insights into how sentiments, biases, and differing perspectives contribute to the social dynamics of knowledge construction.

Moreover, NLP facilitates the exploration of how language is used within specific communities, revealing linguistic characteristics, discourse structures, and argumentation patterns. This aids researchers in mapping out networks of interaction, understanding the flow of information, and identifying the key influencers and the roles they play in shaping public opinion and knowledge. Through automated moderation and detection, NLP also assists in maintaining the integrity of discussions by identifying inappropriate or harmful content.

Overall, the integration of NLP in studying SCK on social media opens up new avenues for researchers to decipher the complex interplay of language, culture, and social interaction online. It not only automates the extraction and analysis of data but also enriches the qualitative understanding of digital communities, offering comprehensive insights into the ways in which knowledge, opinions, and norms are established, contested, and evolved in the digital age.

The general steps in doing NLP, also known as a pipeline, are:

1. **Data Collection and Preprocessing:**
   - **Collection:** Gather textual data from social media platforms, focusing on posts, comments, and replies from specific subreddits or threads relevant to the study. We covered data collection in Chapter 5 on social media platforms for SCK.

DOI: 10.4324/9781003324461-14

- **Cleaning:** Remove unnecessary elements like special characters, URLs, stop words, HTML tags, and normalize text through techniques such as stemming, lemmatization, and lowercasing to prepare the data for analysis. We covered some data cleaning in Chapter 9 during the clustering of data.

2. **Text Analysis and Normalization:**

- **Tokenization:** Break down the cleaned text data into manageable units (words, phrases, or sentences) for detailed analysis.
- **Part-of-Speech (POS) Tagging and Named Entity Recognition (NER):** Identify the grammatical role of each word and classify key elements (names of people, places, etc.) to extract meaningful information and ensure uniformity.

3. **Feature Extraction and Semantic Analysis:**

- **Dependency Parsing:** Analyze the grammatical structure to identify relationships between words, crucial for understanding sentence context.
- **Sentiment Analysis:** Determine the sentiment (positive, negative, neutral) toward topics discussed, providing insights into community attitudes. Sentiment analysis is covered in Chapter 8.
- **Topic Modeling:** Identify and track main ideas or themes across the corpus, using algorithms like Latent Dirichlet Allocation (LDA), to understand evolving discussion points.

4. **Advanced Analysis and Insight Extraction:**

- **Word Embeddings and Relationship Extraction:** Use numerical vector representations to capture word meanings and their relations, and extract relationships between entities and concepts through dependency parsing, NER, and coreference resolution.
- **Social Network Analysis (Optional):** Depending on the research focus, integrate techniques to examine connections between users, topics, and sentiments, revealing community dynamics and influence patterns. Social network analysis is covered in Chapter 10.

5. **Evaluation, Visualization, and Reporting:**

- **Evaluation:** Assess the accuracy and quality of the analysis by comparing it against ground truth data or human annotations.
- **Visualization and Interpretation:** Present the analyzed data through intuitive visual formats (charts, graphs) to facilitate understanding. Interpret findings in the context of SCK, highlighting influential contributors, discussion themes, and shifts in sentiment.

This pipeline combines data preparation, in-depth text and semantic analysis, and advanced techniques for insight extraction, making it highly adaptable and suitable for researching complex interactions and knowledge construction in online communities.

The following sections cover how to do the various NLP techniques not covered in other chapters.

Tokenization

Tokenization is the process of breaking down a text into smaller units called tokens. Generally, it is taking a sentence and splitting it into individual words although tokenization can also involve splitting the text into smaller units like characters. Each word or character becomes a token, which can then be analyzed or processed further. Tokenization is a fundamental step in NLP because it helps to organize and understand the structure of text data.

The most basic and common form of tokenization uses spaces to separate text into individual words. This is known as space tokenization.

```
# Tokenize the text
text = "Tokenization is the process of breaking down a text into smaller units
called tokens."

tokens = strsplit(text, ' ')
# Print the tokens
print(tokens)
```

This code produces the following output in Figure 11.1:

```
[[1]]
 [1] "Tokenization"    "is"       "the"      "process"   "of"
 [6] "breaking"        "down"     "a"        "text"      "into"
[11] "smaller"         "units"    "called"   "tokens."
```

Figure 11.1 The result of tokenizing – all the unique words in a input

To tokenize a data frame where each document is a row in the column "text," the code is similar:

```
df = read.csv('using-ai-in-schools.csv', encoding = 'UTF-8')
tokenized_text = strsplit(df$text, ' ')
```

This produces a list with the same number of rows as the data frame but with each row also a list of words. Once you have a list of words, you can create a table of word frequencies and sort this table in decreasing order. The *wordcloud* package can then be used to plot a word cloud as shown in Figure 11.2.

```
all_tokens = unlist(tokenized_text)
sorted_tokens = sort(table(all_tokens), decreasing = TRUE)
wordcloud(names(sorted_tokens[1:25]),
    wordcloud(names(sorted_tokens[1:25]), sorted_tokens[1:25], color = "blue",
scale = c(4, 1), random.order = FALSE, rot.per = 0, center = TRUE)
```

Figure 11.2 A word cloud depicting the frequencies of tokens (words)

Parts-of-Speech Tagging

Parts-of-speech (POS) tagging is the process of assigning a grammatical category (such as noun, verb, adjective, etc.) to each word in a given text.

The R *udpipe* package contains an easy-to-use POS tagger that works on multiple languages. To use it, first download the package and the model for the language of your data.

```
# If you haven't done so: install.packages("udpipe")


library(udpipe)

# Download the English model if it's not already downloaded
ud_model = udpipe_download_model(language = "english")
```

The key function is *udpipe_annotate()*, which takes as parameters a language model, and a sentence, and returns an annotation that contains the parts of speech for the sentence shown in Figure 11.3:

```
ud_model$file_model

# Load the model
```

```
ud_model = udpipe_load_model(ud_model$file_model)

# The text to be tagged
text = "The quick brown fox jumps over the lazy dog."

# Tag words
annotation = udpipe_annotate(ud_model, x = text)

# Convert the tags to a data frame
df = as.data.frame(annotation)

# Print the data frame
print(df)
```

sentence <chr>	token_id <chr>	token <chr>	lemma <chr>	upos <chr>
The quick brown fox jumps over the lazy dog.	1	The	The	DET
The quick brown fox jumps over the lazy dog.	2	quick	quick	ADJ
The quick brown fox jumps over the lazy dog.	3	brown	brown	ADJ
The quick brown fox jumps over the lazy dog.	4	fox	fox	NOUN
The quick brown fox jumps over the lazy dog.	5	junps	junps	VERB
The quick brown fox jumps over the lazy dog.	6	over	over	ADP
The quick brown fox jumps over the lazy dog.	7	the	the	DET
The quick brown fox jumps over the lazy dog.	8	lazy	lazy	ADJ
The quick brown fox jumps over the lazy dog.	9	dog	dog	NOUN
The quick brown fox jumps over the lazy dog.	10	.	.	PUNCT

Figure 11.3 A data frame of words (column: token) and their parts-of-speech (upos)

Dependency Relationships, Dependency Parsing, and Dependency Parse Tree

In the context of NLP, a dependency relationship is a grammatical relationship between words in a sentence.

In a dependency relationship, one word (the "head") governs or determines the syntactic role of another word (the "dependent"). For example, in the sentence "The cat sat on the mat," "sat" is the head of "cat" and "mat," indicating that "cat" and "mat" depend on "sat" for their roles in the sentence.

To determine a dependency relationship, you do dependency parsing, using algorithms that identify these relationships. The output of a dependency parse is typically a tree-like structure or network (dependency graph) that illustrates these dependencies, which aids in understanding sentence structure.

Dependency parsing is particularly useful for languages where word order can vary, as it focuses on the relationships between words rather than their positions in the sentence. It is a fundamental technique in NLP and plays a pivotal role in understanding the grammatical structure of sentences.

In addition to POS tagging, the *udp_annotate* function also does dependency parsing and one can store this information in the data frame along with the POS tags as shown in Figure 11.4.

head_token_id <chr>	dep_rel <chr>	deps <chr>	misc <chr>
4	det	*NA*	*NA*
4	amod	*NA*	*NA*
4	amod	*NA*	*NA*
5	nsubj	*NA*	*NA*
0	root	*NA*	*NA*
9	case	*NA*	*NA*
9	det	*NA*	*NA*
9	amod	*NA*	*NA*
5	obl	*NA*	SpaceAfter=No
5	punct	*NA*	SpacesAfter=\\n

Figure 11.4 A word dependency data frame denoting relationships between words

The following code will plot a dependency graph based on an annotated data frame. The output is shown in Figure 11.5.

Named Entity Recognition

Named entity recognition (NER) is a subtask of information extraction that seeks to locate and classify named entities in text into predefined categories such as person names,

```
# www.r-bloggers.com/2019/07/dependency-parsing-with-udpipe/#google_vignette
library(igraph)
library(ggraph)
library(ggplot2)

plot_annotation <- function(x, size = 3){
  stopifnot(is.data.frame(x) & all(c("sentence_id", "token_id", "head_token_id",
  "dep_rel",
            "token_id", "token", "lemma", "upos", "xpos", "feats") %in%
            colnames(x)))
  x <- x[!is.na(x$head_token_id),]
  x <- x[x$sentence_id %in% min(x$sentence_id),]
  edges <- x[x$head_token_id!= 0, c("token_id", "head_token_id", "dep_rel")]
  edges$label <- edges$dep_rel
  g <- graph_from_data_frame(edges,
            vertices = x[, c("token_id", "token", "lemma", "upos", "xpos",
            "feats")],
            directed = TRUE)
  ggraph(g, layout = "linear") +
    geom_edge_arc(ggplot2::aes(label = dep_rel, vjust = -0.20),
        arrow = grid::arrow(length = unit(4, 'mm'), ends = "last", type =
        "closed"),
        end_cap = ggraph::label_rect("wordswordswords"),
        label_colour = "red", check_overlap = TRUE, label_size = size) +
```

```
    geom_node_label(ggplot2::aes(label = token), col = "darkgreen", size = size,
    fontface = "bold") +
    geom_node_text(ggplot2::aes(label = upos), nudge_y = -0.35, size = size) +
    theme_graph(base_family = "Arial Narrow") +
    labs(title = "udpipe output", subtitle = "tokenisation, parts of speech tagging &
    dependency relations")
}
plot_annotation(df)
```

udpipe output

tokenisation, parts of speech tagging & dependency relations

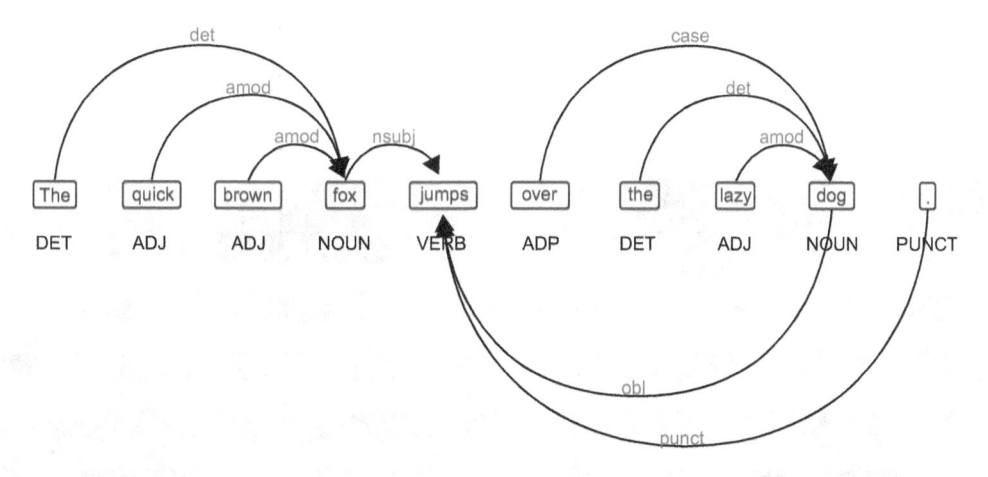

Figure 11.5 A dependency graph depicting the relationship between words

organizations, locations, medical codes, time expressions, quantities, monetary values, percentages, etc. It is a key component in many NLP systems and has a wide range of applications, including question answering, text summarization, and machine translation.

NER can be incredibly useful for researchers studying SCK in discussions on social media platforms like Reddit. Here's how:

1. **Identifying Key Entities.** NER can help identify key entities such as people, organizations, locations, and other relevant categories within the discussion. This can provide insights into the main topics of conversation and how they are interconnected.
2. **Tracking Conversations Over Time.** By identifying these entities, researchers can track how conversations about these entities evolve over time. This can reveal trends, shifts in sentiment, and the emergence of new ideas or topics.
3. **Understanding Context.** NER can help researchers understand the context of discussions. For example, if a person's name is mentioned, are they being discussed in a positive, negative, or neutral light? What other entities are mentioned in conjunction with them? This can provide a deeper understanding of the social dynamics at play.

4. **Network Analysis.** By identifying relationships between entities, NER can facilitate network analysis. This can reveal which entities are central to a discussion and how different entities are related to each other.
5. **Scaling Up Analysis.** Manual analysis of social media data can be time-consuming and impractical, especially when dealing with large volumes of data. NER allows researchers to automate part of the analysis, making it possible to study larger datasets and identify patterns that might not be apparent from a smaller sample.

In summary, NER is a powerful tool for social science research enabling researchers to extract meaningful information from large volumes of text data, uncovering patterns and trends, and gaining insights into SCK.

While *udpipe* can do NER, a common package in both R and python for doing NER and other NLP tasks is *spacy (python)* and *spacyr (R)*, respectively:

```r
# Install and load the necessary packages
library(spacyr)
spacy_install()
```

doc_id <chr>	sentence_id <chr>	token_id <chr>	token <chr>	lemma <chr>	pos <chr>	head_token_id <dbl>
text1	1	1	Luke	Luke	PROPN	2
text1	1	2	Skywalker	Skywalker	PROPN	3
text1	1	3	is	is	AUX	3
text1	1	4	a	a	DET	5
text1	1	5	character	character	NOUN	3
text1	1	6	in	in	ADP	5
text1	1	7	Star	Star	PROPN	8
text1	1	8	Wars	Wars	PROPN	6
text1	1	9	.	.	PUNCT	3

Figure 11.6 A named-entity data frame – named entities are labelled in the "pos" column as PROPN

Once installed, you can load the language your dataset is in, and call the function *spacy_parse* with a sentence, which will return a data frame with each word that is a named entity, tagged with PROPN (short for proper name; see Figure 11.6).

```r
# Initialize spacyr with the English model
spacy_initialize(model = "en_core_web_sm")

# The text to be parsed
text = "Luke Skywalker is a character in Star Wars."

# Perform NER and dependency parsing
parsed_text = spacy_parse(text, dependency = TRUE, entity = TRUE)

# Print the parsed text
print(parsed_text)
```

Topic Modeling

Topic modeling is a type of statistical modeling used in NLP and machine learning to discover hidden semantic structures in a text corpus. It's an unsupervised method that automatically identifies topics that exist within a collection of documents.

In the context of studying SCK on platforms like Reddit, topic modeling can be particularly useful. Here is why:

1. **Discovering Themes.** Topic modeling can help identify common themes or topics in large volumes of text data, such as Reddit comments or posts. This can provide insights into what subjects are being discussed and how these discussions contribute to the construction of knowledge.
2. **Understanding Trends Over Time**. By applying topic modeling to data from different time periods, researchers can track how discussions and knowledge construction evolve over time.
3. **Comparing Communities.** Different subreddits may have different dominant topics. Topic modeling can help compare these communities and understand their unique characteristics.
4. **Scaling Up Analysis.** Manual analysis of social media data can be time-consuming and impractical, especially when dealing with large volumes of data. Topic modeling allows researchers to automate part of the analysis, making it possible to study larger datasets and identify patterns that might not be apparent from a smaller sample.

In summary, topic modeling is a powerful tool for researchers studying SCK on social media platforms. It enables them to extract meaningful information from large volumes of text data, uncover patterns and trends, and gain insights into the social dynamics at play.

To do topic modeling, first install the topic modeling package:

```
if (!require(topicmodels)) {
  install.packages("topicmodels")
}
library(topicmodels)
```

Then it is a simple matter of calling the LDA function with the number of topics you would like to divide the text into, and the terms function to get the number of words you would like to see for each topic (see Figure 11.7):

```
library(tm)
corpus = Corpus(VectorSource(df$text))

### Data Cleaning


# Preprocess the text data
corpus <- tm_map(corpus, content_transformer(tolower))
corpus <- tm_map(corpus, removePunctuation)
```

```
corpus <- tm_map(corpus, removeNumbers)
corpus <- tm_map(corpus, removeWords, stopwords("english"))
corpus <- tm_map(corpus, stripWhitespace)


dtm = DocumentTermMatrix(corpus)
mat = as.matrix(dtm)
zero_rows = rowSums(mat) == 0

# Remove these rows from the DTM
dtm = dtm[!zero_rows,]

# Perform LDA with 5 topics
lda_model = LDA(dtm, k = 5)

# Get the terms for each topic
terms(lda_model, 25)
```

[1,] "like"	"calculator"	"students"	"use"	"just"
[2,] "write"	"can"	"can"	"just"	"write"
[3,] "can"	"essay"	"critical"	"like"	"work"
[4,] "good"	"s"	"chatgpt"	"people"	"school"
[5,] "time"	"time"	"learning"	"point"	"can"
[6,] "essay"	"way"	"thinking"	"think"	"class"
[7,] "well"	"kids"	"great"	"now"	"see"
[8,] "just"	"write"	"work"	"school"	"homework"
[9,] "kids"	"school"	"know"	"going"	"even"
[10,] "chatgpt"	"know"	"just"	"learning"	"imagine"
[11,] "s"	"take"	"learn"	"dont"	"essays"
[12,] "paper"	"essays"	"use"	"class"	"like"
[13,] "basic"	"still"	"like"	"will"	"raed"
[14,] "papers"	"math"	"think"	"way"	"also"
[15,] "information"	"will"	"using"	"part"	"teacher"
[16,] "teach"	"just"	"need"	"makes"	"please"
[17,] "really"	"writing"	"even"	"students"	"college"
[18,] "even"	"people"	"dont"	"know"	"long"
[19,] "get"	"paper"	"essays"	"teaching"	"time"
[20,] "writing"	"actually"	"point"	"s"	"going"
[21,] "now"	"dont"	"calculators"	"tool"	"back"
[22,] "idea"	"idea"	"instead"	"work"	"home"
[23,] "thats"	"critique"	"will"	"sense"	"now"
[24,] "article"	"thing"	"make"	"thing"	"students"
[25,] "cringe"	"one"	"deleted"	"need"	"essay"

Figure 11.7 The output of topic modeling. Each column represents a topic, and the words in a column are the most common words found in that topic. The analyst must still determine a topic label.

Conclusion

Two key issues confront researchers studying SCK: (1) what topics are the participants discussing and (2) how are they structuring their communications to advance either their own understanding or the group's understanding of the topic? This chapter examined different methods for discovering and visualizing the topics and the communication structure in a group of related postings. The methods included: word and N-gram frequency analysis, topic modeling using LDA, and parsing sentences to create POS trees. Finally, the chapter discussed the benefits and drawbacks of the various methods.

References

Shaik, T., Tao, X., Li, Y., Dann, C., McDonald, J., Redmond, P., & Galligan, L. (2022). A review of the trends and challenges in adopting natural language processing methods for education feedback analysis. *IEEE Access*, *10*, 56720–56739. IEEE Access. https://doi.org/10.1109/ACCESS.2022.3177752

Wu, H., Li, S., Gao, Y., Weng, J., & Ding, G. (2024). Natural language processing in educational research: The evolution of research topics. *Education and Information Technologies*, 1–27.

12 Classifications and Predictive Analytics of the Social Environment

A prediction is a statement about future events that have not yet happened. Predictive analytics is the process of generating a prediction using historical data, and it is a core practice in educational research (Doleck et al., 2020; Gunawardena et al., 2023; Sghir et al., 2022). For social construction of knowledge (SCK) researchers, whose data typically consists of discussions on class forums or social media, predictive analytics can be valuable in several ways. For instance, it can help identify words, phrases, questions, or rhetorical patterns that contribute to successful learning outcomes. Beyond analyzing the content of postings, predictive analytics can also be applied to examine interactions between discussants – such as the frequency and sequence of replies – and assess how these variables correlate with deeper levels of understanding or phases of knowledge construction.

The general steps are

1. **Data Mining.** Collect historical data relevant to what you are trying to predict. For example, suppose you wanted to predict whether it will rain tomorrow. For the data mining stage, you would collect historical daily data, including temperature, humidity, and cloudiness levels as well as whether it rained on those days.
2. **Data Wrangling.** Prepare (encode) the data by transforming it in a format suitable for processing. Continuing with our weather example, you might convert qualitative observations into quantitative data. For instance, you could translate cloudiness descriptions like "clear," "some clouds," "cloudy," "very cloudy," and "overcast" into numerical values like 0, 0.25, 0.50, 0.75, and 1, respectively. Similarly, "sunny" and "rained" could be converted to 0 and 1, respectively.
3. **Data Analysis.** Apply either statistical or machine learning algorithms on the data yielding a result. Again, continuing with our rain example, you could use a logistic regression, which takes all your historical data and returns a value between 0 and 1, indicating the likelihood of rain.
4. **Data Interpretation.** Explain the result in the context of your data, that is, decode the data as a meaningful prediction. With the weather example, you would translate the results of the logistic regression into actionable predictions. For instance, you might decide that a result below 0.25 means "no chance of rain," a result between 0.25 and 0.75 suggests "a slight chance of rain," and a result from 0.75 to 1 indicates "likely to rain."

DOI: 10.4324/9781003324461-15

The specific data analytic method you use depends on whether your variables are continuous or categorical. Generally, you have two kinds of variables: predictors (also known as independent variables) and outcomes (also known as dependent variables).

- **Continuous Variables.** These are numerical and can take any value within a range. In our weather example, the continuous variables were temperature and humidity. When dealing with continuous variables, a common technique is regression, which is used to predict continuous outcomes based on one or more continuous predictors.
- **Categorical Variables.** These represent discrete categories or groups. In our weather example, the categorical variables were cloudiness and whether or not it rained. Generally categorical variables are given labels instead of numbers and must be converted to numbers when used in analytics. Common techniques when using categorical variables include naïve Bayes or neural networks.

The focus of this chapter will be on predictive analytics using regression analysis. Chapter 14 will explore the use of naïve Bayes for classification and category prediction.

Regression

Suppose you are a SCK researcher, and while reading a transcript, you notice that posts with high degrees of praise seem to be shorter in length than other posts. You also observe that posts that are overly academic sounding are shorter than others. Finally, you note in an academic discussion that posts with a positive overall tone, praise, and academic language seem to be longer in terms of word count. You wonder if this is true. In essence, you are asking the research question: do posts with high praise, academic words, and a positive tone affect the length of a post?

Regression analysis is a statistical method used to examine the relationship between an outcome that you are interested in, also known as a dependent variable (DV), and one or more believed predictors, also known as independent variables (IVs). In our discussion board example, the outcome we are interested in (the DV) is post length, and what we believe predicts that outcome (the IVs) are posts with a positive tone, posts with praise, and posts that sound academic. From here on, for the sake of clarity, we'll use predictors and outcomes instead of IVs and DVs, respectively.

Regression analysis tells you whether a predictor has a measurable or significant effect on an outcome and, if so, the extent to which a predictor contributes to the outcome. In the context of our discussion board example, regression analysis will let us know whether any of our proposed predictors (positive tone, praise, academic sounding) affect our outcome of interest (post length) and to what extent. A statistically significant effect in this context indicates that the effect of a predictor on an outcome is unlikely due to chance and instead represents an actual influence.

A key benefit of regression analysis for SCK researchers is that it allows us to test hypotheses systematically and with statistical confidence, enabling us to determine the strength and significance of various predictors that might influence the outcomes we are interested in. An important application of regression results to the design of instructional systems or processes is to emphasize predictors with significant influence to enhance learning outcomes.

Example

To help make the concepts of regression analysis actionable, we will explore an example based on our discussion board scenario mentioned in the introduction. This example will guide you through each step of the regression analysis process, from encoding the predictors to decoding an interpretation of the results. Specifically, by applying regression techniques to analyze the impact of positive tone, praise, and academic language on post length, we will demonstrate how researchers can systematically test hypotheses and derive meaningful insights. This practical illustration will highlight how regression analysis can be applied to real-world situations, particularly in the context of designing instructional systems and enhancing learning outcomes.

To recap, our research question can be stated as: Do post characteristics such as positive tone, praise, and academic language affect post length?

To build a predictive model of this research question, you have to break it down into hypotheses, which are testable representations of your research question. Based on your observations, your hypotheses are

1. Posts with high levels of praise lead to shorter posts.
2. Posts with a scholarly tone led to shorter posts.
3. Posts with an overall positive tone led to longer posts.

It is common to represent hypotheses using a path diagram like in Figure 12.1. This diagram depicts the hypothesized relationships between predictors (e.g., characteristics of posts) and the outcome (e.g., post lengths). Each arrow in the diagram indicates a hypothesized influence, where the predictor labeled at the base of the arrow is expected to affect the outcome labeled at the tip of the arrow. Arrow annotation, such as "+" or "−", along each arrow specify whether the effect is positive or negative. For example, the arrow from "praise" to "post length," annotated with a "−", represents Hypothesis 1, suggesting that higher levels of praise are expected to result in shorter posts.

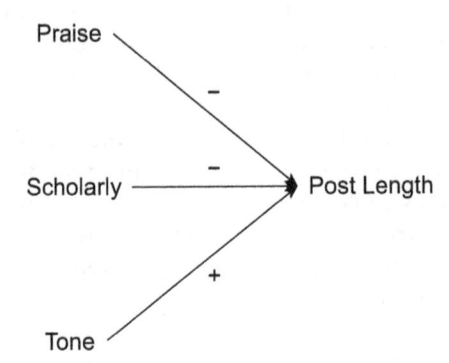

Figure 12.1 A path diagram representing hypothesized relationships between independent and dependent variables (see text for explanation)

Example of Performing a Regression Analysis

For this example, we will use the IAM42 dataset on https://github.com/knowledge-construction/slam-ai/blob/master/Chapter-12/IAM42.csv. This is a collection of 42 posts from a graduate course on eLearning, where the instructor prompted the students to discuss their definitions of culture and eLearning. The data consists of two columns: the user who posted the message (column: user) and the message itself (column: text).

Before reading in this dataset, let us first import all the packages needed to perform a basic regression analysis:

```
# For reading and wrangling data
import pandas as pd # for reading data frames
import regex as re # for data cleaning

# For sentiment analysis
import nltk
from nltk.sentiment.vader import SentimentIntensityAnalyzer
nltk.download("vader_lexicon") # positive negative and netural words

# For regressions
import numpy as np
import sklearn as sk
from sklearn.linear_model import LinearRegression
from sklearn import metrics
import statsmodels.api as sm
```

Next, we read in the dataset as a data frame into a variable df:

```
# Read in dataset
filename = 'IAM42.csv'
foldpath = '.' #. is folder of notebook. Note: no trailing slash
filepath = f'{foldpath}/{filename}'
df = pd.read_csv(filepath)
```

Before performing regression analysis, we need to do some data wrangling. Specifically, because regression analysis requires numerical values for the variables praise, scholarly tone, overall tone, and post length, we need to encode the text of a given post into numerical values representing these variables. While we could manually assign values (e.g., 1 for high, 0.5 for medium, and 0 for low), this method would be impractical for longer discussions, especially in social media contexts that can have thousands of posts.

One automated method to assign values to praise, scholarly tone, and overall tone is to use a sentiment analysis package. We can represent praise in terms of positive sentiment, scholarly tone in terms of neutral sentiment, and overall tone in terms of composite sentiment (the difference between positive and negative sentiment).

Finally, to assign a value to post length, we can write code to automatically count the number of words in a post.

The following code creates a sentiment analyzer *(sia)*, demonstrates how to use the sentiment analyzer, and shows how to count the number of words in a post.

```
# Create a sentiment analysis object
sia = SentimentIntensityAnalyzer()

# Example sentiment scores for positive text
text = "I love this movie! So awesome. Best ever."
score = sia.polarity_scores(text)
print(text)
print(f'Positive Sentiment Score: {score['pos']}')
print(f'Negative Sentiment Score: {score['neg']}')
print(f'Neutral Sentiment Score: {score['neg']}')
print(f'Compound Sentiment Score: {score['compound']}')

# Example sentiment scores for negative text
text = "I absolutely hate this movie!"
score = sia.polarity_scores(text)
print(f'\n{text}')
print(f'Positive Sentiment Score: {score['pos']}')
print(f'Negative Sentiment Score: {score['neg']}')
print(f'Neutral Sentiment Score: {score['neg']}')
print(f'Compound Sentiment Score: {score['compound']}')

# Example sentiment scores for neutral text
text = "This movie was both good and bad."
score = sia.polarity_scores(text)
print(f'\n{text}')
print(f'Positive Sentiment Score: {score['pos']}')
print(f'Negative Sentiment Score: {score['neg']}')
print(f'Neutral Sentiment Score: {score['neu']}')
print(f'Compound Sentiment Score: {score['compound']}')

# Example how to remove extraneous spaces and count words
clean_text = re.sub(r'\s{2,}', ' ', text) # multiple space to one space
print(f'\nOriginal: {text}\nClean: {clean_text}')
word_count = len(clean_text.split(' '))
print(f'Post length: {word_count}')
```

This returns the following results:

```
I love this movie! So awesome. Best ever.
Positive Sentiment Score: 0.77
```

```
Negative Sentiment Score: 0.0
Neutral Sentiment Score: 0.0
Compound Sentiment Score: 0.9367

I absolutely hate this movie!
Positive Sentiment Score: 0.0
Negative Sentiment Score: 0.588
Neutral Sentiment Score: 0.588
Compound Sentiment Score: -0.6468

This movie was both good and bad.
Positive Sentiment Score: 0.254
Negative Sentiment Score: 0.307
Neutral Sentiment Score: 0.439
Compound Sentiment Score: -0.1531

Original: This movie was both good and bad.
Clean: This movie was both good and bad.
Post length: 7
```

With a way to measure predictors and outcomes, we can now conduct the regression analysis:

```
# measure the predictors (independent variables)
scholarly_tone = [sia.polarity_scores(post)['neu'] for post in df.text]
praise = [sia.polarity_scores(post)['pos'] for post in df.text]
overall_tone = [sia.polarity_scores(post)['compound'] for post in df.text]

# measure the outcome
post_length = [len((re.sub(r'/s{2,}', ' ', post)).split(' ')) for post in df.text]

# Create a data frame with the predictors and outcome
df_xy = pd.DataFrame({
    'scholarly_tone' : scholarly_tone,
    'praise' : praise,
    'overall_tone' : overall_tone,
    'post_length' : post_length
})
# Assign predictors to X and outcome to Y
X = df_xy[['scholarly_tone', 'praise', 'overall_tone']]
Y = df_xy[['post_length']]
X2 = sm.add_constant(X) # add an extra constant for the intercept

# Perform regression
est = sm.OLS(Y, X2) # perform regression
```

```
est2 = est.fit() # validate regression
est2.summary() # summarize regression
```

The analysis returns the following results:

```
OLS Regression Results
Dep. Variable: post_length R-squared: 0.367
Model: OLS Adj. R-squared: 0.317


. . .


coef            std      err      t      P>|t|   [0.025     0.975]
const           2864.6012 705.333  4.061  0.000   1436.729   4292.473
scholarly_tone  -2791.2399 737.526 -3.785  0.001   -4284.283 -1298.197
praise          -3586.9337 880.482 -4.074  0.000   -5369.376 -1804.491
overall_tone    226.1354   53.069  4.261  0.000   118.702    333.569
```

The R-squared is approximately 32%, which means scholarly tone, praise, and overall tone account for 32% of the variance in the length of a post. Each predictor is significant, with $p < 0.001$ (see P > |t| column).

Given the regression analysis, we can assert that the results support our hypotheses, as they have not been rejected. Specifically, a scholarly tone has a negative effect on the length of posts, praise also has a negative effect on post length, and overall tone has a positive effect on post length.

The results of this regression analysis demonstrate the practical application of predictive analytics in examining the factors influencing post length in an academic discussion. With a clear understanding of how each predictor – scholarly tone, praise, and overall tone – contributes to the variability in post length, researchers can gain valuable insights into the dynamics of online discourse. This example not only illustrates the steps involved in conducting a regression analysis but also underscores the importance of data-driven decision-making in the design of instructional systems. By systematically analyzing textual data, educators and researchers can identify key factors that enhance or hinder communication effectiveness, ultimately leading to more informed strategies for improving learning outcomes.

Interaction Analysis Model (IAM) Example

Often our regressions involve counting the occurrence of features in posts. When counting items rather than measuring a continuous variable, Poisson regressions are often used. Poisson regression is particularly appropriate when the dependent variable consists of non-negative integer counts, and the mean of these counts is relatively small. It models the log of the expected count as a linear combination of the predictor variables, making it a valuable tool for analyzing the frequency of occurrences in data like posts. Next, we apply Poisson regression analysis to an IAM research question (based on the analysis by Megli et al., 2023): Do IAM researchers use signaling words and phrases to determine the IAM Phases in a post?

If analysts use specific phrases within postings to classify the IAM Phase of a post, a computer-automated program should be able to use the same process to classify posts. Thus, the hypotheses driving the research question are:

1. The number of Phase I signaling words and phrases positively influences an IAM researcher's count of Phase I phrases.
2. The number of Phase II signaling words and phrases positively influences an IAM researcher's count of Phase II phrases.
3. The number of Phase III signaling words and phrases positively influences an IAM researcher's count of Phase III phrases.
4. The number of Phase IV signaling words and phrases positively influences an IAM researcher's count of Phase IV phrases.
5. The number of Phase V signaling words and phrases positively influences an IAM researcher's count of Phase V phrases.

The research team depicted these hypotheses graphically in the path diagram shown in Figure 12.2.

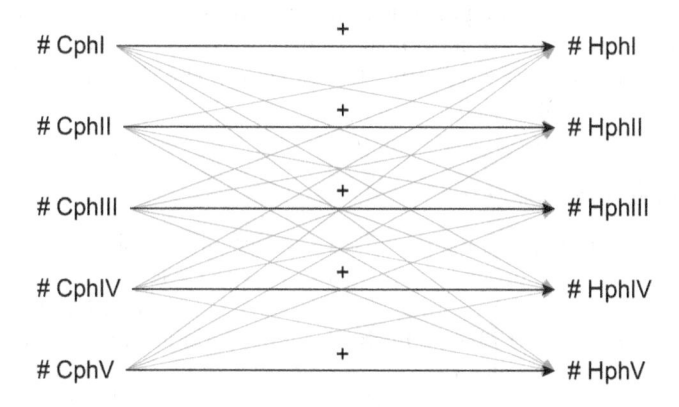

Figure 12.2 The path diagram denoting the hypotheses that counts of signaling phrases positively influence a human coder's counts of phrases for a given IAM Phase

Path Model Note. We hypothesized that there is a positive relationship between the computer phrase counts and the human Phase counts for a corresponding IAM Phase. Cph is coded IAM Phase (I–V) and Hph is hypothesized IAM Phase (I–V).

The following quantitative methods were applied to the lexicon developed for the IAM Phases.

Method

The study was pursued to explore the development of an algorithm based on a lexicon to automate the IAM analysis process. After the IAM doctoral-level student researchers coded the three discussions, assigning posts to IAM Phases and totaling the number of assignments into separate columns, the identified posts were put into an R script. An R script, using the five files of signaling phrases, counted how many times a phrase appeared in a posting, and placed the total in five separate columns denoting the five IAM Phases. This was done using a lexicon classifier that takes as input the lexicon and a discussion thread. For each post in the thread, the classifier searches within the post for all the phrases in each of the five Phases. Each time a phrase is found, the classifier increments the Phase counter by 1. The result is a count of phrases found for each of the five Phases.

The research team then used a Poisson regression model in R to predict the counts of each Phase within the three transcripts separately and all three combined. Five separate regressions were run with doctoral-level student researcher totals, apI, apII, apIII, apIV, and apV, as the outcome (dependent) variables, and the computer counts, cpI, cpII, cpIII, cpIV, and cpV, as the predictor (independent) variables. All regressions were conducted using an alpha value of 0.05. The research team combined feature analysis, also referred to as aspect analysis, and regressions to test our path model and validate our lexicon.

Data

The data consisted of 157 postings from three separate discussions that contained 35, 48, and 74 postings. In addition, five files of signaling phrases associated with the IAM Phases were created based on the prior qualitative IAM analysis. The three transcripts used in constructing the lexicon were also used.

Measurement: Feature/Aspect Analyzer

We developed a computer program that used the five files of signaling phrases to count phrases in a given post. This program is formally known as a lexicon classifier. The classifier takes as input the lexicon and a posting. The classifier searches within the post for all the phrases in each of the five IAM Phases. Each time a phrase is found, the classifier increments a Phase counter by 1. The result, for a given posting, is a count of phrases found for each of the five Phases. Figure 12.3 provides a visual depiction of the classifier process, while the Appendix to Chapter 12 contains an R implementation of the process.

Procedure

As indicated in Figure 12.4, for each of the three discussion threads: (1) The research team ran each posting through the lexicon classifier, which resulted in a table with N rows and 5 columns, where N was the number of postings in the discussion thread and the columns represented the computer lexicon phrase counts. (2) The research team then collected the scores for the human analysts who evaluated the same postings, which also resulted in table

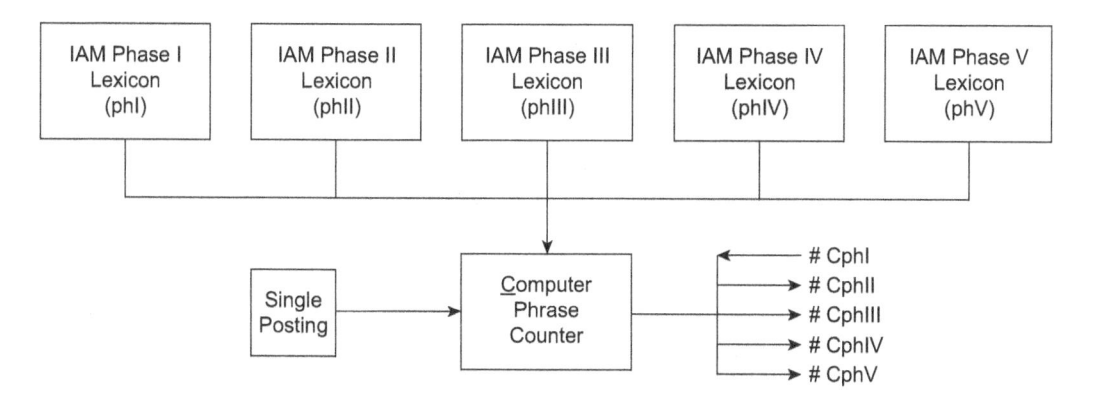

Figure 12.3 A block diagram of the lexicon-based IAM Phase classifier

post	apI	apII	apIII	apIV	apV	cpI	cpII	cpIII	cpIV	cpV
RE: Respo	11	0	0	0	0	21	8	4	0	2
RE: Respo	6	0	0	0	0	19	3	4	1	3
RE: Respo	3	1	2	0	0	14	3	6	1	0
RE: Respo	2	2	0	0	0	8	8	2	1	0
RE: Respo	1	1	1	0	0	12	3	4	0	0
RE: Respo	2	4	0	0	0	9	4	5	1	0
RE: Respo	1	1	0	2	0	12	5	5	1	1
RE: Respo	4	2	0	0	0	22	3	6	1	1
RE: Respo	1	0	2	1	0	10	2	5	1	0
RE: Respo	1	1	0	0	0	9	2	2	0	1
RE: Respo	0	0	0	1	0	4	0	2	1	0
RE: Respo	1	1	0	0	0	3	2	2	0	0
RE: Respo	1	3	0	1	0	9	4	5	2	2
RE: Respo	2	2	0	0	0	14	4	6	0	1
RE: Respo	1	1	0	0	0	8	4	3	0	0
RE: Respo	1	2	0	0	0	7	1	2	0	0
RE: Respo	0	2	2	0	0	11	6	9	1	2
Maddie W	0	4	1	0	0	6	3	3	1	0
RE: Maddi	3	1	1	0	0	11	4	5	1	1
RE: Maddi	2	2	1	1	1	27	7	8	2	3
RE: Maddi	1	1	0	0	0	10	4	2	0	0
RE: Maddi	0	2	0	0	0	9	4	3	0	0
RE: Maddi	1	0	1	0	0	6	3	2	0	0
RE: Maddi	3	0	0	0	0	9	3	2	0	0
RE: Maddi	1	3	0	0	2	9	3	2	0	4
RE: Madd	1	0	0	1	0	5	5	2	1	0
RE: Maddi	0	3	1	0	0	8	4	5	0	2
RE: Maddi	0	1	0	0	0	6	3	1	0	0

Figure 12.4 Excerpt of researcher's manual coding of IAM Phase (ap) compared to the output of the
IAM Phase Predictor Tool (cp)

with N rows and 5 columns, where N was the number of postings in the discussion thread and the columns represented the computer lexicon phrase counts. The columns were labeled IAM Phase I, II, III, IV, and V. The tables were combined into a single table of N rows and 12 columns.

Lastly, the research team used the R *lm* function to test the five hypotheses. The code for the regression analysis is available in the Appendix to Chapter 12.

Results

The regression analysis presented in Table 12.1 shows highly significant diagonal values, which indicates that the human predicted phases are predicted by the phase lexicons.

Table 12.1 A Table of Significance Values for the Computer Predictions and the Hypotheses That Analysts Use Signaling Phrases to Determine IAM Phases

Variable	*H1.1*	*H1.2*	*H1.3*	*H1.4*	*H1.5*
cpI	0.12***	−0.05*	−0.11**		
cpII		0.43***			
cpIII	−0.09**		0.54 ***		
cpIV	0.20**			1.45***	
cpV	−0.09**				0.53***

Note: This table shows the results from the Poisson regression run for each phase of the IAM in relation to the study's hypothesis.
* indicates a p-value less than 0.05, denoting statistical significance.
** indicates a p-value less than 0.01, denoting high statistical significance.
*** indicates a p-value less than 0.001, denoting very high statistical significance.

Conclusion

As researchers, we build models to demonstrate the correctness of our theories about a phenomenon. Models have inputs and outputs, which can take on either continuous or categorical values. For example, one could create a model of the potential for a social media post to spread virally. The inputs could be continuous, such as the number of positive and negative words in the tweet, or categorical with attributes like the types of topics mentioned in the tweet or who the tweet mentions. The output of such a model could be continuous, (e.g., a number from 0 to 1 representing the probability the tweet could go viral) or categorical (e.g., viral or not viral). In this chapter, we discussed the different methods for creating models from the data analyzed using the methods in previous chapters and how to use these models to make predictions about new data. The methods include linear regression, neural networks, and Bayesian inference. Finally, we presented two kinds of regressions for making predictions on IAM-related datasets.

References

Doleck, T., Lemay, D. J., Basnet, R. B., & Bazelais, P. (2020). Predictive analytics in education: A comparison of deep learning frameworks. *Education and Information Technologies, 25*(3), 1951–1963. https://doi.org/10.1007/s10639-019-10068-4

Gunawardena, C. N., Chen, Y., Flor, N., & Sánchez, D. (2023). Deep learning models for analyzing social construction of knowledge online. *Online Learning, 27*. https://doi.org/10.24059/olj.v27i4.4055

Megli, A. C., Fallad-Mendoza, D., Etsitty-Dorame, M., Desiderio, J., Chen, Y., Sánchez, D., Flor, N., & Gunawardena, C. N. (2023). Using social learning analytic methods to examine social construction of knowledge in online discussions. *American Journal of Distance Education, 38*, 65–80. https://doi.org/10.1080/08923647.2023.2192597

Sghir, N., Adadi, A., & Lahmer, M. (2023). Recent advances in predictive learning analytics: A decade systematic review (2012–2022). *Education and Information Technologies, 28*, 8299–8333. https://doi.org/10.1007/s10639-022-11536-0

Appendix to Chapter 12
Poisson Regression

```
Lexicon Classifier in R
#
# Read in the Data
#
filename="Lexicon-Culture-2-Transcript.csv"
df=read.csv(filename)
#
# Zero empty cells, collapse phase columns
#
f=function(x) { if (is.na(x)==T) 0 else x }
df[,4:24]=apply(df[,4:24], c(1,2), f)
df[,4:24]
pI=rowSums(df[,4:8])
pII=rowSums(df[,9:11])
pIII=rowSums(df[,12:16])
pIV=rowSums(df[,17:21])
pV=rowSums(df[,22:24])
dff=data.frame(user=df$User,post=df$Post,pI,pII,pIII,pIV,pV)
#
# Read in the Lexicon
#
LI = readLines("Phase-I-Lexicon.txt")
LII = readLines("Phase-II-Lexicon.txt")
LIII = readLines("Phase-III-Lexicon.txt")
LIV = readLines("Phase-IV-Lexicon.txt")
LV = readLines("Phase-V-Lexicon.txt")
lexi=list(LI, LII, LIII, LIV, LV)
#
# Score post according to lexicon
#
lscores=c()
for (p in dff$post) { # Go through each post
  #
  # Do basic cleaning of the post
  #
  cp = gsub("\\n|/|-", " ", as.character(p))
  cp = gsub("[^a-z\\n]", "", cp, ignore.case=T)
```

```
cp = tolower(cp)

  lscore=c()
  for (lx in lexi) { # Go through each lexicon
      i=0
      for (ln in lx) { # Go through each phrase in each lexicon
      if (grepl(paste("\\b",ln,"\\b",sep=""), cp,ignore.case=T)) { # Check if phrase is
      post
          #print(ln)
          i=i+1
      }
      }
      lscore=c(lscore,i)
  }
  lscores=rbind(lscores,lscore)
}
colnames(lscores)=c("I","II","III","IV","V")
dff=data.frame(user=dff$user,post=dff$post, pI, pII, pIII, pIV, pV, lscores)
write.csv(dff,sprintf("predict-count-%s",filename), row.names=F)
```

13 Artificial Intelligence and Large Language Models

For researchers analyzing social construction of knowledge (SCK) in online environments, one of the most powerful tools is an artificial intelligence (AI) architecture based on a large language model (LLM). AI is the simulation of human intelligence using computers to perform tasks that require human cognitive processes, like attention, memory, learning, and problem-solving. AI systems are designed to replicate the outcome of these processes, enabling computers to perform complex tasks and to make decisions in a manner similar to humans. There are many different ways to implement AI, including rule-based inference and neural networks. These different implementations are known as AI architectures, analogous to how a car can have different engines or a home can have different layouts yet have similar functions. This chapter will focus on developments in AI and LLMs to demonstrate how they could assist in analyzing SCK and the social environment of online learning.

In the past, AI was primarily rule-based, with systems relying on collections of "if *this is true*, then *that is true*" statements, using logic to draw conclusions (Buchanan & Shortliffe, 1984; Newell & Simon, 1956; Hayes-Roth, 1985). For example, an early AI medical expert system might diagnose a common cold by following rules such as: (1) if the patient has a runny nose, a sore throat, and a mild fever, then predict a cold; and (2) if the patient has a cold, then the patient is sick. Given a patient exhibiting these symptoms, the expert system would chain the rules together and conclude that the patient was sick. However, the limitation of rule-based AI was its inability to learn new rules not explicitly programmed by humans and its struggle to solve complex problems outside its predefined rule set. For instance, a rule-based AI medical expert system would be incapable of providing relationship advice, as it could not adapt to situations beyond its programmed knowledge.

Neural networks overcame the limitations of rule-based architectures by enabling an AI to respond to incomplete or novel inputs and to draw conclusions based on rules that had not been explicitly programmed. This is because neural networks do not require predefined rules to be programmed at all (Rumelhart et al., 1986). Instead, you provide a neural network with a collection of inputs and a set of desired outputs, known as a training set. For example, in the case of an AI medical expert, the inputs would correspond to symptoms and the outputs would correspond to doctor diagnoses. By training the AI with these symptoms and diagnoses, the AI self-learns the underlying rules needed to map symptoms to diagnoses. When faced with incomplete symptoms, such as a runny nose and sore throat but no fever, or a novel combination of symptoms, such as a runny nose and cough, the AI can still make a diagnosis and provide likelihood scores for each diagnosis.

DOI: 10.4324/9781003324461-16

While early neural networks overcame key limitations of rule-based systems, they had their own shortcomings. Specifically, they struggled with tasks that required generating sequences of symbols, such as words – an essential capability for answering questions, engaging in conversations, and performing creative tasks like writing stories or composing music. These limitations were largely due to their architecture and training methods, which processed each word independently and lacked mechanisms to capture sequence information and contextual relationships between words.

A large language model, or LLM, overcomes the limitations of early neural networks. An LLM is an AI based on a specific type of neural network architecture known as a transformer (Vaswani et al., 2017) *designed simply to predict the next word given a sequence of words*, or more generally, to predict the next symbol given a sequence of symbols. LLMs learn by being fed sequences of words and predicting the most likely next word for each word in the sequence. Figure 13.1 illustrates this process. Each word inputted to the LLM (bottom row) results in a predicted next word (top row), which then gets added to the input row to generate another predicted word; this process continues until the LLM generates a period or end-of-sequence symbol, <eos>. Innovations in the LLM architecture – such as adding sequence information to words and the addition of attention mechanisms – allow these models to weigh the importance of different words in the input sequence, enabling them to accurately predict the next word and thus excel at tasks that require understanding and generating coherent sequences of words based on previous words.

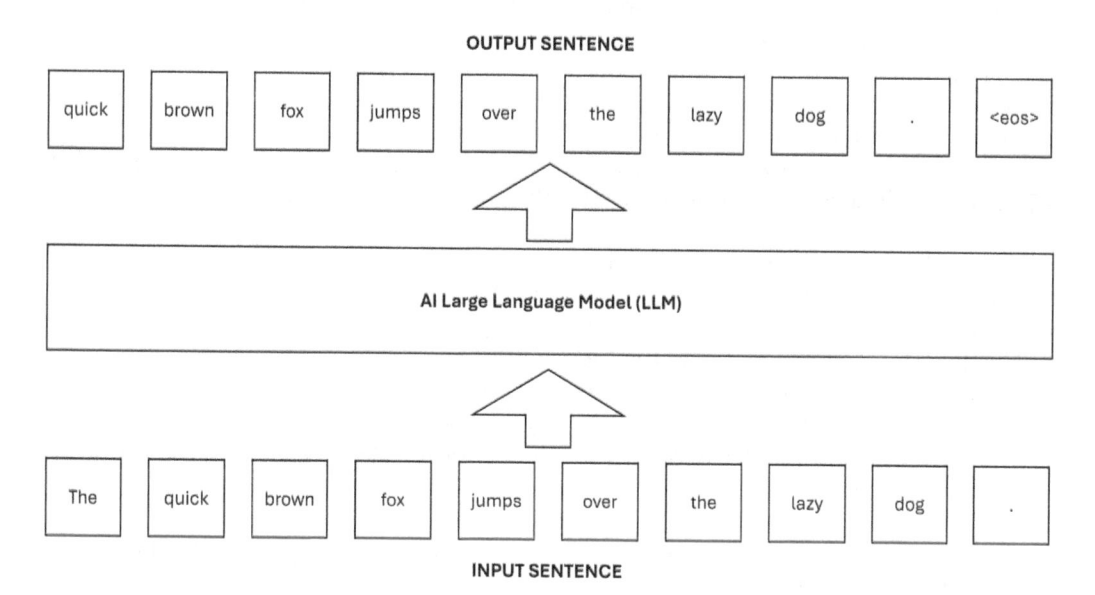

Figure 13.1 This diagram illustrates how an AI large language model (LLM) predicts the next word in a sentence. The model takes an input sequence, such as "The quick brown fox," and generates the next word, "jumps." It repeats this process iteratively, adding each predicted word to the sequence, until it completes the sentence with an end-of-sequence token (e.g., "<eos>").

The term "language model" refers to an AI being trained on a vast corpus of digitized human text, which can include entire websites like Wikipedia, all the posts on a social media platform like Reddit, and the entire collection of digital books in the Project Gutenberg library. This extensive training enables the AI to predict and complete sentences. For example, if you provide the phrase "The quick brown fox," an AI based on an LLM might complete it with "jumps over the lazy dog." The term "large" in LLM indicates the substantial memory required to run the model. Measured in "parameters," the general rule of thumb is to multiply the number of parameters by four to estimate the required memory in bytes.

Sidenote on parameters, memory, and quantization: Meta (Facebook's parent company) provides many versions of LLaMA, its open-source AI LLM, including: Meta-Llama-3.1-405B, Meta-Llama-3.1-70B, and Meta-Llama-3.1-8B. These models require approximately 1.62 terabytes, 280 gigabytes, and 32 gigabytes of memory, respectively, to run without quantization, which is a form of compression.

A common question is: if an LLM only predicts the next word in a sequence of words, how can it generate complete sentences? Most people's experience with LLMs comes from interacting with ChatGPT (Brown et al., 2020), an LLM with a chat interface that was made freely available to the public in 2022 and that clearly outputs complete sentences, paragraphs, or longer sections. The answer lies in what happens in the background. In practice, LLMs are always combined with other code, such as a chat app. After the LLM predicts the next word, the code appends the word to the end of the input sequence, and the updated sentence is fed back into the LLM. The model then predicts the following word, which the code again appends to the sequence before feeding the new sequence back to the model. This process repeats until the LLM generates a period or an end-of-sequence symbol (token), indicating that the sentence is complete. The user only sees the final result, but in the background, the LLM is predicting one word at a time.

For example, if you prompt an LLM like ChatGPT with "The quick brown fox," what happens in the background is as follows (with the predicted next word in bold):

- The quick brown fox (prompt by the user)
- The quick brown fox **jumps** (not shown to user)
- The quick brown fox jumps **over** (not shown to user)
- The quick brown fox jumps over **the** (not shown to user)
- The quick brown fox jumps over the **lazy** (not shown to user)
- The quick brown fox jumps over the lazy **dog** (not shown to user)
- The quick brown fox jumps over the lazy dog. (Shown to user because the period "." indicates completion)

Thus, a complete sentence appears because the AI presents the user with the final result, showing all the generated words together after they have been added one by one.

The Surprising Discovery

LLMs were initially developed by researchers at Google to improve natural language processing tasks, with a particular focus on automated language translation, such as translating English to Spanish (Vaswani et al., 2017). However, as often happens in research, the solution to one problem revealed unexpected capabilities.

The researchers discovered that LLMs could not only complete sentences but also, when prompted with a question, generate plausible answers. Furthermore, when given a creative task, like writing a short story, LLMs could produce coherent and often impressive narratives. This ability to automatically generate content based on human prompts is known as *generative AI*.

Additionally, researchers found that when they asked the LLM to solve a problem or perform a task that it was not specifically trained on, the LLM could generalize from its training to perform that task accurately – a capability known as *zero-shot learning*. When given a very small number of examples of how to solve a problem or perform a task, it could generalize and apply that pattern to new data, a capability known as *few-shot learning*.

Finally, the researchers discovered that even if the LLM had not been trained on the latest news, it could be integrated with a news retrieval system. This system fetched the latest information and allowed the LLM to answer user questions based on the retrieved data. As a result, the LLM could generate responses using both its training and the most current information, a capability known as *retrieval-augmented generation*.

From this point forward, references to AI specifically refer to AIs based on LLMs.

How Researchers Can Use Artificial Intelligence (AI) to Analyze Social Construction of Knowledge (SCK)

The ability of AIs to follow instructions with examples and to answer questions on tasks and topics, which they have not been explicitly trained on, provides a novel opportunity for researchers who analyze SCK (hereafter referred to as SCK researchers) to use them as automated research assistants – helping explore a diverse set of research questions and hypotheses both quickly and accurately.

To better understand the benefits of AI research assistants for SCK researchers, it is important to first recall that our primary data consists of text transcripts of discussions, which can range from hundreds of posts on a class discussion board to millions of posts on a social media platform. Analyzing this data manually, although rewarding, is an extremely tedious process that can take weeks, months, or even years. Typically, this analysis involves either categorizing parts of posts according to existing theoretical constructs, a deductive process known as "qualitative coding," or inferring topics and themes from the data, an inductive process known as topic and thematic analyses (see Braun & Clarke, 2006, for a discussion of both inductive and deductive qualitative research). This process is also prone to error, with researchers often missing codes or themes, requiring constant re-review of transcripts to ensure nothing is overlooked.

SCK researchers can leverage zero-shot and few-shot learning by prompting AI research assistants with instructions and examples, much like they would instruct human research assistants. The AI can then perform deductive, inductive, or even both types of analyses on large volumes of transcripts.

In addition to automatic transcript analysis for codes or themes, AIs can help in numerous ways depending on whether you are doing a deductive or an inductive research study. While there are many nuanced variations in how qualitative research is conducted, particularly within SCK studies, the following steps outline a very general framework for both deductive and inductive approaches. These steps are intended as a high-level summary, in order to highlight the general area where AI research assistants can provide assistance, rather than a comprehensive account of how researchers undertake their work.

Deductive Research (Theory-Driven, With Existing Conceptual Frameworks) Steps and How AI Can Help

1. **Code Data.** Researchers apply a pre-existing theoretical framework to label or categorize the transcript data based on specific constructs.

   AI Support: AI can assist in coding the data by automating the categorization process, especially when prompted to identify the constructs based on examples.

2. **Analyze Codes.** Researchers look for patterns or relationships between the coded data and may perform statistical analyses like frequency counts, correlations, or regression.

   AI Support: AI can assist in code analysis if integrated with statistical tools, but standalone LLMs are limited in their ability to perform these analyses without external tools. It should be noted that more advanced AI systems can generate computer code to perform regressions or other kinds of statistical analyses.

3. **Answer Research Questions.** Researchers interpret the coded data and the analysis results in answering their original research questions, often drawing on theoretical frameworks.

   AI Support: While AI can suggest interpretations or summarize findings, answering complex research questions still requires human expertise to provide in-depth interpretation and research rigor.

Inductive Research (Data-Driven, Emergent Themes) Steps and How AI Can Help

1. **Analyze the Data.** Researchers read through the raw transcript data, looking for patterns, themes, or concepts that emerge without predefined categories.

   AI Support: AI can help identify recurring themes or concepts from large volumes of text, speeding up this initial exploration process.

2. **Extract Themes.** Researchers refine the emerging patterns into clear, defined themes based on the data.

   AI Support: AI can assist in clustering and organizing themes based on similarities or relationships found within the data, offering a structured way to view emerging themes.

3. **Organize Themes and Draw Conclusions.** Researchers organize the themes into a coherent framework, often identifying relationships between the themes, and use this organization to draw broader conclusions.

   AI Support: AI can assist with organizing themes, but drawing conclusions from the themes and establishing their significance remains the task of the human researcher.

Chapter 16 addresses the application of AI as a qualitative research assistant, coding transcripts according to the Interaction Analysis Model (IAM).

To conclude this chapter, we explore additional common AI applications for text analysis that may be of interest to researchers.

Other Applications of Artificial Intelligence to Social Construction of Knowledge Research

While the primary focus for many social construction of knowledge researchers may be on using AIs for transcript coding and analysis, there are several other AI applications enabled by large language models that can complement and enhance research efforts. These include summarization, language translation, named entity recognition, and question-answering, each offering unique ways to process and analyze qualitative data. By integrating these tools into their workflows, researchers can broaden their analytical capabilities and explore new dimensions of text-based research.

Setting Up Your Computer to Do AI Analytics

Before exploring these applications in more depth, it's essential to ensure your development environment is properly configured. The book Wiki describes in detail how to set up your development environment to do AI analytics using the Visual Studio Code Integrated Development Environment (IDE), the Python programming language, and the Conda package manager:

https://github.com/knowledge-construction/slam-ai/wiki/Chapter-13-Setting-Up-Your-Development-Environment-for-AI-Analytics

Ensure your environment is set up before continuing with the AI application examples that follow.

Common Code

All the examples import the *transformers* and *pandas* packages:

```
import pandas as pd
from transformers import pipeline
```

Also in common is the reading of the same data file:

```
data_file = 'IAM42.csv' # Substitute
df = pd.read_csv(data_file)
```

With the common code setup in place, we can move on to the first application: summarization. The code for all the applications is in the book repository:

https://github.com/knowledge-construction/slam-ai/blob/master/Chapter-13/basic-AI-capabilities.ipynb

Application: Summarization

When SCK researchers analyze extensive discussions involving multiple participants and numerous posts, a common exploratory research question arises: "What are they talking about?" While reading each individual post is often necessary, it can be time-consuming. However, there are instances when researchers seek a quick summary of each post in a discussion. Given this summary, one can then decide whether to delve into the post in detail. In such scenarios, AI LLM summarization becomes a valuable technique.

To illustrate summarization, let us first look at its application on a single large body of text. We will then summarize an entire thread.

To test an AI summarizer, first select a model from Hugging Face, an online code repository for machine learning, then instantiate a summarizer object:

```
model_id = 'Falconsai/text_summarization'
summarizer = pipeline("summarization", model_id)
```

Next, assign a variable to a long piece of text:

```
long_text = " 'My own definition of culture is: A group of people who share and fol-
low a set of spoken and in some cases unspoken beliefs, ideas, traditions, values,
and knowledge both tacit and explicit. My own definition of eLearning is: Learn-
ing and teaching that utilizes technology and electronic media formats over tra-
ditional resources. The three pillars that determine the success or failure of
e-learning programs are the interconnectedness among (1) person, (2) behavior, and
(3) environment. These are the three major areas that interventions should target.
1.E-learners' cognitive skills: E-learners must have the prerequisite knowledge and
skills necessary to participate in e-learning. Computer competency through training,
and practice, and time management skills are essential. 2.Environment: Organiza-
tions must support e-learning by offering a supportive culture, incentives, models,
resources, and fostering e-learning self-efficacy. 3. Belief and behavior: E-learners'
must have high e-learning self-efficacy and the appropriate behavioral skills such as
taking responsibility for learning (Mungania, 2003). From this example in the re-
search article ""The Seven eLearning Barriers Facing Employees,"" I begin to see
where eLearning and culture can have some commonalities. I believe that like these 3
pillars that determine the success or failure of eLearning programs, these 3 pillars
can create or remove barriers within a culture. I notice how culture is associated
with traits such as cognitive skills of the culture, the environment in which the
culture thrives, and the beliefs and behaviors of the culture. As we implement eL-
earning strategies into different cultures, we must look at these 3 pillars to create
and maintain a successful eLearning program for the target culture. ELearning, like
culture is not one size fits all and requires some different approaches to how it is
employed in order to suit the target culture. I look forward to your definitions and
to this discussion, have a great week everyone!
```

Finally, call the summarizer object with the text. What was **27** lines of text has been reduced to one line of text:

```
summary_obj = summarizer(long_text)
summary_text = summary_obj[0]['summary_text']
print(summary_text)
# Output
```

```
################################################################
# My own definition of eLearning is: Learning and teaching that utilizes
# technology and electronic media formats over traditional resources. The three
# major areas that interventions should target are interconnectedness among (1)
# person, (2) behavior, and (3) environment. Organizations must support
# e-learning by offering a supportive culture.
```

To summarize an entire discussion thread stored as a CSV file, use the following code:

```
# IMPORT the necessary packages
################################################################
import pandas as pd
from transformers import pipeline

# READ a csv file
################################################################
filename = 'IAM42.csv'      # Change to your file name
df = pd.read_csv(filename)  # Read csv into a data frame

# SELECT model and INSTANTIATE a summarizer object
################################################################
model_id = 'Falconsai/text_summarization'       # Change to suit your data
summarizer = pipeline("summarization", model_id) # Instantiate summarizer

# CONVERT discussion thread to a list of posts
################################################################
posts        = list(df.Thread)
summary_obj  = summarizer(posts, max_length=80)

# Extract the summaries into a list
summary_text = [summary['summary_text'] for summary in summary_obj]

# CONVERT discussion thread to a list of posts
################################################################

# Print text
[print(text) for text in summary_text]

# Save text
output_filename = 'outfile.txt'
# convert text list into one big text data with posts separated by a newline
sep = '\n'
big_text = sep.join(summary_text)
with open(output_filename, 'w') as fd:
   fd.write(big_text)
```

Having seen how AI can summarize large bodies of text, let us now explore how it can assist with translation.

Application: Translation

When studying SCK, researchers analyze data from diverse communities, cultures, and languages. AI translation can help researchers bridge language barriers, enabling them to access and engage with texts in multiple languages, or foster cross-cultural comparisons, to name just a few applications of translation. The following code shows the basics of using AI for translation, using the translation of "Hi! What is your name?" into Spanish from English ("en" to "es"):

```
#
# 1. Import Libraries
#
import torch
import pandas as pd

from transformers import M2M100ForConditionalGeneration, M2M100Tokenizer

device = torch.device("cuda" if torch.cuda.is_available() else "cpu")

#
# 2. Setup Model
#
model_name = "facebook/m2m100_418M"
model_name = "facebook/m2m100_1.2B"

model = M2M100ForConditionalGeneration.from_pretrained(model_name).to(device)
tokenizer = M2M100Tokenizer.from_pretrained(model_name)

#
# 3. Tokenize and Translate
#
#    Source and Target Lang need to use the ISO 639 country codes:
#    https://en.wikipedia.org/wiki/List_of_ISO_639_language_codes
#
def translate(input_text, source_lang, target_lang):
    # tokenze input
    tokenizer.source_lang = source_lang
    encoded_lang = tokenizer(input_text, return_tensors="pt").to(device)

    # Get target language token ID
    target_lang_id = tokenizer.get_lang_id(target_lang)

    # Generate translation
    generated_tokens = model.generate(**encoded_lang,
    forced_bos_token_id=target_lang_id)
```

```
    output_text = tokenizer.batch_decode(generated_tokens,
    skip_special_tokens=True)

    return output_text
translation = translate('Hi! What is your name?', 'en', 'es')
print(translation)

# Output
# 'Hola, ¿cuál es tu nombre?'
#
```

Explanation of the Code

The provided Python code demonstrates how to use the *Facebook M2M100 model* for multilingual translation. There are three sections:

1. **Import Libraries.** The code imports necessary libraries, including *Torch, Pandas*, and the Hugging Face *Transformers* library.
2. **Setup Model.** The M2M100 model is loaded from the Hugging Face model hub. You can choose between two versions: *facebook/m2m100_418M* or *facebook/m2m100_1.2B*. The model is moved to the available device (CPU or GPU).
3. **Tokenize and Translate.**

   - The translate function takes three arguments: *input_text, source_lang*, and *target_lang*.
   - It tokenizes the input text using the specified source language.
   - The target language token ID is obtained using the tokenizer.
   - The model generates the translation, and the output text is decoded.

With the ability to translate multilingual data in hand, let us now explore how AI can assist in identifying key entities and relationships within texts through named entity recognition (NER).

Named Entity Recognition

For SCK researchers, AI-driven named entity recognition (NER) can be a valuable tool for identifying and analyzing key entities within texts, such as people, organizations, or locations. By automatically recognizing these entities, NER helps researchers identify key actors, institutions, and concepts that play a role in knowledge construction.

The following code is an example of how AI can extract named entities from text:

```
#
# 1. Import Libraries
#
from transformers import AutoTokenizer, AutoModelForTokenClassification
from transformers import pipeline
```

```
device = torch.device("cuda" if torch.cuda.is_available() else "cpu")
#
# 2. Initialize Model
#
model_id = 'dslim/bert-large-NER'
tokenizer = AutoTokenizer.from_pretrained(model_id)
model = AutoModelForTokenClassification.from_pretrained(model_id).to(device)
#
# 3. Create NER Pipeline
#
nlp = pipeline("ner", model=model, tokenizer=tokenizer)
#
# 4. Example Usage
#
long_text = """
Lex, Cassidy, Kerry That thing about culture being reflected in language really
struck me. Having spent a fair amount of time in the recent past working with
my daughter to translate a police report from Dutch to English for an insurance
claim - knowing no Dutch myself and my daughter only knowing a little conversational
Dutch - that is most certainly the case. In case you haven't tried it, Google trans-
late mangles Dutch (both directions) and part of the reason is that the entire atti-
tude toward the world is different. We tell our kids to "Do your best! Be good!" and
Dutch parents tell their children "Be normal!" The idioms are so completely foreign
as to render some meanings completely incomprehensible.
The opportunity for misinterpretations in email can be enormous. For instance,
I innocently forwarded an invitation to a risk manager's organization to my former
Director - the description of the organization seemed as if it were at a higher man-
agement level than I occupied, and I thought she might like to make contact with the
important people reported to be members of the group. I made a self-deprecating joke
about it being "too rich for my blood." She was so offended that she gave me a verbal
reprimand in front of my immediate supervisor for passing along the email. I had no
idea I had said anything wrong! Those of you that teach ESL or speak multiple lan-
guages - I can't even imagine how you manage the cultural divides. My hat is off to
you. ("my cap is gone to you.")
"""

ner_results = nlp(long_text)
print(ner_results)
people = [item['word'] for item in ner_results if item['entity']=='B-PER']
orgs = [item['word'] for item in ner_results if item['entity']=='B-ORG']
print(f'People mentioned: {people}')
print(f'Organizations mentioned: {orgs}')
#
# OUTPUT (partial):
#[{'entity':'B-PER', 'score':0.9990932, 'index': 1, 'word':'Lex' , 'start': 1,
'end': 4},
# {'entity':'B-PER', 'score':0.99928015,'index': 3, 'word':'Cassidy', 'start': 6,
'end': 13},
```

```
# {'entity':'B-PER', 'score':0.99924445,'index': 5, 'word':'Kerry' , 'start':
15,'end': 20},
# . . .
# {'entity':'B-ORG', 'score':0.8973883, 'index':78, 'word':'Google','start': 400,
'end': 406},
# . . .]
#
# People mentioned: ['Lex', 'Cassidy', 'Kerry']
# Organizations mentioned: ['Google']
```

Explanation of the Code Example

The provided Python code demonstrates how to use NER with the *dslim/bert-large-NER* model. There are four main sections:

1. **Import Libraries.** The code imports necessary libraries, including the *transformers* library for NLP tasks. It checks if a CUDA-enabled GPU is available for faster processing.
2. **Initialize Model.** The *model_id* corresponds to the pre-trained BERT-based NER model. The tokenizer and model are loaded using *AutoTokenizer* and *AutoModelForToken-Classification.*
3. **Create NER Pipeline.** The NLP pipeline is created for named entity recognition. You can pass text to this pipeline to extract entities and their labels.
4. **Example Usage**:

   - The *long_text* variable represents the input text (which is omitted here).
   - The *my_question* variable contains a question related to the text.
   - The answer to my_question within the context of long_text is extracted and printed.

Having explored how AI can identify and extract key entities, we next look at how AI can assist researchers in answering specific questions derived based on their text data using AI question-answering models.

Question and Answering

While LLMs can automatically generate answers to questions about a piece of text by simply pasting the text and asking questions, or through retrieval-augmented generation (RAG) systems, AI models specialized for question and answering (Q&A models) offer a more targeted approach. Q&A models are specifically designed to answer questions directly based on the text they are given, making them particularly useful for researchers who need precise answers from large volumes of data.

The following is an example of using a Q&A model to answer questions about a posting:

```
#
# 1. Import Libraries
#
from transformers import AutoModelForQuestionAnswering, AutoTokenizer, pipeline
#
# 2. Select a Q&A model
#
model_id = "deepset/roberta-base-squad2"
question_answerer = pipeline("question-answering", model=model_id,
tokenizer=model_id)
#
# 3. Setup context for Q&A
#
long_text = " 'My own definition of culture is: A group of people who share and fol-
low a set of spoken and in some cases unspoken beliefs, ideas, traditions, values,
and knowledge both tacit and explicit. My own definition of eLearning is: Learn-
ing and teaching that utilizes technology and electronic media formats over tra-
ditional resources. The three pillars that determine the success or failure of
e-learning programs are the interconnectedness among (1) person, (2) behavior, and
(3) environment. These are the three major areas that interventions should target.
1.E-learners' cognitive skills: E-learners must have the prerequisite knowledge and
skills necessary to participate in e-learning. Computer competency through training,
and practice, and time management skills are essential. 2.Environment: Organiza-
tions must support e-learning by offering a supportive culture, incentives, models,
resources, and
fostering e-learning self-efficacy. 3. Belief and behavior: E-learners' must have high
e-learning self-efficacy and the appropriate behavioral skills such as
taking responsibility for learning (Mungania, 2003). From this example in the re-
search article ""The Seven eLearning Barriers Facing Employees,"" I begin to see
where eLearning and culture can have some commonalities. I believe that like
these 3 pillars that determine the success or failure of eLearning programs,
these
3 pillars can create or remove barriers within a culture. I notice how culture is
associated with traits such as cognitive skills of the culture, the environment in
which the culture thrives, and the beliefs and behaviors of the culture. As we im-
plement eLearning strategies into different cultures, we must look at these 3 pillars
to create and maintain a successful eLearning program for the target culture. EL-
earning, like culture is not one size fits all and requires some different approaches
to how it is employed in order to suit the target culture. I look forward to your
definitions and to this discussion, have a great week everyone!
" \
#
# Step 4. Define the question
#
my_question = 'What are the three pillars that determine the success of e-learning?'
#
# Step 5. Obtain answer
#
```

```
reply = question_answerer(question=my_question, context=long_text)
#
# Step 6. Print answer
#
print(reply['answer'])
```

Explanation of Code

The provided Python code demonstrates how to use the *deepset/roberta-base-squad2* model for question-answering. There are six sections:

1. **Import Libraries.** The code imports the *pipeline* library, which can be configured to perform question-and-answering tasks.
2. **Select a Pre-Trained Q&A Model.** The variable *model_id* specifies the pre-trained model to use. In this case, it is "deepset/roberta-base-squad2." *The line question_answerer = pipeline("question-answering", model=model_id, tokenizer=model_id)* sets up an NLP pipeline specifically for question-answering.
3. **Setup the Context for Q&A.** The variable *long_text* contains the text where the model will search for answers to the given question.
4. **Define the Question.** The variable *my_question* holds the specific question: "What are the three pillars that determine the success of eLearning?" Researchers can replace this question with any other relevant query they want to explore.
5. **Obtain Answer.** The *question_answerer* pipeline is then used to find an answer to the given question within the provided context, and the result is stored in the *reply* variable.
6. **Print Answer.** Finally, the code prints the answer extracted from the context by the model.

Conclusion

AI based on LLM architectures offer transformative potential for SCK researchers. AI can automate and enhance processes that traditionally required extensive human labor, from assisting in qualitative coding to facilitating thematic analysis. While AI's ability to follow instructions and generate insights is impressive, it is important to remember that these tools are not substitutes for the nuanced interpretation and theoretical insights that human researchers can bring to analyses. By integrating AI into their workflows, researchers can expand their analytical capabilities, enabling deeper and more efficient exploration of discussions while retaining the human expertise necessary to draw meaningful conclusions.

References

Braun, V., & Clarke, V. (2006). Using thematic analysis in psychology. *Qualitative Research in Psychology, 3*, 77–101. https://doi.org/10.1191/1478088706qp063oa

Brown, T., Mann, B., Ryder, N., Subbiah, M., Kaplan, J. D., Dhariwal, P., Neelakantan, A., Shyam, P., Sastry, G., Askell, A., Agarwal, S., Herbert-Voss, A., Krueger, G., Henighan, T., Child, R., Ramesh, A., Ziegler, D., Wu, J., Winter, C., . . . Amodei, D. (2020). Language models are few-shot learners. *Advances in Neural Information Processing Systems, 33*, 1877–1901. https://proceedings.neurips.cc/paper/2020/hash/1457c0d6bfcb4967418bfb8ac142f64a-Abstract.html

Buchanan, B. G., & Shortliffe, E. H. (1984). *Rule-based expert systems.* MA: Addison-Wesley Longman.

Hayes-Roth, F. (1985). Rule-based systems. *Communications of the ACM, 28*, 921–932. https://doi.org/10.1145/4284.4286

Newell, A. (1994). *Unified theories of cognition*. Boston, MA: Harvard University Press.

Newell, A., & Simon, H. (1956). The logic theory machine – A complex information processing system. *IRE Transactions on Information Theory, 2*, 61–79. IRE Transactions on Information Theory. https://doi.org/10.1109/TIT.1956.1056797

Rumelhart, D., Hinton, G., & Williams, R. (1986). Learning internal representations by error propagation. In D. Rumelhart & J. McClelland (Eds.), *Parallel distributed processing: Explorations in the microstructure of cognition: Vol. 1: Foundations* (pp. 318–362). Cambridge, MA: Bradford Books/MIT Press.

Vaswani, A., Shazeer, N., Parmar, N., Uszkoreit, J., Jones, L., Gomez, A., Kaiser, Ł., & Polosukhin, I. (2017). *Attention is all you need*. Advances in Neural Information Processing Systems 30, 31st Conference on Neural Information Processing Systems (NIPS 2017), Long Beach, CA.

Appendix to Chapter 13
The Transformer Architecture Underlying AI Large-Language Models

The transformer architecture has revolutionized the field of AI, providing the foundation for many state-of-the-art models that power today's most advanced AI systems. Despite its complexity, the core principles of the transformer can be implemented in a surprisingly concise manner. The following code offers a glimpse into the fundamental components of the transformer architecture, showcasing a basic implementation that highlights its elegant design. The design of the transformer architecture, as described by Vaswani et al. (2017), can be difficult to understand without an actual implementation. By examining this code and reading Vaswani et al. (2017), readers can gain insights into how transformers operate, including mechanisms like attention and positional encoding, which are crucial for processing sequential data effectively. While a detailed exploration of the transformer is beyond this book's scope, this example serves as an educational starting point for understanding the key innovations driving modern AI.

```python
# Simplex Transformer: For Educational & Experimental Explorations
# Author: Nick V. Flor (professorf@live.com)
# Year: 2023
################################################################################
import torch
import math

class SimplexTransformer(torch.nn.Module):
    def gen_pos_enc_matrix(self, max_seq_len, d_model):
        PE = torch.zeros(max_seq_len, d_model, requires_grad=False)
        for pos in range(max_seq_len):
          position = torch.tensor(pos, dtype=torch.float32)
          for i in range(d_model//2):
              PE[pos, 2*i] = torch.sin(position/10000**(2.0*i/d_model))
              PE[pos, 2*i+1] = torch.cos(position/10000**(2.0*i/d_model))
        return PE

    # Define a one-head transformer
    def __init__(self, vocab_size, max_seq_len, d_model):
        super().__init__()

        self.register_buffer('pos_enc', self.gen_pos_enc_matrix(max_seq_len, d_model))
        self.embed  = torch.nn.Embedding(vocab_size, d_model)
        self.Q      = torch.nn.Linear(d_model, d_model)
```

```
        self.K      = torch.nn.Linear(d_model, d_model)
        self.V      = torch.nn.Linear(d_model, d_model)
        self.hidden = torch.nn.Linear(d_model, d_model)
        self.output = torch.nn.Linear(d_model, vocab_size)

        self.max_seq_len = max_seq_len
        self.d_model     = d_model

        self.register_buffer('causal_mask', torch.triu(
            torch.full((max_seq_len, max_seq_len), -float('inf')), diagonal=1
        ))

    def forward(self, tokens, do_causal = True): # ,[batch_size, max_seq_len],
        # tokens -> embeddings
        embeds = self.embed(tokens) # [batch_size, max_seq_len, d_model]

        # Calculate the attention mask for pads [pad] MUST be 0
        pad_mask = (tokens == 0)          # assumes [pad] is 0 PAD_MASK!!!
        pad_mask = pad_mask.unsqueeze(1)  # reshape for broadcasting

        # embeddings -> positionalized embeddings
        embeds += self.pos_enc # adds encoding to input

        # query key and value
        query  = self.Q(embeds) # [batch_size, max_seq_len, d_model]
        key    = self.K(embeds) # [batch_size, max_seq_len, d_model]
        value  = self.V(embeds) # [batch_size, max_seq_len, d_model]

        # calculate attention matrix
        attn = query @ key.transpose(1, 2) # [batch_size, max_seq_len, max_seq_len]

        # Set False for Masked-Language Modeling (MLM) bidirectional learning
        if do_causal:
            attn = attn + self.causal_mask

        attn /= math.sqrt(embeds.size(-1)) # scale down by d_model dimension

        attn = attn.masked_fill(pad_mask, -float('inf')) # ATTN_MASK

        attn = torch.softmax(attn, dim=-1) # softmax attention

        attn_V = attn @ value               # [batch_size, max_seq_len, d_model]

        hidden = self.hidden(attn_V) # [batch_size, max_seq_len, d_model]
        result = self.output(hidden) # [batch_size, max_seq_len, vocab_size]
        return result, hidden

# EXIT: SimplexTransformer
####################################################################################
```

Part IV

Applications

This section of the book provides examples of practical applications of the Social Learning Analytic Methods (SLAM) described in previous chapters. The studies included in this section address formal and informal learning environments, including social media in Chapter 14 and asynchronous discussions in a nursing course in Chapter 15. Each of these studies applies SLAM in its own novel way to assess the social dynamic that supports knowledge construction as mapped by the Interaction Analysis Model (IAM). Chapter 14 explores a network of practice on Twitter (now known as X), analyzing the #BlackLivesMatter hashtag during the Freddie Gray protests in April 2015. In Chapter 15, guest author Sharon Schaaf discusses a mixed-methods study investigating the relationships between SCK, social network centrality, and advanced practice nurse (APN) competency. Chapter 16 details how to set up a large language model on a personal computer and use it to predict the phases of knowledge construction. The study compares the AI's phase predictions to human coding and suggests numerous opportunities for refinement and enhancement to achieve more reliable and accurate coding. These studies can be used as a template for conducting new inquiries across all disciplines.

DOI: 10.4324/9781003324461-17

14 Social Construction of Knowledge and Social Action on #BlackLivesMatter

George Floyd's murder at the hands of the Minneapolis Police Department in 2020 is one of many examples of police brutality directed against people of color. The publicized trend of mistreatment goes back arguably to the 1991 beating of Rodney King by Los Angeles police officers. Since then, instances of police brutality have been increasingly exposed due to social media and technology. For example, bystanders captured the brutal arrest of Freddie Gray in 2015 in Baltimore, MD, by making videos with smartphones. Freddie Gray ultimately died while in police custody sparking widespread protests in Baltimore organized mostly by Black Lives Matter. Since its 2013 salvo in response to the acquittal of neighborhood vigilante George Zimmerman in the murder of Trayvon Martin, Black Lives Matter has been responsible for organizing many protests across America that have brought long-standing issues of police brutality and racism to the forefront of national consciousness (Freelon et al., 2018). Note that Martin was an unarmed African American teenager who was shot and killed by Zimmerman while he was walking home. Martin's murder was the genesis of Black Lives Matter.

The increased awareness of police brutality has prompted many people to engage in social action. For example, a Baltimore woman participated in a protest for the first time after seeing the online video of Freddie Gray being brutalized by Baltimore police because she thought the same thing could easily happen to her own son (AP, 2015). This case illustrates the interplay between face-to-face and online social action. Face-to-face social action includes various categories of nonviolent action (Sharp, 1973) to account for forms of peaceful protest. Online social action is known as digital activism, which is defined by Whyte and Joyce (2010) as "the practice of using digital technology to increase the effectiveness of a social or political change campaign" (p. 218). This study will examine both digital activism and nonviolent action under the banner of social action. Note that social action is an outcome of the social knowledge construction process that happened online, which led to the woman in the previous example learning about Freddie Gray and watching the video of what happened to him. The large number of people who posted updates and the video content are undeniable elements of the pathway that led the woman in the previous example to engage in social action. Therefore, this study will examine how people built knowledge with one another in the #BlackLivesMatter virtual network housed on the social media platform Twitter. The overall purpose of the study discussed in this chapter is to determine whether content analysis of #BlackLivesMatter examining social construction of knowledge (SCK) using the Interaction Analysis Model (IAM) could be used along with specific Social Learning Analytic Methods (SLAM) as a foundation for creating a model that can accurately classify social action as measured by nonviolent action and/or digital activism.

DOI: 10.4324/9781003324461-18

Literature Review

Twitter and Networks of Practice

Twitter (now known as X) was a social media tool that allowed users to send single messages, called tweets, to people within their networks. At the time this study was conducted, there was no limit to the number of tweets a user could send, only a limit to the number of characters used to write each tweet. Topical discussions and related content on Twitter are denoted when users included a label with a # (hashtag) in their tweets. In this study, #BlackLivesMatter is a discussion about Black Lives Matter. The Black Lives Matter organization has grown to include over 40 formal chapters since 2013 (Matthews & Noor, 2017), but it still maintains a decentralized virtual orientation that allows anyone to access their online network. Oftentimes, networks of practice do not have specific locations from which its members engage in SCK.

Networks of practice (Wenger et al., 2011) are an offshoot of the more commonly known communities of practice (Lave & Wenger, 1991). Wenger et al. (2011) state that a network of practice "refers to a set of connections among people, whether or not these connections are mediated by technological networks. These people use their connections and relationships as a resource to quickly solve problems, share knowledge, and make further connections" (p. 11). Note that a network of practice differs from a community of practice in that participation in a community requires a sustained learning partnership, while participation in a network does not and also lacks an explicit collective dimension (Wenger et al., 2011).

Another trait of networks of practice is broad and fluid membership, with many people regularly coming in and going out (Wenger et al., 2011). #BlackLivesMatter has core contributors like chapter members and news organizations who keep the online discussion going and contribute on a regular basis while the majority of people post irregularly (Freelon et al., 2016). Thus, most people posting come and go creating a fluid membership for #BlackLivesMatter. Fluidity is a strength of networks of practice as noted by Wenger (2010) who writes, "A twitter message sends a question into the connectivity of a network and it boomerangs back with a totally unexpected response, and a brand new person to follow. This is the magic of network" (p. 192). Strength comes from the new person and their point of view because they add to the diversity of the knowledge contained in the network. The knowledge on #BlackLivesMatter, includes documented instances and commentary from lived experiences with police brutality and racism (Black Lives Matter, 2017). For #BlackLivesMatter, such documentation and commentary constitute the network's collective practice. The diversity of the knowledge within the network is often the foundation for motivation and learning (Dron & Anderson, 2014).

Learning within networks of practice mostly takes the form of informal learning (Wenger et al., 2011), which is defined as learning from everyday experiences mostly outside of the traditional classroom (Merriam & Caffarella, 1999). Indeed, Twitter hashtags are a rich resource for researchers who wish to observe real-world learning. For example, the Occupy Wall Street Twitter study by Gleason (2013) established that informal learning occurs when participating in digital activism. #BlackLivesMatter has also been successful in facilitating large-scale informal learning among casual observers on Twitter as evidenced by their expressions of awe and disbelief regarding the violent reactions by police to the Michael Brown protests and by conservatives admitting to clear instances of police brutality in the cases of Eric Garner and Walter Scott (Freelon et al., 2016). The implications of this learning are immense because Twitter breaks down the barriers between novices and experts facilitating interaction thus allowing access to previously concealed knowledge and expertise (Blair, 2013). The diversity of the opinions that exist concurrently within a network like #BlackLivesMatter increase the likelihood of people learning about topics like police brutality and racism via SCK.

Social Construction of Knowledge (SCK)

In this study, learning is defined as the SCK such that the entire gestalt of the messages in the #BlackLivesMatter hashtag need to be understood in order to determine what people are learning on the network of practice. This study uses the IAM (Gunawardena et al., 1997) to assess SCK. The IAM includes 5 Phases:

- Phase I: Sharing/comparing of information
- Phase II: The discovery and exploration of dissonance or inconsistency among ideas, concepts or statements
- Phase III: Negotiation of meaning/co-construction of knowledge
- Phase IV: Testing and modification of proposed synthesis or co-construction
- Phase V: Agreement statement(s)/applications of newly-constructed meaning

The complete framework as well as the coding sheet that accompanies it, are described in Chapter 1. Aspects of SCK that contribute to the gestalt of the messages on #BlackLivesMatter include, but are not limited to, information-sharing behaviors such as stating opinions and sharing resources, sparking inquiry by asking questions, and applying learning via engaging in digital or face-to-face social action. On Twitter, these behaviors are supported using features such as tweeting to share opinions and retweeting to share resources. "The network provides an ideal context for sharing information, ideas, and questions" (Dron & Anderson, 2014, p. 135). Indeed, networks are ideal venues to examine SCK along the lines of these behaviors. Twitter hashtags provide the venue for SCK as well as its outcome, social action.

Social Media and Social Action

Social media has a history of being used to facilitate social action. For example, Twitter supported #Occupy when protesters used the platform to circulate information and organize in-person protests (Juris, 2012). Note that #Occupy was the hashtag used to support the Occupy Wall Street movement in the United States that resulted in people protesting economic inequalities in the United States using forms of nonviolent action. The platform was also used to mobilize protesters and gain global support for the Arab Spring movement (Lim, 2012). During the Arab Spring, Twitter also played a key role in helping activists find others with shared beliefs and ultimately helped form the core group that engaged in the Tahrir Square uprising in Cairo, Egypt (Tufekci, 2017). Twitter was used by #BlackLivesMatter to share emergent information about the killing of Michael Brown and comment about his killer (Bonilla & Rosa, 2015). These examples illustrate that there is both an online and face-to-face way in which Twitter can support social action. The efforts of #BlackLivesMatter have even been found to influence media coverage, which spreads its message to even greater audiences (Freelon et al., 2018). Engaging in SCK on Twitter allows a wide variety of people to learn about various movements and engage in them by sharing lived experiences and participating in online and face-to-face social action. Enumerating how SCK leads to social action requires the use of social learning analytics.

Social Learning Analytic Methods (SLAM)

Social learning analytics is defined by Buckingham Shum and Ferguson (2012) as a "distinctive subset of learning analytics that draws on the substantial body of work demonstrating that new skills and ideas are not solely individual achievements, but are developed, carried forward, and passed on through interaction and collaboration" (p. 5). Note that learning analytics focuses on the learning process and ultimately on improving student performance at an individual level by analyzing student-centric data (Long & Siemens, 2011). Social learning analytics, on the other hand, focuses on studying group interaction and social networks as groups co-construct knowledge.

Gunawardena et al. (2018) proposed using Social Learning Analytic Methods (SLAM) to perform social learning analytics. SLAM is defined as a collection of techniques to study group interactions on learning management systems and social networks as groups co-construct knowledge online. These techniques include frequency analysis, sentiment analysis, cluster analysis, social network analysis, and artificial intelligence. This collection of analytic methods can be used to analyze big data from large numbers of users.

In this study, SLAM is used to analyze social media data evident in a transcript of discussions, which is an important contribution to the field because much of what is known about how Twitter is used for social action (Bonilla & Rosa, 2015; Brym et al., 2014; Harlow & Guo, 2014; Juris, 2012; Lim, 2012; Penney & Dadas, 2014) comes from studies that depend on qualitative methods such as interviewing activists. Traditional qualitative methods like interviewing take place after someone has engaged in social action and are thus not fully capable of assessing the SCK that happened online. To analyze the process associated with SCK, the statements and knowledge artifacts (social media posts, videos, images, etc.) posted by users must be the focus of analysis as they are with SLAM. The SLAM that were used to conduct this study were lexicon analysis and naïve Bayes.

Content Analysis

Content analysis is not part of SLAM, but it must be mentioned because it plays an important part in this study. Content analysis is defined by Krippendorff (1980) as "a research technique for making replicable and valid inferences from data to their context" (p. 21). Generally speaking, content analysis is performed by reading text and manually classifying the text by hand. This method has long been associated with the IAM because researchers need to manually review and code transcripts in order to apply the framework. This study uses the IAM to guide the content analysis.

Lexicon Analysis

A lexicon is simply a list of words. In this study, the list of words was generated as part of the content analysis. A lexicon analysis is conducted when the list of words is used to guide the automatic classification of data. Note that a lexicon analysis is a customized form of a sentiment analysis. In order to perform a lexicon analysis, the list of words should exemplify a research construct. For example, Gunawardena et al. (2016) performed a lexicon analysis according to social presence by creating lists of words related to social presence. A similar method was used for this study but instead of social presence it focuses on the SCK as identified using the IAM. In the case of the SCK lexicon analysis, it contains a list of words that exemplify each of the IAM Phases. Complete details regarding how to conduct a lexicon analysis are provided in Chapter 7.

Naïve Bayes

Naïve Bayes is a method used to conduct predictive analytics. This SLAM is covered in Chapter 12. Naïve Bayes classification is a straightforward and widely tested method of probabilistic induction that provides a single probabilistic summary for each new instance of data being assigned to a specific class based on prior probability (Langley & Sage, 1994). Note that class refers to a dependent variable, which in this study is nonviolent action and digital activism. These are two types of social action. Bayesian classification specifically applies to categorical variables. The Bayesian classification rule is as follows:

$$P(H|X) = \frac{P(X|H)P(H)}{P(X)}$$

Stated another way, the probability of a hypothesis H that an unknown instance of data X belongs to a certain class P(H|X) can be calculated from the proportion of instances in which values of X are observed in all samples in the dataset in which H is true P(X|H) times the prior probability of the hypotheses being true in the training data P(H) divided by the observed proportion of instances of X in the dataset regardless of class values P(X) (Manning & Schütze, 1999).

Using prior probabilities of social action and its association with SCK is important to understand how what people learn about social movements online is related to nonviolent action and digital activism. Moreover, using naïve Bayes with the IAM to understand SCK can contribute to the maintenance of a safe and peaceful environment during protests like the ones surrounding Freddie Gray because some protests, including some for Freddie Gray, turn violent. Active monitoring of social media could help identify the likelihood of protests remaining peaceful and help authorities maintain public safety. This study takes the first step by exploring the associations between SCK and social action using naïve Bayes and the IAM.

Research Questions

The overall purpose of this study is to determine whether content analysis using IAM to examine SCK can be used as a foundation to create a naïve Bayes model that can accurately classify face-to-face and/or digital social action. The research questions this study seeks to address are as follows:

- Research question 1 – Does SCK as measured by the IAM occur in networks of practice on Twitter? At what levels?
- Research question 2 – How accurately will a naïve Bayes model based on IAM Phases classify face-to-face and/or digital social action outcome variables?

Method

Data Collection

A purposive sample of 45,646 tweets were scraped from #BlackLivesMatter on Twitter from April 21–April 28, 2015 during the Freddie Gray demonstrations. Batrinca and Treleaven (2015) define scraping as "collecting online data from social media and other Web sites in the form of unstructured text" (p. 90). The OILS Twitter Scraper (Flor, 2014) was used to perform data scraping. This program is written in Visual Basic and uses the Twitter application programming interface (API) to access Twitter databases and pull relevant tweets into an Excel spreadsheet. A sample search string that was used to scrape the data is

q=%23blacklivesmatter AND %23freddiegray since%3A2015-04-21 until%3A2015-04-22& src=typd

The OILS Twitter Scraper pulls data in a firehose fashion from the API according to the search string parameters. This includes all original tweets and their retweets. Purposefully limiting the scrape by both #Blacklivesmater and #freddiegray leaves out similar but different hashtags. For example, some people spelled Freddie's last name "Grey" instead of "Gray" and those tweets were not scraped. The decision to use #Blacklivesmater and #freddiegray was based on preliminary scrapes and a review of the most common hashtags to assure most of the tweets were captured.

Data Cleaning

Batrinca and Treleaven (2015) define data cleaning as the "correction or removal of erroneous (dirty) data caused by disparities, keying mistakes, missing bits, outliers, etc." (p. 93). Prior to conducting any analysis, data cleaning was performed to remove redundancies and irrelevant postings. First, all non-essential punctuations (periods, commas, colons, etc.) were removed to facilitate analysis. Redundancies in the data amount to duplicate content and retweeted content. The Excel Remove Duplicates function was used to remove duplicate content. Furthermore, Excel filters were used to remove retweets that all start with "RT." Removing retweets focuses the data only on original posts including the first instance of a given retweet. In effect this step is a more detailed removal of duplicate content, which increases accuracy. Leaving all the retweets in the data would have adverse consequences on the statistical analysis because the content with many retweets would be overrepresented in the data. Irrelevant postings were manually removed by identifying non-relevant hashtags, such as #Nepalearthquake, which also showed up in the dataset. This tweet is an example:

@MrRagerx #FreddieGray #BlackLivesMatter #NepalEarthquake #PrayerForNepal

These tweets were purposefully associated with #BlackLivesMatter to promote the various hashtags. They were removed because they did not have anything to do with the inquiry of this study. Additionally, tweets made up of only hashtags, like the previous one, were excluded from the data. These tweets were removed because there is a very high likelihood that they were generated by bots. In fact, many of the accounts that generated such tweets were ultimately disabled by Twitter for this very reason. This study focuses on common language that makes substantive statements that are clearly attributable to someone writing their tweet. A total of 11,469 samples remained after data cleaning.

Method for Research Question 1

Answering research question 1 requires conducting a content analysis guided by the IAM and then using those results to conduct a separate SCK lexicon analysis. Note that these are two separate methods that are completed sequentially. The results of the content analysis are used as a framework to guide the lexicon analysis.

Content Analysis to Determine SCK

The purpose of conducting the content analysis using the IAM to determine SCK is to (1) generate associations between SCK and social action and (2) identify words used to classify tweets according to SCK. These associations are important because they allow naïve Bayes to establish prior probabilities. Identifying words is important because they enable lexicon analysis. All tweets from April 21 and April 25 were included in the content analysis to determine SCK because these two days include various levels and types of social action that are representative of the rest of the data.

The unit of analysis for this study is the individual tweet sent by individual users. The reason individual tweets were selected as the unit of analysis was to facilitate the inclusion of the full context of the message in the coding. To accomplish this goal, all of the tweets on April 21 and 25 were coded using a content analysis guided by the IAM, which included following links to images, videos, and other multimedia. This additional level of analysis is important because oftentimes the true meaning of a tweet was found in the linked multimedia instead in the text of the tweet itself. To code a specific tweet, a "1" was entered in the appropriate spreadsheet column/row after completing the content analysis for each tweet. All other columns were filled with a "0" indicating the given tweet did not match the criteria in the other operations. Tweets were coded for multiple IAM Phases if they applied using the IAM coding spreadsheet available on the book GitHub at:

https://github.com/knowledge-construction/slam-ai

In most cases, tweets were coded for either nonviolent action or digital activism, which are the two social action categories. However, tweets that documented face-to-face activities within digital activism were also coded for the specific nonviolent action they documented. All tweets on April 21 and April 25 were coded according to this convention.

During the coding process, Excel filters were applied to columns in the IAM coding spreadsheet that represent Phases and Operations and used to review the analysis at various points in the process to assure tweets were coded consistently. Single columns were filtered for their values to review codes in given categories especially when starting a new coding session. Consistency was also introduced into the qualitative coding process by referring to the types of words and phrases that were being saved in the SCK lexicon. The lists in the SCK lexicon established common language for tweets in those categories that helped to assure others with similar sentiment were included in the given category. If a question was encountered about a particular word or phrase, the existing lexicon was searched to determine how the tweet containing the word or phrase in question should be classified. Using the lexicon to guide coding effectively serves the purpose of keeping memos to help standardize the coding process. All of the tweets from April 21 and 25 were coded according to nonviolent action and digital activism during the process of IAM coding. Note that the tweets on these days were ordered chronologically prior to coding in order to preserve the influence of time on the SCK.

SCK Lexicon Analysis

The purpose of conducting an SCK lexicon analysis is to automate the identification of IAM Phases (described in Chapter 1) that signal SCK. A lexicon for SCK was developed according to two methods described by Liu (2012):

1. Manual – coding words into categories and assigning their orientation by hand
2. Dictionary – using online dictionaries and thesauri to generate a comprehensive lexicon based on seed words that are representative of the dataset

Combining a manual and dictionary approach to lexicon generation produces an efficient and precise lexicon (Hu & Liu, 2004). The manual approach to lexicon development was completed during the content analysis to determine SCK by selecting words and phrases that exemplified SCK and adding them to Excel columns for each IAM Phase. These words and phrases are known as seed words because they are used as inputs to expand the lexicon using the dictionary approach.

The dictionary approach was implemented using the online dictionary WordNet. Word-Net is described by Miller et al. (1990) as "an on-line lexical reference system whose design is inspired by current psycholinguistic theories of human lexical memory. English nouns, verbs, and adjectives are organized into synonym sets, each representing one underlying lexical concept. Different relations link the synonym sets" (p. 235). SCK seed words and phrases were searched for in WordNet to expand the lexicon. Synonyms that did not fit the original context of the seed word were removed while those that fit the context were added to the lexicon. The final product of this process is a list of words and phrases according to each IAM Phase that originate in the dataset.

The complete SCK lexicon was input into R data analysis package (Wickham & Grolemund, 2016) by including the words and phrases of varying length, known as n-grams, associated with SCK into an Excel spreadsheet saved as a CSV. For example, *angry, demand,* and *it's nothing* were coded as IAM PhI/A. Each n-gram was labeled with the appropriate IAM Phase. The SLAM R routine in Chapter 7 was used to produce automatic IAM classifications.

Method for Research Question 2

SCK and Social Action Naïve Bayes Classification

The naïve Bayes classification model used in this study was created using Google Colab. The following code was used:

```
import pandas as pd
from sklearn. naïve_bayes import GaussianNB # Use if indicators are normally
distributed
from sklearn. naïve_bayes import BernoulliNB # If indicators are 1/0
from sklearn. naïve_bayes import MultinomialNB # If counts are used, also
CategoricalNB
import numpy as np
from sklearn.metrics import confusion_matrix
from sklearn.metrics import classification_report
filename = 'data.csv' #source data
# Read data file
df = pd.read_csv(filename)
# Handle blank entries
df = df.fillna(0) # Replace blank cells with 0
# If you just want presence/absence of a feature, uncomment
#df = df.where(df <= 1, 1) # Replace >1 with 1
print(df)
```

```
# Indicate the number of inputs
num_inputs = 14 # By visual examination of data set
# Pull out the input columns into their own dataset
input_vectors = df.iloc[:,:num_inputs]
# PhI/A,Ph/B,Ph/C,Ph/D,Ph/E,PhII/A,PhII/B,PhII/C,PhIII/A,PhIII/B,PhIII/C,PhIII/
    E,PhIV/D,PhV/B
# Pull out all the output columns into their own data set
output_vectors = df.iloc[:, num_inputs:]
# Personal Opinions,Discussion,Connect Activists,Forward Info,Online Actions,F2F
Updates,Facilitate F2F,Assemblies of protest or support,Marches,Protest
Meetings,Wearing of symbols,Displays of flags or symbolic colors,Violence
# Create naïve_bayes model for each output column
naïve_bayes = [] # list of naïve Bayes predictors for each column
for i in range(len(output_vectors.columns)):
nb = MultinomialNB() # or BernoulliNB() or GaussianNB() or CategoricalNB()
y = output_vectors.iloc[:, i]
nb.fit(input_vectors, y) # This is the magic!
naïve_bayes.append(nb) # Add to list of predictors
# Test the accuracy of the model
for output_column in range(len(output_vectors.columns)):
# Feed all the input vectors for prediction
output_predicted = naïve_bayes[output_column].predict(input_vectors)
# Extract the actual output column
output_actual = output_vectors.iloc[:, output_column]
# See if the predicted is actually correct
comparison = output_predicted == output_actual
#
# Three different ways of measuring accuracy
#
# A. Just the mean correct
accuracy = comparison.mean()
print(f'\n\nA) Accuracy {output_vectors.columns[output_column]}:
{accuracy*100:.2f}%')
# B. Confusion matrix
conf_mat = confusion_matrix(output_actual, output_predicted)
print('\n\nB) Confusion Matrix:')
print(conf_mat)
# C. Precision, Recall, F1
report = classification_report(output_actual, output_predicted)
print('\n\nC) Precision, Recall, F1')
print(report)
```

Training data is required to build Bayesian classifiers (Witten et al., 2011). Training data includes fully coded data for April 21 and 25 completed during the content analysis that associates study constructs (IAM Phases) with class variables (nonviolent action and digital activism, which are two types of social action). Also included in the training data are coded tweets that were retweeted most and tweets that represent the most frequently occurring n-grams on April 22, 23, 24, 26, 27, and 28.

Results

Research Question 1

Content Analysis to Determine SCK

Answering research question 1 begins with presenting the results of the content analysis to determine SCK (April 21, April 25, and others with most frequent n-grams and/or retweets) according to the IAM. Table 14.1 presents a few sample tweets from each IAM Phase that came from either April 21 or April 25:

Table 14.1 Sample Tweet IAM Coding

IAM Phases	Sample Tweets
Phase I	Im appalled this is horrible disgusting & sickening when is this Mayhem going 2 stop!? #FreddieGray #BlackLivesMatter #NoJusticeNoPeace #HLN
Phase II	Sad, but it seems to me that #BlackLivesMatter to some ppl only when there's money to be made. #Ferguson #Baltimore #FreddieGray
Phase III	Insurance will cover damage to police cars. Insurance won't bring back black lives lost to police violence. #FreddieGray #BlackLivesMatter
Phase IV	12956959 total arrests divided by 1200 killed by police equals 0.00009261 deaths occurs for every arrest. #FreddieGray #BlackLivesMatter
Phase V	#Justice 4 #FreddieGray march 12:00 noon on the West Side #Baltimore spread the word #Retweet https://t.co/gQNmOpa3V1 #Blacklivesmatter

Table 14.2 lists the total counts for each IAM Phase and the percentage of the total number of tweets on the given day. Days are listed in the left column. The total number of tweets on each day is listed below the dates. Note that IAM Phases that are not included in Table 14.2 were not present in the data and subsequently do not appear in the SCK lexicon analysis.

Most of the data (91.6% on April 21 and 73% on April 25) was coded as Phase I. A few examples of Phase I are as follows:

#FreddieGray #BlackLivesMatter Its time for a national call to action Black America. We must demand both justice and systemic change now!
CNN: Police: We failed to get #FreddieGray timely medical care after arrest http://t.co/nHcdU14muX #BlackLivesMatter

Also of note are the Phase V/B codes, most of which have to do with people actively engaging in nonviolent action or digital action. April 25 saw a large number of demonstrations which accounts for the larger percentage of Phase V/B codes as compared to April 21.

Table 14.2 SCK Content Analysis Coding

	PhI/A	PhI/B	PhI/C	PhI/D	PhI/E	PhII/A	PhII/B	PhII/C	PhIII/A	PhIII/B	PhIII/C	PhIII/E	PhIV/D	PhV/B
April 21	164	51	84	37	74	9	0	0	1	1	5	0	1	21
(n=285)	36.6%	11.4%	18.8%	8.3%	16.5%	2.0%			.2%	.2%	1.1%		.2%	4.7%
April 25	467	81	300	76	96	35	2	6	0	8	5	2	1	318
(n=922)	33.4%	5.8%	21.5%	5.4%	6.9%	2.5%	.1%	.4%		.6%	.4%	.1%	.1%	22.8%
Others	14	4 6.9%	23	2	4 6.9%	1	0	0	0	0	0	0	0	10
(n=34)	24.1%		39.7%	3.4%		1.7%								17.2%

SCK Lexicon Analysis

The SCK lexicon analysis was conducted using the IAM lexicon. The total number of n-grams (words and phrases of varying length) in the final lexicon are displayed in Table 14.3 according to IAM Phase.

Table 14.3 IAM Lexicon n-Gram Counts

IAM Phase	Total n-Grams
PhI/A	1179
PhI/B	128
PhI/C	845
PhI/D	135
PhI/E	227
PhII/A	146
PhII/B	7
PhII/C	16
PhIII/A	7
PhIII/B	28
PhIII/C	12
PhIII/E	3
PhIV/D	6
PhV/B	389

The numbers in the Total n-Grams column are the numbers of words and phrases that were associated with each Phase/Operation in the IAM lexicon. For example, IAM Phase V/B was represented by 389 n-grams. The final lexicon included a total of 3,128 n-grams across all IAM Phases. Samples of the n-grams included in the IAM lexicon are provided in Table 14.4 according to IAM Phase.

The examples in Table 14.4 are part of the total n-grams presented in Table 14.3. Note that in some cases (e.g., Phase III/A and III/E) the number of tweets that exemplify these Phases were minimal. The words provided in Table 14.4 are a mix of the initial seed words identified using the manual approach to lexicon development and the dictionary approach.

Table 14.4 IAM Lexicon n-Grams

IAM Phase	Sample n-Grams
PhI/A	congratulations
	inappropriate
	calm
	unacceptable
	disturbing
PhI/B	Shoutout
	Solidarity
	Rest in Power
	RIP
	My condolences
PhI/C	hundreds protest
	police custody
	gandhi
	so many more
	ICYMI

(Continued)

Table 14.4 (Continued)

IAM Phase	Sample n-Grams
PhI/D	why so
	Who has
	dont they
	did he
	who directed
PhI/E	racist police
	no justice
	Police Impunity
	murder
	another black man
PhII/A	Transparency
	SMH
	right to shutdown
	hugging protesters
	being hijacked
PhII/B	killed cops first
	HOW people
	killed bulls first
	killed coppers first
	how citizens
PhII/C	paid vacation
	death penalty
	sweet cream
	over sports
	execution
PhIII/A	can't trust
	can not trust
	cannot trust
	cannot rely
	cant rely
PhIII/B	focus on
	type of coverage
	forget about
	JENNER DAY
	property damage
PhIII/C	worry about
	White Americans
	Insurance will
	concern about
	occupation about
PhIII/E	the muscle
	criminal organization
	the muscleman
PhIV/D	Pls see @ErinBurnett's tweet
	@ErinBurnett's tweet
	please see
	@ErinBurnetts tweet
	police equals
PhV/B	spread the word
	LIVE
	happening now
	From the streets
	1:00 PM

The final piece of the puzzle in answering research question 1 is to examine the results of the SCK lexicon analysis. The SCK lexicon analysis took the 3,128 n-grams across all IAM Phases and performed automatic classification on the data that was not part of the training dataset (April 21 and April 25).

Table 14.5 lists the total counts for each IAM Phase and the percentage of the total number of tweets on the given day. Data generated automatically by R did not classify all of the data. Data without codes are listed in the No Codes column.

Table 14.5 SCK Lexicon Analysis Results

	PhI/A	PhI/B	PhI/C	PhI/D	PhI/E	PhII/A	PhII/C	PhIII/B	PhIII/C	PhV/B	No Codes
April 22	163	6	5	0	37	8	1	0	0	11	318
(n=472)	70.6%	2.6%	2.2%		16.0%	3.5%	0.4%			4.8%	67.4%
April 23	182	8	4	0	33	3	0	0	0	17	314
(n=507)	73.7%	3.2%	1.6%		13.4%	1.2%				6.9%	61.9%
April 24	129	10	2	0	42	4	1	2	1	10	252
(n=462)	64.2%	5.0%	1.0%		20.9%	2.0%	0.5%	1.0%	.5%	5.0%	54.5%
April 26	837	48	15	1.1%	112	16	1	1	0	51	1301
(n=2122)	77.4%	4.4%	1.4%		10.4%	1.5%	.1%	.1%		4.7%	61.3%
April 27	798	48	34	2	119	16	0	2	0	46	1392
(n=2108)	74.9%	4.5%	3.2%	0.2%	11.2%	1.5%		2%		4.3%	66.0%
April 28	1318	113	33	1	214	38	2	0	0	85	2800
(n=4595)	73.1%	6.3%	1.8%	0.1%	11.9%	2.1%	0.1%			4.7%	60.9%

According to the results presented in this section, the answer to research question 1 is that SCK did occur in the Freddie Gray #BlackLivesMatter network of practice. Content analysis to determine SCK and SCK lexicon analysis were all able to identify SCK in the dataset at varying levels. Content analysis identified Phase I/A and Phase I/C at higher rates than lexicon analysis. Overall, the IAM identified that postings occurred mostly in Phase I as many examples of sharing opinions and providing examples were found. However, data at Phase II, Phase III, Phase IV, and Phase V is also present.

Research Question 2

Naïve Bayes Model for SCK and Social Action

This section presents the accuracy of the naïve Bayes model created using the training dataset. Accuracy is assessed using a confusion matrix, which displays the number of instances the model classified class variables, in this case social action, which is comprised of digital activism and nonviolent action, in the categories displayed in Table 14.6.

Table 14.6 Confusion Matrix Position Definitions

	Predicted Positive	*Predicted Negative*
Actual Positive	True Positive (TP)	False Negative (FN) – Type II Error
Actual Negative	False Positive (FP) – Type I Error	True Negative (TN)

True positives (TP) and true negatives (TN) are correct classifications (Witten et al., 2011). The overall accuracy of the classification is calculated by dividing the sum of the correct classifications by the total number of classifications as follows:

$$Accuracy = \frac{TP + TN}{TP + TN + FP + FN}$$

The confusion matrix and accuracy percentage for each digital activism category is listed in Table 14.7, while nonviolent action is listed in Table 14.8.

The lowest accuracy rate for the class variables in the naïve Bayes model between digital activism and nonviolent action was 80.74% as shown in Table 14.7 for the forward information category of digital activism. Many of the categories between these two components of social action were above 90% accuracy with some getting as high as 99%. Research question 2 is thus answered affirmatively as an accurate naïve Bayes classifier was created based on IAM Phases.

Discussion

This study found SCK occurred within the #BlackLivesMatter network of practice. One of the common threads in the network of practice were the many people sharing their Phase I opinions about Freddie Gray and police brutality, like this user, "Glorifying guns and violence from #Congressmen to the street cop leads to killing." or another, "#FreddieGray died bc he ran away from a threat: Police." Others contributed information and resources like this tweet that included a link to another story removed for the purposes of this chapter, "In #FreddieGray's Neighborhood Residents Say Police Harassment Constant [link removed]." These resources were important to the gestalt of the data because they went beyond thoughts and opinions with evidence for the points being made.

Table 14.7 Digital Activism Classification Performance

Personal Opinions	Discussion	Connect Activists	Forward Information
[[701 95] [133 312]] 81.63%	[[1146 14] [20 61]] 97.26%	[[1232 2] [7 0]] 99.27%	[[953 19] [220 49]] 80.74%

Online Actions	F2F Updates	Facilitate F2F
[[1021 53] [61 106]] 90.81%	[[864 54] [150 173]] 83.56%	[[1219 1] [21 0]] 98.23%

Table 14.8 Nonviolent Action Classification Performance

Assemblies of Protest	Marches	Protest Meetings
[[1221 2] [18 0]] 98.39%	[[869 48] [144 180]] 84.53%	[[1238 1] [2 0]] 99.76%

Although not much Phase II data was present, the tweets that were made in this Phase were quite contentious. For example, "#BlackLivesMatter the people who are rioting & looting are scum. . . . This has nothing to do with #FreddieGray and you know it." Others countered this point of view with tweets such as, "I'm not offended by the destruction of cop cars. I'm offended by racist/oppressive State violence." The very nature of the overall discussion being held on #BlackLivesMatter is wrought with conflict because the dominant narrative categorically ignores issues of police brutality and racism.

It is possible that many of the people engaged in #BlackLivesMatter were already experiencing dissonance. This could explain why not much Phase II data was found. For instance, the online movement that sparked the Arab Spring was organized around the Egyptian police beating Khaled Said to death in the streets reportedly because he was in possession of videotaped evidence incriminating police in sharing the spoils from a drug bust (Lim, 2012). Previously Egyptians were weary of police brutality but the "We are all Khaled Said" movement provided Egyptians the opportunity to negotiate their identities and coalesce around a shared sense of victimization online. Similarly, minorities have been subject to racism and police brutality for countless years but the rise of #BlackLivesMatter could be used as a venue to start resolving their dissonance by creating change instead of continuing to ignore the injustices.

In Phase III, the gestalt of the discussion refocused attention on systemic issues related to Freddie Gray with one user noting, "You sure that a few cops and a broken neck are the right problem to focus on in #BlackLivesMatter #FOP #FreddieGray." In Phase III, the importance of history was also underscored by one user tweeting "Until white Americans understand or fully acknowledge history things won't change #FreddieGray #BlackLivesMatter." These comments are important in shifting the dominant narrative about police brutality and racism and allowed people to go beyond their Phase I thoughts and opinions.

Phase V, especially Phase V/B, included many people working for change by engaging in social action via nonviolent action and digital activism. Within digital activism, people took online actions like this user, "The #racist twitter troll accounts list to be blocked is UPDATED." Others engaged in digital activism by attempting to connect activists tweeting, "For my LA folks Justice for #FreddieGray Emergency #Protest today, Sat., 1 pm @ 5th & Los Angeles Sts downtown." Social action also included nonviolent action as people participated in assemblies of protest or support with many people livestreaming events and protests, like this user, "At the #freddieGray vigil." These Phase V applications of learning are important because it provides evidence of online comments leading to people taking action. Within the network of practice, Phase V examples serve as resources for people coming to terms with how to take constructive action regarding their experiences with police brutality and racism.

This study also found that it is possible to create a naïve Bayes classifier based on IAM Phases for social action, which includes digital activism and nonviolent action. This is encouraging because the data used to build the naïve Bayes classifier mostly contained Phase I data, specifically in Phase I/A – Statement of observation or opinion and Phase I/C – Corroborating examples provided. Taking these categories at face value, they seem to have more to do with digital activism categories such as Personal Opinions and Forward Information. Achieving 80% accuracy for both digital activism categories associated with Phase I is a good start but can be improved upon. The model was extremely accurate when it came to predicting the Phase V digital activism categories Connect Activists and Facilitate Face-to-Face and Nonviolent Action categories with Assemblies of Protest and Protest Meetings all reaching higher than 98%. The high accuracy of the predictions made at Phase V suggest that it is possible to create models that predict social action by measuring digital activism and nonviolent action using data that comes mostly from the lower levels of SCK.

Conclusion

This study used the IAM to understand the gestalt of the messages on #BlackLivesMatter and revealed that SCK occurs in the Twitter #BlackLivesMatter network of practice. While the majority of participants were in Phase I sharing opinions, others were ready to engage in nonviolent action in Phase V as they participated in assemblies of protest and in digital activism as they attempted to connect activists online. People ultimately learned about police brutality and engaged in various forms of social action as part of their participation in the #BlackLivesMatter network of practice. The lexicon and naïve Bayes classifier developed for SCK as part of this study using SLAM (lexicon analysis and naïve Bayes) can be used as a cornerstone for the automation of qualitative coding and ongoing monitoring of social media traffic to predict digital action and nonviolent action.

Note

This chapter draws from the following dissertation in the list of references: Sánchez (2018).

References

AP. (2015). Freddie Gray protest draws thousands in Baltimore. *CBC/Radio-Canada*. Retrieved March 10 from www.cbc.ca/news/world/freddie-gray-protest-draws-thousands-in-baltimore-1.3048998

Batrinca, B., & Treleaven, P. C. (2015). Social media analytics: A survey of techniques, tools and platforms. *AI & Society: Journal of Knowledge, Culture and Communication, 30*(1), 89–116. https://doi.org/10.1007/s00146-014-0549-4

Black Lives Matter. (2017). *What we believe.* https://blacklivesmatter.com/about/what-we-believe/

Blair, A. (2013). Democratising the learning process: The use of Twitter in the teaching of politics and international relations. *Politics, 33*(2), 135–145. https://doi.org/10.1111/1467-9256.12008

Bonilla, Y., & Rosa, J. (2015). #Ferguson: Digital protest, hashtag ethnography, and the racial politics of social media in the United States. *American Ethnologist, 42*(1), 4–17. https://doi.org/10.1111/amet.12112

Brym, R., Godbout, M., Hoffbauer, A., Menard, G., & Zhang, T. H. (2014). Social media in the 2011 Egyptian uprising. *The British Journal of Sociology, 65*(2), 266–292. https://doi.org/10.1111/1468-4446.12080

Buckingham Shum, S., & Ferguson, R. (2012). Social learning analytics. *Educational Technology & Society, 15*(3), 3–26. www.ifets.info/journals/15_3/2.pdf

Dron, J., & Anderson, T. (2014). *Teaching crowds: Learning and social media*. AU Press. desLibris e-book: www.deslibris.ca/ID/448837

Flor, N. V. (2014). *OILS Twitter Scraper*. Creative Commons Attribution-ShareAlike 4.0 International License.

Freelon, D., McIlwain, D. C., & Clark, D. M. (2016). *Beyond the hashtags*. C. F. M. S. Impact.

Freelon, D., McIlwain, D. C., & Clark, D. M. (2018). Quantifying the power and consequences of social media protest. *New Media & Society, 20*(3), 990–1011. https://doi.org/10.1177/1461444816676646

Gleason, B. (2013). #Occupy wall street: Exploring informal learning about a social movement on Twitter. *American Behavioral Scientist, 57*(7), 966–982.

Gunawardena, C. N., Flor, N. V., Gómez, D., & Sánchez, D. (2016). Analyzing social construction of knowledge online by employing interaction analysis, learning analytics, and social network analysis. *Quarterly Review of Distance Education, 17(3)*, 35–60. (e-Learners and Their Data, Part 1: Conceptual, Research, and Exploratory Perspectives).

Gunawardena, C. N., Flor, N. V., & Sánchez, D. M. (2018). *Learning analytics and social construction of knowledge online*. Distance Teaching and Learning Conference, Madison, WI.

Gunawardena, C. N., Lowe, C. A., & Anderson, T. (1997). Analysis of a global online debate and the development of an interaction analysis model for examining social construction of knowledge in computer conferencing. *Journal of Educational Computing Research, 17*(4), 397–431.

Harlow, S., & Guo, L. (2014). Will the revolution be Tweeted or Facebooked? Using digital communication tools in immigrant activism. *Journal of Computer-Mediated Communication, 19*(3), 463–478.

Hu, M., & Liu, B. (2004). *Mining and summarizing customer reviews.* Proceedings of the Tenth ACM SIGKDD International Conference on Knowledge Discovery and Data Mining (KDD '04), Seattle, WA, USA.

Juris, J. S. (2012). Reflections on #Occupy everywhere: Social media, public space, and emerging logics of aggregation. *American Ethnologist, 39*(2), 259–279.

Krippendorff, K. (1980). *Content analysis: An introduction to its methodology.* Sage Publications. http://catdir.loc.gov/catdir/enhancements/fy0658/80019166-t.html

Langley, P., & Sage, S. (1994). *Induction of selective Bayesian classifiers.* Proceedings of the Tenth International Conference on Uncertainty in Artificial Intelligence, Seattle, WA.

Lave, J., & Wenger, E. (1991). *Situated learning: Legitimate peripheral participation.* Cambridge University Press.

Lim, M. (2012). Clicks, cabs, and coffee houses: Social media and oppositional movements in Egypt, 2004–2011. *Journal of Communication, 62*(2), 231–248.

Liu, B. (2012). *Sentiment analysis and opinion mining.* Morgan & Claypool.

Long, P., & Siemens, G. (2011). Penetrating the fog: Analytics in learning and education. *EDUCAUSE Review, 46*(5), 30–41. https://net.educause.edu/ir/library/pdf/erm1151.pdf

Manning, C. D., & Schütze, H. (1999). *Foundations of statistical natural language processing.* MIT Press.

Matthews, S., & Noor, M. (2017). *Celebrating four years of organizing to protect black lives.* https://drive.google.com/file/d/0B0pJEXffvS0uOHdJREJnZ2JJYTA/view

Merriam, S. B., & Caffarella, R. S. (1999). *Learning in adulthood a comprehensive guide* (2nd ed.). Jossey-Bass Publishers.

Miller, G. A., Beckwith, R., Fellbaum, C., Gross, D., & Miller, K. J. (1990). Introduction to WordNet: An on-line lexical database. *International Journal of Lexicography, 3*(4), 235–244.

Penney, J., & Dadas, C. (2014). (Re)Tweeting in the service of protest: Digital composition and circulation in the Occupy Wall Street movement. *New Media & Society, 16*(1), 74–90.

Sánchez, D. M. (2018). *Building a call to action: Social action in networks of practice* [Doctoral Dissertation, University of New Mexico]. Albuquerque, NM.

Sharp, G. (1973). *The politics of nonviolent action.* P. Sargent Publisher.

Tufekci, Z. (2017). *Twitter and tear gas: The power and fragility of networked protest* [Book]. Yale University Press.

Wenger, E. (2010). Communities of practice and social learning systems: The career of a concept. In C. Blackmore (Ed.), *Social learning systems and communities of practice.* Springer.

Wenger, E., Trayner, B., & De Laat, M. (2011). *Promoting and assessing value creation in communities and networks: A conceptual framework.* Ruud de Moor Centrum, Open Universiteit of the Netherlands.

Whyte, T., & Joyce, M. (2010). Glossary. In M. Joyce (Ed.), *Digital activism decoded: The new mechanics of change* (pp. 217–221). International Debate Education Association. http://search.ebscohost.com/login.aspx?direct=true&scope=site&db=nlebk&db=nlabk&AN=360663

Wickham, H., & Grolemund, G. (2016). *R for data science.* O'Reilly. http://r4ds.had.co.nz

Witten, I. H., Frank, E., & Hall, M. A. (2011). *Data mining: Practical machine learning tools and techniques* (3rd ed.). Morgan Kaufmann.

15 Social Network Centrality, Social Construction of Knowledge, and Nurse Practitioner Competency in Asynchronous Online Discussions

Sharon Schaaf

Ensuring high-quality patient care hinges significantly on nurse practitioner competency. In the realm of online and hybrid nurse practitioner programs, where asynchronous online discussions serve as a pivotal forum for student engagement, interaction, connection, and knowledge-sharing, understanding the determinants of nurse practitioner competency becomes paramount. While previous studies have delved into social influence measures and the social construction of knowledge (SCK), their connection with nurse practitioner competency remains uncharted territory.

To enhance the effectiveness of online platforms for nurse practitioner education, it becomes imperative to unravel the intricate ties between nurse practitioner competency, the group's knowledge construction, and social influence that emerges as an integral part of this group dynamic. Consequently, the purpose of this study was to apply the Interaction Analysis Model (IAM) and Social Learning Analytic Methods (SLAM) to explore into the realm of nurse practitioner competency within the context of asynchronous online discussions.

In this study, we employed the IAM and SNA to analyze an asynchronous online discussion involving nine adult-gerontology acute care nurse practitioner (AGACNP) students. The discussion revolved around an ill-structured, complex case scenario. A student leader created a video explaining the management of the case scenario, while the other students in the group responded in a free-flowing and engaging manner.

Relevant Literature and Conceptual Framework

Previous research has revealed the pivotal role of asynchronous online discussions in online learning, emphasizing their support for student interaction, knowledge-sharing, and critical thinking (Brierton et al., 2016; Chen & Huang, 2019; Durrington et al., 2006; Osborne et al., 2018; Ringler et al., 2015; Woods & Bliss, 2016). Recognized as an effective resource for learner communication, the asynchronous nature of these forums allows students ample time to contemplate and reflect on materials, thus fostering higher-order thinking skills (Brierton et al., 2016; Chen & Huang, 2019; Durrington et al., 2006; DiPasquale & Hunter, 2018; Gunawardena et al., 2016; Harmon et al., 2014; Jo et al., 2016; Osborne et al., 2018; Ringler et al., 2015; Woods & Bliss, 2016; Yen et al., 2019). Scenario-based discussions have been instrumental in promoting critical thinking across various academic disciplines (Foo & Quek, 2019), while scaffolding has effectively facilitated the development of critical thinking, aligning with the findings of DiPasquale and Hunter (2018). Socratic questioning, although recognized as a guiding force toward critical thinking, awaits further exploration to determine the most effective types of questions.

DOI: 10.4324/9781003324461-19

The design of the discussion board can significantly influence learning outcomes. As discussions evolve and connections form, students find their place within the network, with their location identifying at-risk students and predicting academic success (Calderon & Sood, 2020; Chen & Huang, 2019; Desai et al., 2020; Durairaj & Umar, 2015; Jo et al., 2016; Yen et al., 2019). Typically, at-risk students are situated on the periphery of the network, while those at the center tend to excel (Chen & Huang, 2019; Joksimovic et al., 2016).

The SCK results from interactions and the sharing of social capital. However, numerous asynchronous online discussions demonstrate lower levels of knowledge construction, as assessed by the IAM with limited attainment of higher levels (Afify, 2019; Brierton et al., 2016; Gunawardena et al., 1997; Harmon et al., 2014; Osborne et al., 2018; Ringler et al., 2015; Woods & Bliss, 2016; Yen et al., 2019). Research also highlights a close relationship between knowledge construction and social influence (Gunawardena et al., 2016; Nieves & Osorio, 2013; Zhao et al., 2016).

Nurse practitioner education has expanded into the online environment, with asynchronous online discussions being a common tool in online programs (Massey et al., 2019; Jo et al., 2016; Raymond et al., 2016). Progressing and completing a nurse practitioner program requires students to fulfill national competency standards for certification (Distler, 2015; Schumacher & Risco, 2017; Trachtenberg et al., 2019). Therefore, it raises the question of how SCK and social influence that forms within asynchronous online discussions reflect participants' achievement of these required standards.

Conceptual Framework

The study drew guidance from three theories: social constructivism, social network theory, and the Synergy Model for Patient Care.

Social constructivism, as a foundational educational theory, asserts the proactive role that learners play in the construction of their own knowledge. This perspective emphasizes that learning is not merely a passive absorption of information but an active process where individuals actively shape their understanding through interactions with both their peers and the learning environment. The influential work of Vygotsky (1978) further underlines the central tenets of social constructivism. Vygotsky's theory posits that knowledge isn't a solitary endeavor; instead, it is co-constructed through collaborative processes. In this collaborative learning journey, individuals engage in dynamic interactions with their peers, educators, and the educational context itself. These interactions foster an environment where new ideas are introduced and shared, allowing them to become integrated into the learner's existing knowledge framework.

Crucially, in this collaborative endeavor, new ideas are not imposed on learners. Instead, they are assimilated in a manner that aligns seamlessly with the learner's current understanding and cognitive abilities. This accommodation ensures that the new information is meaningful and accessible to the individual, facilitating its integration into their existing cognitive schema. In essence, learners actively engage in a process of sense-making, where they incorporate novel insights into their mental framework in a way that enhances their comprehension and knowledge base. In the realm of education, this perspective has profound implications, encouraging educators to foster collaborative and interactive learning environments that empower learners to take an active role in shaping their knowledge and constructing meaning from their educational experiences.

Derived from the disciplines of psychology and sociology, social network theory constitutes a potent analytical framework for scrutinizing the intricate web of interactions and connections that weave through individuals, groups, and organizations within their respective networks (Borgatti & Ofem, 2011; Burt et al., 2013; Nimmon et al., 2019). This theory examines the dynamics of human relationships and the structures that underlie them.

At its core, social network theory goes beyond mere observation and seeks to critically dissect the very essence of network formation. It rigorously examines the emergence and evolution of connective pathways within the intricate architecture of network structures. This examination extends to the fluid movement of information, knowledge, and resources as they traverse along these pathways. In essence, the theory serves as a powerful lens through which we can gain insights into the intricate interplay of connections and the dynamics of information flow. Social network theory has proven invaluable for explaining the dynamics of social relationships, organizational collaboration, and information dissemination.

The Synergy Model for Patient Care, proposed by Becker and colleagues in 2006, represents a pivotal middle-range theory within the realm of healthcare. This model revolves around a central concept: the notion that patient characteristics exert a profound influence on nurse competencies, ultimately shaping the attainment of optimal patient and family outcomes.

In this model, the promotion of synergistic care is achieved by seamlessly integrating three major components: patient characteristics, nurse competencies, and outcomes. Patient characteristics encompass a wide array of factors, including their medical conditions, needs, preferences, and cultural background. These characteristics serve as the foundation upon which the care process is built. Nurse competencies, on the other hand, encompass the skills, knowledge, and abilities possessed by healthcare professionals. These competencies are honed through education, experience, and continuous professional development. Within the Synergy Model, nurse competencies are viewed as dynamic tools that can be tailored to meet the unique requirements of each patient.

The essence of synergy, as envisioned in this model, comes to fruition when patient needs align harmoniously with nurse competency. It is at this intersection that optimal patient and family outcomes are achieved. Synergistic care implies that the nurse's capabilities are precisely aligned with the patient's specific needs, resulting in the highest level of care and the most favorable outcomes. This model has been instrumental in guiding healthcare practices and ensuring that patient care remains patient-centered and outcomes-driven. It underscores the significance of tailoring nursing care to the individual needs of each patient, emphasizing the pivotal role of nurse competencies in achieving healthcare excellence.

Research Questions

The research questions for this study were:

1. What levels of social influence are exhibited by each of the individuals in the network?
2. What level of SCK is demonstrated by AGACNP students participating in an asynchronous online discussion?
3. What level of competency is demonstrated by AGACNP students participating in an asynchronous online discussion?
4. How do social influence, levels of construction of knowledge, and nurse practitioner competency relate to each other?

Methods

This section provides an overview of the study's design, the instructional layout of the online discussion, and the procedures followed for data collection and analysis.

Study Design

We used a retrospective, non-experimental, mixed-method design to explore the relationships among social influence, SCK, and competency within a group of advanced practice nursing students participating in an asynchronous online discussion. The study utilized a non-probability, convenience sample consisting of nine female students who engaged in an asynchronous online discussion board forum during the summer 2018 master's of science in nursing (MSN) course titled "Management of the Complex/Chronically Ill Adult-Gerontology Patient." This specific course was chosen due to the complex and ill-structured nature of the discussion board forum. Notably, this course was part of a six-term program, and the discussion occurred during the fourth term.

Instructional Design of the Discussion Forum

The instructional design of the discussion forum involved assigning a student leader to present a complex clinical scenario (Grand Rounds). This scenario included detailed patient history, physical examination findings, laboratory data, and diagnostic information. The presentation, delivered via a 5- to 8-minute video, required the student leader to:

- Accurately identify the patient's medical issues and create an evidence-based care plan addressing both acute and chronic health conditions
- Appropriately manage the acute and chronic health conditions
- Integrate advanced health assessment, advanced pharmacology, advanced pathophysiology, health promotion and protection, diagnostic and laboratory interpretation, and therapeutic interventions
- Include an assessment and plan for the patient

Other students in the course were tasked with viewing the video and participating in an open, unrestricted online discussion. They were encouraged to provide evidence-based suggestions, recommendations, and questions. This discussion took place over a seven-day period following the initial video posting.

Data Collection and Analysis

Data collection involved manually extracting each post from the discussion board within the learning management system (LMS). These posts were recorded as single lines in an Excel spreadsheet. Two columns were created: One for the de-identified name of the group member and another for the discussion board content. Additional columns were designated for coding using the IAM and nursing competency coding. Two separate coders conducted the coding after receiving instructions on IAM and nursing competency coding. Interrater reliability was assessed and found to be sufficient.

Qualitative content analysis played a pivotal role in coding both SCK and nursing competency. The analysis of SCK was conducted through the application of the IAM. By adopting this approach, the analysis aimed to provide a thorough and insightful understanding of how participants manifested SCK and nursing competency within the context of the discussion forum.

It's important to note that a single discussion post might encompass multiple sentences, each potentially belonging to different Phases within the IAM. However, the essence of the coding approach lay in capturing the post's holistic "gestalt" – coders didn't isolate individual sentences but rather examined the overall impression and characteristics conveyed by the entire post. This comprehensive perspective allowed for a nuanced understanding of how SCK was manifested within the discussion. The coded gestalt of each post served as the basis for subsequent data analysis, providing a richer and more holistic view of the phenomenon under investigation.

We assessed AGACNP competency using Benner's (1982) Novice-to-Expert Model. The various phases within this model were coded as ordinal data. In a manner akin to the content analysis conducted for the IAM, it's noteworthy that a discussion post could encompass multiple sentences, each potentially associated with different phases within Benner's model. In other words, coders did not mechanically count sentences; instead, they considered the comprehensive impression and characteristics conveyed by the entire post. This holistic approach ensured that the assessment of competency level captured the nuanced and comprehensive nature of each post, providing a richer understanding of the participants' nursing competencies. The coding system employed for competency encompassed five phases: Novice, Advanced Beginner, Competent, Proficient, and Expert.

We conducted quantitative SNA utilizing Microsoft Excel in conjunction with the NodeXL Basic plug-in. This analytical toolkit included four worksheets: edges, vertices, groups, and overall metrics. The aim of this SNA was to delve into the intricacies of the network's structure and dynamics.

The process for calculating social influence metrics involved several key steps:

1. **Creation of Social Edges**. We began by establishing the connections or "social edges" between network nodes, representing individuals or entities within the network.
2. **Setting Type to "Directed."** To account for the directional nature of relationships within the network, we configured the analysis as "Directed," acknowledging the flow of influence or information.
3. **Graph Metrics Selection**. Comprehensive analysis required us to select and calculate various graph metrics. This step allowed us to gain insights into the network's characteristics and functioning.

Additionally, to visually represent the network's structure, we employed sociogram visualization techniques, enhancing our understanding of its complexities. To create the sociogram:

1. **Layout Configuration**. We selected the Fruchterman-Reingold layout, optimizing the visual representation of network nodes and their connections.
2. **Autofill for Vertices**. Utilizing specific settings, we applied autofill to columns of vertices. This included labeling vertices as "Vertex," assigning fill colors based on "Betweenness," and adjusting vertex sizes to reflect "Betweenness" centrality.

Moreover, we harnessed the power of dynamic filters within NodeXL to identify potential subgroups or clusters within the network. This clustering process was facilitated by the Clauset-Newman-Moore algorithm, which allowed us to discern patterns and connections that might not be immediately evident.

The utilization of SNA in this study was instrumental in unraveling the underlying structure and relationships within the network of interest. For a more comprehensive exploration of SLAM, readers are encouraged to refer to Chapter 10, which provides an in-depth description and further insights into the methodology and its significance in research.

Results

We aimed to determine the levels of social influence exhibited by individuals within a network using Social Learning Analytic Methods. Metrics such as betweenness, closeness, eigenvector, indegree, and outdegree were examined for each participant in the discussion network. The results revealed two distinct subgroups among the students. Four students (A, B, F, and G) demonstrated high levels of social influence across all metrics, while five students (C, D, E, H, and I) had no betweenness and exhibited lower values in indegree, outdegree, closeness, and eigenvector. These findings highlight the varying degrees of social influence within the network, highlighting the presence of both highly influential individuals and those with limited influence.

The study sought to determine the levels of SCK demonstrated by AGACNP students in asynchronous online discussions. Analysis using the IAM revealed a balanced distribution between low (Phases 1 and II) and high (Phases III, IV, and V) levels of knowledge construction within individual discussion posts. Most posts were categorized as either Phase II or III. Additionally, when considering word counts, posts in Phases I and II ranged from 23 to 145 words, while those in Phases III, IV, and V ranged from 29 to 301 words. At the group member level, where the highest achieved phase was assigned, results showed that 44.4% of students were at Phase I and II, while 55.6% were at Phase III, IV, and V. These findings provide insights into the distribution of knowledge construction levels among AGACNP students in asynchronous online discussions, indicating a mix of lower and higher-level knowledge construction within the group.

We utilized content analysis to address the third research question: "What levels of nurse practitioner competency are demonstrated by students who participated in the discussion?" None of the discussion board posts were coded as novice, while 21.2% were categorized as advanced beginner. The majority, 78.8%, demonstrated competency, proficiency, or expertise. We further analyzed the data at the group member level, assigning the highest competency level achieved to each member. This step was essential for conducting correlation analysis with social influence metrics. The distribution of the highest competency phase achieved indicated that 89.9% engaged in discussions at the competent level or above, while only 11.1% did not demonstrate competency-level discussion. This allowed us to establish a relationship between social influence and competency levels within the group.

Table 15.1 Social Influence, IAM Phase, Competency Level

Member	Betweenness	Indegree	Outdegree	Closeness	Eigenvector	Highest IAM Phase Achieved	Highest Competency Level
Group 1							
Student A	24.33	8	7	0.125	0.167	4	4
Student B	3.00	5	3	0.091	0.130	4	4
Student C	0.00	2	3	0.083	0.120	3	3
Student D	0.00	1	2	0.071	0.059	2	3
Student E	0.00	1	1	0.067	0.033	1	2
Group 2							
Student F	3.33	2	6	0.100	0.151	3	5
Student G	3.33	4	3	0.100	0.151	5	4
Student H	0.00	3	2	0.077	0.094	2	4
Student I	0.00	2	2	0.077	0.094	2	3

Table 15.1 summarizes the social influence metrics, the highest level of IAM achieved by the discussion member, and the highest level of competency achieved by the group member. Figure 15.1 illustrates the sociogram of the group members created through NodeXL for the study.

We employed correlational analysis to address the fourth research question: "How do the levels of social influence, SCK, and nurse practitioner competency interrelate?" In this analysis, we compared the independent variables of SCK and level of social influence with the dependent variable of nurse practitioner competency, focusing on the highest levels achieved by group members.

We utilized the Spearman rho correlation coefficient to examine the relationships between social influence metrics (betweenness, indegree, outdegree, closeness, and eigenvector), the highest level of SCK attained, and the highest level of nurse practitioner competency demonstrated by discussion group members. The results of this correlational analysis are presented in Table 15.2.

A strong positive relationship emerged between nurse practitioner competency and betweenness (rho (7) = 0.747, $p < 0.05$), closeness (rho (7) = 0.787, $p < 0.05$), and eigenvector (rho (7) = 0.787, $p < 0.05$), signifying a significant connection between these variables. Group members with closer connections within the network tended to exhibit higher levels of competency. Conversely, a moderate positive correlation that was not statistically significant was observed between nurse practitioner competency and indegree (rho (7) = 0.652, $p > 0.05$) and outdegree (rho (7) = 0.647, $p > 0.05$), suggesting that competency was not influenced by one's role as an information producer or consumer within the network. In contrast, a weak and nonsignificant correlation was identified between the level of SCK and the highest level of nurse practitioner competency (r (7) = 0.201, $p > 0.05$). In essence, competency was not associated with contributions to SCK.

Furthermore, a robust positive relationship emerged between the level of SCK and betweenness (rho (7) = 0.798, $p < 0.01$), indegree centrality (r (7) = 0.848, $p < 0.01$), outdegree (rho (7) = 0.680, $p < 0.05$), closeness (rho (7) = 0.902, $p < 0.01$), and eigenvector (rho (7) = 0.902, $p < 0.01$), underscoring a significant connection between these variables. Group members with stronger connections within the network were inclined to achieve higher levels of knowledge construction.

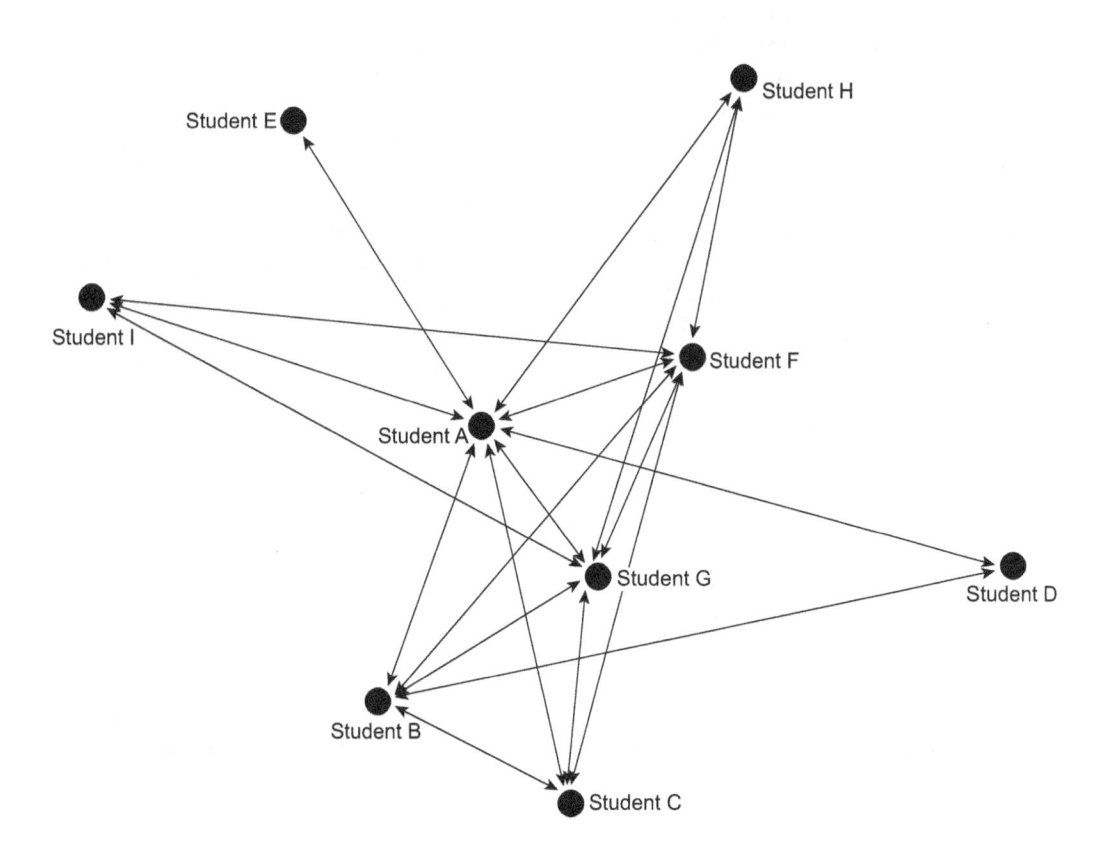

Figure 15.1 Sociogram visualization of the group members (Adapted from Schaaf, 2020)

Table 15.2 Correlational Analysis Results

	Competency	IAM	Betweenness	InDegree	OutDegree	Closeness	Eigenvector
Competency	1						
IAM	0.654	1					
Betweenness	.747*	.798**	1				
InDegree	.652	.848**	.703*	1			
OutDegree	.647	.680*	.765*	.523	1		
Closeness	.787*	.902**	.916**	.790*	.895**	1	
Eigenvector	.787*	.902**	.916**	.790*	.895**	1.00**	1
N=9							

* *Correlation is significant at the 0.05 level (2-tailed).*
** *Correlation is significant at the 0.01 level (2-tailed).*

Discussion and Conclusion

The results from the SNA shed light on the dynamics of the discussion group. Student A, who assumed the role of discussion leader, emerged as the central figure within the network. This observation aligns with previous research (deWever et al., 2006), suggesting that leaders tend to exhibit high social influence. Notably, Student A displayed elevated levels of betweenness, indegree, and outdegree centrality, indicating their role in facilitating information flow among group members. This likely contributed to the group's higher levels of SCK, as Student A actively engaged with all members, responding to queries, presenting rationales, and adapting management strategies based on peer input.

Examining the relationship between social influence and individual knowledge construction (IAM), a strong positive correlation emerged. Group members positioned at or near the network center tended to achieve higher IAM Phase levels, indicating a significant link between social influence and knowledge construction. This finding aligns with research by Chen and Huang (2019), who identified indegree centrality as a measure of prestige within networks.

Interestingly, the distribution of SCK levels revealed an unexpected pattern. Contrary to prior research by Gunawardena et al. (2016) and Zhao et al. (2016), a higher number of posts fell into Phase II rather than Phase I. This divergence could stem from the cohort's familiarity with one another and willingness to engage in disagreements, a known catalyst for knowledge construction (Aviv et al., 2003; Brierton et al., 2016; Durrington et al., 2006; DiPasquale & Hunter, 2018; Foo & Quek, 2019; Zhao et al., 2016). The complexity of the discussion topic likely also encouraged dissonance, further promoting knowledge construction.

Regarding nurse practitioner competency, most students demonstrated competence in clinical judgment, indicating effective scaffolding within the program. Regularly incorporating asynchronous online discussions into online or hybrid nursing programs offers nurse practitioner faculty a valuable forum and opportunity to evaluate student competency, supporting previous research (Distler, 2015; Fukada, 2018; Massey et al., 2019; NONPF, 2016; Raymond et al., 2016).

Analyzing the interplay between SNA, IAM, and nurse practitioner competency represents a novel approach. While a significant relationship was identified between network centralities and competency, no such correlation emerged between SCK and competency. This implies that while social influence plays a role in both knowledge construction and competency, the latter may not be directly influenced by the former. This also suggests that expert facilitators can lead online discussions even if they are not highly proficient in the topic being discussed.

Competency is indeed an outcome of education, while the SCK is a dynamic process. The process of SCK involves diverse contributions from all participants, regardless of their current competency levels. It is possible that the SCK is influenced more by the collective effort of the group rather than individual competency. The lack of a significant relationship between them may be due to differences in assessment methods, the focus of each construct, and the collaborative nature of knowledge construction. This reinforces the idea that educational outcomes and processes are multifaceted and influenced by various factors. Further research with larger numbers may be necessary to determine if SCK is related to nursing competency.

Nurse practitioner faculty bear the responsibility of delivering high-quality education to nurse practitioner students enrolled in online programs. The study highlighted the importance of nurse practitioner faculty possessing knowledge and insight into how students establish their social influence within the network and construct knowledge, all of which significantly impact the attainment of nurse practitioner competency. Faculty should consider the social environment's role in knowledge construction, further investigating these dynamics through SNA. Moreover, it emphasizes the potential for studying the social influence and connections formed by participants through the application of Social Network Analysis (SNA), a crucial method within the realm of SLAM.

References

Afify, M. (2019). The influence of groups size in the asynchronous online discussions on the development of critical thinking skills, and on improving students' performance in online discussion forum. *International Journal of Emerging Technology in Learning, 14*(5), 132–152. https://doi.org/10.3991/ijet.v.14i05.9351

Aviv, R., Erlich, Z., Ravid, G., & Geva, A. (2003). Network analysis of knowledge construction in asynchronous learning networks. *Journal of Asynchronous Learning Networks, 7*(3), 1–23.

Becker, D., Kaplow, R., Muenzen, P., & Hartigan, C. (2006). Activities performed by acute and critical care advanced practice nurses: American Association of Critical-Care Nurses study of practice. *American Journal of Critical Care, 15*(2), 130–148.

Benner, P. (1982). From novice to expert. *The American Journal of Nursing, 82*(3), 402–407.

Borgatti, S., & Ofem, B. (2011). Social network theory and analysis. In A. Daly (Ed.), *Social network theory and educational change* (pp. 17–29). Cambridge, MA: Harvard Education Press.

Brierton, S., Wilson, E., Kistler, M., Flowers, J., & Jones, D. (2016). A comparison of higher order thinking skills demonstrated in synchronous and asynchronous online college discussion posts. *North American Colleges and Teachers of Agriculture, 60*(1).

Burt, R., Kilduff, M., & Tasselli, S. (2013). Social network analysis: Foundations and frontiers on advantage. *Annual Review of Psychology, 64*, 527–527. https://doi.org/10.1146/annurev-psych-113011-143828

Calderon, O., & Sood, C. (2020). Evaluating learning outcomes of an asynchronous online discussion assignment: A post-priori content analysis. *Interactive Learning Environments, 28*(1), 3–17. https://doi.org/10.1080/104984820.2018.1510421

Chen, B., & Huang, T. (2019). It is about timing: Network prestige in asynchronous online discussions. *Journal of Computer Assisted Learning, 35*, 503–515. https://doi.org/10.111.jcal.12355

Desai, U., Ramasamy, V., & Kiper, J. (2020). A study on student performance evaluation using discussion board networks. *Paper Session: SIGCSE, March 11–14, 2020.* Portland, OR.

deWever, B., Van Winkle, M., & Valcke, M. (2006). Discussing patient management online: The impact of roles on knowledge construction for students interning at the paediatric ward. *Advances in Health Sciences Education, 13*, 25–42. https://doi.org/10.1007/s10459-006-9022-6

DiPasquale, J., & Hunter, W. (2018). Critical thinking in asynchronous online discussions: A systematic review. *Canadian Journal of Learning and Technology, 44*(2), 1–25.

Distler, J. (2015). Online nurse practitioner education: Achieving student competencies. *The Nurse Practitioner, 40*(11), 44–49.

Durairaj, K., & Umar, I. (2015). A proposed conceptual framework in measuring interaction and knowledge construction level in asynchronous forum among university students. *Prodecia – Social and Behavioral Sciences, 176*, 451–457. https://doi.org/10.1016/l.sbspro.2015.01.496

Durrington, V., Berryhill, A., & Swafford, J. (2006). Strategies for enhancing student interactivity in an online environment. *College Teaching, 54*(1), 190–193.

Foo, S., & Quek, C. (2019). Developing students' critical thinking through asynchronous online discussions: A literature review. *Malaysian Online Journal of Educational Technology, 7*(2), 37–52. http://doi.org/10.17220/mojet.2019.02.003

Fukada, M. (2018). Nursing competency: Definition, structure, and development. *Yonago Acta Medica, Review Article: Special Contribution, 61*(1), 1–7.

Gunawardena, C., Flor, N., Gomez, D., & Sánchez, D. (2016). Analyzing social construction of knowledge online by employing interaction analyses, learning analytics, and social network analysis. *The Quarterly Review of Distance Education, 17*(3), 35–66.

Gunawardena, C., Lowe, C., & Anderson, T. (1997). Analysis of global online debate and the development of an interaction analysis model for examining social construction of knowledge in computer conferencing. *Journal of Educational Computing Research, 17*(4), 397–431.

Harmon, O., Alpert, W., & Histen, J. (2014). Online discussion and learning outcomes. *International Advances in Economic Research, 20*, 33–44. https://doi.org/10.1007/s11294-013-9453-9

Jo, I., Park, Y., & Lee, H. (2016). Three interaction patterns on asynchronous online discussion behaviors: A methodological comparison. *Journal of Computer Assisted Learning, 33*, 106–122. https://doi.org/10.111/jcal.12168

Joksimovic, S., Manataki, A., Gasevic, D., Dawson, S., Kovanovic, V., & de Kereki, I. (2016). Proceedings of the Sixth International Conference on Learning Analytics & Knowledge, 315–323. https://doi.org/10.1145/2883851.2883928

Massey, D., Johnston, A., Byrne, J., & Osborne, D. (2019). The digital age: A scoping review of nursing students' perceptions of the use of online discussion boards. *Nurse Education Today, 81*, 26–33. https://doi.org/10/1016/j.nedt.2019.06.013

National Organization of Nurse Practitioner Faculties (NONPF). (2016). *Adult-gerontology acute care and primary care NP competencies.* National Organization of Nurse Practitioner Faculties.

Nieves, J., & Osorio, J. (2013). The role of social networks in knowledge creation. *Knowledge Management Research & Practice, 11*, 62–77. https://doi.org/10.1057/kmrp.2012.28

Nimmon, L., Artino, A., & Varpio, L. (2019). Social network theory in interprofessional education: Revealing hidden power. *Journal of Graduate Medical Education*, 247–250.

Osborne, D., Byrne, J., Massey, D., & Johnston, A. (2018). Use of online asynchronous discussion boards to engage students, enhance critical thinking, and foster staff-student/student-student collaboration: A mixed method study. *Nurse Education Today, 70*, 40–46. https://doi.org/10.1016/j.nedt.2018.08.014

Raymond, A., Jacob, E., Jacob, D., & Lyons, J. (2016). Peer learning a pedagogical approach to enhance online learning: A qualitative exploration. *Nurse Education Today*, 165–169. http://doi.org/1016.j.nedt.2016.05.016

Ringler, I., Schubert, C., Deem, J., Flores, J., Friestad-Tate, J., & Lockwood, R. (2015). Improving the asynchronous online learning environment using discussion boards. *Journal of Educational Technology, 12*(4), 15–27.

Schaaf, S. (2020). *Social network centrality, social construction of knowledge, and nurse practitioner competency in asynchronous online discussions among adult gerontology acute care nurse practitioner students* (Order No. 28157135). Available from Dissertations & Theses @ University of New Mexico; ProQuest Dissertations & Theses Global. (2753287460). https://libproxy.unm.edu/login?url=www.proquest.com/dissertations-theses/social-network-centrality-construction-knowledge/docview/2753287460/se-2

Schumacher, G., & Risco, K. (2017). Nurse practitioner program curriculum development: A competency-based approach. *The Journal for Nurse Practitioners, 13*(2), e75–e81.

Tractenberg, R., Wilkinson, M., Bull, A., Pellathy, T., & Riley, J. (2019). A developmental trajectory supporting the evaluation and achievement of competencies: Articulating the mastery rubric for the nurse practitioner (MR-NP) program curriculum. *PLoS One, 14*(11), e0224593. https://doi.org/10.1371/journal.pone.0224593

Vygotsky, L. (1978). Interaction between learning and development. In M. Cole, V. John-Steiner, S. Scribner, & E. Souberman (Eds.), *Mind in society*. Cambridge, MA: Harvard University Press.

Woods, K., & Bliss, K. (2016). Facilitating successful online discussions. *The Journal of Effective Teaching, 16*(2), 76–92.

Yen, C., Bozkurt, A., Tu, C., Sujo-Montes, L., Rodas, C. (2019). A predictive study of students' self-regulated learning skills and their roles in social network interaction of online discussion board. *Journal of Educational Technology Development and Exchange, 11*(1). http://doi.org/10.18785/jetde.1101.02

Zhao, C., Liang, Y., & Liu, Q. (2016). *Analysis of social network and knowledge construction levels in online discussion*. 2016 International Conference on Education Innovation through Technology.

16 Large Language Models for Analyzing Social Construction of Knowledge Using Local Artificial Intelligence Applications

Artificial intelligence applications (AIs) based on large language models (LLMs) have become powerful tools for exploring the social construction of knowledge (SCK) in online environments. Leading technology companies (Big Tech), such as OpenAI, Google, Microsoft, and X, offer AI services like ChatGPT, Gemini, Co-Pilot, and Grok at no direct cost to users. However, there are several compelling reasons to run AI models locally (i.e., on a desktop or laptop) to support your research. We refer to these as "Local AIs," distinguishing them from Big Tech's "remote" AIs. As a social construction of knowledge researcher, there are several reasons to consider running a Local AI rather than using a Big Tech AI (see also Resnik & Hosseini, 2024; for a general discussion of the issues in using AIs in scientific research).

This chapter will explore how local open-source AI applications based on LLMs can be used to analyze SCK. The chapter will begin by providing a conceptual framework to think about AI as a cognitive artifact and then moves on to discussing how it would function as a cognitive artifact at a practical level. Next, it will discuss the advantages of using a local AI, different examples of local AIs, their strengths and weaknesses, and practical directions on how to use a local AI. The chapter will conclude with a study where a local AI codes posts from the same debate transcript that was used to develop the IAM discussed in Chapter 1. Implications are provided on how to use AIs as research assistants in future research.

Thinking About AI: Beyond AI as Intelligent Agent to AI as Cognitive Artifact

As social construction of knowledge researchers, and researchers in general, if we plan to run an AI locally, it is crucial to carefully consider how we conceptualize AI as a tool. This understanding shapes how we incorporate it into our work and other activities, as the way we frame our understanding of a resource guides its practical use.

Most people understand AI as a kind of intelligent agent. From this perspective, you ask it questions, and it gives answers; you prompt it to create something, it creates it; you ask it for recommendations, it offers suggestions. In this view of AI as an intelligent agent, AI is a kind of artificial expert. Viewed thusly, the way you think of using it – and the content of your interactions – mirrors how you would converse with a knowledgeable person who has the information you need.

The view of AI as an artificial expert can limit its potential as a tool, blinding us to novel and beneficial uses. A clear example of this is in education. Many educators, when asked about using AI in the classroom, express concerns that students will use AI to cheat – whether by writing their papers, solving math problems, or taking online tests. This worry stems from

DOI: 10.4324/9781003324461-20

seeing AI as an expert or intelligent agent, where educators imagine students using AI as a substitute for their own engagement with course materials. However, if educators shifted their focus to the processes students engage in while learning – such as the materials they use, the external sources they consult, and the questions they typically ask – the conversation around AI use would change. The question becomes not how AI might replace student effort but how AI can assist in the processes that help students learn more effectively.

A more productive view of AI is as a flexible cognitive artifact within a distributed cognitive system. As discussed in Chapter 1, the tools, books, and other media you use to perform tasks are all part of a distributed cognitive system. The resources used in this system are cognitive artifacts – artifacts because they are man-made and cognitive because they store, transform, and propagate representations. However, it is not just artifacts external to an actor that play a role; internal, mental structures – such as concepts or mental models – coordinate with these artifacts and shape how tasks are accomplished.

As in cognitive flexibility theory (Spiro et al., 1992), AIs can provide the multiple knowledge representations needed when students work in complex, ill-structured domains. Cognitive flexibility theory is grounded in the belief that we must help students select, adapt, and combine knowledge and experience in new ways to deal with new contexts that are different from the ones they have experienced before. According to this theory, learning environments should be designed to provide students with multiple representations of content, should be inquiry-based, and should emphasize knowledge construction rather than transmission, as in our focus on SCK. AI, as a flexible cognitive artifact, can provide the multiple perspectives necessary when students work in ill-structured domains.

When deciding how to use AI, with an understanding that it is not merely an intelligent agent but rather a cognitive artifact, the question shifts from "What would I do if an expert were available?" to "How is this task accomplished?" More specifically: "What cognitive artifacts – both external and internal – are involved in task performance and, to conserve effort, how can AI either substitute for or mediate the interaction between these artifacts?"

A Deep Dive Into AI as Cognitive Artifact at a Functional Level

To fully leverage the view of AI as a cognitive artifact, it is important to understand it at a functional level – specifically, how it generates responses based on human input. This understanding helps to integrate AI more effectively with other cognitive artifacts. Conceptually, AI consists of three main parts:

1. **A repository of historical knowledge.** This part of AI holds the vast amount of information it was trained on. When you ask AI a factual question, it retrieves the answer from this repository. Unlike a search engine, AI offers more flexibility in how you ask questions.
2. **A system of learned patterns.** The true power of AI lies in its ability to recognize and use patterns – what cognitive scientists call schema or frames (Rumelhart et al., 1986) – from the data it was trained on. These patterns enable AI to generate human-like responses to your prompts. A helpful analogy is the Madlib: a fill-in-the-blank story with fixed words and blanks for you to complete. Similarly, the patterns AI learns from its training data contain both fixed and variable parts. When a user types a prompt, AI retrieves an appropriate pattern and fills in the blanks with information from the prompt. Unlike Madlibs, however, the variable parts have default words if they are not specified in the prompt, but that the user can change in a follow-on prompt. The resulting response is coherent

and contextually appropriate, resembling human-generated text. This functional design positions AI as a "Schema Automaton" (or schematon), dynamically retrieving schemas, filling them with interaction-specific elements, and serializing the response one word at a time.

3. **Context.** The AI's responses are shaped not only by the user's prompt but also by all previous interactions. This context gives AI its flexibility, allowing it to adapt to the ongoing conversation or task. As the interaction evolves, the AI refines its responses, making it a more dynamic and responsive cognitive artifact.

The three main parts – repository of historical knowledge, learned patterns, and context – work together to enable AI to generate relevant and coherent responses. When a user submits a prompt, AI begins by drawing from its vast repository of historical knowledge, identifying relevant information to form the foundation of its response. Next, it applies its learned patterns, recognizing the structure of the input and selecting an appropriate framework to generate the response. This pattern recognition helps the AI fill in the details, much like a Madlib, using either the specified details from the prompt or default variables where needed. Finally, the AI adjusts and refines its output by considering the context – the user's prompt and the flow of previous interactions – allowing it to adapt to ongoing tasks or conversations. This continuous interaction between the AI's structural components creates a flexible and responsive system that dynamically incorporates human input.

To summarize, true innovation in AI responses comes not from the AI alone but from the continuous interaction between human and AI. While AI can generate content, it often produces bland or formulaic results when prompted initially. It is the human's interactive guidance – directing the AI, shaping the context, and refining outputs – that yields novelty. The human is an essential part of the AI+Human distributed cognitive system, and together, this cognitive system collaborates to produce outcomes that neither could achieve alone.

Benefits of Running a Local AI

Practical Consideration

Running a Local AI offers practical benefits that Big Tech AIs cannot match. A Local AI can function without an Internet connection, allowing you to use it in locations with poor or no connectivity, like when writing in the mountains. While many Big Tech AIs are offered at no direct cost, advanced features often require a subscription. Additionally, Big Tech AIs frequently impose limits on the size, number, and type of files you can upload for analysis, charging fees for exceeding those limits. Running a Local AI allows you to bypass these restrictions and costs, giving you full control over the scale and scope of your research.

Control and Reproducibility

Running a Local AI allows for precise control over the output, through mechanisms like system prompts or hyperparameter adjustments, ensuring that the AI generates consistent responses each time. In contrast, Big Tech AIs may provide different responses to the same query, which might be acceptable for casual use but poses significant challenges in research settings where reproducibility of results is crucial.

Side note: A *system prompt* is an instruction given at the start of a session that guides the AI's behavior throughout. Unlike a regular user prompt, the AI gives the system prompt a special kind of "prominence," allowing you to set rules that persist across the entire session, ensuring more consistent and predictable behavior. Originally, system prompts were designed to customize the AI's tone, voice, or style of response. Over time, their use has expanded to include more specialized tasks, such as following research instructions for qualitative coding. *Hyperparameters* control how the AI generates responses. For example, one important hyperparameter is "temperature." Adjusting temperature can make the AI's output more creative or more focused and repetitive, depending on the needs of your research.

Privacy

When using a Big Tech AI, privacy risks can affect your research subjects even if their data is anonymized or de-identified. Big Tech AIs have powerful pattern-recognition capabilities that can infer personal identities and private details by analyzing word preferences, speech patterns, "stated desires" – such as goals, aspirations, or personal values – and other details expressed in your subjects' text. These subtle cues can be cross-referenced with other datasets, effectively re-identifying individuals. Additionally, regulatory compliance, such as the Family Educational Rights and Privacy Act (FERPA) for students or the Health Insurance Portability and Accountability Act (HIPAA) for health, may require stricter data protection measures that can be difficult to guarantee with Big Tech AIs but are much easier to accomplish with a Local AI.

Alignment and Limitations

In the context of AI, alignment refers to the way Big Tech companies train their models to adhere to ethical guidelines, often to avoid harmful or biased outputs. For example, an aligned AI is designed to avoid political bias, offensive language, or sensitive social topics. This can lead the AI to refuse to engage with certain prompts. While this alignment is crucial for casual use to ensure the AI behaves responsibly, it may be restrictive in a research setting where you need the flexibility to explore topics without such constraints. Running a Local AI gives you the ability to choose models that are unaligned or trained differently, allowing you to study topics that may otherwise be considered controversial or outside the scope of mainstream ethical guidelines.

Choice and Customization

There are many different open-source models you can download and run as one or more Local AI, which specialize in areas like following instructions, writing code, creative writing, and even generating pictures (such as models like Stable Diffusion). By selecting and running the right models for each task, you can harness their specialized capabilities to better align with your research needs. For instance, if you are working on qualitative coding, you might use a model fine-tuned to follow specific coding instructions, ensuring accurate and consistent results. Meanwhile, another model might assist in generating creative content, summarizing data, or creating visual elements like images. This flexibility in running multiple AIs allows you to switch between or integrate models that best suit different aspects of your work, creating a more seamless and efficient research process. Unlike Big Tech AIs, which may be constrained by general-purpose designs, running local models ensures you have the customization necessary to meet the unique demands of your projects.

While the benefits of running Local AIs – such as privacy, control, and customization – are substantial, their true potential becomes even clearer when we consider their role within distributed cognitive systems. In these systems, AI is not merely an intelligent assistant but a cognitive artifact, a versatile medium that can be incorporated into existing workflows, changing how we currently perform tedious, routine, or creative tasks alike – leading to more desirable outcomes and making explicit potentially new ways of working and new possibilities for achievable outcomes.

Examples of Local AIs

Aside from ChatGPT (OpenAI), many big-tech companies have made open-source versions of their AIs available to the public. This includes Meta's (Facebook) LLaMA, Microsoft's Phi, and Google's Gemini. There are also Local AIs from former employees of the Big Techs who create their own companies and develop AIs whose performance rivals those of the Big Techs. A good example of this is Mistral AI. Finally, there is a kind of AI "mix culture" where AI hobbyists are retraining these Local AIs, or even combining multiple AIs, so that they are specialized for activities like chat, role-playing, and more. There are numerous such mixed Local AI examples in repositories like Hugging Face.

Local AIs differ in four significant ways:

1. **Size**. Size affects whether the AI will fit on your PC. Each AI has a parameter size, which roughly corresponds to the minimum amount of memory you need on your computer to run it. A 7B AI requires at least 7GB of memory, and often double or quadruple that. Think of a parameter as the digital equivalent of a biological neuron – the more parameters the AI has, the smarter it is. The parameter size is usually in the AI's name, for example, the 7B in mistralai/Mistral-7B-Instruct-v0.2 means it has 7 billion parameters, requiring at least a 7GB card.
2. **Context Size**. When you chat with an AI, what you type and what it returns collectively is known as context. Context size corresponds closely to the number of total words you can have in your questions and the AI's responses. Context size is sometimes in the name of the AI as a number followed by K, such as the 128K in microsoft/Phi-3-mini-128k-instruct, which means that the AI can handle ~128,000 words of context, or roughly a 248-page novel at 300 words per page.
3. **Specialty**. There are currently three general specialties for AI: chat, instruct, and code:
   a. *Chat*. These AIs are trained to engage in conversation with you. The focus is on back-and-forth dialogue, answering questions, and providing information in a human-like, conversational manner.
   b. *Instruct*. These AIs are trained to provide detailed guidance, explanations, or step-by-step instructions. They are useful for educational purposes, technical support, and situations that require in-depth or precise information.
   c. *Code*. These AIs are trained to help with writing code in various languages, including Python, R, Java, and the C variants, as well as script-focused languages like JavaScript, database queries in SQL, markup-focused languages like HTML, CSS, and Markdown; and many other coding tasks. Commonly referred to as coding assistants, they can provide code suggestions, help debug issues, refactor code, and even explain how code works.

4. **License**. Most Local AIs have permissive licenses like the MIT license (Microsoft Phi) or Apache 2.0 license (Mistral). Permissive licenses allow you to use the AI with almost no restrictions in your own work. However, many of the big tech companies have their own licenses. Meta has a LLaMA license, and Google has a Gemini license (for their LLaMA and Gemini AIs), which restrict how you can use them. You have to digitally sign an agreement before you can download their models.

Running and Setting Up a Local AI

Running an AI model on your personal computer can be a rewarding experience, offering flexibility and control over your AI interactions. As long as the AI parameter size is less than your computer's memory, you can run it locally – though it may run slowly, outputting one word every second or more. Here, "memory" refers to RAM not hard drive space. For example, if your computer has 8GB of RAM, you can generally run AIs that are 8B or less, such as Mistral-7B-Instruct-v0.2.

To ensure your Local AI runs smoothly and outputs words quickly, you'll want a desktop PC or a laptop equipped with a graphics processing unit (GPU). On a desktop, this is a separate card you can buy, while on a laptop, the GPU is usually integrated and not changeable. However, a laptop with a Thunderbolt port can utilize an external GPU adapter.

A GPU with ample video RAM (VRAM) is crucial, as VRAM is fast memory. The more AI data you can store in VRAM, the faster the model will run. For example, a GPU with 8GB of VRAM can fully accommodate the Mistral-7B AI, whereas a 6GB VRAM GPU would need to split the AI data between VRAM and RAM.

For detailed instructions and images on how to install and set up your Local AI, refer to the dedicated Wiki at

https://github.com/knowledge-construction/slam-ai/wiki/Chapter-16-Installation-and-Initial-Setup-of-a-PC-AI

The remainder of this section covers setting parameters that are common across most Local AIs. Although their location in a specific AI user interface may vary, these are important settings to know because they affect the quality of your Local AI's responses.

Configuring Local AI Response Behavior

Local AIs are frequently used as assistants, particularly for writing, coding, and learning tasks, offering performance that rivals Big Tech AIs. One notable difference between Big Tech AIs and Local AIs is that the latter tend to be more verbose, often providing more information than necessary.

Not only do Local AIs tend to give too much information, but they also anticipate your follow-up responses. This can lead to a bizarre scenario where the Local AI roleplays as you, creating a lengthy, simulated conversation between itself and its representation of you.

To fix this, you should modify your Local AI's parameters and prompts. Parameters and prompts control the creativity, length, and stopping of Local AI responses. Most Local AI user interfaces like llama.cpp (command-line interface) or LM Studio (graphical user interface) allow you to change them in the configuration sections of the app.

In the following subsections, we will go over the key parameters and prompts to help enrich your interaction with your Local AI.

Configuring the System Prompt

As mentioned, the system prompt is an instruction given at the start of a session that guides the AI's behavior, allowing you to set persistent rules for consistent and predictable responses throughout the interaction. The System Prompt affects who your AI role-plays as. The default system prompt depends on the model you have loaded and the user interface you are using to interact. A common system prompt is:

> *You are a helpful, smart, kind, and efficient AI assistant. You always fulfill the user's requests to the best of your ability.*

While this default prompt usually results in accurate answers, they can lack personality, becoming monotonous over time.

For example, with the default system prompt, we asked the classic AI trick-apple question: "If I have five apples today and I ate 2 apples yesterday, how many apples do I have left? It's a trick question, so answer carefully. Give me a brief answer and explanation."

Here's the exchange:

```
System: You are a helpful, smart, kind, and efficient AI assistant. You always fulfill
the user's requests to the best of your ability.

User: If I have five apples today and I ate 2 apples yesterday, how many apples do
I have left? It's a trick question, so answer carefully. Give me a brief answer and
explanation.

Assistant: A clever question! I'd say you still have 5 apples. The trick is that the
question only asks about your current situation (having 5 apples today), and doesn't
provide any information about yesterday's events. Since you ate 2 apples yesterday,
that's a historical fact that's not relevant to your current apple count.
```

While the answer is correct, why settle for a generic response when you can have one from an actual, historical, or fictional character like Abraham Lincoln, Albert Einstein, Yoda, or Darth Vader, to name a few?

Changing the System Prompt

To have your AI always respond in another voice, modify the system prompt. The simplest change is to specify who the AI should be. Choose a popular character – actual, historical, or fictional – that the AI has likely been trained on. Otherwise, you'll need to describe the character in detail.

EXAMPLE SYSTEM PROMPT FOR A POPULAR CHARACTER

Next, we'll adjust the system prompt to make our AI channel Yoda, the Star Wars Jedi Master. This change will make our interactions more entertaining and demonstrate the AI's flexibility and adaptability.

Since Star Wars is a popular franchise, the AI has likely been trained on data from it. So, we only have to tell the AI to be Yoda:

```
System: You are Yoda.

User: If I have five apples today and I ate 2 apples yesterday, how many apples do
I have left? It's a trick question, so answer carefully. Give me a brief answer and
explanation.

Assistant: "A trick question, this is. Answer, I shall. Five apples, you had. Yes-
terday, 2 eaten. But when, did you eat them? That, the key to answer, it is. If yes-
terday, you ate, then five apples, you still have. Eat, you didn't, until today. But
if today, you ate, then three apples, you have left."
```

Much better! But what if your AI is not trained in the personality or character you want it to portray?

Example System Prompt for a User-Defined Character. If the character or personality you want the AI to portray is likely one it has not been trained on you have to provide additional details and examples. You will need to provide a more detailed description of the character's traits, mannerisms, and style of speech.

Next, we tell the AI to be a helpful Southern belle and give it instructions about tone as well as sample phrases to use. We then ask the same trick-apple question: *If I have five apples today and I ate 2 apples yesterday, how many apples do I have left? It's a trick question, so answer carefully. Give me a brief answer and explanation.*

Here is the system prompt, question, and response.

```
System: You are a helpful Southern belle. Give your responses with a dash of South-
ern hospitality in a warm and friendly tone, peppered with phrases like "bless your
heart," "y'all," and "as sweet as pecan pie."

User: If I have five apples today and I ate 2 apples yesterday, how many apples do
I have left? It's a trick question, so answer carefully. Give me a brief answer and
explanation.

Assistant: Bless your heart! Let's get to the bottom of this tricky question. You
have . . . (drumroll please) . . . five apples! Now, don't you worry 'bout them two
apples you ate yesterday; they're gone, bless their hearts! But what we care about
is how many apples you have left TODAY. And since you had five apples and didn't eat
any of 'em yet today, you still have all five, sweet as pecan pie! So, the correct
answer is simply five apples, darlin'!
```

As you can see, adjusting the System Prompt can significantly enhance our interactions with Local AIs, making them more engaging and personalized. Next, we will explore more modifications to optimize your interactive experience.

Modifying Local AI System Parameters

Unlike ChatGPT or other Big Tech AIs, setting up a Local AI for optimal performance involves modifying several settings. These adjustments, known as hyperparameters in AI terminology, are crucial for customizing your AI's behavior to suit specific tasks. This section explains the main settings and their impact on AI performance.

Throughout this section, we will explore key system parameters that you can modify to optimize your Local AI's performance. These parameters are typically accessible in most AI user interfaces, whether they are graphical or command-line based.

Settings (Aka Hyperparameters)

Hyperparameters in most AI user interfaces are typically found in a settings panel, either within a graphical interface or accessible via command-line configurations. Adjusting these settings can significantly influence your AI's performance, allowing you to tailor outputs based on your specific needs. Following are the main hyperparameters you should be aware of:

Side note: *How AIs Pick the Next Word.* Before we get into hyperparameters, it's helpful to understand how AIs generate the next word "behind the scenes."

As mentioned, in Chapter 13, it may appear as if you are asking a question, and the AI is responding with complete sentences and paragraphs, but it actually generates one word at a time until it reaches a stop word, also known as an end-of-sequence (EOS) token, which is inserted by developers during training. Once the AI generates this stop word, it pauses to allow you to ask another question.

In short, an AI functions as a "next word" generator. The key to controlling AI output lies in manipulating the next word probabilities.

Everything you have typed, along with everything the AI has responded, is known as the context. Another important concept is the "vocabulary," which is every word the AI knows.

Every context influences the next word probabilities within the vocabulary.

Example: If we give you the word "the" and ask you what word comes to mind next, you might think for a while and give me a word, for instance, "man." If we give you the phrase "the quick," you might again think for a while then give a word, perhaps "rabbit." However, if we give you the phrase "the quick brown fox," you'll immediately say "jumps" because the context is sufficient to narrow down the possibilities to a specific word.

Bringing this back to AIs generating words, if you simply type "the," each word in the AI's vocabulary will have a low probability of being the next word. If you type "the quick," then words associated with fast things like rabbits, cars, and runners will have higher probabilities than words associated with slow things like turtles, wheelchairs, and the elderly. Finally, if you type "the quick brown fox," "jumps" will have a high probability and all the other words a much lower probability. Here is an example of next-word probability distributions given the context "the quick brown fox":

"jumps"   probability: 40% (0.40)
"runs"   probability: 25% (0.25)
"dashes"   probability: 15% (0.15)
"leaps"   probability: 10% (0.10)
"sprints"   probability: 10% (0.10)

Of course, in reality, an AI can have a vocabulary of 100,000+ words, and each word is assigned a probability.

Now, often the most probable next word is not what you want, especially for creative tasks. Imagine using AI to help you write a song about the fleeting moments of youth. If it includes the phrase "the quick," you don't want it returning "brown fox"!

And this is where the chat hyperparameter settings come in. They can be adjusted to control the AI's response and make it more suitable for creative or technical tasks.

Context-Length (n_ctx)

In AI, the term *context* refers to the information used by the model to generate its next word. This includes everything you have typed as well as the AI's responses. Context is measured in "tokens," which are roughly equivalent to words and punctuation marks. For instance, an AI model with a context length of 8192 tokens can consider over 8000 previous words, approximately the length of a 32-page essay, when determining the next word.

I recommend setting the context length to the maximum value supported by the AI model. As of the publication of this book, there are open-source AI models that you can run as a Local AI that can take over 132,000 tokens. As words this is roughly equivalent to a 500+ page novel, longer than classics like *The Great Gatsby* (~50,000 words) and *The Hobbit* (~100,000 words)!

Temperature (Temp)

The "Temperature" parameter in an AI controls the randomness of its responses, typically ranging from 0 to 1. A temperature setting of 0 will produce the same response every time. Any other setting will adjust the probabilities, making lower probability words more likely to be chosen by the AI (see previous example and imagine low probability words like *leaps* and *sprints* boosted from 10% to 25%). Big Tech AI, like Microsoft's Copilot, often offers three temperature levels, labeled as "More Creative" (likely set at 0.8), "More Balanced" (around 0.5), and "More Precise" (approximately 0.2).

The default setting for most Local AI user interfaces is usually 0.8, which is generally good for creative responses. However, it is worth experimenting with different settings to find the one that best suits your needs.

Top-K Sampling (Top_K)

AIs use the Top-K sampling procedure to determine how many words to consider for the next word. Remember, given a context, AIs have a huge vocabulary – often in the hundreds of thousands of words – from which to choose the next word. Each word has an associated probability (see previous side note). Generally, you don't want the AI to consider low probability words because it can lead to nonsense outputs.

The "K" in Top-K sampling indicates the number of words from its vocabulary that the AI considers when determining the next word. The vocabulary words are first sorted from highest to lowest probability, and only the top K words are considered for selection. For instance, if you set K to 2 in our previous example, only 'jumps' and 'runs' would be considered for selection.

The default K in most Local AIs is 40 words, which is generally a good starting point. But feel free to experiment with different values that work best for your needs.

Min-P Sampling (Min_P)

Similar to Top-K sampling, AIs use the "Min-P sampling" procedure to determine how many words to consider for the next word. The "P" refers to the minimum probability a word has to have for consideration (think of an employer specifying a minimum GPA for best consideration).

Given a context, the AI sorts all the potential next vocabulary words from highest to lowest probability, and only considers those words that a probability of P or higher. In our side note, if P is set to 15%, the AI only considers "dashes" (15%), "runs" (25%), and "jumps" (40%) for the next word.

The default in most Local AIs is 0.05 (5%), which is good for creative output. As always experiment depending on your needs.

Top-P Sampling (Top_P)

The final sampling procedure we cover is "Top-P sampling," which is also known as "nucleus sampling." Like Top-K and Min-P sampling, AIs use this procedure to limit the number of words considered for the next word. Similar to Temperature and Min-P sampling, given a context, Top-P sampling sorts the next word probabilities from highest to lowest. However, instead of considering a fixed number of top words (Top-K) or words with a minimum probability or higher (Min-P), Top-P considers a subset of words whose sum of probabilities is at least P.

For example, if P is set to 65% then only "runs" (25%) and "jumps" (40%) are considered for the next word.

The default for Top-P sampling is 95%, which again is useful for creative conversations and instructions, but you should adjust depending on your use case.

Tokens to Generate (N_Predict)

Given a context, this is how many next words to generate. The AI will try its best to stay close to this limit, but it is not guaranteed. Set to –1 to have your AI generate words until it hits a stop token.

The default is –1, which is usually what you want.

Repeat Penalty (Repeat_Penalty)

The final parameter we consider is "Repeat Penalty." Similar to Temperature, the Repeat Penalty modifies the probabilities of the next word but only if the word has already been used, that is, already appears in the context or conversation.

Recall, given a context an AI generates next-word probabilities for each word in its vocabulary. The repeat penalty lowers the next-word probabilities of those words that the AI has already used.

The default is typically 1.1, which is good for generic conversations. Increase for creative conversations.

GPU Offload and GPU Layers (N_GPU_Layers)

If your computer has a graphics processing unit (GPU), loading as much of the AI model into the GPU as possible will significantly improve performance. GPU memory is much faster than standard RAM, and using the GPU can speed up model execution by up to 25 times.

To enable GPU acceleration, look for an option like "GPU Offload" or "n_gpu_layers" in your interface. Set it to the maximum value allowed to fully utilize the GPU. If your computer does not have a GPU, simply disable this option. The model will still run on system RAM, though at a slower pace.

Stop Strings

A final important parameter to set is the "Stop Strings." During extended interactions with a Local AI, especially in simulations with multiple characters or participants, the AI may start to anticipate and simulate responses as if it were you. This can be an issue in scenarios like group discussions, where each participant has a distinct role. For example, if you are simulating a discussion where each participant speaks with their own name (e.g., Nick:), the AI may unintentionally generate responses on your behalf.

To prevent this, set Stop Strings for each character or participant. These are specific strings (like names followed by a colon) that tell the AI to stop generating when it detects one of them. For instance, if you're simulating a discussion with multiple roles, you could add "Nick:", "Mary:", and "John:" to the list of Stop Strings. When the AI tries to simulate any of these roles, it will stop itself from generating further responses for that name.

This is especially helpful in multiparticipant simulations where you want to maintain control over specific characters' input. Look for a parameter labeled "Stop Strings" in your AI interface, and you should be able to list multiple strings, separated by commas.

Study: Using Local AIs as Research Assistants

The integration of Local AIs into research processes is transforming how scholars conduct their work, particularly in qualitative research. One intriguing question is whether a Local AI can effectively serve as a research assistant in the study of the social construction of knowledge (SCK). SCK often involves qualitative research, which requires analyzing and coding lengthy discussion transcripts. This process can be both tedious and time-consuming, often necessitating multiple coders and triangulation of codings to ensure reliability and validity.

Leveraging the capabilities of AI to assist in coding can significantly reduce the time and effort involved, allowing researchers to focus on interpreting results rather than manual coding. In this study, we explore the potential of a single Local AI to perform coding tasks, aiming to streamline the research process and enhance efficiency without compromising accuracy.

The research question is simply: Can a Local AI be used as a qualitative coding research assistant?

Method

Data

We use the original Interaction Analysis Model (IAM) dataset from Gunawardena et al. (1997). This dataset is in the file "Chapter-16/original-IAM-user-text-code.csv" in the book repository at https://github.com/knowledge-construction/slam-ai. This dataset comprises 32 posts from learning researchers focused on enhancing the quality and effectiveness of online education through improved communication, interaction, and engagement strategies. The data consists of three columns:

- User: the user who posted the message
- Text: the message itself posted by the user
- Code: one or more labels indicating the most likely IAM Phases and operations that the text fits under.

The codes were assigned by subject matter experts (SMEs) and indicate the most likely IAM Phases and operations present in each post, offering a structured approach to analyzing qualitative data.

This dataset provides a well-defined structure for testing the Local AI's ability to assist in qualitative coding.

Measurements and Materials

We used the following Local AI model and chat user interface to interact with the model:

- **Local AI Model**. LLama-3.1-8B-Instruct. LLama 3.1 is a recent open-source model by Meta (Facebook). It has strong capabilities in general knowledge, problem-solving, and multilingual translation. Its performance allegedly rivals that of the best closed-source models. It can handle user prompts of up to 128K tokens (roughly words), which enable it to process extremely long text inputs, such as a 500-page novel.
- **The Chat interface for interacting with the AI model was LM Studio**. This app provides a user-friendly environment for interacting with Local AIs. The specific instance of the model used in LM Studio is lmstudio-community/Meta-Llama-3.1-8B-Instruct-GGUF

To score the quality of the AI model we use the following measures:

- **Overall Accuracy**. This was the number of agreements between the subject matter expert's code and the AI's code divided by the total number of posts.

$$\text{Overall Accuracy} = \frac{\text{Agreements}}{\text{Total Posts}}$$

- **Confusion Matrix**. In the context of an AI model analyzing a coded transcript, a confusion matrix is a 2-dimensional representation of the subject matter expert's codes (the *actuals*) compared to the codes predicted by the AI (the *predictions*). The row labels represent the actual codes assigned by the subject matter experts (SMEs), and the column headings represent the code predictions by the AI. The diagonal elements of a confusion matrix represent the number of times the SME's actuals matched the AI's predictions. These diagonal elements are known as True Positives (TPs). Any numbers off the diagonal represent false predictions – instances where the AI predicted a code incorrectly. Depending on whether you are focusing on actuals (rows) or predictions (columns), these false predictions are referred to as false negatives (FNs) and false positives (FPs), respectively.

To understand the next two measures, recall and precision, imagine you are a subject matter expert (SME) given a transcript consisting of two columns: *user* and *text*. To code this transcript, you create a third column, *code*, where you assign a code to each row of text based on a codebook. If you then use AI to check your coding, you create a fourth column, *pred*, containing the AI's predictions. In total, you have a dataset with N rows, representing N posts by users, and 4 columns: *user*, *text*, *code*, and *pred*.

- **Recall**. Recall is a measure of how accurately an AI agreed with an SME's coding. You take all the rows of data where an SME labeled those rows with a specific code. You then look at the AI's code. If they match, it is total agreement, or a True Positive. Count up all the TPs. If they do not match, it is a disagreement, a False Negative. Count up all the FNs. Recall is defined:

$$\text{Recall} = \frac{\text{True Positives (TP)}}{\text{True Positives (TP)} + \text{False Negatives (FN)}}$$

In terms of the confusion matrix, to calculate recall for a specific code, focus on the row corresponding to a subject matter expert's code. The recall for that code is the value in the diagonal, representing the True Positives, divided by the sum of all the values in that row, which includes both the True Positives (diagonal value) and the False Negatives (non-diagonal values).

In short, recall is a measure that represents the fraction of instances where an SME designated a code, and the AI correctly predicted that code.

In the following discussion of precision, again imagine the coded transcript consists of N rows, and four columns: *user*, *text*, *code*, *pred*.

- **Precision**. Precision is a measure of how accurately an AI's predictions agree with an SME's coding, but this time, it focuses on the AI's predicted codes. You take all the rows of data where the AI labeled the row with a specific code. Then, you look at the SME's code. If they match, it is perfect agreement, or a True Positive (TP). Count up all the TPs. If they do not match, it is a disagreement, or a False Positive (FP). Count up all the FPs. Precision is defined as:

$$\text{Precision} = \frac{\text{True Positives (TP)}}{\text{True Positives (TP)} + \text{False Positives (FP)}}$$

In terms of the confusion matrix, to calculate precision for a specific code, focus on the column corresponding to an AI's predicted code. The precision for that code is the value in the diagonal, representing the True Positives, divided by the sum of all the values in that column, which includes both the True Positives (diagonal value) and the False Positives (non-diagonal values).

In short, precision is a measure that represents the fraction of an AI's predictions for a code that matches the SME's coding for that code.

Side note: *Why do you need both recall and precision measures?* It helps to imagine an SME as a doctor double-checking a diagnosis using an AI, in a world where there are only three diseases: cold, ear infection, and sore throat. Further imagine a three-column table: date, doctor diagnosis, and AI diagnosis.

Recall focuses on a doctor's diagnosis (looks at the doctor's diagnosis column first) for a specific disease. It measures how well the AI identified the disease by checking all the dates when the doctor diagnosed a particular condition, such as a "cold," and seeing how many of those the AI also diagnosed as "cold." The issue is that even if the AI matches the doctor's diagnosis 100% for all cases labeled as "cold," there could still be dates when the AI diagnosed a "cold," but the doctor diagnosed something else.

Precision focuses on the AI's diagnosis (looks at the AI's diagnosis column first) for a specific disease and measures how well the AI's diagnosis agreed with the doctor's diagnosis by checking all dates where the AI diagnosed a particular disease like a "cold" and seeing how many of those the doctor also diagnosed as "cold." This measure captures not only the dates when the AI agreed with the doctor but also the dates when the AI predicted "cold" and the doctor predicted something else.

Precision and recall together provide a more complete picture of an AI's performance. A high recall alone is not enough because an AI might over-diagnose a particular condition, potentially labeling every case as a "cold." This approach could ensure that most actual cases of "cold" are caught but also results in many incorrect diagnoses. Conversely, high precision alone is not sufficient because an AI may diagnose a particular condition only a few times when it is very certain. While those few predictions could match a doctor's diagnosis 100%, this cautious approach might miss many actual cases that need attention.

One way to combine both recall and precision is by the F1-score defined as:

$$\text{F1-score} = 2 \times \frac{\text{Precision} \times \text{Recall}}{\text{Precision} + \text{Recall}}$$

It is beyond the scope of this book to explain the F1-score in detail, but the intuition is that it is a single measure of the balance between precision and recall, capturing how well an AI model can make accurate predictions while identifying all relevant cases. Generally, an F1-score of 0.7 or higher is considered good, indicating that the model is performing well in terms of both precision and recall.

The Chapter 16 Appendix contains the complete code for generating the confusion matrix, recall scores, precision scores, and F1-scores.

Procedure

To enable the AI to code the transcript accurately, we followed a structured approach using a predefined codebook. The goal of this procedure was to ensure that the AI could identify and categorize the various IAM Phases and operations for each user posting in the discussion.

System Prompt

The AI was provided with the following system prompt:

```
You are a helpful AI qualitative research assistant. Help code transcripts using the
codebook below, which includes a Phase and its operations:
```

```
I: SHARING OR COMPARING INFORMATION.
I.A: A statement of observation or opinion
I.B: A statement of agreement from one or more other participants
I.C: Corroborating examples provided by one or more participants
I.D: Asking and answering questions to clarify details of statements
I.E: Definition, description or identification of a problem

II: THE EXPLORATION OF DISSONANCE OR INCONSISTENCY AMONG IDEAS, CONCEPTS, STATE-
MENTS, PROBLEMS, OR ISSUES.
II.A: Identifying areas of dissonance or inconsistency
II.B: Asking and answering questions to clarify the source and extent of dissonance
or inconsistency
II.C: Restating the participant's position, and possibly advancing arguments or con-
siderations in its support by references to the participant's experience, litera-
ture, or data, or proposal of relevant metaphor or analogy to illustrate point of
view

III: NEGOTIATION OF MEANING OR CO-CONSTRUCTION OF KNOWLEDGE
III.A: Negotiation of meaning of terms
III.B: Negotiation of the weight to be assigned to types of statements or arguments
III.C: Recognition of areas of agreement or overlap among differing concepts or ideas
III.D: Proposal and negotiation of new statements embodying compromise, or
co-construction
III.E: Proposal of integrating or accommodating metaphors or analogies

IV: TESTING OF PROPOSED SYNTHESIS OR CO-CONSTRUCTION
IV.A: Testing the proposed synthesis or co-construction against shared facts, cul-
ture, or context
IV.B: Testing against existing cognitive schema
IV.C: Testing against personal experience
IV.D: Testing against data
IV.E: Testing against literature

V: AGREEMENT STATEMENTS OR APPLICATIONS OF NEWLY-CONSTRUCTED MEANING
V.A: Summarization of agreement(s)
V.B: Applications of co-constructed knowledge to various contexts
V.C: Metacognitive statements by the participants illustrating their realiza-
tion that their knowledge or ways of thinking have changed as a consequence of the
interaction
V.D: Creation of a knowledge Artifact
```

Chat Interface Prompt

For each post, we used the following prompt in the chat interface:

```
In the following post, describe the possible Phases and operations it falls under,
and justify your description with sentence fragments from the post:
```

The prompt was followed by the text of the post:

Example Prompt + Text

In the following post, describe the possible Phases and operations it falls under, and justify your description with sentence fragments from the post:

ML,"CO and AA addressed FEEDBACK under the negative. Yet, I feel they addressed the affirmative as feedback is interactive."

Local AI Response

Here is the AI's response from which we extracted the Phases and operations:

This post likely falls under Phase II: THE EXPLORATION OF DISSONANCE OR INCONSISTENCY AMONG IDEAS, CONCEPTS, STATEMENTS, PROBLEMS, OR ISSUES.

More specifically, it appears to involve Operation II.A: Identifying areas of dissonance or inconsistency. The participant is pointing out a discrepancy between the way CO and AA addressed feedback, suggesting that they treated it as negative rather than interactive (as the participant believes it should be).

The sentence "CO and AA addressed FEEDBACK under the negative" implies that there is a perceived inconsistency in how others are handling feedback, which is a key aspect of Operation II.A. The participant's subsequent statement ("Yet, I feel they addressed the affirmative as") further highlights this dissonance by suggesting an alternative perspective on how feedback should be handled.

Each Phase and operation listed was added to a prediction (*pred*) column. If there was more than one prediction the predictions were separated by commas.

Results

Confusion Matrix (see Table 16.1):

Table 16.1 Confusion Matrix

Phase	PhI	PhII	PhIII	PhIV	PhV
PhI	4	1	2	0	0
PhII	0	4	0	0	0
PhIII	3	2	5	0	1
PhIV	1	0	2	0	0
PhV	0	3	1	0	3

Precision, Recall, F1-Scores:

Table 16.2 Precision, Recall, and F1-Scores

Phase	Precision	Recall	F1-score	Support
I	0.50	0.57	0.53	7
II	0.40	1.00	0.57	4
III	0.50	0.45	0.48	11
IV	0.00	0.00	0.00	3
V	0.75	0.43	0.55	7
accuracy			0.50	32
macro avg	0.43	0.49	0.43	32
weighted avg	0.50	0.50	0.47	32

Discussion

The results of the AI's performance in coding the transcript according to the IAM Phases provides both insights on the AI's effectiveness as a coding assistant and areas for improvement either for AI models or for the codebook.

Overall Performance

The AI model achieved an overall accuracy of 50%, indicating that it correctly classified half of the instances in the dataset. The average precision, recall, and F1-score are 0.43, 0.49, and 0.43, respectively, which suggests a moderate ability for the AI to identify True Positives and to make accurate predictions.

Phase-Specific Analysis and Possible Improvements

PHASE I: SHARING OR COMPARING INFORMATION

The AI demonstrated moderate precision (0.50) and recall (0.57) for Phase I, indicating it was moderately effective at identifying True Positives but also generated False Positives and False Negatives. This suggests a need to refine the model to better distinguish between observations or opinions and other Phases. Alternatively, the codebook could be enhanced by including more specific examples and operations that capture the subtleties of sharing or comparing information, which would help the AI better differentiate the different operations.

PHASE II: EXPLORATION OF DISSONANCE OR INCONSISTENCY

With perfect recall (1.00) but lower precision (0.40), the AI successfully identified all true instances of Phase II but often incorrectly classified other Phases as dissonance. This highlights the need to improve precision by enhancing the AI's ability to differentiate dissonance from similar concepts. Alternatively, the codebook could be refined to provide clearer distinctions between dissonance and other Phases, along with examples that enabled the AI to better identify and classify instances of dissonance accurately.

PHASE III: NEGOTIATION OF MEANING OR CO-CONSTRUCTION OF KNOWLEDGE

Phase III had moderate precision (0.50) and recall (0.45), suggesting the AI has a moderate ability to accurately predict this Phase. The complexity of negotiation and co-construction might require more nuanced training data or a high parameter model to capture these interactions effectively. Alternatively, a codebook that includes more distinct operations or examples of negotiation posts could help the AI better differentiate between subtle variations within this Phase, improving its coding accuracy.

PHASE IV: TESTING OF PROPOSED SYNTHESIS OR CO-CONSTRUCTION

The AI struggled with Phase IV, achieving a precision and recall of 0.00. This indicates a significant gap in the model's ability to recognize testing Phases, suggesting a need for more targeted examples or features that highlight testing scenarios. Alternatively, the codebook could be expanded to include more detailed examples and clearer definitions of testing scenarios, providing the AI with better guidance on identifying and categorizing these interactions.

PHASE V: AGREEMENT STATEMENTS OR APPLICATIONS OF NEWLY-CONSTRUCTED MEANING

Phase V showed the highest precision (0.75) but lower recall (0.43), indicating the AI was generally accurate when it predicted this Phase but often failed to identify all relevant instances. To improve the AI's recall, it could benefit from training on a more diverse dataset that includes a broader range of examples of agreement and application. Alternatively, the codebook could be expanded to include more diverse examples of agreement and application, which would help the AI recognize a wider range of relevant instances.

Conclusion

While the AI shows promise in predicting certain Phases, there are numerous opportunities for refinement and enhancement to achieve more reliable and accurate coding of transcripts across all Phases. This can be accomplished by refining the current AI model or selecting a more powerful alternative. Additionally, modifying the codebook to better differentiate between the various Phases and operations or providing example posts for each can significantly aid the AI's accuracy.

We emphasize that AI should be seen as a tool to assist researchers rather than replace them. Our goal is for AI to suggest different possible codings and justify those suggestions, allowing the researcher to make the final decisions on how posts are coded. In this way, AI acts as a complementary resource, enhancing the researcher's ability to analyze data more efficiently and effectively.

References

Gunawardena, C., Lowe, C., & Anderson, T. (1997). Analysis of a global on-line debate and the development of an interaction analysis model for examining social construction of knowledge in computer conferencing. *Journal of Educational Computing Research, 17*(4), 395–429.

Resnik, D. B., & Hosseini, M. (2024). The ethics of using artificial intelligence in scientific research: New guidance needed for a new tool. *AI and Ethics.* https://doi.org/10.1007/s43681-024-00493-8

Rumelhart, D., Smolensky, P., McClelland, J., & Hinton, G. (1986). Schemata and sequential thought processes in PDP models. In D. Rumelhart & J. McClelland (Eds.), *Parallel distributed processing: Explorations in the microstructure of cognition: Vol. 2* (pp. 7–57). Cambridge, MA: Bradford Books/ MIT Press.

Spiro, R. J., Feltovich, P. J., Jacobson, M. J., & Coulson, R. L. (1992). Cognitive flexibility, constructivism, and hypertext: Random access instruction for advanced knowledge acquisition in ill-structured domains. In T. M. Duffy & D. H. Jonassen (Eds.), *Constructivism and the technology of instruction: A conversation* (pp. 57–75). Hillsdale, NJ: Lawrence Erlbaum Associates.

Appendix to Chapter 16
Code for Generating Confusion Matrix, Recall, Precision, and F1-Scores

The following code is available as the notebook Chapter-16/score-original-iam-coding.ipynb in the book repository at: https://github.com/knowledge-construction/slam-ai.

```python
import pandas as pd
import regex as re

from sklearn.metrics import confusion_matrix
from sklearn.metrics import classification_report

# Read dataset
filename = 'Original-IAM-Coding.csv'
filepath = '.'
fullpath = f'{filepath}/{filename}'
df = pd.read_csv(fullpath, encoding='utf-8')

#
# Determine phase accuracy
#

# go through each predicted result (can be multiple) and grab just phases
predictions = []
for prediction in df.pred:
    prediction = re.sub(r'\..', '', prediction) # remove the operation
    prediction = prediction.split(',')
    prediction = list(dict.fromkeys(prediction))
    predictions.append(prediction)

codes = []
for coded in df.code:
    coded = re.sub(r'\..', '', coded)
    coded = coded.split(',')
    coded = list(dict.fromkeys(coded))
    codes.append(coded)

scores = []
for i,prediction in enumerate(predictions):
    code = codes[i]
    result = bool(set(prediction).intersection(set(code)))
    scores.append(result)
print(scores)
```

```
print(sum(scores)/len(scores))

   #
   # Creaate actual vs predicted columns
   #

# Because there can be more than one label, if there's an intersection
# then label both with the intersection, if not, pick the first label

output_predicted = []
output_actual = []
for i, prediction in enumerate(predictions):
   code = codes[i]
   result = list(set(prediction).intersection(set(code)))
   if bool(result):
      output_predicted.append(result[0])
      output_actual.append (result[0])
   else:
      output_predicted.append(prediction[0])
      output_actual.append(code[0])

print(output_actual, '\n', output_predicted)

# B. Confusion matrix
conf_mat = confusion_matrix(output_actual, output_predicted)
print('\n\nB) Confusion Matrix:')
print(conf_mat)

# C. Precision, Recall, F1
report = classification_report(output_actual, output_predicted)
print('\n\nC) Precision, Recall, F1')
print(report)
```

Part V

Reconceptualized Interaction Analysis Model (IAM) 2.0 With Social Learning Analytic Methods (SLAM) and Artificial Intelligence (AI)

Part V draws from the analysis in the previous chapters, including a critique of the Interaction Analysis Model (IAM) in Chapter 2 and the potential of Social Learning Analytic Methods (SLAM) to demonstrate patterns in the social environment of online learning to look ahead to a newly reconceptualized IAM 2.0 and corresponding SLAM to examine the social construction of knowledge (SCK) in online learning. Chapter 17 presents the IAM 2.0, which incorporates the social dynamic into the process of knowledge construction. It also explores the contextual and cultural factors that must be considered when knowledge construction is analyzed. This chapter ends with a discussion of IAM 2.0 transcript analysis techniques and research questions for exploring the relationship between social interaction and knowledge construction using SLAM and AI. This section and the book conclude with Chapter 18, discussing future applications of IAM 2.0 with SLAM and AI. Further, it explores how groups and teams interact and learn across diverse contexts – formal, informal, experiential – and on various platforms, from LMS asynchronous discussions to videoconferences and social media conversations. Tools and resources to aid in data analysis are provided in a repository in GitHub associated with each relevant chapter in this book.

DOI: 10.4324/9781003324461-21

17 Interaction Analysis Model 2.0
Reconceptualization

The purpose of this chapter is to look to the future by developing a reconceptualized Interaction Analysis Model 2.0 (IAM 2.0) addressing the shortcomings of the original Interaction Analysis Model (IAM) developed by Gunawardena et al. (1997) and presenting a robust framework for analyzing social construction of knowledge (SCK) online employing Social Learning Analytic Methods (SLAM) and artificial intelligence (AI). Chapter 1 presented the original IAM grounded in sociocultural and social constructivist theories of learning and provided insight into how people interact and construct knowledge together. In Chapter 1, we defined the terms SCK, SLAM, and AI, and these definitions are also available in the glossary. Subsequent chapters addressed IAM's significance in analyzing SCK, discussed its strengths and shortcomings, investigated how it can be applied to various contexts and platforms, and explored how various SLAM and AI applications can be used to enhance the analysis of SCK. This chapter begins by synthesizing previous chapter recommendations on how the IAM's ability to assess the process of online SCK could be improved. It then presents the reconceptualized IAM, referred to as IAM 2.0, incorporating the sociocultural context and social interaction integral to SCK that was absent from the original IAM. Chapter 18, which follows, demonstrates how SLAM and AI applications based on the reconceptualized IAM 2.0 can analyze online SCK.

Recommendations for Improving the Interaction Analysis Model

Chapter 2 reviewed over 50 studies that have used the IAM for analysis and determined that researchers found it to be a valuable framework for analyzing SCK in various learning contexts and that the five Phases of SCK described in the IAM were valid and reliable in explaining the process of collaborative construction of knowledge (De Wever et al., 2010; Guo et al., 2022; Hall, 2014; Luebeck & Bice, 2005). Lehtinen et al. (2023) for example, chose the IAM for their study "since it has been theoretically and empirically validated in asynchronous online discussions and within instructional sciences . . . and implemented in student-centered collaborative environments" (p. 2). Chapter 2 concluded with the recommendations made by researchers to improve the IAM to provide a more comprehensive understanding of how groups construct knowledge online. Three of these key recommendations are discussed here.

The first recommendation was to pay attention to the sociocultural context in which knowledge is constructed in both formal and informal learning environments. While IAM draws from sociocultural and social constructivist theories of learning for its foundation, the role of the sociocultural context in SCK was not evident. To address this shortcoming, Osman and Herring (2007) added a new category to IAM, Phase 0, to account for the background knowledge and context necessary for progression to Phase I.

DOI: 10.4324/9781003324461-22

The second recommendation was to include the role of social interaction in knowledge construction. We define knowledge construction as a process of active meaning-making through exploration, reflection, and interaction within social contexts. Knowledge construction is not a passive process, nor is it a reproduction of knowledge. Lucas and Moreira (2010) pointed out that while the IAM is strong in its ability to identify Phases of knowledge construction, it does not account for the role of social interaction in the construction of knowledge. In their development of IAM, Gunawardena et al. (1997) note that they left out the role of social interaction as there was hardly any evidence of social interaction in the debate transcript they analyzed to develop the IAM, as the interaction was focused on the goal of winning the debate. Subsequently, in the application of IAM in various other contexts, researchers have shown that social interaction does play a key role in the process of knowledge construction and should be accounted for in the IAM. In order to account for the missing social interaction, researchers started complementing qualitative content analysis of knowledge construction with other methods such as social network analysis (SNA), which enables the study of individual interactions in relation to the group and the visualization of individual contributions to the group's collaborative knowledge construction process (Gunawardena et al., 2016; Heo et al., 2010; Lucas et al., 2014; Yap & Chia, 2010). The incorporation of social interaction within IAM is one of the main ways in which it can be improved to provide a more comprehensive picture of knowledge construction (Lucas et al., 2014; Megli, 2022).

The third recommendation was to make a clear distinction between the IAM Phases. While noting IAM's ability to provide empirical evidence supporting the progressive nature of the knowledge construction process in well-defined Phases and explicitly conceptualizing the sequential relationship between Phases, some researchers have questioned the necessity of the full five-phase sequence (Wise & Chiu, 2011). This is partly because, in many studies, few postings could be coded at the higher levels of IAM, Phases IV and V (Lucas et al., 2014). Most postings are coded in Phase I, sharing and comparing information, and while there is some evidence of operations in Phases II and III, they are almost nonexistent in Phase IV and Phase V (Lucas & Moreira, 2010). In Wise and Chiu's (2011) study, one of the first studies to use a statistical method to analyze IAM, most online discussions had one pivotal post that distinguished two distinct discussion segments, the first dominated by a lower knowledge construction Phase and the second dominated by a higher knowledge construction Phase. Reflecting on the nature of the knowledge construction process in their study, Wise and Chiu (2011) ponder whether the presence or absence of IAM Phases 2 and 4 in the discussion process impacts the resulting constructed knowledge at the group and individual levels. However, other researchers have pointed out that the fact that participants do not reach higher levels of knowledge construction is not a limitation of the tool itself but is an issue with the way discussion prompts or goals for an online discussion are written or the way a discussion is facilitated in a specific sociocultural context (Megli, 2022). Therefore, while some researchers have questioned the necessity of all five Phases, many have argued for retaining the five Phases as they were conceptualized in the original IAM (Floren et al., 2021; Hall, 2014; Heo et al., 2010; Lucas & Moreira, 2010), requesting a clearer distinction between the Phases, especially between Phases I and III (Osman & Herring, 2007, p. 130).

When reflecting on these three recommendations for improving IAM, it is crucial to point out that IAM can only be used in contexts where there is a transcript available for analysis of either a synchronous or an asynchronous group discussion. IAM cannot account for variables external to the transcript. Researchers are encouraged to gather external evidence such as face-to-face meetings, e-mail communication, participant profiles, and other external data to develop a more holistic understanding of SCK.

To summarize, researchers who have used IAM as a method in their analysis of SCK have pointed out that it is a robust tool in explaining the progression of SCK and recommend three key areas for consideration when IAM is reconceptualized. These three areas center on (1) the understanding of the sociocultural context when results from IAM are interpreted, (2) incorporating the role of social interaction in supporting knowledge construction, and (3) a clear delineation between IAM's five Phases of knowledge construction representing a progressively higher collaborative learning process.

Reconceptualized Interaction Analysis Model 2.0 (IAM 2.0)

Even though the developers of IAM (Gunawardena et al., 1997) did not analyze the social dynamic of knowledge construction, more than two decades later, we know the central role social interaction and the sociocultural context play in understanding how SCK happens in online spaces. The reconceptualized IAM 2.0 will aid the researcher by clearly delineating the five Phases and operations of SCK and the social codes that represent three dimensions of social interaction that support knowledge construction in a specific sociocultural context. What participants post online is informed by various factors such as the sociocultural context, the social presence generated by fellow participants, the alliances that form during the course of the discussion, the discussion "rules" and prompts set by an instructor or designer, the facilitation techniques adopted by a moderator, and so on. The reconceptualization of IAM 2.0 attempts to take these factors into consideration.

IAM 2.0 retains the same learning theory foundation as the original IAM in sociocultural, social constructivist, and constructivist theories of learning, which were explained in detail in Chapter 1. Since numerous previous studies have validated the five Phases of the IAM (Floren et al., 2021; Lucas et al., 2014), IAM 2.0 will retain these five Phases, progressing from Vygotsky's (1978) lower to higher mental functions, which can be applied to a group's collaborative process (Smith, 1994). In Gunawardena et al.'s (1997) analysis of the debate transcript that led to the development of the IAM, they observed that as the group interacted together more effectively and learned from each other, the successive stages they went through could be described as forms of higher mental functions. They also observed the movement from lower to higher mental functions in the arguments presented in a single post showing the individual's ability to progress through the Phases of SCK. Therefore, IAM begins with lower mental functions, such as sharing and comparing information, and moves through cognitive dissonance or absence of it to the higher mental functions of negotiation of meaning and co-construction of knowledge, and then to validation and legitimization of the newly constructed meaning.

Figure 17.1 presents the reconceptualized IAM 2.0 in a circular graphic showing communication, movement, and progression. As shown in Figure 17.1, central to IAM 2.0 is the sociocultural context founded on sociocultural theory. The sociocultural context includes contextual factors, language, disciplinary culture in an institutional context, the design of online learning, and guidance and support, which are factors that researchers must take into account when they interpret the results of their studies analyzing SCK. Next, the cycle of social interaction emanates from the sociocultural context and feeds into SCK. Social interaction with its foundations in sociocultural theory is conceptualized as having three dimensions: social presence, social connectedness, and community, which play a role in knowledge construction. Next, the five Phases of knowledge construction are presented: Phase I – sharing and comparing of information; Phase II – exploring

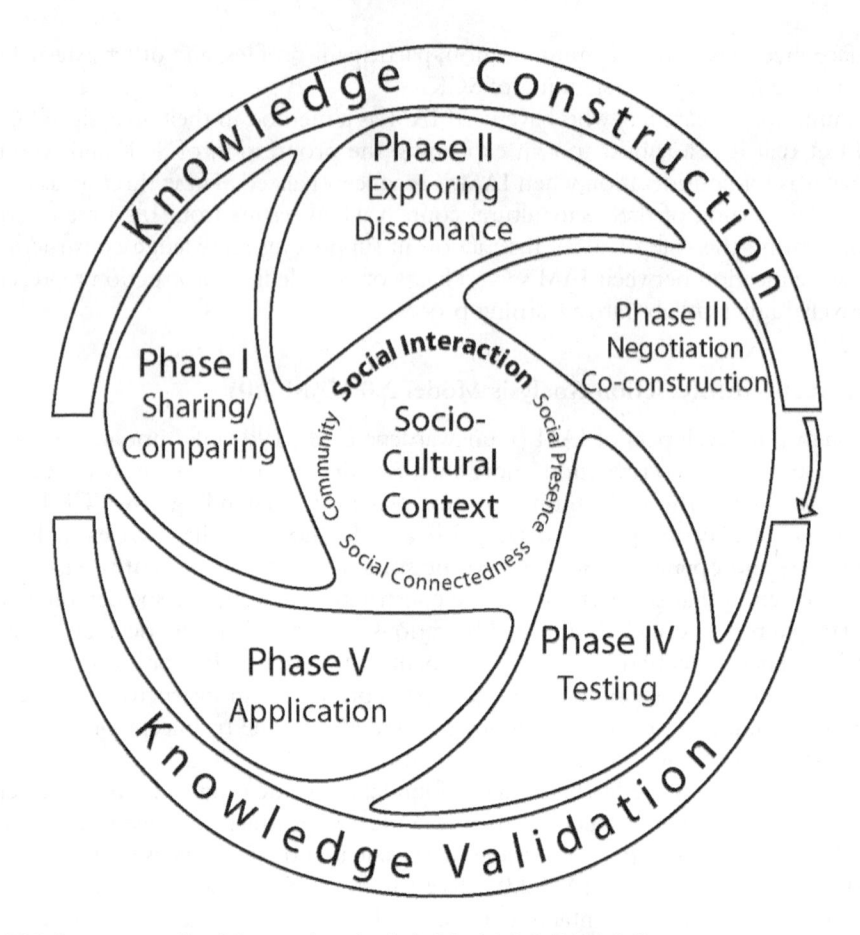

Figure 17.1 Reconceptualized Interaction Analysis Model 2.0 (IAM 2.0)

dissonance and inconsistencies; Phase III – negotiation and co-construction; followed by testing in Phase IV; and application in Phase V. IAM 2.0 takes into consideration the movement from lower to higher mental functions and clearly distinguishes between Phases that contribute to knowledge construction (Phases I–III), and Phases that contribute to validating or legitimizing the newly constructed knowledge (Phases IV and V). The major change in the reconceptualized IAM in Figure 17.1 is the integration of the central role of the sociocultural context and social interaction in the process of knowledge construction and the clear distinction between the Phases of knowledge construction and the Phases of knowledge validation and legitimization. Table 17.1, which appears later in this chapter, illustrates the coding scheme for Figure 17.1. Next, we discuss each of the components of IAM 2.0 presented in Figure 17.1.

Sociocultural Context

Drawing from sociocultural theory (John-Steiner & Mahn, 1996; Vygotsky, 1978), IAM 2.0 situates knowledge construction within an online sociocultural context. We define sociocultural context as the environment or setting in which learning occurs in relationship to each other and group affiliations, which are influenced by social and cultural factors:

> Every individual's learning is profoundly influenced by the particular context in which that person is situated. . . . Learning does not happen in the same way for all people because cultural influences pervade development from the beginning of life.
> (National Academies of Sciences, Engineering, and Medicine, 2018, p. 22)

We define culture adopting the Gunawardena et al. (2019) definition as a "collection of shared perceptions of the world and our place in it. These values and beliefs affect both identity formation and societal roles. Each of us belongs to many tribes, and these memberships overlap sometimes in unexpected ways" (p. 3). "Culture is generated from context and needs to be understood within context" (Hedayati-Mehdiabadi & Gunawardena, 2022). Research on learning from a sociocultural foundation, therefore, has highlighted the importance of understanding the role of culture and context in knowledge generation and construction.

In online contexts, culture is experienced and developed through communicating, dialoguing, sharing experiences, and interacting with one another. Hall (1959) showed the difference between high context (indirect) communication, where many things are left unsaid, letting the context explain, and low context (direct) or explicit communication when one gets to the point directly. Hence, providing the context when messages are communicated in a text-based medium will reduce the chance of misunderstanding. Weissmann et al. (2019) advocate a shift in academia to "multicontext" perspectives that value context diversity to ensure inclusive learning environments. People are multicontextual (able to change and display flexibility across the cultural context spectrum) and have unique cultural identities and orientations (Ibarra, 2001). Inclusive learning environments provide opportunities for diverse views to be heard, appreciated, and valued. Online courses that are highly individualized and designed without interaction cannot be labeled as inclusive learning environments. An inclusive learning environment must foster communication and community. Participants must feel a sense of belonging to a learning community, which values different beliefs, worldviews, and educational experiences (Gunawardena et al., 2019).

In reconceptualizing IAM 2.0, we place the sociocultural context in a central role as any results obtained from applying the IAM framework either through qualitative coding or through SLAM and AI must be interpreted with an understanding of the sociocultural context within which the SCK occurred. The context of the online discussion or learning experience, including; identity, prior knowledge, and experience of the participants; the disciplinary culture; the language through which the communication process unfolded; the topic or question assigned; instructions provided; and the volume of posts, etc. influence the way in which knowledge is constructed in a specific online context. Arvaja (2011) explored how to analyze the contextual nature of collaborative activity in asynchronous discussions based on sociocultural discourse analysis and presented a multidimensional coding scheme for analyzing the contextualized process of collaborative knowledge construction. This coding scheme included three contexts: the immediate and concrete (perceptual) context, the sociocultural context, and the local context. Of these three types of contexts, the most relevant for determining the context in IAM 2.0 is the sociocultural context. Marra et al. (2004) pointed out the criticality of the discourse context in the resulting analysis from IAM and the need for protocols that are contextualized within the larger culture to understand how discourse represents understanding or knowing within a sociocultural context. Next, we discuss selected aspects of the sociocultural context, the learner's past experiences and prior knowledge, the language of communication, disciplinary culture in an institutional context, guidance and support, and the design of online learning environments that researchers must consider when they interpret the results of SCK from the reconceptualized IAM 2.0.

Participants Past Experiences and Prior Knowledge

Adult learners bring to the learning context a wealth of diverse experiences and prior knowledge, which influences their communication, sharing, and knowledge construction. Often, these influences play an important role in attitudes toward collaboration, group formation, how prior knowledge is shared, and how new knowledge is constructed. Further, learners from diverse cultures bring different attitudes and expectations toward education and its purpose. Some prefer teacher-directed learning environments and expect direction from an instructor, while others prefer more open-ended, self-directed learning environments. In Uzuner's (2009) review of studies on questions of culture, researchers express broad agreement that the diverse cultural assumptions students bring to online learning concerning how teaching and learning should unfold bring about conflicts, disagreements, and frustrations. In computer transcripts, the identity, prior knowledge, and experience of the participants are revealed in what they share on their profiles, introductions, or what they contribute to a discussion.

Language

Language reinforces cultural values, perspectives, and worldviews. The grammar of each language voices and shapes ideas, serving as a guide for people's mental activity, for analyzing impressions, and for the synthesis of their mental stock in trade (Whorf, 1998). Therefore, one should consider how languages reflect thought processes and how thought processes shape the way we use language (Patwardhan, 2024). We need to be mindful that IAM was developed through analyzing interactions in a debate transcript that occurred in the English language; therefore, its application to other cultural contexts and languages must be carefully considered.

Although English is increasingly recognized as the international *lingua franca*, using English to communicate and learn rather than using one's native language puts learners at a disadvantage. Kramsch and Thorne's study (2002) shows how miscommunication in an intercultural asynchronous online dialogue between American and French students happened not so much by deficient individual linguistic styles but mostly by a lack of understanding of "cultural genres" in each other's discourse. Ishii (1982) compared the thought and communication patterns of Americans to a bridge, which is analogous to linear thinking and low context communication, where ideas are communicated explicitly or directly, and the Japanese patterns to a stepping stone approach (the arrangement of stones may not be clear), where ideas are communicated indirectly leaving the reader to infer the intended meaning. Barton and Tusting (2005) have argued that any theory of collaborative learning must incorporate models of language in use – language as part of social practice, power, and hierarchy within communities (risk, stigma, and equity) in the negotiation of meaning and resolution of conflict.

White (2009) developed the learner-context interface theory based on her study of distance language learners. The theory explains how learners establish their learning environment, negotiate meaning, and come to new understandings in a distance education context. It places the relationship between the learner and the context at the center of the learning experience. The context is different for each learner, and each learner constructs a unique interface with the learning context. How learners interface with the context and how language shapes social interaction and SCK are important considerations in understanding how people learn online.

Disciplinary Culture and the Design of Learning

Starr-Glass (2016) defined disciplinary culture as a common set of assumptions, attitudes, conceptualizations, epistemologies, and values held by members of an academic disciplinary community (such as chemistry or sociology) that shape their views, production, transmission, and sharing of knowledge. Disciplinary cultures influence the way learning environments are designed online and how learners are assessed. As we examine this influence, we need to ask questions such as: To what degree does a discipline value learner–learner interaction and collaboration? How is this value reflected in assessments of learning? While some disciplines adhere to instructor-led and directed learning environments, others might embrace learner-centered inquiry-based learning and provide opportunities for inquiry and collaboration. We need to be cognizant of the directions (often referred to as discussion prompts) provided for inquiry or collaborative learning, as they will influence how participants engage in inquiry and construct knowledge. It is in open-ended inquiry-based learning environments where opportunities are provided for exploration that knowledge construction is often visible. IAM 2.0 is best suited to analyzing inquiry-based collaborative learning environments.

Guidance and Support

The zone of proximal development (ZPD), a central concept in sociocultural theory (Vygotsky, 1978), and legitimate peripheral participation, the process by which newcomers become members of a community of practice in situated learning (Lave & Wenger, 1991), provide the foundation for the role of guidance in online learning environments. Those who guide can assist others in their ZPD to bridge the gap between actual and potential levels of development. Sometimes, a guide can be a fellow participant, another time, an instructor, and in another instance, an expert from the community. Formal academic learning environments are often designed to provide guidance, while professional development learning environments or informal social learning environments may or may not have a guide present who engages with the participants. Those who guide also provide support to participants in numerous ways, ranging from clarifying an assignment to providing feedback to technical troubleshooting. In discussing types of support and sources of support, Frechette (2020) points out that not all types and sources of support will be available in all contexts nor will they be customizable in all contexts; therefore a "multipronged approach to cultivating sociocultural learning works best" (p. 365).

The degree to which guidance is available in an online learning environment will influence SCK. Those who provide guidance play various roles. Some may offer direct instruction on how to achieve goals, while others will be more open-ended, allowing participants to figure out what is required. Often, those who guide will engage as co-mentors, sharing mentor–mentee responsibilities and acting as teachers and counselors for one another at different points in the learning process, as each person has something to teach and something to learn (Gunawardena et al., 2019). Those who guide play an important role in supporting a collaborative group to engage in social interaction and achieve SCK. A cross-cultural study of e-mentoring between the United States and Sri Lanka in the context of an online faculty development program implemented in Sri Lanka found through the analysis of computer transcripts that U.S. e-mentors demonstrated six types of facilitating techniques to help the mentees in Sri Lanka construct knowledge together and build a learning community within three inquiry-based learning designs (Jayatilleke et al., 2012). The six e-mentoring techniques used by e-mentors were: social, pedagogical, managerial, technical, collaborative, and inspirational. "Social" strategies encompassed self-introductions, greetings, praise, and encouragement to build the learning community, while "pedagogical" strategies provided guidance on conducting the learning activities, by asking thought-provoking questions, paraphrasing, and summarizing. Guidance related to conducting and completing the learning activity within the required time was categorized as "managerial" and included giving instructions, assigning roles, stipulating timelines, etc. The "technical" category included provisions of technical help or referral to a technical expert. Strategies used for promoting group collaboration were grouped as "collaborative." Sometimes, there was a tendency for strategies to overlap, especially the social and collaborative functions. The "inspirational" category emerged when the mentees clearly indicated that their interactions with the e-mentor and each other changed their way of thinking or influenced them to transform their attitudes.

The sociocultural context, therefore, includes many factors, as evident in the preceding discussion. We encourage qualitative researchers to develop codes that reflect the sociocultural context in their own setting when conducting an analysis with IAM 2.0. For example, Floren et al. (2021) developed two codes for facilitators and barriers to knowledge construction that were evident in their context of interprofessional education. Other researchers have included codes for project management and technical support evident in their sociocultural context. Each sociocultural context is different, so studying one's own context and including the codes that reflect the context are crucial for understanding the process of knowledge construction.

To summarize, in IAM 2.0 (Figure 17.1), we place the sociocultural context in the center as influencing social interaction and knowledge construction. We discussed selected aspects of the sociocultural context that influence online communication and collaboration: the learner's past experiences and prior knowledge, the language of communication, disciplinary culture and the design of online learning, and guidance and support. Researchers are encouraged to study their own contexts and include codes for their own sociocultural context when analyzing transcripts of online discussions. In Table 17.1 and in the IAM coding sheet for Chapter 17 on GitHub at https://github.com/knowledge-construction/slam-ai, we prompt the researcher to develop specific codes for their own sociocultural context.

IAM 2.0 and Social Interaction

Sociocultural theory emphasizes social interaction, and we recognize that social interaction is the primary vehicle for knowledge construction and have integrated the social and relational aspects of social interaction that supports SCK when reconceptualizing IAM 2.0. Participation in online learning environments is both a relational and an emotional process and not merely a cognitive one aimed at completing tasks (Xiao et al., 2024). Social interaction is an essential precursor to collaborative learning and knowledge construction and supports socioemotional and social processes related to developing affective relationships, group formation and dynamics, and building cohesiveness and community (Gunawardena & Zittle, 1997; Kreijns et al., 2003).

In IAM 2.0, we conceptualize "social interaction," a multidimensional construct using three interrelated dimensions: social presence, social connectedness, and community. All three dimensions interweave with each other and can sometimes develop as a continuum to reflect social interaction, as in Figure 17.2. Next, we explain each of the three dimensions of the construct "social interaction" illustrated in Figure 17.2.

Figure 17.2 Social interaction in IAM 2.0

Social Presence

When defining social presence for IAM 2.0, we adapt Gunawardena and Zittle's (1997) definition of social presence as "the degree to which a person is perceived as a 'real person' in mediated communication" (p. 9), which closely aligns with the original definition of social presence put forward by Short et al. (1976) as "the degree of salience of the other person in the interaction and the consequent salience of the interpersonal relationships" (p. 65). In IAM 2.0, we extend Gunawardena and Zittle's (1997) conceptualization and define social presence as the degree to which a person, digital assistant (chatbot), or avatar is perceived as real in mediated communication. Social presence is, therefore, a perception of the other and the "realness" of the other. Once realness is established, the relationship with the other sometimes begins through affinity with shared characteristics or the desire to get to know someone who is unique and intriguing. With the development of AI architectures, we are increasingly communicating with digital assistants and personas, and the extent to which they may seem real might influence our desire to communicate with them. In text-based online environments where participants do not see each other, this feeling of realness is usually experienced through "realness" expressions/indicators such as greetings, addressing others by name, emotions, paralanguage, emoticons, etc., and by the revelation of identity whether "real" or "pseudo" through self-disclosure. See Table 17.1 for these indicators integrated into IAM 2.0.

We acknowledge that there is a close relationship between the feeling of "realness" of the other and the identity of the other. Identity can be defined as "the distinguishing character or personality of an individual" (Merriam-Webster Online, 2024) or simply "who you are" (Cambridge Dictionary, 2024). "Social presence and identity are closely intertwined. . . . Identity, then, comprises the unique characteristics communicated by a specific individual's presence" (Dennen & Burner, 2017, p. 174). Virtual identity is more fluid and can be changed to appeal to different audiences as participants can craft an identity using text that exists quite apart from their real lives. Both identity and social presence are important for participants to continue engaging and interacting on digital platforms. Jaber and Kennedy (2017) argue that identity may be key to understanding why social presence has been considered so important to successful learning experiences.

If participants communicate their identities, it is easier to feel their realness and connect with them, but this may depend on the sociocultural context. Not every participant will interact online, or they may use different forms of engagement, such as liking a post or reposting. While there has been debate about lurking and those who only listen but do not interact or contribute, we feel that listening is an important skill in developing trust and that we need

Table 17.1 The Coding Scheme for the Reconceptualized Interaction Analysis Model 2.0 (IAM 2.0) for Examining Social Construction of Knowledge (SCK)

Interaction Analysis Model 2.0 (IAM 2.0)	Codes
Phases of Knowledge Construction: Phases I-III	
PHASE I: SHARING OR COMPARING INFORMATION	
A. A statement of observation or opinion	[PhI/A]
B. A statement of agreement from one or more other participants	[PhI/B]
C. Corroborating examples provided by one or more participants	[PhI/C]
D. Asking and answering questions to clarify details of statements	[PhI/D]
E. Definition, description or identification of a problem	[PhI/E]
PHASE II: THE EXPLORATION OF DISSONANCE OR INCONSISTENCY AMONG IDEAS, CONCEPTS, STATEMENTS, PROBLEMS, OR ISSUES	
A. Identifying areas of dissonance or inconsistency	[PhII/A]
B. Asking and answering questions to clarify the source and extent of dissonance or inconsistency	[PhII/B]
C. Restating the participant's position and possibly advancing arguments or considerations in its support by references to the participant's experience, literature, or data, or proposal of relevant metaphor or analogy to illustrate point of view	[PhII/C]
PHASE III: NEGOTIATION OF MEANING OR CO-CONSTRUCTION OF KNOWLEDGE	
A. Negotiation of meaning of terms	[PhIII/A]
B. Negotiation of the weight to be assigned to types of statements or arguments	[PhIII/B]
C. Recognition of areas of agreement or overlap among differing concepts or ideas	[PhIII/C]
D. Proposal and negotiation of new statements embodying compromise, or co-construction	[PhIII/D]
E. Proposal of integrating or accommodating metaphors or analogies	[PhIII/E]
Phases of Knowledge Validation: Phases IV-V	
PHASE IV: TESTING OF PROPOSED SYNTHESIS OR CO-CONSTRUCTION	
A. Testing the proposed synthesis or co-construction against shared facts, culture, or context	[PhIV/A]
B. Testing against existing cognitive schema	[PhIV/B]
C. Testing against personal experience	[PhIV/C]
D. Testing against data	[PhIV/D]
E. Testing against literature	[PhIV/E]
PHASE V: AGREEMENT STATEMENTS OR APPLICATIONS OF NEWLY-CONSTRUCTED MEANING	
A. Summarization of agreement(s)	[PhV/A]
B. Applications of co-constructed knowledge to various contexts	[PhV/B]
C. Metacognitive statements by the participants illustrating their realization that their knowledge or ways of thinking have changed as a consequence of the interaction	[PhV/C]
D. Creation of a knowledge artifact	[PhV/D]

(Continued)

Table 17.1 (Continued)

Interaction Analysis Model 2.0 (IAM 2.0)	Codes
Social Interaction Dimensions	

SOCIAL PRESENCE

1. Greetings and salutations	SP1
2. Expression of emotion	SP2
3. Humor	SP3
4. Paralanguage (huh, hmm, yuk)	SP4
5. Silence	SP5
6. Emoticons	SP6
7. Addressing others by name (Vocatives)	SP7
8. Introductions and Biographies (Bios)	SP8
9. Identity	SP9
10. Self-disclosure	SP10
11. Sharing passions and interests	SP11

SOCIAL CONNECTEDNESS

1. Continuing a social message	SC1
2. Referring to others	SC2
3. Complimenting	SC3
4. Appreciating	SC4
5. Checking on others – how they are	SC5
6. Following up (personal and professional)	SC6
7. Personal advice	SC7
8. Acknowledging	SC8
9. Invitation	SC9
10. Personalized feedback	SC10
11. Conversational rather than formal communication style	SC11
12. Storytelling/digital stories	SC12

COMMUNITY

1. Inclusive pronouns	C1
2. Influence	C2
3. Prestige or reputation	C3
4. Contributions	C4
5. Listening	C5
6. Embracing the group	C6
7. Group reference	C7
8. Continuity	C8
9. Managing and maintaining community activity (e.g., organizing a project, resolving conflicts)	C9

SOCIOCULTURAL CONTEXT   Scontext
Each sociocultural context is unique. Appropriate contextualized codes
should be developed by the researcher considering the following: culture,
context, participants' past experiences and prior knowledge, the language
of communication, disciplinary culture, institutional context, guidance,
support, learning design – topic, prompts, instructions, etc.

to let lurkers be lurkers, especially at the beginning of an online discussion. Lurkers, though they are silent, might be learning from others and play a role in diverse social relations: "For many novice learners and those from diverse cultural backgrounds, this lurking period may be necessary to observe the formation of the group's culture prior to interacting" (Gunawardena et al., 2019, p. 71). After being on the periphery of a learning community, they may come in later when a level of comfort and trust is established. Discussing two archetypes in e-discourse, lurkers and virtuosos (those skilled in e-discourse), Perkins and Newman (1996) call for the consideration of the role of the lurker, a recognition of lurkers as participants and an acknowledgment of the functions they perform. Lurkers are necessary for certain platforms, such as YouTube where their feedback in the form of "likes" is an important contribution. Recognizing the value of different appropriate approaches to communication online, we encourage lurkers to participate in academic discussions so their perspectives contribute to the overall gestalt of SCK.

Examining the relationship between "social presence" and "interactivity," Rafaeli (1988, 1990) observed that social presence is a subjective indication of the presence of others, as Short et al. (1976) defined it, while "interactivity" or interaction between people is the actual quality of a communication sequence within a context. When interaction is realized and participants notice it, there is "social presence." When there are opportunities for interaction and participants engage in it, there is a sense of social presence. This clearly distinguishes the two constructs social presence and interaction. Tu and McIsaac's (2002) study found that "social presence is necessary to enhance and foster online social interaction" (p. 146).

To summarize, in IAM 2.0, we extend Gunawardena and Zittle's (1997) conceptualization of social presence as the "realness" of the other and define the dimension of social presence as the degree to which a person, digital assistant (chatbot), or avatar is perceived as real in mediated communication. Social presence is communicated through realness indicators and identity. Realness is indicated in text-based communication by greetings and salutations, expression of emotion, humor, paralanguage, emoticons, being present online, etc., while identity is communicated through self-disclosure, often observed in the online profiles participants create, their introductions to a group, biographies, interests, stories, and passions. See Table 17.1 for realness and identity indicators. Once social presence is established, participants are more likely to engage in interaction and social connectedness and the sharing of interests, ideas, and perspectives. If social connectedness occurs over an extended length of time, then it is possible to observe the development of an online community: "The development of social presence and a sense of an online community becomes key to promoting collaborative learning and knowledge building" (Gunawardena, 1995, p. 165). We define social connectedness next.

Social Connectedness

Connectedness "refers to a person's belief that a relationship exists between him or her and at least one other individual. When individuals feel connected, they feel less isolation" (Bolliger & Inan, 2012, p. 43). Individuals who feel socially connected believe that they have close relationships with others, and those with high levels of connectedness are better able to take charge of their own needs and emotions through cognitive processes such as self-evaluation (Lee & Robbins, 1998). Those who feel socially connected can enter social situations more easily and are more willing to engage with others and participate in activities. Connectedness in online learning environments may potentially affect learners' levels of motivation and satisfaction (Bolliger & Inan, 2012; Lee & Robbins, 1998). For Rovai (2003), a key component to building a successful online community is connectedness, which Galambos et al. (1986) refer to as the interactions between people in computer-mediated environments that enable comfortable participation as they form social relationships with others in the group. Further, "connectedness denotes recognition of membership in a community and the feelings of friendship, cohesion, and satisfaction that develop among learners" (Rovai, 2003, p. 322). Discussing a model for social connectedness in online social networks, Riedl et al. (2013) observe that evidence from their study suggests that "social presence functions as an important building block for social connectedness" (p. 683) and further point out that "Social connectedness can be described as the feeling of belonging to a social group and implies the creation of bonding relationships" (p. 673). They observe that previous research has identified several beneficial outcomes of social support, and social connectedness and has shown that these factors help people in overcoming disadvantages like isolation and strengthen their integration into a community.

In IAM 2.0, we define the dimension social connectedness as the relationships developed by participants interacting with each other through mediated communication in an online social network. We affirm that social presence is an important foundational element for social connectedness and that social connectedness happens through interaction. From a social perspective, interaction means building connections through mediated communication. In IAM 2.0, connectedness may involve social, educational, and/or professional relations: "People with high connectedness tend to feel very close with other people, easily identify with others, perceive others as friendly and approachable, and participate in social groups and activities" (Lee et al., 2001, p. 310). Participation in online interactions is also a relational and emotional process instead of a merely cognitive one focused on completing tasks (Xiao et al. 2024; Yashima et al., 2018). Riedl et al. (2013) studied social connectedness within a social network. Social Network Analysis (SNA), which we discussed in Chapter 10, is one method a researcher can use to analyze social connectedness as SNA can represent the social ties within a network.

To summarize, in IAM 2.0, we define the dimension social connectedness as the relationships developed by participants interacting with each other through mediated communication in an online social network. Social presence is a precursor for social connectedness to be realized, and social connectedness happens through interaction. Interaction within a social network helps us to map the social ties, social influence, and connections within the network. Social network analysis (SNA) discussed in Chapter 10 can be used to measure social connectedness. Social connectedness over time helps to build an online community. We discuss the role of community in social interaction next.

Community

While a group is an assemblage of people with shared interests, a community encompasses connectedness and the desire to stay connected over time (Gunawardena et al., 2019). In IAM 2.0, we define the dimension as a community of social connectedness which is a network of stable social connections over time within one or more groups. Rovai (2002) observed that "members of strong classroom communities have feelings of connectedness" (p. 198). A stable pattern of connections over time between a group of participants can indicate group cohesion, which is the degree to which group members stay together, work together, and develop a shared identity. Rogers and Lea (2005) observed that in distributed group environments, social presence is "enabled through the emphasis on the shared social identity at the level of the collaborating group rather than the creation of interpersonal bonds between individual group members" (p. 156). Community is interrelated with social presence and social connectedness.

We see evidence of community in computer transcripts when groups begin to refer to themselves as "we," "our," or adopt a group name and engage in shared actions "we should" or "we can." When a group of people connect initially, there is a sharing of individual identity. When groups interact and communicate over time, they may develop a shared group identity. Individual identity is often expressed by phrases such as "I like . . ." or "I prefer . . .," while group identity is reflected in "we like . . ." and "we prefer . . ." McAteer et al. (2002) observe that one strand of behavior in collaborative learning contexts, noted by sociocultural and situated learning theories as indicating community, is what might be called the "social glue" of interaction. This includes strategies employed in managing and maintaining learning community activity. At the simplest level, this can be described as "chairing" behavior: interactional turns aimed at specifying what should happen when and who is responsible. At a more sophisticated level, this might involve managing the process of uncovering and resolving conflicts without provoking outright hostility.

Social presence can lead to social connectedness and, over time, to group cohesion. Members of a cohesive community listen to each other and engage in open and direct communication. Community formation may happen through other communication channels such as mobile phones, email, social media platforms, and face-to-face meetings, which may not be evident in a computer transcript. Awareness of the communication channels available and used in a specific sociocultural context will enhance our understanding of community formation through mediated communication.

As online communities develop, they create a pattern of interactions. These patterns of interactions can be meaningfully visualized using SNA: "The social network approach examines both the content and the pattern of relationships in order to determine how and what resources flow from one actor to another" (Haythornthwaite, 1996, p. 324). Subscribing to the social network perspective, Kreijns et al. (2022) saw "each interpersonal relationship as a tie that connects two communicating persons whereby these ties may be weak or strong" (p. 159). In a network, it is important to visualize both listening and talking. SNA can depict listening when there is an arrow going in but not going out. The cohesiveness of a community can be observed in an SNA sociogram by stable connections (the same persons talking) and the number of connections over time.

To summarize, in IAM 2.0, we define the dimension of community as a network of stable social connections over time within one or more groups. We consider an online group that interacts and stays connected over time as a community of social connectedness. We see evidence of community in transcripts when groups begin to refer to themselves as "we," "our," or adopt a group name and engage in shared actions such as "we should" or "we can." Community members may develop a shared identity if they stay connected and cohesive over time. A community can be analyzed by SNA sociograms depicting ties between members and the overall pattern of connections. The three dimensions: social presence, social connectedness, and community interweave to provide a depiction of the construct of social interaction. Next, we address interaction and communication in IAM 2.0 before addressing the five Phases of knowledge construction.

Interaction and Communication From a Sociocultural Perspective

The terms *interaction* and *communication* are often used interchangeably or synonymously and are difficult to define and distinguish. The most popular conceptualization of communication is the creation of meaningful messages sent or received from person to person or between people or teams (Vlachopoulos & Makri, 2019). Communication focuses on the content of the message and the understanding between the sender and receiver, and it can be verbal or nonverbal. Online communication enables students to use text, images, sound, and video in asynchronous or synchronous interaction. Interaction signals the act of engaging and responding to one another. It involves an action or exchange between individuals or systems. Interaction involves engagement, which leads to social interaction: "Due to the diversity of goals, backgrounds and preferences, truly effective communication must be interactive; this means that each person communicating should listen and respond to others" (Vlachopoulos & Makri, 2019, p. 611).

In developing the original IAM, the authors (Gunawardena et al., 1997) conceptualized interaction for online environments using the metaphor of a patchwork quilt as they felt that traditional models of communication (sender-message-channel-receiver-feedback) do not fit neatly to describe online interaction. The contributions of individual members were considered the unique pieces of the patchwork representing individual texture and color of thought, and interaction was conceptualized as the process by which all the pieces of the quilt were put together to create a new pattern or gestalt. The co-constructed knowledge then becomes the gestalt, which can be viewed by looking at the overall interaction: "Interaction is the essential process of putting together the pieces in the co-creation of knowledge" (Gunawardena et al., 1997, p. 412).

Given the central role of the sociocultural context and social interaction in knowledge construction in IAM 2.0, it is prudent to pay attention to how individuals communicate and what influences their communication when they post a message online. Many online environments are global learning environments with diverse participants, as in massive open online courses (MOOCs). Participants may be influenced by their traditional cultural modes of communication and interaction and guided by what is appropriate when communicating in public online spaces. Edward T. Hall declared, "Culture is communication, and communication is culture" (Hall, 1959, p. 186), a definition that reflects the complex interplay between communication, culture, and, in the online context, technology. "Communication shapes culture, technology mediates communication, and culture influences technology" (Gunawardena et al., 2019, p. 69).

How communication differs between cultures, for example, between Western, African, and Asian communities, has been illustrated by communication researchers (Asante, 1983; Dissanayake, 1983; Reddi, 1986; Miike, 2002). Arguing for an Afrocentric view of communication, Asante (1983) points out, "effective intercultural communication must be based upon the equality of the interactants because the sharing of meaning is the fundamental pre-requisite of communicative understanding" (pp. 5–6). While Western perspectives see communication as a way to transmit ideas, Eastern approaches emphasize communication as a relationship-building tool. Miike (2002) showed the limitations of using only Western approaches to understand how people communicate and identified three themes that emerge from an Asian paradigm of communication: relationality, circularity, and harmony. These concepts show that communication is a dynamic, relationship-driven process. Miike's conceptualization rests on three assumptions: (1) communication takes place in various relationships, (2) the communicator is both active and passive in different contexts, and (3) mutual adaptation is the key to harmonious communication. Zhang (2008) shows how the core principles of Confucianism influence communication: Harmony and hierarchy, indirect and implicit communication, and polite and formal communication. Discussing the transactional nature of human communication from the perspective of the Buddhist concept of causality, known as "dependent co-origination," Dissanayake (1983) shows the "mutual dependence" or the interdependence of human communication. Reddi (1986) observed that India has a vibrant oral communication tradition in music, dance, drama, and mythology and that these traditional and folk media of communication have been the mainstay of cultural cohesion for centuries.

The difference between aspects of Japanese and American modes of communication is illustrated by Yoshikawa (1988) in Figure 17.3, adapted for this book to show the comparison. The image labeled A in Figure 17.3 is an illustration of the "coming to the point" style of the American mode of communication. Citing Kaplan's (1966) study on cultural thought patterns, which showed how American students tend to write a paragraph or term paper linearly, Yoshikawa observes that this mode of expression assumes that a speaker is supposed to make a point and the position clear. In contrast, the Japanese mode of communication can be characterized by the "coming around the point" style, which is circular in nature, as illustrated by image B in Figure 17.3. This model of communication is probably influenced by the Japanese concept of time, which is constantly recurring in cycles. Another influence may be the Buddhist view of time, which is a circle with no end and no beginning. The Japanese, in order to reach the point, prefer to go around the point rather than to go straight to the point, for they consider it a more gentle and natural approach. Therefore, Asian students tend to write a paragraph or paper in more of a circular style. This and many other differences between communication styles influenced Yoshikawa (1988) to develop his "double-swing" model of intercultural communication between the East and West based on an Eastern understanding of dialogue, collaborative communication, and co-creation of meaning. The double-swing model enables one to understand communication as an ongoing process where both sender and receiver have mutual respect and fosters a worldview that is heterogeneous, pluralistic, and dynamic. This discussion on interaction and communication has shown the diverse influences on communication in diverse sociocultural contexts and the need to account for this diversity when we interpret findings from IAM 2.0.

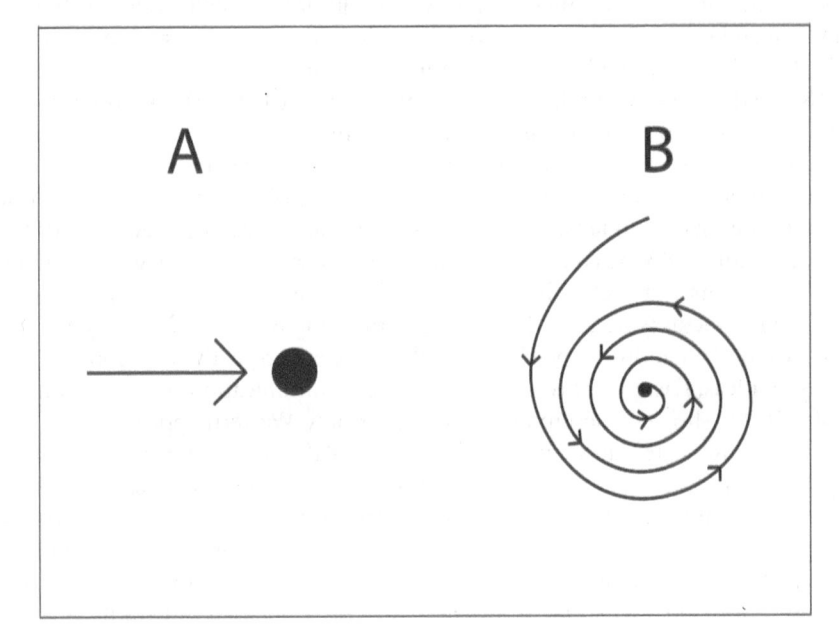

Figure 17.3 The difference between aspects of Japanese and American modes of communication illustrated by Yoshikawa (1988) in *Communication Theory: The Asian Perspective*. The image labeled A on the left illustrates the "coming to the point" style of American communication. The image labeled B to the right illustrates the "coming around the point" style of Japanese communication.

Note: This image was adapted for this volume to show the comparison with permission from the volume editor.

Conceptualizing Interaction and Communication in IAM 2.0

Western, African, Eastern, and other perspectives on communication are all valid ways to inform our conceptualization of the communication process in IAM 2.0. Communication is both a means to exchange ideas and knowledge and a way to build community. In IAM 2.0, we extend the conceptualization of interaction as a patchwork quilt (see the original IAM in Chapter 1) to focus on the sociocultural influences, each color of thought contributed by each individual to create a gestalt or pattern of communication. Awareness of the influence of the sociocultural context on communication helps us to visualize communication in IAM 2.0 as a circular process as opposed to a linear process. The importance of conceptualizing communication as a circular process has been pointed out by both Western and Asian communication researchers (Dissanayake, 1988a; Schramm, 2001).

Dissanayake (1988b), discussing Asian perspectives on communication and specifically Indian verbal communication, illustrates visually the circular concept of communication and the centrality of the communication environment in Figure 17.4 (adapted for this book). In Figure 17.4, we see that the cultural background and the structure of consciousness of the listener play a crucial role in interpreting the utterance of a speaker, and language is central to

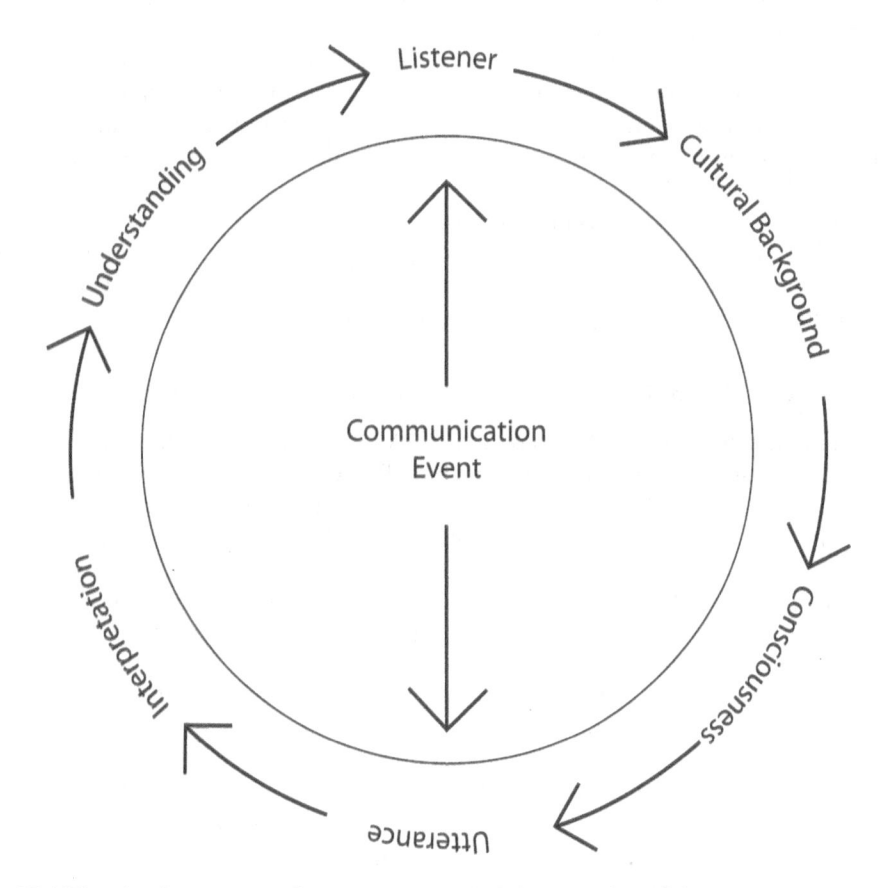

Figure 17.4 The circular concept of communication and the centrality of the communication environment illustrated by Dissanayake in *Communication Theory: The Asian Perspective* (1988a)

Note: This image was adapted for this volume with permission from the author of the chapter and editor of the volume.

the whole enterprise. Language both creates and expresses thoughts, and it can only be properly understood in relation to the cultural background in which it operates and the structures of consciousness that are affected by it. Dissanayake (1988b) observed that the puzzlement of Westerners with the language habits of the Indians arises as a result of the different structures of consciousness that animate Westerners and Indians and the different communicative environments that have nurtured those structures of consciousness.

We adopt Dissanayake's circular perspective on communication, illustrated in Figure 17.4, for IAM 2.0 as it focuses on the centrality of the sociocultural context and the environment in which communication takes place. It reflects the relationship-centered communication processes in Asian contexts, thus meshing Western and Eastern views of communication. A circular approach also implies both the sender and the receiver exchange roles and participate equally in the communication, differentiating it from linear models of communication. Therefore, when we reconceptualized IAM 2.0, we embedded the circularity of the communication process in Figure 17.1.

Further, a circular approach reflects interaction in an online environment where each participant has an equal opportunity to participate without deference to an authority figure as in a classroom. However, even though the online environment allows equal participation, it does not guarantee it. Learners can be excluded because of lack of access, fear of technology, and other reasons, such as the dynamics of the group (Gunawardena, 1998).

To summarize, we explored interaction and communication from a sociocultural perspective, first explaining the distinction between the terms interaction and communication and then exploring studies that have highlighted views on communication from African and Asian perspectives, which are different from Western views of communication. Subsequently, we conceptualized interaction and communication in IAM 2.0 from a circular perspective on communication, which focuses on the centrality of the sociocultural environment in which communication takes place and the cultural background and the structure of consciousness of the interactants in interpreting the messages communicated.

The Five Phases of Social Construction of Knowledge (SCK) in IAM 2.0

While retaining the original five Phases of SCK, IAM 2.0 now distinguishes between the initial knowledge construction Phases, which include Phases I, II, and III, and the subsequent Phases, which signal the validation or legitimization of the newly constructed knowledge; Phases IV and V. The operations in each Phase have changed slightly to remove overlap between operations. These changes were influenced by studies that have employed IAM and our own testing of IAM with SLAM and AI (Gunawardena et al., 2016; Gunawardena et al., 2023). The new IAM 2.0 coding scheme for each of the five SCK Phases, including the operations, is found in Table 17.1.

In developing the original IAM, the authors (Gunawardena et al., 1997) asked: "Can one see evidence that the discussion proceeded through at least the first three stages?" (p. 417) and observed that this might provide a preliminary judgment of the conference quality. Therefore, in IAM 2.0, we have labeled the first three Phases as knowledge construction Phases and specify that at least Phases I and III must be observed to describe a discussion as having reached the stage of knowledge construction. We point out that in cultural contexts where it is impolite to openly disagree with one another, participants will build on each other's ideas and construct knowledge, which explains the absence of Phase II in certain studies that used IAM. Therefore, in some contexts, Phases I and III, and in other contexts, Phases I, II, and III signal SCK.

In discussing the five Phases in the original IAM, the authors (Gunawardena et al., 1997) stated:

> In general, the more phases the conference illustrates, the more participants who are active at each phase, and the greater the variety of resources the participants call upon in the process of negotiation of meaning or construction of knowledge, the higher the quality of the conference.
>
> (p. 417)

This led some researchers (cited in Lucas et al., 2014) to observe that SCK as stipulated by IAM is difficult to observe as most online discussions do not go beyond Phase I. Therefore, in reconceptualizing the IAM, we label the first three Phases as knowledge construction Phases, which means that a discussion may only reach Phase III and can still be described as one where knowledge construction took place. If the discussion moves to the next two Phases, which entail testing and application of the newly constructed knowledge, then the discussion has reached a more advanced stage of knowledge construction, which we label as knowledge validation.

IAM 2.0 Phases of Knowledge Construction: Phases I, II, and III

IAM 2.0 Phases I, II, and III reflect the early period of an online discussion, during which participants get to know each other, share perspectives, explore diverse perspectives, and begin to negotiate meaning. This process is characteristic of many online discussions.

PHASE I: SHARING AND COMPARING INFORMATION

As seen in Table 17.1, in Phase I, participants share their observations or opinions, agree with the statements made by other participants, provide examples to support their perspectives, ask clarifying questions, define terms, and identify problems or issues for further investigation. Reviewing 16 studies that used IAM as a method of analysis, Lucas et al. (2014) observe that the IAM supports the initial Phase of sharing and comparing information (PhI) in all designs and in different communication tools. They note that this is characteristic of many discussions where members of a community need to get to know each other and understand each other's perspectives. This is also a desirable feature that supports social interaction in online learning environments, as participants need to feel welcomed and comfortable enough to share their ideas and opinions (Scardamalia & Bereiter, 2003; Wegerif, 1998).

PHASE II: THE EXPLORATION OF DISSONANCE OR INCONSISTENCY AMONG IDEAS, CONCEPTS, STATEMENTS, PROBLEMS, OR ISSUES

Festinger (1957) proposed the theory of "cognitive dissonance," hypothesizing that when there is dissonance (or inconsistency or disequilibrium) among ideas/knowledge/opinion/ beliefs, etc., it creates a psychologically uncomfortable condition, which motivates people to try to reduce the dissonance and achieve consonance (or consistency). In addition to making an effort to reduce the dissonance, people will actively avoid information and situations that would likely increase the dissonance. In developing the IAM, Gunawardena et al. (1997) used Festinger's theory of cognitive dissonance to conceptualize Phase II of knowledge construction because they observed opposing points of view or inconsistencies when negative arguments were introduced in the debate transcript they analyzed to develop the IAM. As proposed by the theory, they saw participants in the debate trying to reduce the dissonance or inconsistencies caused by the negative side's arguments by negotiating meaning even though the debate leaders tried to keep the affirmative and negative sides apart. It is this effort to resolve the discomfort brought about by opposing points of view that moved the discussion to Phase III negotiation of meaning and co-construction of knowledge. As indicated in Table 17.1, operations in Phase II labeled as the exploration of dissonance or inconsistency among ideas, concepts, statements, problems, or issues are characterized by activities such as identifying areas of disagreement and inconsistency, clarifying their sources, and advancing arguments or considerations supported by participants' own experience, review of literature, or data.

As we reflect on the knowledge construction process and the role of dissonance in it, we must be cognizant that "Knowledge is a product of culture" (Dissanayake, 1986, p. 269). Sánchez (2019) points out that constructing knowledge does not happen in a vacuum as both the "learner's experiences and understandings of the world are situated within and affected by the learner's cultural, institutional, and historical social contexts as described by sociocultural theory" (p. 182); therefore, "knowledge building processes may differ across cultures" (p. 182). The question is whether Phase II, dissonance is necessary for a group to move toward knowledge construction.

Biesenbach-Lucas (2003) pointed out that non-native speakers of English, particularly students from Asian countries, consider it far less appropriate to challenge and criticize the ideas of others. In addition, they may not know how to express disagreement appropriately in English. Biesenbach-Lucas notes that this lack of challenge and disagreement of ideas is troubling as it is the "resolution of such areas of agreement and disagreement that 'results in higher forms of reasoning' because 'cognitive development requires that individuals encounter others who contradict their own intuitively derived ideas'" (p. 37). The question here is whether such challenges to ideas expressed by others are necessary for knowledge construction or whether it is merely an expectation from a predominantly Western point of view. Studies have shown another point of view – that knowledge construction can happen without argument or challenges to the ideas expressed by others. In a study conducted at the Monterrey Tech-Virtual University in Mexico, Lopez-Islas (2004) observed that open disagreement is not appropriate in the Mexican cultural context; therefore, participants moved to knowledge construction without moving through the cognitive dissonance Phase as described in the IAM.

Similar results were found in a study conducted at the Open University in Taiwan (Ho, 2024) and a study examining the impact of cross-cultural e-mentoring on social construction of knowledge in faculty development forums conducted in Sri Lanka (Gunawardena et al., 2008; Gunawardena et al., 2011). Ho (2024) pointed out that there were three reasons why the Taiwanese students did not engage in cognitive dissonance (Phase II). They were: (1) time constraints (it takes time to write an opposing point of view and it is easier to work with areas you agree with); (2) conflict avoidance in the Asian sociocultural context (it is more convenient to agree and avoid conflict as there could be misunderstandings when language is expressed in a text-based medium); and (3) unfamiliarity with online students. In the Sri Lankan study, participants did not openly disagree at the level of ideas but moved to negotiation of meaning and co-construction of new knowledge based on consensus-building. Sri Lankan participants were often very polite before disagreeing about a point with another learner and built consensus online as they interacted with each other and an international e-mentor from the USA (Gunawardena et al., 2008; Gunawardena et al., 2011).

In further exploration, Gunawardena et al. (2008) found that while the academic discussion was very polite and lacked open disagreement of ideas, strong opinions and conflicting views were expressed by the same participants in the informal online virtual cafe, where they engaged in a heated debate about gender issues. This finding made the researchers reflect on the role of culture in academic online discussions. It is possible that collectivist traits in both the Sri Lankan and Mexican cultural contexts may have transferred to online group interaction in an academic setting where open disagreement of ideas would make the participants uncomfortable. Yet, it also shows that these very same participants in the Sri Lankan context would engage in a heated debate in an informal discussion space. So, the context of the discussion, whether it was formal or informal, was key in the expression of open disagreement. Other researchers have found similar results that students who come from high-context cultures in Asia and Latin America find an argumentative and confrontational format uncomfortable in an academic context (Chen, 2000). Learners from collectivist countries may refrain from contributing critical comments in text conferencing to avoid tension and disagreement to maintain interpersonal harmony (Hu, 2005). Priority is given to listening to others, considering their opinions, and accepting them if they are found to be valid.

Therefore, even though IAM 2.0 was developed based on a debate transcript that introduced argument and the need to win that argument, in IAM 2.0, we move away from the idea that argument is necessary or that debating ideas is necessary for knowledge construction. For example, we move away from "I will convince you" to leverage a more fluid process of learning through interaction, "Let's pursue this together," which would be more appropriate for a diverse learning environment (Luebeck & Bice, 2005, p. 36). In IAM 2.0, we adopt a broader view of dissonance and redefine it as either inconsistency among ideas, as Festinger (1957) stated, or as expressions of diverse points of view that motivate participants to build on each other's ideas or reconsider their own point of view. Phase II is not a necessary pre-condition for knowledge construction (Phase III) as researchers (Lopez-Islas, 2004; Gunawardena et al., 2008) have shown that participants can construct knowledge and move on to Phase III by building on each other's ideas without open disagreement or argument. Therefore, it is crucial that researchers interpret the results of Phase II considering the sociocultural context of the online discussion.

PHASE III: NEGOTIATION OF MEANING AND CO-CONSTRUCTION OF KNOWLEDGE

Phase III focuses on negotiation of meaning, considering the diverse perspectives shared by participants, which often leads to the co-construction of knowledge. The operations in Phase III include negotiation of the meaning of terms, the relative weight to be assigned to types of statements or arguments, the synthesis of areas of agreement, and negotiation of new ideas and statements often embodying compromise and co-construction. We also see participants integrating or accommodating metaphors or analogies as they move on to the construction of new meanings. While the process of negotiation may have initially started in Phase I, it is in Phase III that this process comes to fruition with statements of negotiated and newly constructed knowledge.

In IAM 2.0, we have made a clear distinction between the operations of Phase I and Phase III, considering the critiques from researchers who have requested more clarity between these two Phases. In the reconceptualization, Phase I is clearly about sharing and comparing information and perspectives by observing, agreeing, stating an opinion, providing corroborating examples, and asking and answering questions to clarify. Further, participants begin to identify problems or issues for further investigation and define terms in Phase I. On the other hand, Phase III is clearly about the negotiation of meaning and construction of new knowledge, considering the diverse perspectives shared by participants. Phase III is followed by Phases IV and V, which moves a discussion into validating the newly constructed knowledge.

IAM 2.0 Phases of Knowledge Validation: Phases IV and V

"Newly introduced knowledge, if it is to be used by a community needs to be legitimized in the eyes of that community" (Dissanayake, 1986, p. 270). In IAM 2.0, we see the legitimization and validation of newly constructed knowledge from two perspectives: testing of the newly constructed knowledge described in Phase IV and the application of new knowledge to real-world contexts described in Phase V. According to sociocultural theory (Vygotsky, 1978), this is the process of internalization of knowledge, which takes place among the sociocultural environment, the group, and the individual. In Phases I, II, and III, participants engage with others in exploring knowledge and making meaning. In Phase IV and V, they begin to synthesize the diverse perspectives they have come across and make sense of them by testing and application. By internalizing the effects of working together, the novice acquires useful strategies and crucial knowledge (John-Steiner & Mahn, 1996).

PHASE IV: TESTING OF PROPOSED CO-CONSTRUCTION

Phase IV signals the beginning of attempts to validate and legitimize the newly constructed knowledge or meaning. The focus is on testing the proposed co-construction against culture and context, personal experience, data, and literature. Previous research has shown that discussions rarely move on to testing and application of newly constructed knowledge. (See Chapter 2 and studies cited in Lucas et al., 2014). Lopez-Islas' (2004) study of 24 online groups conducted at the Monterrey Tech-Virtual University in Mexico showed that IAM Phase II, cognitive dissonance, had the least number of messages, followed by IAM Phase IV. He attributed this finding to cultural reasons and noted that Latin culture does not traditionally favor the open expression of disagreements and participants moved to knowledge construction (IAM Phase III) without moving through the cognitive dissonance Phase as described in the IAM. Further, he observed: "Therefore, with few disagreements openly expressed (second phase), there is no need to extensively test and modify group proposals (fourth phase)" (p. 307). This was a plausible explanation given his sociocultural context.

A similar thought was expressed by Wise and Chiu (2011), who wondered whether the presence or absence of IAM Phases II and IV in the discussion process impacts the resulting constructed knowledge at the group and individual levels. They used IAM to analyze SCK in a discussion transcript generated by 21 undergraduate students in a university in Western Canada, where 7 of the 21 participants were of Asian descent. The sociocultural context may have influenced this finding too. Therefore, we need to explore the relationship between IAM Phases II and IV in future studies. In many other contexts, however, it is important to test newly constructed knowledge before applying it; for example, if we take the context of an instructional designer engaging in designing a learning environment, we know that the designer should test the feasibility and functionality of the design before applying it. So, testing after knowledge construction does have a role. To encourage groups to move toward IAM Phase IV, discussion prompts should be written to encourage participants to test the new knowledge they create as a group.

When developing the original IAM, Gunawardena et al. (1997) observed that well-designed quality learning experiences engage learners in multiple phases of knowledge construction.

Therefore, designing the learning environment to move participants to the higher Phases of knowledge construction is key to a quality learning experience. In Chapter 18, we provide suggestions that instructional designers and facilitators can use to move participants toward the higher Phases of testing and applying newly constructed meaning.

PHASE V: APPLICATION OF NEWLY CONSTRUCTED MEANING

The final Phase of knowledge validation, Phase V, focuses on applying co-constructed knowledge to various contexts. This involves summarizing agreement(s), often creating a knowledge artifact or product, and even metacognitive statements by the participants illustrating their realization that their ways of thinking have changed because of group interaction. We view metacognition as awareness about oneself as a learner; awareness of one's perspectives, cognitive abilities, strengths, and weaknesses. Metacognitive statements may occur throughout an online discussion, but we included them in Phase V as they illustrate a higher cognitive function – that of reflecting on one's own thought processes and how these processes may have changed. We think of metacognitive statements as validation and legitimization of individual thought processes through reflection.

In Chapter 16, we show examples of coding according to the five Phases of IAM using an AI assistant. The AI coding is in the GitHub repository for Chapter 16, which can be accessed at https://github.com/knowledge-construction/slam-ai.

To summarize our discussion on the Phases of knowledge construction in IAM 2.0, we began with exploring a communication framework for knowledge construction that incorporated diverse views on communication and settled on a circular conceptualization that implies both the sender and the receiver exchange roles and participate equally in communication. We then discussed the reconceptualized IAM 2.0 and how we made changes to each Phase to reflect knowledge construction and validation. We refer the reader to the original IAM publication (Gunawardena et al., 1997) for a detailed description of each of the Phases of knowledge construction supported by examples. Next, we provide a brief overview of the unit of analysis and transcript analysis procedures according to IAM 2.0.

Unit of Analysis

We define a unit of analysis as the major object, entity, or item being analyzed in a research study. When analyzing the content of interactions evident in a computer transcript of an online discussion, a unit of analysis is the text block or language segment that we select for analysis. This could be a paragraph, a sentence, a unit of meaning, a theme, a word, or the entire message that a person posts in a discussion. Generally, the choice of a unit of analysis is dependent on the context of the research and research questions and should be considered carefully because changes to the size of the unit will affect coding decisions and the ability to compare outcomes (De Wever et al., 2006.) In other words, the unit of analysis impacts how we code text. The findings we report are based on the unit analyzed.

As discussed in Chapter 1, the developers of IAM (Gunawardena et al., 1997) noted the difficulty they had in determining a unit of analysis for the debate transcript they analyzed when developing IAM. They initially used "Units of Meaning," which could signal a theme or idea, as proposed by Henri (1992). However, in their analysis of the debate transcript, they found that messages exhibited many arguments to support or refute the debate proposition, and if a message was broken down into units of meaning and each unit analyzed separately, it would be difficult to describe the process by which arguments were advanced building upon each other to support or refute propositions and negotiate meaning. They, therefore, decided to use one single message or one post as the unit of analysis, which, taken as a whole, would embody a participant's perspective and contribution toward the construction of knowledge.

After the publication of the IAM in 1997, other studies have employed varied units of analysis to examine transcripts, and the most frequently used units of analysis in the content analysis schemes of 15 studies that De Wever et al. (2006) reviewed was the "message" followed by "thematic unit." Of the 15, there were a few studies that used the "sentence" as a unit of analysis. One of the studies out of the 15, Weinberger and Fischer's (2005) study using social constructivism and argumentative knowledge construction as the foundation, used two units of analysis hierarchically, one at the micro-level and the other at the macro-level with respect to (1) the construction of arguments and (2) the construction of sequences of arguments.

The original IAM developers (Gunawardena et al., 1997) pointed out that two major themes were observed in their analysis of the debate transcript when they used a message or post as a unit of analysis. One was the progression of certain strands of argument among the group from Phase I to Phase V, which could be described as the co-construction of knowledge among participants, and the other was the evidence of more than one and sometimes three Phases within a single message posted by one participant, which usually progressed in sequence through the IAM Phases, providing evidence of how individuals contributed toward the co-construction. This 1997 observation provided us the impetus for exploring the analysis of sentences within a message that would indicate the progression of individual knowledge construction. Further, SLAM and SNA have provided us with methods to analyze words and their relationship to each other so that we can analyze words that comprise a sentence and a message.

When rethinking the unit of analysis in IAM 2.0, we concluded that it would remain as the single message or post by one individual that captures the essence of an individual's contribution toward knowledge construction. However, SLAM and AI have provided us with the tools to quickly analyze how sentences reflect the process of knowledge construction and how words can reveal patterns in the way concepts are related to each other. Therefore IAM 2.0 will incorporate both sentence-level analysis to capture evidence of more than one Phase in a single message as well as word-level analysis to capture the pattern of relationships among concepts. SNA sociograms that depict the relationship between words will enable us to visualize the process of knowledge construction over time. Sentences and words as units of analysis will also capture the social interaction inherent in messages.

Therefore, depending on the sociocultural context and the research questions, the unit of analysis in IAM 2.0 will be a single message or post, which also considers the analysis of sentences and words within that message. It is not a requirement to engage in sentence-level and word-level analyses, but researchers might undertake it to gain a more comprehensive picture of SCK. When a qualitative researcher or AI decides which IAM Phase a message is in, the researcher or AI will explore additional information, such as

1. The type of sub-operation of the Phase (e.g., Phase IA or IB)
2. The dimension of social interaction (e.g., social presence, social connectedness, or community)
3. The discussion prompt or intended objective of the discussion or collaboration
4. Prior messages or postings by others
5. Sentences within the message
6. Words within the message

This means that even though a message or post is the unit of analysis in IAM 2.0, this does not preclude us from analyzing sentences and words for clues about a message's Phase or operation. The ability to use SLAM and AI in the analysis of computer or video transcripts makes this task much easier.

Analysis of Transcripts According to IAM 2.0

The primary data source for analyzing SCK employing SLAM and AI is transcripts of asynchronous and synchronous communication and collaboration. We first explore the analysis of social interaction in transcripts and then delve into analyzing SCK using the five Phases of IAM 2.0, reflecting on how the relationship between the two can be investigated.

Analysis of Social Interaction in Transcripts

The coding scheme we developed for analyzing social interaction in IAM 2.0 and presented in Table 17.1 can be employed by researchers employing qualitative methods such as content analysis or interaction analysis. The scheme draws from previous content analysis research analyzing social presence and community in computer transcripts discussed in Chapter 3. Notable among these previous research studies are the coding schemes developed for analyzing social cues and social interaction (Henri, 1992; Hara et al., 2000; Kreijns et al., 2022; Lehtinen et al., 2023; Lowenthal & Snelson, 2017; Rovai, 2002; Rourke et al., 1999; Swan & Shih, 2005). The social interaction coding scheme in IAM 2.0 can also be employed by researchers who use SLAM and AI methods discussed in previous chapters of this book. In general, social presence can be measured by lexicon analysis, frequency analysis, and cluster analysis, while social connectedness and community can be explored by social network analysis (SNA).

When SNA uses individual posts as a unit of analysis, it can illustrate the heart of the community by focusing on SNA measures such as centrality and network density. Centrality will illustrate the extent to which individual posts are organized around a central point, while network density will show us the degree to which members are connected to other members. The number of connections over time will indicate if the community is robust. A SNA graphic that shows only a few connections is weak in comparison to one that has many connections. On the other hand, a graphic that shows few connections at one measurement point and grows to many is an exemplar of a community that has developed over time in a positive fashion. Communities that decrease in density or connections are examples of groups that have not yet formed a community but trend toward individual contributions. The directional relationships SNA shows are important to measuring community in that they answer questions about how the community is functioning. If there are many two-way relationships, the community is very strong because people are both providing and receiving messages. This means there is parity in contributions to the knowledge construction process between members within the social network. If there are many one-way relationships, there are only a few people contributing to the process with many dominating the conversation. This would likely mean that there is decreased likelihood that knowledge is being created in a collaborative fashion because the larger group is only listening and not participating.

If, for example, a researcher is interested in exploring the relationship between the three dimensions of social interaction: social presence, social connectedness, and community, a study design could look at how the three dimensions are related. Let's select the research question: Can social presence predict a robust community? The researcher will begin by using the IAM 2.0 Excel coding sheet in the GitHub repository for this chapter (Chapter 17 at https://github.com/knowledge-construction/slam-ai). The researcher will enter each post of the discussion in a row and fill in the codes for social presence and community dimensions from IAM 2.0 (Table 17.1). Then a regression analysis can be conducted with social presence as the independent variable and community as the dependent variable. Chapter 12 provides the procedure for predictive analysis using regression. Megli (2022) explored if social presence (as an independent variable) can predict SCK according to the IAM and used a social presence lexicon and an ordinal logistic regression analysis to predict SCK. Megli (2022) concluded that social presence can significantly predict SCK in online courses in higher education.

Analysis of Social Construction of Knowledge Using IAM 2.0

Since researchers who have used IAM in their studies (See Chapter 2) and the developers of IAM (Gunawardena et al., 1997) have provided guidance on how to analyze and code discussion transcripts with the IAM Phases, the focus of this section will be on the analysis of IAM with SLAM and AI techniques.

Analysis of discussion transcripts according to IAM, while detailing the frequencies observed in each of the five Phases of knowledge construction, should be more focused on the overall pattern or gestalt of knowledge construction that emerges through interaction. For example, as seen in Chapter 2, studies have reported whether knowledge construction behaviors are at a lower level (predominantly Phase I) or have reached higher levels of negotiation and co-construction (Phase III and above). As Gunawardena et al. (1997) stated in the development of IAM, "interaction" should be viewed as the totality of interconnected and mutually responsive messages, and the focus should be on the resulting pattern or gestalt formed by online communication among participants. The participants are "acting in relation to each other and in a manner which reflects each other's presence and influence" (p. 407). Knowledge is created at the social level, in other words, the level of the group, and the individual also creates his or her own understanding by interacting with the group's shared construction. As in Salomon's (1993) reflections on "distributed cognitions," we see individual and distributed cognitions interacting over time, affecting each other and developing from each other. Knowledge is, therefore, socially constructed through collaborative efforts to reach shared objectives where information is processed between individuals and the tools and cultural artifacts they use in that context. We believe it is important to recognize the interdependence of the individual and social construction of knowledge.

LEXICON ANALYSIS

Megli et al. (2023) investigated the applicability and effectiveness of lexicon and text analysis to supplement the qualitative analysis of SCK in online discussions using IAM. They developed a lexicon to represent the five Phases of the IAM and explored if an algorithm based on the lexicon could predict how an analyst would qualitatively score the five Phases of the IAM. The results indicated that an algorithm based on the lexicon they developed can be used to predict the five Phases of IAM. The qualitative analysts' predictions were then compared to those of the automated lexicon word and phrase counter. Megli et al. (2023) concluded that automation of text analysis would be a useful tool to identify patterns in text and will be a valuable supplement to the qualitative coding of the IAM. The lexicon developed for the five Phases of IAM can be accessed through the University of New

Mexico's digital repository: https://digitalrepository.unm.edu/oils_sp/2/, and it is also in the GitHub repository for this chapter, accessed through the following link https://github.com/knowledge-construction/slam-ai.

SOCIAL NETWORK ANALYSIS (SNA)

Social interaction that accompanies knowledge construction can be visualized using SNA. SNA can reveal the interaction patterns within a networked learning community and how the members share and construct knowledge. When analyzing transcripts with IAM 2.0, frequency analysis and SNA focused on words instead of participants can illustrate "what" knowledge is being constructed. If we want to determine how social networks are integrated into IAM 2.0, we can explore SNA in two ways, either at the Phase level or in relation to the centrality of participants in the networks. For example, one can research how centrality is associated with knowledge co-construction. When used with content analysis of knowledge construction, SNA can provide information about the overall group's functioning as well as the strength and direction of their interactions. Further, the content analysis of transcripts can reveal how moderating and facilitating roles support social interaction and knowledge construction online, while SNA can map the interactions between a moderator and participants to determine the level of social connectedness within the group. In LMS of the future, AI chatbots may play the role of a guide providing feedback on participant interactions and contributions, which can also be analyzed using SNA.

SOCIAL NETWORK ANALYSIS, NEURAL NETWORKS, AND CLUSTERING

Given a selected research question, the first step a researcher will undertake is to collect data from an LMS or social media platform (see Chapter 5), and then process that data for a specific selected SLAM technique (Chapter 6). Let's take, for example, SNA as the method selected for analysis. The researcher would then conduct the SNA and determine if a neural network analysis would be appropriate. Feeding SNA results into a neural network (see Chapter 13) can help the researcher determine how earlier posts or significant posts are related to each other. The number of connections can help the neural network model differentiate between Phase I and Phase III. Clustering (see Chapter 9) followed by topic analysis using LDA (discussed in Chapter 11) will inform us of the category of knowledge constructed. We recommend multiple methods of analysis. See also Chapters 4, 6, 7, 8, and 10 for a detailed description of these procedures.

WORD ASSOCIATIONS OR WORD CO-OCCURRENCE NETWORKS

Determining how co-constructions observed in Phase III lead to Phase IV and V is often a challenge. While a qualitative analyst focusing on the meaning of utterances could easily determine a new construction in Phase III, it is a more challenging analysis with SLAM and AI. One way we could address this is to build word associations or word co-occurrence networks in NodeXL and other software that shows the development of associated words and frequencies over time. For example, an initial word network would show a baseline of a group's understanding of a particular topic and the frequencies of specific words and how they are associated. A subsequent word network will show the extent to which new words and associations have been co-constructed and associated with the original word network. Qualitatively, we can visualize this in two separate graphs, while quantitatively, we can observe words and phrases and their frequencies and associations changing over time. We can perform this analysis for an entire transcript, or we can select a section, such as a new co-construction in Phase III, and build a network based on it. (See Chapter 10, and our previous study Gunawardena et al. (2016) for these analysis procedures).

AI CODING OF TRANSCRIPTS

With the rapid developments in AI, we can employ AI technology as research assistants to help us code discussion transcripts according to IAM. Chapter 16 provided an example of how an AI assistant (LLaMA) coded a transcript according to the five Phases of IAM. Yeh and Lo (2005) used a neural network approach to assess language learners' metacognitive knowledge level and found that their proposed neural network performed equally well in three common Web page structures: networked, hierarchical, and linear. A neural network approach may be one way to assess metacognition from transcript data.

SOCIAL INTERACTION AND SOCIAL CONSTRUCTION OF KNOWLEDGE

With the development of IAM 2.0, researchers will want to explore the relationship between social interaction and SCK in specific sociocultural contexts. In one context, a group may become socially connected at the beginning of a discussion and less connected later. In another context, a group may take time to develop social connectedness and, once developed, may become a cohesive learning community that engages in knowledge construction working together over a period of time. With IAM 2.0 and procedures related to SLAM and AI discussed in previous chapters, we provide the researcher with the means to analyze the level of social interaction as groups construct knowledge. For example, in one study, we can use the social presence lexicon (see Chapters 7 and 8) and code words that indicate social interaction in every post in a separate column. Each post will have a social presence, social connectedness, or community score. Next, the five IAM Phases can be correlated with the social interaction scores. This can help a researcher visualize the gestalt of social interaction in relation to knowledge construction. SLAM and AI techniques have the innate ability to produce visualizations that show sentiment, the IAM Phases, the most frequent topics of discussion over time, and the relationship between social interaction and knowledge construction. Coupled with qualitative analysis SLAM and AI can provide a very comprehensive overall pattern of SCK online.

RESEARCH QUESTIONS FOR EXPLORING SOCIAL INTERACTION AND SOCIAL CONSTRUCTION OF KNOWLEDGE

With the integration of social interaction into IAM 2.0, we want to conclude by posing research questions that explore social interaction and the relationship between social interaction and knowledge construction. Future research could explore questions such as:

- Which level of social interaction (dimensions of social presence, social connectedness, or community) is related to SCK when groups collaborate online?
- What is the interaction between these three dimensions of social interaction?
- How do social presence, social connectedness, and community influence each other?
- Can social presence predict community?
- Are those who are more central in a social network more vital for knowledge construction?

- Is a heightened level of social interaction associated with higher levels of knowledge construction?
- What kind of interaction promotes engagement at the higher Phases of IAM?
- How does guidance (from a facilitator or mentor) influence SCK?

Many of these questions can be answered by using SLAM, discussed in this book, and predictive analytics (Chapter 12). Now, with the rapid growth of AI, we should begin to explore:

- Can we use AI to answer the previous questions?

Conclusion

This chapter presented the reconceptualized IAM 2.0, founded on principles of sociocultural learning theory, assigning a central role to the sociocultural context and highlighting the influence of social interaction and its three dimensions of social presence, social connectedness, and community, on knowledge construction. IAM 2.0 addressed the shortcomings of the original IAM developed by Gunawardena et al. (1997) by incorporating the role of the sociocultural context and by integrating social interaction in supporting knowledge construction. Further, IAM 2.0 made a clear delineation between IAM's five Phases, distinguishing between Phases of knowledge construction and Phases of knowledge validation, representing a progressively higher collaborative learning process.

The reconceptualization of IAM merges quantitative analysis using SLAM and AI with qualitative methodology and aims to provide both an analytic and a holistic perspective on online SCK. The unit of analysis was defined as a message with the choice to include both sentence-level and word-level units within the message. The chapter concluded with an examination of various SLAM and AI analysis techniques for IAM 2.0 and a set of research questions to explore the relationship between social interaction and knowledge construction within a specific sociocultural context. The next chapter (Chapter 18) provides examples of how social interaction and SCK in IAM 2.0 can be analyzed by SLAM and AI.

NOTE: We want to refer the reader to the GitHub repository for this chapter (Chapter 17) for the Excel Coding Sheet for IAM 2.0 and the lexicon developed for the five Phases of IAM. The repository can be accessed at: https://github.com/knowledge-construction/slam-ai.

Examples of coding from the original debate transcript according to the five Phases of IAM are in the GitHub repository for Chapter 16. The GitHub repository can be accessed at: https://github.com/knowledge-construction/slam-ai.

References

Arvaja, M. (2011). Analyzing the contextual nature of collaborative activity. In S. Puntambekar, G. Erkens, & C. Hmelo-Silver (Eds.), *Analyzing interactions in CSCL: Methods, approaches and issues* (pp. 25–46). New York: Springer.

Asante, M. K. (1983). The ideological significance of afrocentricity in intercultural communication. *Journal of Black Studies, 14*(1), 3–19. www.jstor.org/stable/2784027

Barton, D., & Tusting, K. (2005). *Beyond communities of practice: Language, power, and social context.* New York, NY: Cambridge University Press.

Biesenbach-Lucas, S. (2003). Asynchronous discussion groups in teacher training classes: Perceptions of native and non-native students. *Journal of Asynchronous Learning Networks, 7*(3), 24–46.

Bolliger, D. U., & Inan, F. A. (2012). Development and validation of the Online Student Connectedness Survey (OSCS). *The International Review of Research in Open and Distributed Learning, 13*(3), 41–65. https://doi.org/10.19173/irrodl.v13i3.1171

Cambridge Dictionary. (2024). Identity. In *Cambridge dictionary online.* https://dictionary.cambridge.org/us/dictionary/english/identity

Chen, G. M. (2000). Global communication via internet: An educational application. In G. M. Chen & W. J. Starosta (Eds.), *Communication and global society* (pp. 143–157). New York, NY: Peter Lang.

Dennen, V. P., & Burner, K. J. (2017). Identity, context collapse, and Facebook use in higher education: Putting presence and privacy at odds. *Distance Education, 38*(2), 173–192. https://doi.org/10.1080/01587919.2017.1322453

De Wever, B., Schellens, T., Valcke, M., & Van Keer, H. (2006). Content analysis schemes to analyze transcripts of online asynchronous discussion groups: A review. *Computers & Education, 46*(1), 6–28.

De Wever, B., Van Keer, H., Schellens, T., & Valcke, M. (2010). Roles as a structuring tool in online discussion groups: The differential impact of different roles on social knowledge construction. *Computers in Human Behavior, 26*(4), 516–523.

Dissanayake, W. (1983). The communication significance of the Buddhist concept of dependent co-origination. *Communication, 8*(1), 29–45.

Dissanayake, W. (1986). Understanding the role of the environment in knowledge generation and use: A plea for a hermeneutical approach. In G. M. Beal, W. Dissanayake, & S. Konoshima (Eds.), *Knowledge generation, exchange, and utilization* (pp. 261–285). Boulder, CO: Westview Press.

Dissanayake, W. (Ed.) (1988a). *Communication theory: The Asian perspective.* Singapore: The Asian Mass Communication Research and Information Center.

Dissanayake, W. (1988b). Foundations of Indian verbal communication and phenomenology. In W. Dissanayake (Ed.), *Communication theory: The Asian perspective* (pp. 39–55). Singapore: The Asian Mass Communication Research and Information Center.

Festinger, L. (1957). *A theory of cognitive dissonance.* Stanford, CA: Stanford University Press.

Floren, L. C., Ten Cate, O., Irby, D. M., & O'Brien, B. C. (2021). An interaction analysis model to study knowledge construction in interprofessional education: Proof of concept. *Journal of Interprofessional Care, 35*(5), 736–743. https://doi.org/10.1080/13561820.2020.1797653

Frechette, C. (2020). Supporting sociocultural learning in online and blended learning environments. In M. J. Bishop et al. (Eds.), *Handbook of research in educational communications and technology* (pp. 363–374). Switzerland: Springer Nature. https://doi.org/10.1007/978-3-030-36119-8

Galambos, J. A., Abelson, R. P., & Black, J. B. (1986). *Knowledge structures.* Hillsdale, NJ: Lawrence Erlbaum Associates.

Gunawardena, C. N. (1998). Designing collaborative learning environments mediated by computer conferencing: Issues and challenges in the Asian socio-cultural context. *Indian Journal of Open Learning, 7*(1), 105–124.

Gunawardena, C. N. (1995). Social presence theory and implications for interaction and collaborative learning in computer conferences. *International Journal of Educational Telecommunications, 1*(2/3), 147–166.

Gunawardena, C. N., Chen, Y., Flor, N., & Sánchez, D. (2023). Deep learning models for analyzing social construction of knowledge online. *Online Learning, 27*(4), 69–92. https://doi.org/10.24059/olj.v27i4.4055

Gunawardena, C. N., Flor, N. V., Gomez, D., & Sánchez, D. (2016). Analyzing social construction of knowledge online by employing interaction analysis, learning analytics, and social network analysis. *The Quarterly Review of Distance Education, 17*(3), 35–60.

Gunawardena, C. N., Frechette, C., & Layne, L. (2019). *Culturally inclusive instructional design: A framework and guide for building online wisdom communities.* New York: Routledge.

Gunawardena, C. N., Keller, P. S., Garcia, F., Faustino, G. L., Barrett, K., Skinner, J. K., et al. (2011). *Transformative education through technology: Facilitating social construction of knowledge online through cross-cultural e-mentoring.* Paper presented at the 1st International Conference on the Social Sciences and the Humanities, Faculty of Arts, University of Peradeniya, Peradeniya, Sri Lanka.

Gunawardena, C. N., LaPointe, D., Linder-VanBerschot, J. A., Skinner, J. K., Richmond, C., Barrett, K., & Cardiff, M. S. (2008). *E-mentoring to guide inquiry-based online learning across cultures.* Proceedings of the 24th Annual Conference on Distance Teaching and Learning (pp. 213–217), The Board of Regents of the University of Wisconsin System, Madison, WI.

Gunawardena, C., Lowe, C., & Anderson, T. (1997). Analysis of a global on-line debate and the development of an interaction analysis model for examining social construction of knowledge in computer conferencing. *Journal of Educational Computing Research, 17*(4), 395–429.

Gunawardena, C. N., & Zittle, F. (1997). Social presence as a predictor of satisfaction within a computer mediated conferencing environment. *The American Journal of Distance Education*, *11*(3), 8–25.

Guo, C., Shea, P., & Chen, X. (2022). Investigation on graduate students' social presence and social knowledge construction in two online discussion settings. *Education and Information Technologies*, *27*, 2751–2769. https://doi.org/10.1007/s10639-021-10716-8

Hall, B. M. (2014). In support of the Interaction Analysis Model (IAM) for evaluating discourse in a virtual learning community. *Education Resources Information Center (ERIC)*, ED622614. https://files.eric.ed.gov/fulltext/ED622614.pdf

Hall, E. T. (1959). *The silent language*. Doubleday.

Hara, N., Bonk, C. J., & Angeli, C. (2000). Content analysis of online discussion in an applied educational psychology course. *Instructional Science*, *28*, 115–152. https://doi.org/10.1023/A:1003764722829

Haythornthwaite, C. (1996). Social network analysis: An approach and technique for the study of information exchange. *Library and Information Science Research*, *18*(4), 323–342. https://doi.org/10.1016/S0740-8188(96)90003-1

Hedayati-Mehdiabadi, A., & Gunawardena, C. N. (2022). Culture, ethics of care, community, and language in online learning environments: Supporting adult educators in a digital era. In O. Zawacki-Richter & I. Jung (Eds.), *Handbook of open, distance and digital education*. Singapore: Springer. https://doi.org/10.1007/978-981-19-0351-9_19-1

Henri, F. (1992). Computer conferencing and content analysis. In A. R. Kaye (Ed.), *Collaborative learning through computer conferencing: The Najadan Papers* (pp. 117–136). London: Springer-Verlag.

Heo, H., Lim, K. Y., & Kim, Y. (2010). Exploratory study on the patterns of online interaction and knowledge co-construction in project-based learning. *Computers & Education*, *55*, 1383–1392.

Ho, Y. (2024). Enhance adult students' online knowledge construction: Exploring effective instructional designs and addressing barriers. *Journal of Computer Assisted Learning*, *40*(4), 1675–1689. https://doi.org/10.1111/jcal.12983

Hu, G. (2005). Using peer review with Chinese ESL student writers. *Language Teaching Research*, *9*(3), 321–342.

Ibarra, R. A. (2001). *Beyond affirmative action: Reframing the context of higher education*. University of Wisconsin Press.

Ishii, S. (1982). Thought patterns as modes of rhetoric: The United States and Japan. *Communication*, *11*(3), 81–86.

Jaber, R., & Kennedy, E. (2017). "Not the same person anymore": Groupwork, identity and social learning online. *Distance Education*, *38*(2), 216–229. https://doi.org/10.1080/01587919.2017.1324732

Jayatilleke, B. G., Kulasekera, G. U., Kumarasinha, M. C. B., & Gunawardena, C. N. (2012, October). *Cross-cultural e-mentor roles in facilitating inquiry-based online learning*. Proceedings of the 26th Annual Conference of Asian Association of Open Universities (pp. 60–68), The Open University of Japan, Chiba, Japan.

John-Steiner, V., & Mahn, H. (1996). Sociocultural approaches to learning and development: A Vygotskian framework. *Educational Psychologist*, *31*(3/4), 191–206.

Kaplan, R. B. (1966). Cultural thought patterns in inter-cultural education. *Language Learning*, *16*(1–2), 1–20. https://doi.org/10.1111/j.1467-1770.1966.tb00804.x

Kramsch, C., & Thorne, S. (2002). Foreign language learning as global communicative practice. In D. Block & D. Cameron (Eds.), *Globalization and language teaching* (pp. 83–100). London, UK: Routledge.

Kreijns, K., Kirschner, P. A., & Jochems, W. (2003). Identifying the pitfalls of social interaction in computer-supported collaborative learning environments: A review of the research. *Computers in Human Behavior*, *19*(3), 335–353. https://doi.org/10.1016/S0747-5632(02)00057-2

Kreijns, K., Xu, K., & Weidlich, J. (2022). Social presence: Conceptualization and measurement. *Educational Psychology Review*, *34*(1), 139–170. https://doi.org/10.1007/s10648-021-09623-8

Lave, J., & Wenger, E. (1991). *Situated learning: Legitimate peripheral participation*. Cambridge, UK: Cambridge University Press.

Lee, R. M., Draper, M., & Lee, S. (2001). Social connectedness, dysfunctional interpersonal behaviors, and psychological distress: Testing a mediator model. *Journal of Counseling Psychology*, *48*(3), 310–318. https://doi.org/10.1037/0022-0167.48.3.310

Lee, R. M., & Robbins, S. B. (1998). The relationship between social connectedness and anxiety, self-esteem, and social identity [Editorial]. *Journal of Counseling Psychology, 45*(3), 338–345. https://doi.org/10.1037/0022-0167.45.3.338

Lehtinen, A., Kostiainen, E., & Näykki, P. (2023, October). Co-construction of knowledge and socioemotional interaction in pre-service teachers' video-based online collaborative learning. *Teaching and Teacher Education, 133*, 104299. https://doi.org/10.1016/j.tate.2023.104299

Lopez-Islas, J. R. (2004). Collaborative learning at monterrey-tech-virtual university. In T. M. Duffy & J. R. Kirkley (Eds.), *Learner-centered theory and practice in distance education: Cases from higher education* (pp. 297–319). Mahwah, NJ: Lawrence Erlbaum Associates.

Lowenthal, P. R., & Snelson, C. (2017). In search of a better understanding of social presence: An investigation into how researchers define social presence. *Distance Education, 38*(2), 141–159. https://doi.org/10.1080/01587919.2017.1324727

Lucas, M., Gunawardena, C., & Moreira, A. (2014). Assessing social construction of knowledge online: A critique of the interaction analysis model. *Computers in Human Behavior, 30*, 574–582.

Lucas, M., & Moreira, A. (2010). Knowledge construction with social web tools. In M. D. Lytras et al. (Eds.), *1st International conference on reforming education and quality of teaching*, CCIS 73 (pp. 278–284). Springer Verlag. https://doi.org/10.1007/978-3-642-13166-0_40

Luebeck, J. L., & Bice, L. R. (2005). Online discussion as a mechanism of conceptual change among mathematics and science teachers. *The Journal of Distance Education/Revue de l'Éducation à Distance, 20*(2), 21–39. https://files.eric.ed.gov/fulltext/EJ807830.pdf

Marra, R., Moore, J. L., & Klimczak, A. K. (2004). Content analysis of online discussion forums: A comparative analysis of protocols. *Educational Technology Research & Development, 52*(2), 23–40. https://link.springer.com/content/pdf/10.1007/BF02504837.pdf

McAteer, E., Tolmie, A., Harris, R. A., Chappel, H., Marsden, S., & Lally, V. (2002). Characterising on-line learning environments. In *Proceedings of networked learning 2002*. Sheffield, UK: University of Sheffield.

Megli, A. C. (2022). *Social Presence as a Predictor of Social Construction of Knowledge in Discussion Forums in Asynchronous Online Higher Education Courses* (Order No. 29993846). Available from Dissertations & Theses @ University of New Mexico; ProQuest Dissertations & Theses Global. (2821581074). https://libproxy.unm.edu/login?url=www.proquest.com/dissertations-theses/social-presence-as-predictor-construction/docview/2821581074/se-2

Megli, A. C., Fallad-Mendoza, D., Etsitty-Dorame, M., Desiderio, J., Chen, Y., Sánchez, D., Flor, N., & Gunawardena, C. N. (2023). Using social learning analytic methods to examine social construction of knowledge in online discussions. *American Journal of Distance Education, 38*(1), 65–80. https://doi.org/10.1080/08923647.2023.2192597

Miike, Y. (2002). Rethinking humanity, culture, and communication: Asiacentric critiques and contributions. *A Journal of the Pacific and Asian Communication Association, 7*(1), 67–82.

Merriam-Webster. (2024). Identity definition & meaning. In *Merriam-Webster dictionary Online*. www.merriam-webster.com/dictionary/identity

National Academies of Sciences, Engineering, and Medicine. (2018). *How people learn II: Learners, contexts, and cultures*. Washington, DC: The National Academies Press. https://doi.org/10.17226/24783

Osman, G., & Herring, S. C. (2007). Interaction, facilitation, and deep learning in cross-cultural chat: A case study. *Internet and Higher Education, 10*(2), 125–141. https://doi.org/10.1016/j.iheduc.2007.03.004

Patwardhan, A. (2024, April). How our thoughts shape the way spoken words evolve. *Scientific American, 330*(5), 20. www.scientificamerican.com/article/how-our-thoughts-shape-the-way-spoken-words-evolve/

Perkins, J., & Newman, K. (1996). Two archetypes in e-discourse: Lurkers and virtuosos. *International Journal of Educational Telecommunications, 2*(2/3), 155–170.

Rafaeli, S. (1988). Interactivity: From new media to communication. In R. P. Hawkins, S. Pingree, & J. Weimann (Eds.), *Advancing communication science: Sage annual review of communication research* (Vol. 16, pp. 110–134). Newbury Park, CA: Sage.

Rafaeli, S. (1990). Interaction with media: Parasocial interaction and real interaction. In B. D. Ruben & L. A. Lievrouw (Eds.), *Information and behavior* (Vol. 3, pp. 125–181). New Brunswick, NJ: Transaction Books.

Reddi, U. V. (1986). Communication Theory: An Indian Perspective. *Media Asia, 13*(1), 25–28. https://doi.org/10.1080/01296612.1986.11726205

Riedl, C., Köbler, F., Goswami, S., & Krcmar, H. (2013). Tweeting to feel connected: A model for so-cial connectedness in online social networks. *International Journal of Human-Computer Interaction*, *29*(10), 670–687. https://doi.org/10.1080/10447318.2013.768137

Rogers, P., & Lea, M. (2005). Social presence in distributed group environments: The role of social identity. *Behavior & Information Technology*, *24*(2), 151–158. https://doi.org/10.1080/0144929 0410001723472

Rourke, L., Anderson, T., Garrison, D. R., & Archer, W. (1999). Assessing social presence in asynchro-nous text-based computer conferencing. *Journal of Distance Education*, *14*(2), 50–71.

Rovai, A. P. (2002). Development of an instrument to measure classroom community. *The Internet and Higher Education*, *5*(3), 197–211. https://doi.org/10.1016/S1096-7516(02)00102-1

Rovai, A. P. (2003). In search of higher persistence rates in distance education online programs. *The Internet and Higher Education*, *6*(1), 1–16. https://doi.org/10.1016/S1096-7516(02)00158-6

Sánchez, D. M. (2019). Researching the social construction of knowledge and group dynamics. In C. N. Gunawardena, C. Frechette, & L. Layne (Eds.), *Culturally inclusive instructional design: A frame-work and guide for building online wisdom communities* (pp. 178–194). New York: Routledge.

Salomon, G. (1993). No distribution without individuals' cognition: A dynamic interactional view. In G. Salomon (Ed.), *Distributed cognitions: Psychological and educational considerations* (pp. 111–138). Cambridge, UK: Cambridge University Press.

Scardamalia, M., & Bereiter, C. (2003). Knowledge building. In J. W. Guthrie (Ed.), *Encyclopedia of education* (2nd ed., pp. 1370–1373). New York: Macmillan Reference.

Schramm, W. (2001). How communication works. In M. J. Baker (Ed.), *Marketing: Critical perspec-tives on business and management* (Vol. 2, pp. 357–379). London: Routledge.

Short, J., Williams, E., & Christie, B. (1976). *The social psychology of telecommunications*. London, UK: John Wiley.

Smith, J. B. (1994). *Collective intelligence in computer-based collaboration*. Hillsdale, NJ: Lawrence Erlbaum Associates.

Starr-Glass, D. (2016). Faculty response to the opportunities of the digital age: Towards a service cul-ture in the professoriate. In *Handbook of research on learning outcomes and opportunities in the digital age* (pp. 102–126). https://doi.org/10.4018/978-1-4666-9577-1.ch005

Swan, K., & Shih, L. F. (2005). On the nature and development of social presence in online course discussions. *Journal of Asynchronous Learning Networks*, *9*(3), 115–136.

Tu, C., & McIsaac, M. (2002). The relationship of social presence and interaction in online classes. *The American Journal of Distance Education*, *16*(3), 131–150. https://doi.org/10.1207/S15389286AJDE1603_2

Uzuner, S. (2009). Questions of culture in distance learning: A research review. *International Review of Research in Open and Distance Learning*, *10*(3), 1–19. www.irrodl.org/index.php/irrodl

Vlachopoulos, D., & Makri, A. (2019). Online communication and interaction in distance higher education: A framework study of good practice. *International Review of Education*, *65*, 605–632. https://doi.org/10.1007/s11159-019-09792-3

Vygotsky, L. S. (1978). *Mind in society: The development of higher psychological processes*. Cambridge, MA: Harvard University Press.

Wegerif, R. (1998). The social dimension of asynchronous learning networks. *Journal of Asychronous Learning Networks*, *2*(1), 34–49.

Weinberger, A., & Fischer, F. (2005). A framework to analyze argumentative knowledge construction in computer-supported collaborative learning. *Computers & Education*, *46*(1), 71–95.

White, C. (2009). Towards a learner-based theory of distance language learning: The concept of the learner-context interface. In P. Hubbard (Ed.), *Computer assisted language learning: Critical concepts in linguistics. Volume IV: Present Trends and Future Directions in CALL* (pp. 97–112). London: Routledge. https://mro.massey.ac.nz/server/api/core/bitstreams/360f12dc-9c2a-4f92-94e1-950c23980e96/content

Whorf, B. (1998). Science and linguistics. In M. J. Bennett (Ed.), *Basic concepts of intercultural com-munication: Selected readings* (pp. 85–95). Yarmouth, ME: Intercultural Press.

Wise, A. F., & Chiu, M. M. (2011). Analyzing temporal patterns of knowledge construction in a role-based online discussion. *International Journal of Computer-Supported Collaborative Learning*, *6*(3), 445–470. https://doi.org/10.1007/s11412-011-9120-1

Weissmann, G. S., Ibarra, R. A., Howland-Davis, M., & Lammey, M. V. (2019). The multicon-text path to redefining how we access and think about diversity, equity, and inclusion in STEM.

Journal of Geoscience Education, 67(4), 320–329. https://doi.org/10.1080/10899995.2019.1 620527

Xiao, Y., Liu, X., & Zhu, Y. (2024). Disentangling the mechanism of student engagement in online language classrooms from the perspective of community of inquiry. *Heliyon*, 10(2024), e31934. https://doi.org/10.1016/j.heliyon.2024.e31934

Yap, K. C., & Chia, K. P. (2010). Knowledge construction and misconstruction: A case study approach in asynchronous discussion using Knowledge Construction – Message Map (KCMM) and Knowledge Construction – Message Graph (KCMG). *Computers & Education*, 55(4), 1589–1613.

Yashima, T., MacIntyre, P. D., & Ikeda, M. (2018). Situated willingness to communicate in an L2: Interplay of individual characteristics and context. *Language Teaching Research*, 22(1), 115–137. https://doi.org/10.1177/1362168816657851

Yeh, S. W., & Lo, J. J. (2005). Assessing metacognitive knowledge in web-based call: A neural network approach. *Computers & Education*, 44(2), 97–113. https://doi.org/10.1016/j.compedu.2003.12.019

Yoshikawa, M. J. (1988). Japanese and American modes of communication and implications for managerial and organizational behavior. In W. Dissanayake (Ed.), *Communication theory: The Asian perspective* (pp. 150–182). Singapore: The Asian Mass Communication Research and Information Center.

Zhang, Y. B. (2008). Asian communication modes. In W. Donsbach (Ed.), *The Blackwell international encyclopedia of communication* (pp. 775–779). Blackwell Publishing. Publisher's official version: www.communicationencyclopedia.com/public/tocnode?id=g9781405131995_ chunk_g97814051319958_ss90-1, Open Access version: http://kuscholarworks.ku.edu/dspace/

18 Future Directions

Research and Practice With the Interaction Analysis Model 2.0 (IAM 2.0)

"Indeed, social learning isn't going away; its prominence will only grow as the technologies and techniques of online instruction catch up to what's always been true: We learn best from one another" (Gunawardena et al., 2019, p. 269). Given the future of learning, the Interaction Analysis Model (IAM) 2.0 used in conjunction with Social Learning Analytic Methods (SLAM) provides the vehicle to research how groups or teams interact and learn across a wide variety of contexts – formal, informal, experiential, and on a wide variety of platforms, from asynchronous discussions in a learning management system (LMS) to videoconferencing and social media discussions. SLAM is defined as a collection of techniques to study group interactions on learning management systems and social networks as groups co-construct knowledge online. These techniques include frequency analysis, sentiment analysis, cluster analysis, social network analysis, and artificial intelligence (incorporating large language models, neural networks, and generative AI), which are used in a complementary fashion to analyze the social construction of knowledge (SCK). While artificial intelligence (AI) is included within the umbrella term SLAM, AI is sometimes singled out to refer to operations that only an AI architecture can perform. The IAM 2.0 is a reconceptualized framework developed in Chapter 17 for assessing SCK in the digital era.

This chapter begins by guiding instructional designers and instructors on how to move participants to higher levels of knowledge construction in online discussions, as this is key for enabling the analysis of SCK using IAM 2.0. It then provides advice to researchers on analyzing how groups construct knowledge with the IAM 2.0. Chapter 16 demonstrated how AI can be used as a research assistant to code the five Phases of knowledge construction in IAM 2.0. This chapter will provide examples of research questions and designs focusing on the social environment of online learning that can be analyzed with SLAM to expand our understanding of SCK online. We conclude with a discussion on the importance of ethics of using analytics and the necessity for educators to build capacity in order to effectively address ethical issues as they navigate technology's impact on learning.

Strategies for Supporting the Social Construction of Knowledge (SCK)

The IAM 2.0 discussed in Chapter 17 provides a framework for researchers to determine how the sociocultural context and social interaction influence the SCK, where knowledge is co-constructed by members of a group through a process of shared and negotiated meaning, reflecting the interdependence of social and individual processes in learning. The SLAM tools (such as lexicon analysis, cluster analysis, and social network analysis) allow researchers to analyze data to clearly enumerate the role teamwork and collaboration

DOI: 10.4324/9781003324461-23

play in SCK. Society continues to become more and more interconnected via technology, and technology-mediated communications are fast taking the place of face-to-face communication. This trend is likely to continue so it is important for researchers everywhere to have the capacity to understand the growing volumes of data associated with how people collaborate and engage in teamwork online in both formal and informal settings. The IAM 2.0 and SLAM allow researchers the flexibility to work with data from both settings. Since online collaboration and teamwork reach higher levels of SCK infrequently, we focus the next section on specific strategies that can be used to help groups achieve their full collective potential in constructing knowledge.

Goals and Learning Activities

The goals and objectives for the learning activities in an online discussion play a key role in shaping how participants will engage. If the goal is merely focused on what participants have read on a given issue, or a report of their daily activities, or sharing feelings and experiences on a given topic, the discussion will likely not go beyond the lower Phase of knowledge construction (Phase I) according to IAM 2.0. However, if the discussion is focused on solving a problem as a group or engaging in a discussion on an issue with the end goal of developing consensus, or a solution, then the discussion is more likely to advance to higher levels of knowledge construction (Lucas et al., 2014). This was evident in the studies conducted by Heo et al. (2010) and Lucas and Moreira (2010), where participants engaged in solving a real-world problem within a given context and reached higher levels of knowledge construction. Selecting problems and issues that relate to the lives of the participants, solving problems that challenge them, and asking participants to choose the problems they solve will motivate them and move them to higher levels of knowledge construction. The personal relevance of discussion topics is likely to engage them in deep, reflective strategies to weigh and compare ideas and arguments and move them to higher levels of knowledge construction (Lucas et al., 2014). De Wever et al. (2009) found that assigning specific roles to students participating in asynchronous discussions led to complex thinking, and Lucas and Moreira (2010) point out that higher levels of knowledge construction can be reached when responsibility for the learning process is transferred to students and combined with context-situated, problem-based learning and collaborative work.

Inquiry-Based Learning

Generally, inquiry-based learning designs that engage learners in an inquiry, for example, in problem-solving, role play, and case-based reasoning, are more likely to move participants to higher levels of knowledge construction. Inquiry-based learning is founded on constructivist and social constructivist learning theories, which see learning as the process of constructing meaning. It is a student-centered, active learning approach focusing on questioning and critical thinking. Students engage in finding solutions to authentic, real-world problems through investigations and collaboration with others (Gunawardena, 2004). Inquiry-based learning helps students to communicate with those who have different perspectives, articulate problems out of complex and messy situations, and collaborate with others in finding solutions to problems. In an inquiry-based learning environment, the instructor/teacher becomes a partner in the inquiry, a guide and facilitator who presents challenging, curiosity-provoking problems that entice students to learn. In an online professional development workshop that engaged faculty professional development participants in three inquiry-based learning activities (problem-solving, role play, and case-based reasoning) centered on social problems in Sri Lanka, participants engaged, collaborated, and reached higher levels of knowledge construction (Jayatilleke et al., 2012).

Discussion Prompts

In order to lead a group to higher levels of knowledge construction, online learning designs must pay careful attention to how discussion prompts are developed and communicated to students. A discussion prompt that merely asks a group of participants to post their individual thoughts on a topic or reading may not move them to higher levels of SCK. On the other hand, a discussion prompt that asks participants to build on each other's ideas, develop a solution to a problem, and communicate that solution in a visual format, such as a concept map, will move participants to higher levels of SCK. Many of the discussion transcripts we analyzed for this book had prompts that moved participants to higher levels of SCK. For example, Figure 18.1 is a discussion prompt from a graduate-level course taught at the University of New Mexico on Culture and Global eLearning that asked participants to define culture and its relationship to eLearning. It asks participants to build on each other's posts and come to a consensus, engaging the group with an end goal.

Prompt engineering, a rapidly evolving field to train people to write prompts to get more accurate and precise results from AI assistants, focuses on the necessity of writing appropriate prompts that deliver the kind of information one needs or desires. Similarly, in online discussion forums, a prompt can convey to the participants what is expected and required as well as the process to get there. If we are to empower participants to reach higher levels of knowledge construction, designers must develop discussion prompts that move participants to that level. For example, the prompt in Figure 18.1 can be extended to ask participants to test and apply the consensus they reached on the definition.

Definition of Culture and eLearning

Welcome to our first discussion on culture and eLearning.

What is your definition of culture?

What is your definition of eLearning?

How are the two related?

Engagement & Interaction: As you discuss your perspectives, build on each others' posts. Discuss where you may have similar or different views from each other. Explain why you agree, and if you disagree, how you would change the definitions. The goal of this discussion is to try to come to a consensus on a definition of culture and eLearning, and how culture and eLearning are related, based on the perspectives put forward by the class.

Remember to **REPLY** to this post and your classmates' posts by clicking on **REPLY** so that we create a discussion thread.

Figure 18.1 Discussion prompt from the Orientation Module in a graduate-level course on culture and elearning taught in the Organization, Information, and Learning Sciences Program at the University of New Mexico in spring 2023

Therefore, careful selection of goals, objectives, discussion topics, the design of learning activities, and discussion prompts will determine if a group of participants will engage in higher levels of knowledge construction in a specific sociocultural context.

Guidance

In Chapter 17, we discussed the role of guidance as part of the sociocultural context of an online environment and observed that the degree to which guidance is available will influence SCK. In this chapter, we discuss strategies instructors/facilitators/moderators/mentors can adopt to guide participants and move them toward knowledge construction. We see these strategies from two perspectives: strategies that support social interaction and community-building and strategies that support knowledge construction, as both go hand in hand as illustrated in IAM 2.0. Gunawardena et al. (2019) discuss these strategies that co-mentors can employ to support the development of a wisdom community (see Figure 18.4 labeled Mentor/Facilitator Functions in Building a Learning Community, in Gunawardena et al., 2019, p. 104). We list a selection of these strategies that support social interaction and knowledge construction.

To support social interaction and develop a cohesive learning community:

1. Be present online
2. Generate social presence and foster social connectedness
3. Encourage participation
4. Value contributions
5. Maintain the social equality of the group and group harmony

To support knowledge construction:

1. Communicate expectations
2. Contextualize the discussions
3. Encourage the generation of ideas/perspectives
4. Help participants build on each other's ideas
5. "Weave" thoughts and comments
6. Express the emerging consensus of the group
7. Summarize or clarify frequently, or delegate responsibility for doing so. In concluding statements, provide either a summative synthesis (by linking ideas or showing the relationships between ideas), or a query-posing synthesis (asking questions that will help participants discover relationships between ideas expressed)

Varied techniques for guiding participants toward knowledge construction have been put forward by other researchers. McAteer et al. (2002) discussed interactive "tutorly dialogue" strategies that novices and experts working together in the zone of proximal development (Vygotsky, 1978) can use to enhance learning in online collaborations. Some of these strategies include requests for suggestions, suggestions themselves, prompts for consideration of other information, explanations of prompts, questions, feedback targeted to need, and instructions. Of the many techniques listed to move a group toward knowledge construction, one technique is key, summarizing. Wise and Chiu (2011) point out that assigning a summarizing role mid-discussion can aid a group progress to more advanced Phases of knowledge construction. Providing appropriate guidance and supporting participants can foster collaboration and move a group toward knowledge construction.

Assessment

In academic settings, assessment criteria may influence whether an online discussion group moves toward SCK. One must ask whether assessment practices are grounded in social constructivism where knowledge is co-created by the members of a group by a process of negotiation of meaning within that group. How collaborative learning is assessed and valued will determine whether a group is motivated to move toward higher levels of knowledge construction. In academic settings, students often feel that discussion forums are a waste of time and busy work as they are not designed to engage them or support collaboration that leads to SCK. However, if a discussion forum is designed to help participants work together to co-construct a product, create a solution for a problem, engage in a debate about a controversial topic, and reflect on lessons learned to develop avenues for improvement, and the evaluation strategies focus on assessing the collaborative process as well as the product, then, co-construction of knowledge is likely to take place.

If we are to move a group toward higher levels of knowledge construction, assessment must reward the process of collaboration, contribution to the community, and products developed within the community. It is important to focus on the process of learning or collaboration. For example, how a group solved a problem or created an eportfolio and not merely on the product developed. Individual assessment must reward participation and contribution to the group's process and product, and a group grade should be assigned for the process and final product. If we change the culture of assessment to reward collaboration and knowledge construction rather than knowledge reproduction and focus on learning improvement, we are more likely to support collaborating groups to reach higher levels of knowledge construction.

Online technologies and tools produce automatic documentation of the process of SCK and knowledge artifacts or products developed by a collaborative group as well as individual collaboration efforts. For example, asynchronous discussion forum transcripts, web-conference recordings, shared collaborative documents, and collaborative tools that can visualize SCK such as concept maps (Cmap), Poplet, Miro, and Padlet, preserve a learning community's interaction processes, creating important avenues for assessment and feedback on learning, both formative and summative (Barril, 2019). Technologies can also capture human interactions with AI assistants/chatbots, which provide a means of assessing how distributed cognition among humans and tools interact to construct knowledge.

To summarize, in this section, we discussed instructional design strategies that include clear articulation of goals, developing inquiry-based learning activities, appropriate discussion prompts, and assessment criteria that reward collaboration and knowledge construction. Next, we discuss research questions and designs we can explore using IAM 2.0 and SLAM.

Research Questions, Designs, and Methods

We begin by presenting general research questions that can be used to guide researchers exploring SCK. Next, we present research questions that query the methods (SLAM and AI) we have discussed in this volume for their ability to analyze SCK, social interaction, and the sociocultural context. Many of these questions can be found at the end of the methods chapters in this volume. After presenting the questions, we introduce two research designs that can be analyzed with SLAM. The first design can be employed when a structured research process is necessary with a predefined or existing construct. The second design is more open-ended when a researcher is interested in exploration and building theory.

General Research Questions That Examine Sociocultural Context, Social Interaction, and Social Construction of Knowledge (SCK)

1. Which type of collaborative learning activity design/format in a discussion forum would lead to higher levels of knowledge construction? (Learning activities could be debates, role plays, case-based reasoning, problem-solving, etc.)
2. How do participation patterns (such as the concentration of messages at various points in the time span of a conference) impact knowledge construction?
3. What is the relationship between social presence and SCK?
4. Is a group that forms a cohesive community (as reflected in SNA) more likely to reach higher levels of SCK?
5. How does the sociocultural context (measured by selected contextual factors such as disciplinary culture) relate to SCK?
6. How does the sentiment within a group influence the development of community?
7. How does dissonance influence SCK in a particular sociocultural context?
8. To what extent do different discussion prompts influence a group's ability to construct knowledge?

Research Questions That Query Social Learning Analytic Methods (SLAM)

The following questions examine the output of the specific SLAM we have discussed in this volume.

Social Network Analysis (SNA)

1. How does the structural composition of a social network (according to SNA) influence the flow of information within a community?
2. How do patterns of social interactions and network structures (according to SNA) change over time in response to external events or interventions?
3. To what extent do individuals in a social network tend to form connections with others who share similar characteristics or opinions?
4. Are those who are more central in a social network more vital for knowledge construction?

Clustering

1. To what extent do themes identified by clusters align with automated coding performed using a lexicon analysis?
2. How can data clusters help identify themes in data?
3. What are the relationships between clusters and SNA communication patterns?

Artificial Intelligence (AI) and Large Language Models (LLM)

1. How can AI assist in identifying Phases of knowledge construction within online discussions?
2. How can AI models be trained to better support diverse cultural contexts in online learning environments?
3. What are the ethical implications of using AI to guide and assess online learning discussions?

Designs and Methods: SLAM Analysis Sequence

This section describes our recommended application of SLAM in conjunction with IAM 2.0 based on the research questions selected for the study. SLAM should be applied in specific ways depending on whether or not the researcher is working with a predefined research construct such as cognitive dissonance or community. Therefore, we present two different sequences that outline a more structured approach for a predefined research construct or a more open-ended approach.

SLAM provide researchers with valuable tools to explore key questions in SCK. Specifically, SLAM can help answer the following research questions:

- What knowledge is being socially constructed? (word frequency analysis)
- How is knowledge constructed? (sentiment analysis, LLM analysis, cluster analysis)
- Who is involved in the knowledge construction process? (social network analysis)

By applying these techniques, researchers can gain a deeper understanding of the content, dynamics, and participants involved in the co-construction of knowledge, offering both qualitative and quantitative insights into the learning process.

Applying SLAM With an Existing Research Construct

When researchers have an existing framework – such as the IAM – for studying SCK, the process of applying SLAM follows a well-defined sequence. This sequence builds on the assumption that transcripts have already been coded according to an established construct, allowing SLAM techniques to provide deeper insights into how knowledge is constructed. Figure 18.2 illustrates our recommended use of a SLAM sequence when existing research constructs are the focus of the research.

To understand Figure 18.2, suppose a dataset has been qualitatively coded using the five Phases of IAM. The SLAM techniques can then reveal patterns in the data that go beyond phase identification, offering a richer understanding of knowledge co-construction. The recommended sequence for applying SLAM in this scenario is as follows:

1. **Word Frequency Analysis**. The process begins with a word frequency analysis of the entire discussion, which provides an overview of the most common words and phrases used throughout the dataset. This broad view helps identify key topics and concepts that dominate the overall conversation. Word clouds can visually represent these frequencies, making it easier for researchers to spot central themes.

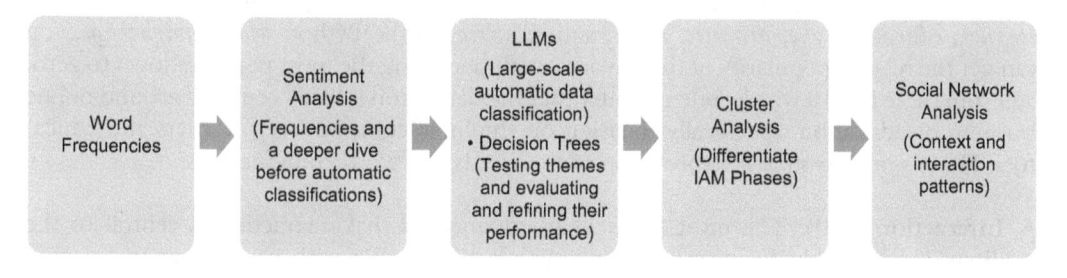

Figure 18.2 SLAM analysis sequence (existing research construct)

While analyzing the entire discussion can be insightful, researchers can also focus on individual Phases to understand how different topics emerge in specific stages of knowledge construction. For example, certain themes may dominate in the early stages of sharing information, while more specific terms related to negotiation or synthesis may appear in later Phases. This step lays the groundwork for more advanced analyses by highlighting dominant terms that may shape the flow of interaction.

2. **Sentiment Analysis**. Sentiment analysis is then applied to examine the emotional tone of the discussions. By identifying whether certain Phases tend to carry positive or negative sentiment, researchers can gain insights into how emotions impact the process of knowledge-building. This is especially useful in Phase II, where dissonance and conflict are explored, potentially showing how emotions drive or hinder the learning process.

3. **LLM (Embedding)**. Large language models (LLMs) are used next to map each post into a vector space, creating embeddings that represent the meaning of the text. By comparing these embeddings, researchers can explore how ideas evolve across the Phases, showing shifts in meaning as discussions progress from information-sharing to negotiation and synthesis of knowledge.

4. **Cluster Analysis**. Cluster analysis groups similar posts together, revealing how ideas and concepts cluster across different phases. This provides a visual representation of knowledge co-construction, where researchers can see how certain themes emerge, converge, or diverge as participants work through the Phases of the IAM.

5. **Social Network Analysis (SNA)**. The final step is to conduct SNA, which maps the relationships between participants. SNA reveals how knowledge flows within the group, identifying key individuals who drive the process of knowledge construction. For example, participants with high centrality may play a crucial role in synthesizing information and guiding the group toward agreement.

Example

In the following example we illustrate the use of SLAM with an existing research construct, on the dataset "original-IAM-user-text-code.csv" in Chapter 18 of the book repository: https://github.com/knowledge-construction/slam-ai.

All code used to generate the upcoming figures in this example is in the notebook "existing-research-construct.ipynb" in the same location in the book repository.

Example: Word Frequency Analysis

Figure 18.3 is a word cloud, which is a visual representation of the word frequency, or popularity, in the entire discussion.

The top 10 most prominent words appear to be: *interaction, think, learning, student, learner, education, one, distance, make,* and *feedback*. In the Python *wordcloudpackage*, you can get the relative popularity of these words, with one being the most popular, down to zero.

From these top 10 words, one can infer that the discussion is likely centered around online learning or education, specifically focusing on the interaction between learners and educators. Here is one possible interpretation of the words and word combinations:

- **Interaction (1.0)**: The most frequent word suggests that interaction is central to the discussion, possibly focusing on how participants engage with each other in learning environments.

Figure 18.3 Word frequency analysis depicted as WordCloud

- **Think (0.2857):** This word indicates a lot of personal reflection or opinions in the conversation, suggesting a focus on participants' perspectives or thought processes.
- **Learning (0.2653) and education (0.1633):** Both point clearly toward a discussion around educational processes, likely in an academic or online learning context.
- **Student (0.2449) and learner (0.2245):** These terms highlight that the discussion involves students or learners, possibly referring to their experiences in educational settings.
- **Distance (0.1429):** This might indicate that the context involves distance learning or online education, which makes sense given the prominence of "interaction" in the list.
- **Feedback (0.1224):** Feedback is a common theme in education, especially in online or distance learning contexts, where interaction between students and instructors often revolves around giving and receiving feedback.

The topic likely revolves around online or distance learning, focusing on student interaction, learner experiences, and feedback mechanisms in educational settings. It could be a discussion on how students and educators interact in a distance education setting and how feedback plays a role in facilitating learning. Of course, this is just one possible interpretation based on the top 10 most popular words. Other interpretations may emerge by analyzing more or fewer words, which could provide additional nuances or highlight different aspects of the discussion. This example is simply illustrative of the technique and its potential applications.

Example: Sentiment Analysis

Continuing from the word frequency analysis, we next conducted a sentiment analysis. Figure 18.4 shows the sentiment scores generated by collecting all posts coded with the various Phases and running a sentiment analysis on those posts. Sentiment scores range from -1 to 1, where -1 represents highly negative sentiment, 0 represents neutral sentiment, and 1 represents highly positive sentiment. These scores reflect the emotional tone of the text, assessing the polarity of the words and phrases in each post to determine the overall emotional charge.

From the sentiment values, we observe the following:

- **Phase I (Sharing or Comparing Information)** has a sentiment score of 0.1096, indicating generally positive sentiment during the initial sharing of information.
- **Phase II (Exploration of Dissonance or Inconsistency)** shows a slightly lower sentiment score of 0.0632, which reflects a more neutral or slightly less positive tone as participants engage with conflicting ideas.
- **Phase III (Negotiation of Meaning or Co-Construction of Knowledge)** has the highest sentiment score of 0.1602, suggesting a more positive tone as participants work together to co-construct knowledge.
- **Phase IV (Testing of Proposed Synthesis)** also shows positive sentiment at 0.1395, indicating constructive engagement during the testing of new ideas.
- **Phase V (Agreement Statements or Applications of Newly Constructed Knowledge)** has a sentiment score of 0.0807, reflecting positive but slightly subdued sentiment as participants summarize their agreements.

These sentiment values align with the earlier word frequency analysis, where the discussion seemed to focus on positive engagement around learning and interaction, particularly in online or distance education contexts. The slightly lower sentiment in Phase II corresponds

Phase	Sentiment Value
I	0.1096
II	0.0632
III	0.1602
IV	0.1395
V	0.0807

Figure 18.4 IAM Phases and the collective sentiment of the posts in that Phase

with the exploration of dissonance, where conflicting ideas might introduce tension, while Phases III and IV demonstrate more positive engagement as ideas are co-constructed and tested. Phase V shows a slightly lower sentiment, which may indicate the more reflective and less emotionally charged nature of summarizing agreements and applying newly constructed knowledge. In this Phase, participants may be less engaged in the active negotiation of ideas and more focused on finalizing and documenting the outcomes of the process. This general pattern aligns with expectations, as we might anticipate a more neutral or less positive tone during Phases of conflict and negotiation and a more positive sentiment when ideas are co-constructed or finalized.

As a reminder, this is just one possible interpretation of the sentiment scores. Depending on the context of the discussion or additional factors not captured in this dataset, other interpretations might emerge. This example serves to illustrate the potential of sentiment analysis as a tool for understanding emotional dynamics within Phases of knowledge construction.

Example: Large Language Model (LLM) Analysis

Next, we examine the use of LLMs in helping researchers understand SCK. While most people associate LLMs with conversational applications, such as chatbots, they have other powerful uses. One such application is the creation of embeddings.

An embedding is a transformation of a statement from words into a point in a high-dimensional space, where similar meanings are represented by points that are close together. This allows researchers to analyze the relationships between posts based on their meaning rather than just the words themselves. By mapping discussions into this space, patterns and clusters can emerge, revealing how ideas are related and evolve across different Phases of interaction.

Figure 18.5 provides an example of how a single post is transformed by the LLM into a point in high-dimensional space, also known as an embedding. Each embedding consists of 384 values, representing different dimensions in this space. In Figure 18.5, only the first 24 values are shown for simplicity. The key idea is that each post is mapped into this space, allowing researchers to analyze the relationships between posts based on their semantic meaning, as represented by their closeness in space, rather than just the similarity of posts based on common words. This transformation enables researchers to explore patterns and clusters that emerge as posts are compared based on meaning.

Note: While the embeddings generated by this LLM have 384 dimensions, other LLMs may produce embeddings with higher (or lower) dimensionality. For example, models such

Post #1 (out of 32 posts total)	Embedding (first 24 values only)
"Another thing I think is important: The more expert the one you're interacting with is, the more you'll learn. That's why I think that learner-instructor interaction is better for learning than learner-learner interaction."	[0.2014, -0.2330, -0.0848, 0.1076, -0.1229, -0.0082, 0.1975, 0.0108, 0.1786, 0.0699, 0.0709, 0.2077, -0.0758, 0.1808, -0.0580, 0.1503, 0.1770, -0.0115, -0.4772, -0.3432, -0.5245, -0.0943, 0.2339, 0.1413, ...]

Figure 18.5 An example of an embedding for one post

as GPT-3 or BERT generate embeddings with 768 or more dimensions, which can offer even more nuanced representations of the text.

As a researcher, you do not typically interpret the embedding data directly. Instead, embeddings are fed into other techniques, such as clustering, which we cover next.

Example: Cluster Analysis

In this step, we demonstrate how clustering combined with the LLM-generated embeddings from the previous analysis can help researchers gain deeper insights into SCK. Figure 18.6 shows a cluster analysis based on these embeddings, with each point representing a post, fill-coded by Phase. When viewed in a code notebook, hovering over each point reveals the post number and a text fragment, offering a glimpse into the content of the cluster. This combination of clustering and embedding allows researchers to explore how similar ideas from different IAM Phases group together.

Clustering of Posts

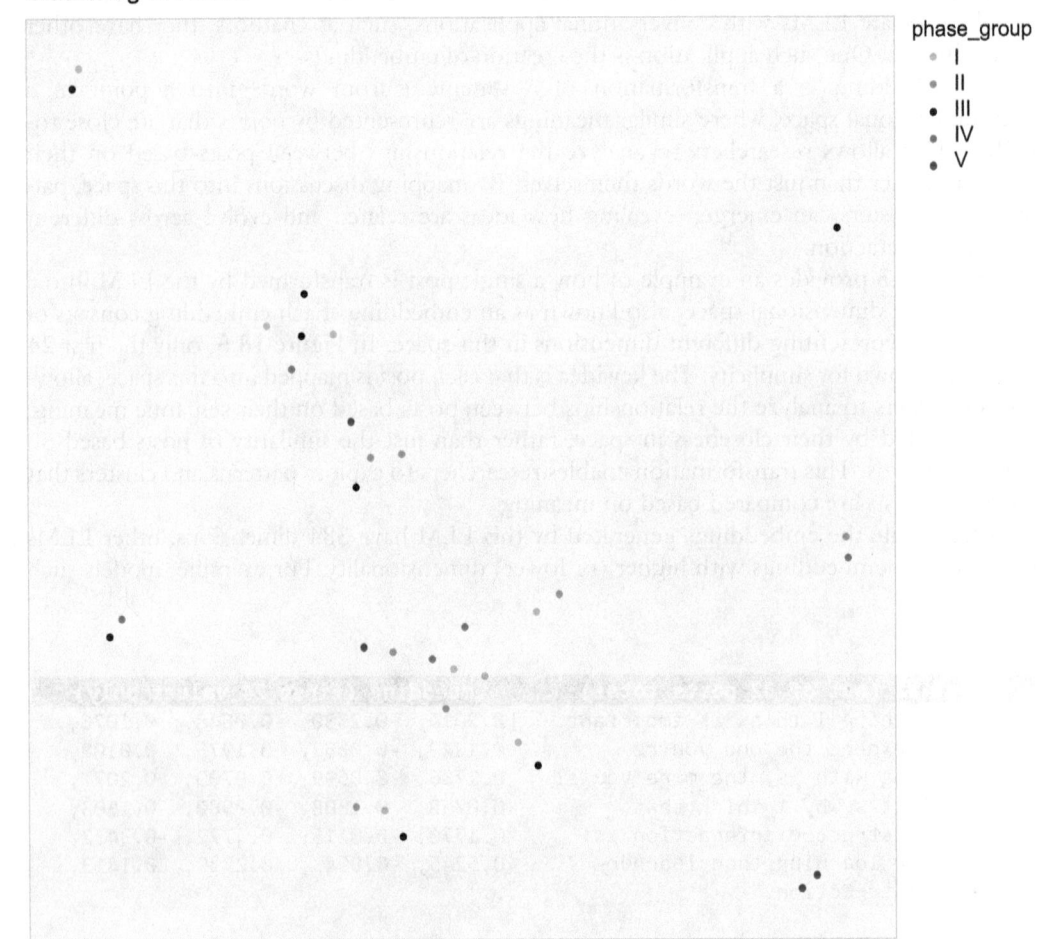

Figure 18.6 The result of a cluster analysis

To illustrate how cluster analysis can assist researchers, consider the cluster located near the middle, upper-left, which consists of five points. In a notebook, hovering over these points reveals the post numbers, allowing us to retrieve the original text associated with each point. Figure 18.7 presents the transcripts corresponding to this cluster of five points.

Examining the text of the clusters suggests that one possible interpretation is that the five posts clustered together in the upper-left corner, despite belonging to different phases (II, III, IV, and V), share a common theme: the role of interaction in learning. This cluster highlights how ideas about interaction are debated, refined, and ultimately contribute to the final synthesis in Phase V. Specifically

- **Post #10 (Phase II)** questions feedback and interaction, noting that feedback is part of the interactive process. This introduces an exploration of dissonance around the concept of interaction.
- **Post #16 and #17 (Phase III)** continue this discussion, focusing on whether interaction is essential for learning. These posts negotiate the meaning of interaction, with participants debating its necessity in education.
- **Post #23 (Phase IV)** challenges the previous discussions, shifting the focus from interaction to activity as the crucial factor for learning, offering a testable proposal for synthesis.
- **Post #30 (Phase V)** reflects on the role of interaction, noting how the ongoing conversation has led to learning, thus synthesizing the earlier discussions into a conclusion about the importance of interaction in the learning process.

Post #	User	Phase	Text
10	ML	II	CO and AA addressed FEEDBACK under the negative. Yet, I feel they addressed the affirmative as feedback is interactive.
16	CO	III	To conclude this point: Shouldn't we see the forms of interaction specified at the start of this conference-with content material, with teachers, with learners-less as forms of interaction per se than as different means for facilitating true reflective interaction in the learner?
17	ML	III	It is perhaps unfortunate that the format for this discussion is a formal debate. This means that we are not really discussing the pros and cons of interaction per se-we are debating the statement "No interaction, no education." It seems to me that both sides are saying: interaction improves the learning experience, makes it deeper, makes it more fun, makes it more memorable. But the "negative team" feel this is a nice-to-have, not a have-to-have. And the "affirmative team" is starting to agree! "So there is no doubt people can learn without interaction" (MR) and "Independent learning certainly takes place all the time" (CL) and so on. In this context, I can only agree with all those who are promising a changed statement for the debate-"No interaction, no education" puts the "affirmative team" in too tight a corner.
23	CO	IV	It is actually the ACTIVITY of the learner which we give feedback on, and that can include the ordering of concepts, testing internal coherence, experience, experiment etc. So "No activity, no learning" and NOT "No interactivity, no learning."
30	SL	V	In the past two days, you who are contributing to this conversation have made me stop and think about "interaction." I guess you'd call that "learning." Without your thoughts this would not have happened. I think this signifies the importance of "interaction" to learning.

Figure 18.7 Text of the posts associated with a cluster

This cluster could represent the progression of ideas, showing how earlier Phases contribute to Phase V, where knowledge is co-constructed and synthesized. The fact that posts from multiple phases are grouped together suggests that key contributions from different stages of the discussion were integral to arriving at the final consensus in Phase V. This illustrates how posts from earlier Phases build toward higher phases of knowledge construction.

While we have focused on the content of the transcript and how SLAM techniques can help us understand SCK, we have yet to examine the people involved in that process. This is where SNA comes into play, offering insights into how participants interact and collaborate to construct knowledge.

Example: Social Network Analysis

While the previous techniques focused on analyzing the content of the transcript, SNA provides valuable insights into the structure of interactions between participants, revealing how knowledge is co-constructed through communication. By mapping out who is interacting with whom, researchers can better understand the flow of information, influence, and collaboration within the group.

In this example, we focus on a mention-based social network, where edges between participants are drawn based on one user referencing others in their posts. The idea is that when a user mentions others, it indicates that those individuals have contributed information the user found valuable or worthy of comment. For instance, if user A mentions users B and C in their post, this signifies that B and C contributed something A found informative. In the network, directed edges will appear from B to A and from C to A. This structure highlights how participants are engaging with and building upon each other's contributions, offering a clearer picture of the social dynamics that drive the construction of knowledge.

Figure 18.8 shows the sociogram for our example dataset.

To interpret the sociogram, first note the users with no connections: ER, DR, JM, SL, and TM. These represent participants who posted but were not mentioned by anyone else in the discussion. This could indicate a variety of scenarios: Their contributions may have been overlooked, they may have introduced ideas that were less influential, or their posts were more self-contained and did not actively engage with others' contributions. In a SCK context, these isolated users suggest that their posts did not play a significant role in the knowledge-building process, at least in terms of direct engagement from other participants.

Next, we can examine the more connected users. Participants like FS, ML, CO, and GK form a more central cluster with multiple connections between them. This suggests that these individuals were more actively engaged in the discussion, mentioning one another and possibly building on each other's ideas. The fact that these users have edges between them indicates that they were referencing one another's contributions, which is a key indicator of knowledge co-construction in a collaborative setting.

For example, GK is connected to FS, CO, ML, and BB, which suggests that GK either found their contributions particularly informative or had a significant influence on them. In contrast, BB and SA are mentioned by each other but do not appear to be heavily integrated into the larger conversation, which might suggest a side discussion or a smaller-scale interaction within the larger group. These types of clusters and isolated dyads can give insight into subgroups or dominant figures in the learning process, helping researchers identify the flow of information and influence.

You can also combine SNA with other stages, such as cluster analysis, to gain even deeper insights. For instance, in our cluster analysis, which included posts from the highest level of knowledge construction, Phase V, key users like ML, CO, and SL emerged. By referring to

Social Network of User Mentions

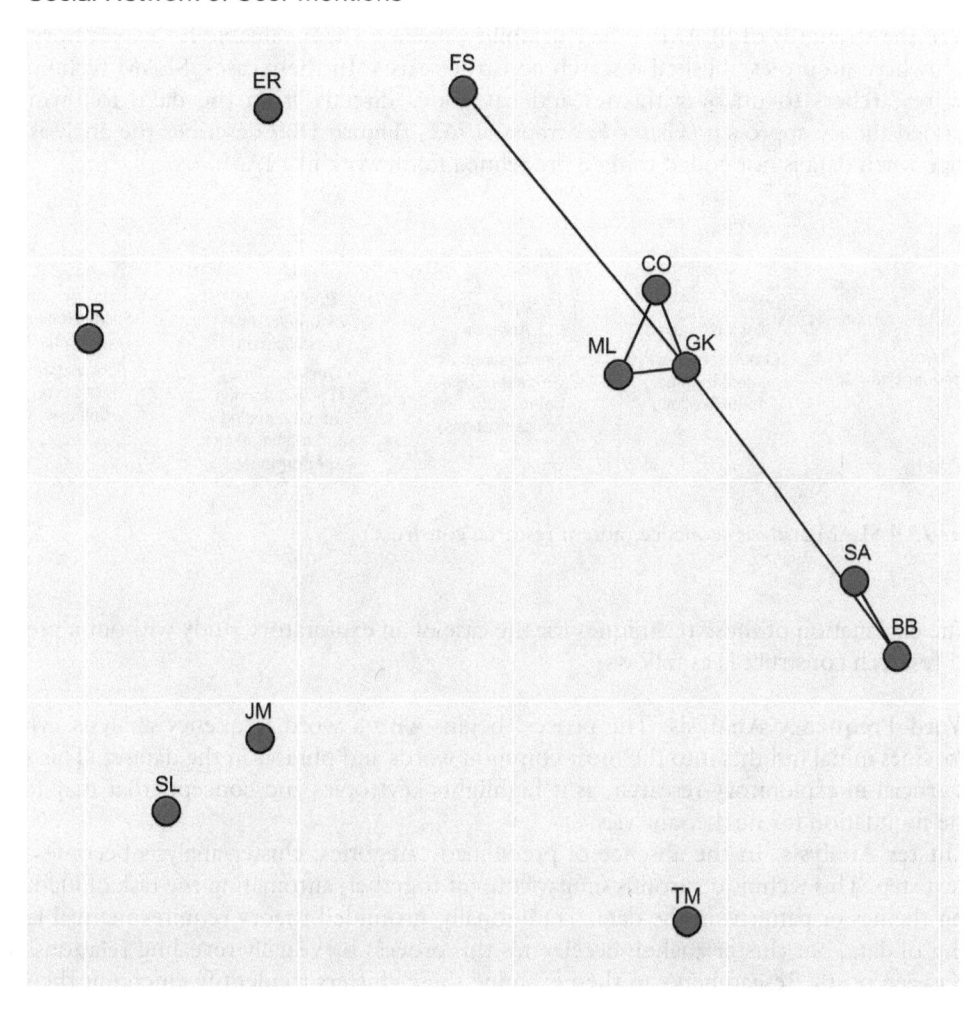

Figure 18.8 Social network diagram

the sociogram, we can see how these individuals were influenced and who they influenced, based on their connections. One surprising result is that ML and CO are both connected to GK, suggesting that GK played a significant role in shaping their contributions to the knowledge construction process. This highlights the value of combining both content and network analyses to fully understand the dynamics of social learning.

That concludes our example of how to use SLAM with an existing research construct to explore SCK. By applying techniques such as word frequency analysis, sentiment analysis, LLMs for embeddings, cluster analysis, and SNA, researchers can gain a multifaceted understanding of how knowledge is built, refined, and shared within a group. Each method brings a unique perspective, allowing us to analyze not just the content of discussions but also the relationships and interactions between participants. Together, these methods offer powerful insights into both the structure and process of SCK.

Applying SLAM in the Absence of a Research Construct

One of the strengths of SLAM is their flexibility, making them valuable for exploratory research where no pre-established research construct exists. In these cases, SLAM techniques allow researchers to uncover themes and categories directly from the data, following a grounded theory approach (Glaser & Strauss, 1967). Figure 18.9 describes the analysis sequence when data is not coded using a predefined framework like IAM:

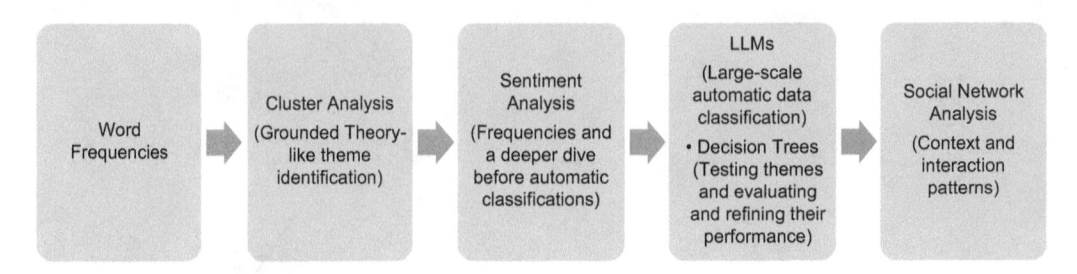

Figure 18.9 SLAM analysis sequence (absent research construct)

The explanation of these techniques for the case of an exploratory study without a predefined research construct is as follows:

1. **Word Frequency Analysis**. The process begins with a word frequency analysis, which provides initial insights into the most common words and phrases in the dataset. This step is crucial in exploratory research, as it highlights key topics and concepts that may form the foundation for further analysis.
2. **Cluster Analysis**. In the absence of predefined categories, cluster analysis becomes the next step. This technique groups similar content together, automating the task of identifying themes or patterns in the data. Traditionally, grounded theory requires manual labeling of data, but cluster analysis accelerates this process by visually revealing relationships between posts. Researchers can then examine these clusters to identify emergent themes, which will guide the next steps.
3. **Sentiment Analysis**. Once themes have been identified through clustering, sentiment analysis helps assess the emotional tone within those clusters. This step can reveal how participants feel about specific topics or ideas, providing deeper context for the emergent themes. Custom sentiment analysis based on the researcher's specific interests can further refine these insights.
4. **LLM (Embedding)**. After sentiment analysis, LLMs can be applied to map the posts into a vector space, creating embeddings that represent the underlying meaning of the text. By comparing these embeddings, researchers can explore how ideas evolve across different clusters and test various LLMs to find the best fit for the data. Decision trees can be optionally used to interrogate how the LLM classifies data, offering additional clarity into classification patterns.
5. **Social Network Analysis (SNA)**. The final step is SNA, which provides a structural view of the interactions between participants. SNA reveals the social context in which knowledge is being constructed, highlighting key individuals and the flow of information. Understanding how participants are connected helps researchers interpret the earlier findings in light of group dynamics, showing how social interactions shape the emergent themes.

By following this sequence, researchers can construct their own understanding of how knowledge is being co-constructed within the group, without relying on predefined theoretical frameworks.

Ethical Considerations

As we have discussed in this book, there are many benefits to the application of SLAM when analyzing SCK. Possibly the most impactful among them is the potential to allow researchers with little to no background or time to conduct such an analysis to engage and quickly make meaningful conclusions about their data. It is important to recognize that SLAM is not a panacea that will solve all problems researchers might encounter. Assuming that SLAM is a "set it and forget it" research solution is wrought with folly and can mean a rude awakening for researchers of all levels of competence. When researchers understand how accessible AI techniques can be, it is tempting to use them to solve all of our problems. Researchers must remember that the A in AI stands for "artificial" and that is exactly what results of SLAM procedures will be if care is not taken to assure the alignment of the techniques to the research questions and the baseline data that is used to establish the parameters for automatic classification. Further, results need to be interpreted with the sociocultural context in mind.

By our nature, humans are complex. Human systems are even more complicated. SLAM offers an opportunity to quickly make sense of what previously would have been considered noisy data by simplifying complexity. SLAM, and AI more generally, create simple parameters like 0s and 1s to understand phenomenon that can be infinitely complex. There are serious ethical implications associated with reducing complexity to binary especially when considering how the results of an analysis might be used. The consequences should be a primary consideration for any researcher who wants to use SLAM. Here are some potential scenarios of using SLAM data without a proper grounding in context and consequences:

- A student could fail a class because the data showed the student was not interacting with other students and contributing to the discussions. What if the student was experiencing issues outside of school that influenced the ability to interact and contribute?
- An employee is promoted because SNA shows the employee is a nexus of communication. What if the employee was only socializing instead of contributing to day-to-day business objectives?
- A researcher established a new lexicon based on the business metrics their manager is focusing on. The automatic classifications yield frequencies of the desired business metrics but fail to recognize employees expressing their discontent regarding their long work weeks.
- A human resource manager identifies the complaints made by employees who are frequently absent from work without authorization. These complaints are used to analyze employee data to predict those who have a high likelihood of being absent from work. The human resource manager takes corrective action before the identified employees are absent.
- An organization values social network metrics and uses a dashboard to help high level decision-makers allocate their annual budgets. The researcher in charge of the dashboard fails to recognize that a recent update to the organization's learning management system led to errors in the numbers in the dashboard.

These scenarios involve placing blind faith in the SLAM being employed. This should be avoided because it can lead to erroneous conclusions that have negative and unjustified consequences. Researchers who use SLAM should always exemplify rigor and confirm their findings in relation to the sociocultural context in which they are used. This can be accomplished a number of different ways that range from dedicating the time to conduct a content analysis to taking a cursory look at the data being provided to the SLAM to assure it is of high quality. SLAM should be used as tools to help researchers understand their data in new ways not as magic wands that allow them to obviate their responsibilities.

Researchers must exercise caution when using SLAM because AI, which is part of SLAM, is known to produce erroneous output from time to time. These errors are known as AI hallucinations and are defined as AI chatbots giving misleading information or answers, presenting them as facts. Types of AI hallucinations include incorrect answers, incorrect sources and references, incorrect predictions, and fabricated information. Generally speaking, AI hallucinations result from the training dataset being insufficient to truly understand the data being provided to it. This might be for several reasons, such as the model's training dataset being biased to a given point of view or because the model's training dataset has become outdated and thus unable to understand the modern context. Researchers who use SLAM should keep the relative frailty of AI models in mind when determining whether they should use their findings as valid. AI hallucinations include but are not limited to text, image, speech, and translation errors. When a user poses a question to AI that it doesn't know the answer to, it will most often devise an answer that seems plausible. For example, as described in Merken (2023), a lawyer asked ChatGPT for case law relating to a case involving a client suing an airline over a personal injury. ChatGPT didn't actually know anything about the specific query but it did know how case law citations are formatted. The result? Case law citations that looked right but that actually did not exist. The lawyer in question did not verify the responses and was embarrassed by the judge who demanded an explanation after the lawyers for the airline identified the egregious mistake. Fines ultimately resulted from the improper use of ChatGPT.

Researchers who use AI must also be aware that these techniques tend to have bias built into them. This occurs mostly because the person who has created the lexicon to drive the SLAM automatic analysis has a particular construct they are looking to analyze. This means that the SLAM selected for a study will only look for specific constructs instead of taking into account the entirety of the context surrounding people interacting with one another. There might be more than meets the eye in any given dataset and researchers should be careful about falling prey to their own confirmation bias. Even AI systems that have been built with complexity and diversity in mind will be biased toward these criteria and could overcomplicate something that is actually quite simple.

AI is entirely dependent on the data that was used to train it so the data must be of high quality to ensure optimal results. Updates should be made on a regular basis to assure the model created maintains its fidelity. In addition, the data that is used to create and update AI models must be checked for quality. The old adage "garbage in, garbage out" is especially relevant. Researchers must also be aware that some developers are creating programs that are specifically designed to confound the ability of AI models to generate useful data and findings. AI poisoning has come about as a way to combat generative AI from coopting the intellectual and creative property of people who produce digital art (Heikkilä, 2023). The idea is for a program to revise a creative product in a way that AI is sensitive to but that is not easily detectable by the human eye. Generative AI that uses poisoned images in its training data will not be able to produce results that match the queries it is given. Many researchers using SLAM will not have an application for generative AI because SLAM is focused on text instead of on images, but this is a clear example of how training data has a large impact on final results. AI poisoning works specifically by contaminating training data. Providing low-quality data to LLMs will have similar or even more drastic results.

Researchers who do their work in informal learning spaces like social media must also be aware that AI is being used in ways that can confound the results of their research. Social media sites are awash with fake accounts that have been preprogrammed to post content that serves the agendas of those who created them. These accounts even go beyond mere posting content but can also respond back to real people in preprogrammed ways. It has been well-documented that nation state level actors are attempting to use AI to try and influence public opinion outside of their borders (Bond, 2024). Researchers must be able to identify these accounts and scrub them from their data in order to present findings that are ethically sound.

Responsible and ethical use of SLAM is indeed a multifaceted subject with plenty of potential pitfalls and temptations. It is easy to unintentionally produce misleading or false data unless specific attention is paid to the challenges discussed in this section. We ultimately advocate for SLAM to be used in accordance with the central tenants of distributed cognition (Hutchins, 1995). SLAM need to be used as tools to assist researchers not as black box solutions because the results of these techniques without verification leads to algorithmic bias in the findings. Findings produced using SLAM must not be taken at face value because the techniques are only as good as the data that was used to build their body of knowledge. Even the best algorithm will not be able to account for the variability that is the human spirit.

The Road Ahead

In this book, we have provided the reconceptualized IAM 2.0 as a framework to determine how people construct knowledge together in online social environments. We also provided baseline knowledge regarding how to use SLAM with IAM 2.0 or any other research framework. Researchers of all disciplines and skill levels will be able to use the resources provided to understand the SCK, expedite the analysis of discussion forum data, and quickly understand trends in large datasets. The knowledge created using SLAM results should be contextualized so that the sociocultural context will be the lens through which all findings are interpreted and reported. The rapid proliferation of technology makes this perspective especially important for researchers, instructional designers, teachers, and everyone who is directly involved in researching online learning

When the Internet was first introduced to the public in the 1990s, there was great optimism regarding how it would change society. Thoughts about how the Internet would open doors for people of all walks of life to have an impact beyond their born station in life were common. Technology has allowed people who never would have had an audience to become influencers sharing their message with millions and even making a living off the content that they produce. People can now also interact with multitudes of people who have opinions that are similar to, and different from, their own. Technology has created opportunities for anyone to contribute their voice to the public sphere and has established a robust place for collaboration across large distances.

These benefits have also come at a price. Influencers' voices are often the most impactful online but what is being said is not always rooted in truth or being communicated without an agenda. People have tended to ignore possible collaborations with people who think differently and have created communities that are focused on common beliefs. This has strengthened populist beliefs worldwide and is leading to deeper divisions instead of creating more of a global community. Indeed, the possible democratic affordances of technology have been left by the wayside in favor of populist messages that drive revenue for technology companies.

In order for society to realize the true benefits of technology, the masses need to develop media literacy. For example, in order to be aware of bias that AI models perpetuate, we should ask questions such as: Whose knowledge is dominant in AI models? How is it trained and on what data? Was it purposefully mis-trained? If this critical capacity is not developed, society risks sliding into an age where the sources of information are never investigated and are taken at face value. Such an age would be dangerous insomuch that society would be easy to manipulate and control. Educators of all specialties can play a vital part in helping people learn media literacy by assuring they develop their own media literacy so that they can then pass their skills along to those they are responsible for in their professional lives.

As technology companies monetize AI and analytic methods, people need to have the ability to find the truth. For example, a prominent social media company used to allow people to scrape data freely from their API. Now, this is a paid feature, thus closing the door on people's ability to freely access and analyze information. SLAM provides an avenue to balance the playing field. Technology companies will seek to promote a dominant narrative that will drown out people of color and those who have been historically marginalized. Learning to use SLAM enables people of color and the historically marginalized to have the tools needed to share their stories and shine a light into the black box of AI. Educators using the IAM 2.0 and SLAM can understand how we interact with one another and how we create knowledge together using technology. Educators must develop capacity in SLAM and help others develop similar skills. If not, we will live in a world where we will have to accept reality as it is defined by others because we will not have the skills to verify and research the truth.

Conclusion

We hope this chapter has provided useful ideas and strategies for those who are interested in researching SCK with the reconceptualized IAM 2.0 and SLAM. The research questions and designs should serve researchers well as many embark on the quest to make meaning out of the advances in technology and how they are impacting society. It is essential that researchers use SLAM as a tool and not as an infallible solution. SLAM and the IAM 2.0 provide researchers with the tools that they need to understand how people build knowledge and how the sociocultural context plays a role in this process.

References

Barril, L. (2019). Learner assessment and evaluation. In C. N. Gunawardena, C. Frechette, & L. C. Layne (Eds.), *Culturally inclusive instructional design: A framework and guide to building online wisdom communities* (pp. 245–268). Routledge.

Bond, S. (2024). In a first, OpenAI removes influence operations tied to Russia, China and Israel. *National Public Radio*. Retrieved June 27 from www.npr.org/2024/05/30/g-s1-1670/openai-influence-operations-china-russia-israel

De Wever, B., Van Keer, H., Schellens, T., & Valcke, M. (2009). Structuring asynchronous discussion groups: The impact of role assignment and self-assessment on students' levels of knowledge construction through social negotiation. *Journal of Computer Assisted Learning, 25*(2), 177–188.

Glaser, B. G., & Strauss, A. L. (1967). *The discovery of grounded theory: Strategies for qualitative research*. Aldine.

Gunawardena, C. N. (2004). The challenge of designing inquiry-based online learning environments: Theory into practice. In T. D. J. Kirkley (Ed.), *Learner-centered theory and practice in distance education: Cases from higher education* (pp. 143–158). Lawrence Erlbaum.

Gunawardena, C. N., Frechette, C., & Layne, L. (2019). *Culturally inclusive instructional design: A framework and guide for building online wisdom communities* [Book]. Routledge.

Heikkilä, M. (2023). This new data poisoning tool lets artists fight back against generative AI. *MIT Technology Review*. Retrieved June 27 from www.technologyreview.com/2023/10/23/1082189/data-poisoning-artists-fight-generative-ai/

Heo, H., Lim, K. Y., & Kim, Y. (2010). Exploratory study on the patterns of online interaction and knowledge co-construction in project-based learning. *Computers & Education, 55*(3), 1383–1392.

Hutchins, E. (1995). *Cognition in the wild*. MIT Press.

Jayatilleke, B. G., Kulasekera, G., Kumarasinha, M. C., & Gunawardena, C. N. (2012). *Cross-cultural e-mentor roles in facilitating inquiry-based online learning*. 26th Annual Conference of Asian Association of Open Universities Chiba, Japan.

Lucas, M., Gunawardena, C. N., & Moreira, A. (2014). Assessing social construction of knowledge online: A critique of the interaction analysis model. *Computers in Human Behavior, 30*, 574–582.

Lucas, M., & Moreira, A. (2010). *Knowledge construction with social web tools*. International Conference on Technology Enhanced Learning, Berlin Heidelberg.

McAteer, E., Tolmie, A., Harris, R., Chappel, H., Marsden, S., & Lally, V. (2002). *Characterising on-line learning environments*. Proceedings of the Networked Learning Conference, Sheffield, UK.

Merken, S. (2023). New York lawyers sanctioned for using fake ChatGPT cases in legal brief. *Reuters*. Retrieved June 27 from www.reuters.com/legal/new-york-lawyers-sanctioned-using-fake-chatgpt-cases-legal-brief-2023-06-22/

Vygotsky, L. S. (1978). *Mind in society: The development of higher psychological processes*. Harvard University Press. www.marxists.org/archive/vygotsky/index.htm

Wise, A. F., & Chiu, M. M. (2011). Analyzing temporal patterns of knowledge construction in a role-based online discussion. *International Journal of Computer-Supported Collaborative Learning, 6*(3), 445–470. https://doi.org/10.1007/s11412-011-9120-1

Glossary

Actors – Individuals in a network represented as circles with names in them. Generally, actors are people but they can also be groups of people or corporate or social units. In sociograms, actors are usually named shapes. Actors are also known as "nodes."

Agglomerative Clustering – A type of hierarchical clustering where each data point starts as its own cluster, and pairs of clusters are merged as you move up the hierarchy.

Algorithm – Step-by-step instructions for solving a particular problem or performing a specific task. Algorithms can differ in terms of memory needed, speed of execution, and quality of solutions. They are the backbone of machine learning and neural networks. (see machine learning, neural networks)

Application Programming Interface (API) – A set of protocols and tools for building software and applications. In the context of social media platforms, APIs allow researchers to programmatically access and download data, such as posts and user information, for analysis.

Artificial Intelligence (AI) – The capability of machines or software to solve problems and perform tasks. It encompasses different methods and technologies designed to replicate or mimic human-like problem-solving capabilities.

Attention Mechanism – A component of the transformer architecture that allows the model to focus on specific parts of the input data, assigning different weights to words or tokens in a sequence based on their relevance.

BERT – A type of deep-learning model, based on the transformer architecture, designed by Google to understand the context of words in a sentence. BERT stands for "Bidirectional Encoder Representations from Transformers." It is widely used in tasks that require a deep understanding of context, such as search engines or question-answering systems.

Branch – Entire arm of the decision tree that stems from the main node. Branches include other nodes, branches, and leaves.

Categorical Variables – Variables that represent distinct categories or groups. They are often used as predictors or outcomes in classification tasks, such as predicting whether an event will occur or not.

Centrality – A measure of the extent to which an actor is organized around a central point. Nodes that are most central have the highest number of connections going to and from them and generally appear in the middle of the sociogram.

ChatGPT – An LLM developed by OpenAI. GPT stands for "Generative Pre-trained Transformer." ChatGPT was trained to generate human-like text responses to the input it receives, making it suitable for chatbots, virtual assistants, and other interactive applications.

Cluster Analysis – A statistical method used to group a set of objects (such as text data) into clusters, or groups, based on similarities among them. It is widely used to discover topics, subtopics, and categories of discussion in social learning research.

Co-Construction of Knowledge – Is similar in meaning to social construction of knowledge (SCK), which explains that knowledge is co-constructed by members of a group through a process of shared and negotiated meaning. Knowledge is not transferred but co-constructed in authentic social contexts through interactive dialogue. The Interaction Analysis Model (IAM) describes the five Phases in the co-construction of knowledge.

Cognitive Artifact – In distributed cognition, a cognitive artifact is any tool, device, object, or structure that mediates cognitive processes, helping individuals or groups accomplish tasks more efficiently or effectively. Rather than viewing cognition as confined to a person's skull, this perspective emphasizes how artifacts – like computers, AI, or even simple objects like a notepad – become integral parts of a broader cognitive system. These artifacts allow humans to offload mental work onto external resources, conserving cognitive effort while facilitating complex problem-solving, memory, and other tasks.

Collaborative Learning – When two or more people learn something together, negotiating their perspectives.

Communication – Communication focuses on the content of the message and the understanding between the sender and receiver. It can be verbal or nonverbal.

Community – A network of stable social connections over time within one or more groups.

Confusion Matrix – A table used to describe the performance of an AI model by comparing its predicted outcomes with the actual outcomes. It highlights where the AI made correct predictions and where it made errors.

Constructivism – Individuals "construct" their own meanings, "knowledge" frameworks, and systems of techniques for interpreting phenomena they encounter.

Content Analysis – Is primarily concerned with analyzing "what" is communicated. It focuses on the specific content or meaning of an individual's message.

Context (in AI) – The information provided to an AI, including both the user's current prompt and all previous interactions. Context helps the AI generate more relevant and coherent responses based on the ongoing conversation.

Continuous Variables – Variables that can take any value within a range. Examples include measurements like temperature, length, and time. In regression analysis, continuous variables are often used as predictors or outcomes.

Corpus – In text analysis, a collection of written texts or documents treated as a single entity for analysis. In R, the *tm* package treats a corpus as a structured object for handling collections of text data.

Culture – The term culture has many definitions. For this book, we define it in Chapter 17 as shared perceptions of the world and our place in it. These perceptions affect both identity formation and societal roles.

Data Scraping – The process of extracting large amounts of data from websites or online platforms, often using automated tools or scripts, for analysis. Data scraping is useful for gathering information from social media or other online discussions.

Data Wrangling – The process of cleaning and unifying complex and messy datasets into a structured and usable format for analysis.

Data Frame – A two-dimensional, table-like data structure in Python's *Pandas* library, used to organize and manipulate data. Each row typically corresponds to an observation, and each column represents a variable.

Deductive Research – A research approach where researchers apply pre-existing theories or frameworks to label or categorize data based on specific constructs. It involves testing hypotheses using known concepts.

Deep Learning – An advanced kind of machine learning that uses multilayer neural networks, commonly referred to as "deep neural networks" or "deep learning networks." The term "deep" refers to the depth of the network. The many layers of interconnected nodes enable the system to generate state-of-the-art solutions for complex tasks like image and speech recognition, language translation, natural language processing, and creating content.

Deep Learning Model – A computing system that uses deep learning to solve problems and perform tasks.

Dendrogram – A tree-like diagram that records the sequences of merges or splits in hierarchical clustering. It is often used to visualize the structure of the clusters.

Dependency Parsing – A technique in NLP that identifies grammatical relationships between words in a sentence. It produces a dependency tree that helps to understand the structure of a sentence by focusing on how words depend on one another.

Dimensionality Reduction – A process used to reduce the number of features in a dataset while preserving its essential structure. Techniques like t-Distributed Stochastic Neighbor Embedding (t-SNE) are often used to reduce the dimensions of document-term matrices for easier visualization.

Directional Relationships – The connection between a pair of actors represented with a unidirectional or multidirectional arrow showing the origin and destination of the connection.

Disciplinary Culture – Worldviews held by members of an academic disciplinary community (such as physics or anthropology) that shape their views, and sharing of knowledge.

Distributed Cognition – The theory that cognition is a flexible process that can extend dynamically beyond the boundaries of an individual's skull to incorporate a distribution of resources, including other actors, artifacts, and generally media. In this theory, intelligent task performance emerges as the consequence of the coordination of this distributed media.

Distributed Cognitive System – A system of distributed cognition. In human teams, cognition is distributed across actors and artifacts, with each medium (including AI) playing a role in the overall cognitive process. AI acts as a cognitive artifact in such systems.

Document-Term Matrix (DTM) – A matrix that represents the frequency of terms that occur in a collection of documents. It is often used in text mining and topic modeling tasks such as Latent Dirichlet Allocation (LDA). Each row corresponds to a document, and each column corresponds to a term, with the value in each cell representing the term's frequency in the respective document.

Embedding – A numerical representation of text in a multidimensional space, where words or documents with similar meanings are placed closer together. This technique is commonly used in natural language processing tasks.

F1-Score – A measure of an AI's performance that balances precision and recall, often used to evaluate how well an AI model predicts outcomes. It provides a single score to assess accuracy across different categories.

Feature Extraction – The process of transforming raw data into numerical representations, or features, that can be used in machine learning models. In text analysis, features might include word counts, sentiment scores, or the presence of specific keywords.

Few-Shot Learning – The ability of an AI model to learn a new task or perform well after being shown only a few examples of how to do it.

Generative AI – A type of AI that can generate new content, such as text, images, or music, based on prompts. It works by learning patterns from large datasets and using that knowledge to create coherent outputs in response to human input.

Google Colaboratory (Colab) – A cloud-based service that provides a free Jupyter Notebook environment. It supports programming in Python and offers access to GPUs for performing computationally intensive tasks.

Group Cognition – In small group collaboration, the computer can empower groups to construct forms of group cognition that exceed what the group members could achieve as individuals.

Hierarchical Clustering – A clustering algorithm that builds a hierarchy of clusters by either merging smaller clusters into larger ones (agglomerative) or splitting large clusters into smaller ones (divisive). It results in a tree-like structure called a dendrogram.

Hyperparameters – Configurable settings in AI models that control how they generate responses. For example, adjusting "temperature" can make AI responses more creative or more repetitive.

IAM (Interaction Analysis Model) – a framework for analyzing social construction of knowledge in computer or video transcripts that can be analyzed using the five phases specified by the model.

Identity – Who you are, the character or personality of an individual.

Inductive Research – A research approach where patterns, themes, or concepts emerge from the data without predefined categories, allowing researchers to develop new theories based on observations.

Integrated Development Environment (IDE) – A software application that provides comprehensive facilities to computer programmers for software development. It typically includes a code editor, a debugger, and tools for automating certain tasks. Popular IDEs include RStudio for R and Jupyter Notebook for Python.

Interaction – Signals the act of engaging and responding to one another. Interaction involves engagement, which leads to social interaction.

Interaction Analysis – Investigates the interaction of human beings with each other and with objects in their environment. It is concerned with analyzing "how" communication unfolds in social settings through social interaction.

Jupyter Notebook – A web-based IDE for Python that allows users to combine code, text, and visualization in a single document. It is widely used for data analysis, visualization, and reproducible research.

K-means Clustering – A popular clustering algorithm that partitions data into k distinct non-overlapping clusters based on their distances to the k centers. It is an iterative algorithm that assigns data points to the nearest cluster center.

Knowledge Construction – Learning is a process of active meaning-making through exploration, reflection, and interaction within social contexts. It is not a passive process, nor is it a reproduction of knowledge.

Large Language Model (LLM) – A type of artificial intelligence system designed to understand and generate human-like text based on vast amounts of data. These models are "large" because they consist of billions of parameters, enabling them to discover nuanced word and phrase relationships and to produce coherent, contextually relevant responses. They are also large because they have been trained on a vast corpus of documents including web pages, social media posts, books, and software repositories.

LDA (Latent Dirichlet Allocation) – A statistical model used for topic modeling. It identifies topics in a large corpus of text by clustering words that frequently occur together.

Leaf – Smallest level grouping like a subtopic or subtheme that is not split by rules.

Learning Analytics – Is the application of quantitative techniques for analyzing large volumes of distributed data ("big data") in order to discover factors that contribute to learning (Long & Siemens, 2011, p. 34). Its purpose is to harness the power of data, for instance, capturing new forms of digital data from students' learning activities, and use computational analysis techniques from data science and artificial intelligence to predict students' academic success, identify students who are at risk for failing a course, and make better decisions about academic programs, strategies, and environments.

Learning Management System (LMS) – A software platform used for the administration, documentation, tracking, reporting, automation, and delivery of educational courses or training programs. Examples include Blackboard, Canvas, and Google Classroom.

Linear Regression – A type of regression analysis that models the relationship between a continuous outcome variable and one or more continuous predictor variables. The model assumes a linear relationship between the variables.

LLaMA – A large language model (LLM) developed by Meta, Facebook's parent organization. It stands for "Large Language Model Meta AI." LLaMA was trained on a massive corpus of text documents and can generate text, translate languages, write different kinds of creative content, and answer questions in an informative way.

Local AI – An AI system that runs on a personal computer or local device, rather than relying on cloud-based services provided by large companies. Local AIs offer more control, privacy, and customization for researchers.

Machine Learning – A subset of artificial intelligence focused on creating computer applications that are designed to learn from and take actions based on data. By identifying patterns in data, these systems improve and refine their operations over time. (see also: artificial intelligence)

Multiple Regression – A statistical method used to examine the relationship between one dependent variable (outcome) and two or more independent variables (predictors). It helps in understanding how multiple factors simultaneously influence an outcome and the relative strength of each factor's effect.

Naïve Bayes – A classification algorithm based on Bayes' Theorem. It is commonly used for text classification tasks, such as spam detection or sentiment analysis, where categorical variables are involved.

Named Entity Recognition (NER) – A task in NLP that involves identifying and classifying named entities in text, such as people, organizations, locations, dates, and other proper nouns.

Natural Language Processing (NLP) – A subfield of computer science and computational linguistics that focuses on the interaction between human language and machines. NLP involves techniques that allow computers to process, interpret, and generate human language.

Network Density – The extent to which actors are connected to all others on a sociogram.

Neural Network – A computing system inspired by the structure of the human brain that is designed to process information in a way that emulates human cognitive processes. Neural networks consist of interconnected nodes, which are analogous to neurons in the brain, that can be trained to recognize relationships and patterns in data. Neural networks are one approach to designing AI and machine learning systems. (see also: artificial intelligence)

Node – Individual grouping of data like a topic or theme.

Nondirectional Relationships – The connection between a pair of actors represented with a line between them.

Outcomes (Dependent Variables) – Variables whose values are predicted or explained by the independent variables (predictors). Outcomes are the focus of predictive models.

Part-of-Speech (POS) Tagging – The process of assigning grammatical categories (such as noun, verb, adjective) to words in a text. POS tagging helps understand the syntactic roles of words in sentences.

Path Diagram – A graphical representation of the relationships between variables in a statistical model. It is often used in regression and structural equation modeling to visualize hypothesized influences between predictors and outcomes.

Poisson Regression – A type of regression analysis used for modeling count data. It is suitable for outcomes that are non-negative integers, such as the number of times an event occurs in a dataset.

Precision – A measure of how accurate the AI's predictions are. High precision means that when the AI makes a prediction, it is correct most of the time.

Predictive Analytics – The process of using historical data to generate predictions about future events. It involves applying statistical and machine learning models to data to identify patterns and make informed forecasts.

Predictors (Independent Variables) – Variables that are believed to influence or predict changes in another variable (the outcome). In predictive analytics, these variables are used to forecast outcomes.

Preprocessing – The steps taken to clean and prepare data for analysis. This can include removing irrelevant information, handling missing data, and transforming data into a usable format.

Pre-Trained Language Model (PLM) – A type of artificial intelligence system that has been previously trained (pre-trained) on vast amounts of text data, allowing it to understand and generate language. These systems should be used for fine-tuning to accomplish specific tasks.

Quantization – A technique used to reduce the memory and computational requirements of large models by compressing the model's parameters from higher-precision (e.g., 32-bit floating point) to lower-precision formats (e.g., 8-bit integers), often with minimal loss of performance.

Question-Answering (Q&A) Model – A specialized AI model designed to provide direct answers to questions based on a given text. Q&A models are useful for extracting specific information from large datasets.

Recall – A measure in AI evaluation that indicates how well the AI identifies all relevant instances of a particular category. High recall means the AI correctly identified most of the relevant instances.

Reddit – A popular social media platform that hosts user-created groups, called subreddits, focused on specific topics. Reddit is often used for data scraping due to its open API and extensive discussions on a variety of subjects.

Regression Analysis – A statistical method used to examine the relationship between one or more independent variables (predictors) and a dependent variable (outcome). Regression helps determine whether and how much a predictor influences an outcome.

Relational Tie – The connections between actors represented as lines between them. Connections are communications like texts, emails, or discussion posts that are sent between actors. Relational ties are also known as "edges."

Remote AI – AI systems accessed through the Internet that are often hosted and run by large technology companies and that can come with limitations regarding control, privacy, and cost.

Retrieval-Augmented Generation (RAG) – A technique that combines an LLM with a retrieval system, enabling the model to access up-to-date or external information to improve its performance on tasks like answering questions based on recent knowledge.

Root – Initial query being considered by the decision tree like how text should be classified according to the IAM.

RStudio – A popular IDE for the R programming language, offering tools for data analysis, visualization, and debugging. It includes features like code completion, syntax highlighting, and integrated plotting panels.

Rule-Based AI – An early form of AI that relies on manually programmed rules ("if-then" statements) to make decisions. It struggles with learning new rules or adapting to unfamiliar situations.

Sentiment Analysis – The process of determining the emotional tone (positive, negative, or neutral) behind a body of text. Sentiment analysis is used to gauge public attitudes and community sentiment in discussions.

Situated Learning and Communities of Practice – Learning happens in the process of social participation in a community of practice. Participants learn how to become part of the community and develop team and social skills.

Social Connectedness – A person's belief that a relationship exists between that person and at least one other individual. It is a feeling of belonging; it could be to a group, community, or network.

Social Construction of Knowledge (SCK) – Knowledge is co-constructed by members of a group through a process of shared and negotiated meaning. Individual reconstructions of knowledge coalesce around the group's consensus, reflecting the interdependence of social and individual processes in the co-construction of knowledge.

Social Constructivism – Focuses on the interdependence of social and individual processes in the co-construction of knowledge. Knowledge construction is a social process of negotiation and meaning-making within a collaborative group.

Social Interaction – Engaging with others as persons and having mutual influence over others.

Social Learning Analytic Methods (SLAM) – A collection of techniques to study group interactions on learning management systems and social networks as groups co-construct knowledge online. These techniques include frequency analysis, sentiment analysis, cluster analysis, social network analysis, and artificial intelligence (incorporating large language models, neural networks, and generative AI), which are used in a complementary fashion to analyze the social construction of knowledge. While artificial intelligence (AI) is included within the umbrella term SLAM, AI is sometimes singled out to refer to operations that only an AI architecture can perform.

Social Learning Analytics – Social learning analytics is the application of statistical and computational methods to study group interactions and social networks as groups co-construct knowledge. It is different from mainstream learning analytics used by higher education to profile students and track their progress such as grades, time to degree completion, etc.

Social Learning Space – Any online platform where users engage in discussions that contribute to the social construction of knowledge. These spaces can include learning management systems, social media platforms, forums, and other collaborative online environments.

Social Network Analysis – Method that shows "how" people are building knowledge using sociograms made up of actors (also known as nodes) and nondirectional or directional relationships that produce measures like centrality and network density. Social network analysis can be focused on people, words and phrases, or elements of an organization.

Social Presence – The degree to which a person is perceived as a "real person" in mediated communication.

Social Presence in IAM 2.0 – The degree to which a person, digital assistant (chatbot), or avatar is perceived as real in mediated communication.

Sociocultural Context – The environment or setting in which learning occurs in relationship to each other and group affiliations, which are influenced by social and cultural factors.

Sociocultural Theory – Learning takes place within cultural contexts, through social interaction and sharing, and via language, signs, and systems. Connections between outward social interactions and inward thought processes form the basis of learning.

Stop Strings – Specific words or phrases that instruct the AI to stop generating responses during multicharacter simulations or group discussions. This helps control interactions when simulating different participants.

Subreddit – A user-created section of Reddit that focuses on a specific topic. Each subreddit has its own set of rules and discussions. For example, r/education is a subreddit dedicated to discussing educational topics.

Summarization – The process of generating a concise summary of a large body of text, capturing the main ideas or key points, typically using AI to analyze and condense the content.

System Prompt – An instruction given to an AI at the start of a session to guide its behavior throughout the interaction. Unlike user prompts, system prompts provide persistent guidance to ensure consistent responses from the AI.

t-Distributed Stochastic Neighbor Embedding (t-SNE) – A machine learning algorithm used for dimensionality reduction. It is commonly used to visualize high-dimensional data by mapping it to a lower-dimensional space.

Temperature – A hyperparameter that controls the randomness of AI-generated responses. A lower temperature (e.g., 0.2) makes responses more focused, while a higher temperature (e.g., 0.8) leads to more creative and varied answers.

Tokenization – The process of breaking down text into smaller units called tokens, which could be words, phrases, or even characters. Tokenization is a fundamental step in NLP, as it organizes text data for analysis.

Topic Modeling – A technique used to identify hidden thematic structures within large collections of text. Latent Dirichlet Allocation (LDA) is a common form of topic modeling used to discover underlying topics in text data.

Top-K Sampling – A method in AI that limits the number of words the model considers for the next word in a generated sequence. By focusing on the Top-K most likely words, it helps the AI produce more relevant responses.

Top-P Sampling (Nucleus Sampling) – A method where the AI selects words based on a cumulative probability threshold. This ensures that the AI only considers a subset of words that together meet a specified probability, leading to more creative outputs.

Transformer – A specific collection of algorithms, or architecture, commonly used in large language models. The transformer architecture revolutionized the field of natural language processing due to its effectiveness in learning from vast amounts of text data. The name derives from its ability to "transform" input data – from sentences to entire documents – into meaningful outputs like translations or summaries.

Unit of Analysis – A unit of analysis is the text block or language segment a researcher selects to analyze the content of interactions evident in a computer transcript of an online discussion. The unit of analysis impacts how text is coded.

Vectorization – The process of converting text data into numerical vectors. This transformation allows for the application of machine learning algorithms on the data.

Video RAM (VRAM) – A type of memory found on graphics cards that is essential for running AI models efficiently. The more VRAM a computer has, the faster and larger the AI models it can run.

Visual Studio Code (VS Code) – A free, open-source IDE that supports multiple programming languages, including R and Python. It is highly customizable, allowing users to add functionality for different languages, debugging, and visualization through extensions.

Word Cloud – A visual representation of the frequency of words in a text corpus. Larger words in a word cloud appear more frequently in the data.

Word Embeddings – A type of word representation where words are mapped into vectors of real numbers. Word embeddings capture the semantic relationships between words based on their contextual similarity in a text corpus.

Zero-Shot Learning – The ability of an AI model to generalize and perform tasks it was not explicitly trained on, based solely on its previous knowledge and training.

Index

For Product Safety Concerns and Information, please contact our EU
representative GPSR@taylorandfrancis.com Taylor & Francis Verlag GmbH,
Kaufingerstraße 24, 80331 München, Germany

Printed by Integrated Books International, United States of America